GCSE Business Studies

NEIL DENBY

AND

PETER THOMAS

 Hodder & Stoughton

A MEMBER OF THE HODDER HEADLINE GROUP

Order queries: please contact Bookpoint Ltd, 39 Milton Park, Abingdon, Oxon OX14 4TD. Telephone: (44) 01235 400414, fax: (44) 01235 400454. Lines are open from 9.00–6.00, Monday to Saturday, with a 24 hour message answering service. Email address: orders@bookpoint.co.uk

A catalogue record for this title is available from The British Library

ISBN 0 340 712120

First published 1998
Impression number 10 9 8 7 6 5 4 3 2 1
Year 2003 2002 2001 2000 1999 1998

Copyright © 1998 Neil Denby and Peter Thomas

All rights reserved. No part of this publication may be reproduced or transmitted in any form or by any means, electronic or mechanical, including photocopy, recording, or any information storage and retrieval system, without permission in writing from the publisher or under licence from the Copyright Licensing Agency Limited. Further details of such licences (for reprographic reproduction) may be obtained from the Copyright Licensing Agency Limited, of 90 Tottenham Court Road, London W1P 9HE.

Cover illustration by Jo Hassall

Editorial, design and production by Hart McLeod, Cambridge

Printed in Great Britain for Hodder & Stoughton Educational, a division of Hodder Headline Plc, 338 Euston Road, London NW1 3BH by Scotprint, Musselburgh, Scotland.

For a full list of acknowledgements please see page 234

Contents

Introduction   What is Business Studies?   iv

SECTION 1 The ownership and control of business

Unit 1	Sole traders	1
Unit 2	Partnerships	6
Unit 3	Limited companies	10
Unit 4	Franchises	17
Unit 5	Co-operatives	21
Unit 6	Public sector organisations	25
Unit 7	Business size	31
Unit 8	Business growth	36

SECTION 2 The aims and objectives of business

| Unit 9 | Business objectives | 41 |
| Unit 10 | Stakeholders' objectives | 46 |

SECTION 3 The management of people within a business

Unit 11	Internal organisation	50
Unit 12	Managers and management	55
Unit 13	Business decision making	61
Unit 14	Motivation	68
Unit 15	Labour requirements	73
Unit 16	Recruitment and selection	78
Unit 17	Training and development	86
Unit 18	Employment contract and pay and conditions	89
Unit 19	Industrial relations	92
Unit 20	Employment and the law	95

SECTION 4 The sources, uses and management of finance

Unit 21	Sources and uses of finance	98
Unit 22	Business plans	103
Unit 23	Costs and revenue in business	107
Unit 24	Break even analysis	112
Unit 25	Cash flow forecast	115
Unit 26	Profit and loss account	118
Unit 27	Balance sheets	122
Unit 28	Business ratios	125
Unit 29	Methods of improving profitability	129

SECTION 5 Production

Unit 30	Resources and the production chain	132
Unit 31	Choosing the right scale	135
Unit 32	Manufacturing methods and strategies	138
Unit 33	Efficiency and innovation	141
Unit 34	Quality management	145
Unit 35	Locating the business	148

SECTION 6 Marketing

Unit 36	Analysing the market	153
Unit 37	Researching the market	159
Unit 38	Consumer behaviour	168
Unit 39	The marketing mix: price	175
Unit 40	The marketing mix: product and the product life cycle	183
Unit 41	The marketing mix: promotion	188
Unit 42	The marketing mix: place – distribution	196
Unit 43	The marketing mix: protecting the consumer	202

SECTION 7 The external environment and business

Unit 44	The external costs and benefits of business activity	208
Unit 45	Business and changes in economic policies	211
Unit 46	Business and the state of the economy	215
Unit 47	Business and Europe	218
Unit 48	Business within the international environment	220

SECTION 8 Preparing for GCSE assessment

| Unit 49 | The examination papers | 223 |
| Unit 50 | Coursework | 228 |

INDEX   232

Introduction

What is Business Studies?

Most students of Business Studies have their first encounter with the subject at the age of 14, when choosing options in a secondary school. Few will have much idea as to what the subject is about. Some think that it is Information Technology or some variant of it, as much work may be carried out in an IT room. Some think that it is typewriting and office skills. Some think that it is accounting skills. Some think that it is going to equip them to become millionaires and some, more realistically, think that it may equip them to run a corner shop or small business.

Look at the images on the cover of this book – sport, new technology, communications, target setting, international trade, transport, statistics – what do you think that they have to do with business? All of these are concerned with the business of getting the right product or service to the consumer at the right time and at the right price.

HOW TO USE THIS BOOK

This book is designed to be used by students of the NEAB GCSE syllabus in Business Studies. This syllabus follows the national criteria for Business Studies and so covers the same ground as all other GCSE syllabuses in Business Studies. It will therefore prove to be an excellent resource for any Business Studies GCSE and also for GNVQ Part 1. The NEAB syllabus is divided into sections – these are reflected in the way the book has been divided. The unit approach is designed so that units can be learned separately or together and in whatever order suits your learning style.

Codebreakers: Some words in the text are **highlighted**. These are explained in the Codebreakers boxes. Many words are used in a particular way or have a particular meaning in Business Studies. They are like using a sort of code, so this box gives definitions and explanations to help you break the code.

Handy hints: You will also find some boxes like this. Handy hints give pointers to how to do better in examinations or coursework or on business methods and techniques or give tips on how to remember things, work them out or present them.

Did you know?: Another type of box is the 'did you know?'. Did you know boxes contain extra information that is either useful or interesting and will help you to place the learning in the real world.

Activity

Within each unit there are many different types of activities to help your learning. Look for the following symbols:

 means a piece of written work for completion in class or at home.

 means a piece of homework.

 means an investigation – something to go and find out.

 means a piece of work using Information Technology; many of these are linked directly to the NEAB Certificate of Achievement in IT. Further details of this scheme can be obtained from the NEAB.

 means a piece of work that can be done either as preparation for coursework, for example practising skills and methods that could be used for coursework, or to help with your coursework directly. Some suggestions show how the knowledge in the unit can be applied to help with your coursework.

Activities are often marked to show the level of difficulty:

› **1** Thought starters – to get you thinking and easy tasks for everyone.

›› **2** A harder task, although all students should still be able to complete it.

››› **3** A task that is harder or requires more thought or detailed explanation. This is so that you can really show how good you are.

WHAT DO WE NEED?

We only need certain things in order to survive – these are the only things that are referred to in Business Studies as '**needs**'; everything else is called a '**want**'. We need:

- water
- food
- protection from the weather.

However, we also 'want' a lot of other things – things that will provide us with variety, comfort, entertainment, enjoyment; things that we can use or 'consume'.

Over the years, these goods and services have been produced first by specialist craftsmen and women, then with the help of machinery and technology so that, in the sophisticated economies of the developed world, a huge variety of goods and services are available to fulfil our every want and need.

The diagram below shows the complex relationship between all the ingredients that are needed to produce goods and services.

Activity

Draw up a table showing:

- what work your grandparents and their generation did
- what work your mother and father and their generation do
- what work you would like to do.

How do you think the pattern of work has changed?

Handy hints

When a task involves drawing up a table, always do it in rough first so that you know how many columns and how many rows you will need and how much space you need for each. In this way your final table will always look neat.

WHAT IS BUSINESS IN THE BUSINESS OF DOING?

Business exists to find out what people's wants and needs are and to try to make sure that the goods and services wanted are available at the right time, in the right place and at the right price.

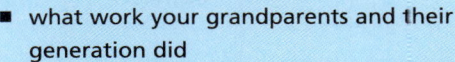

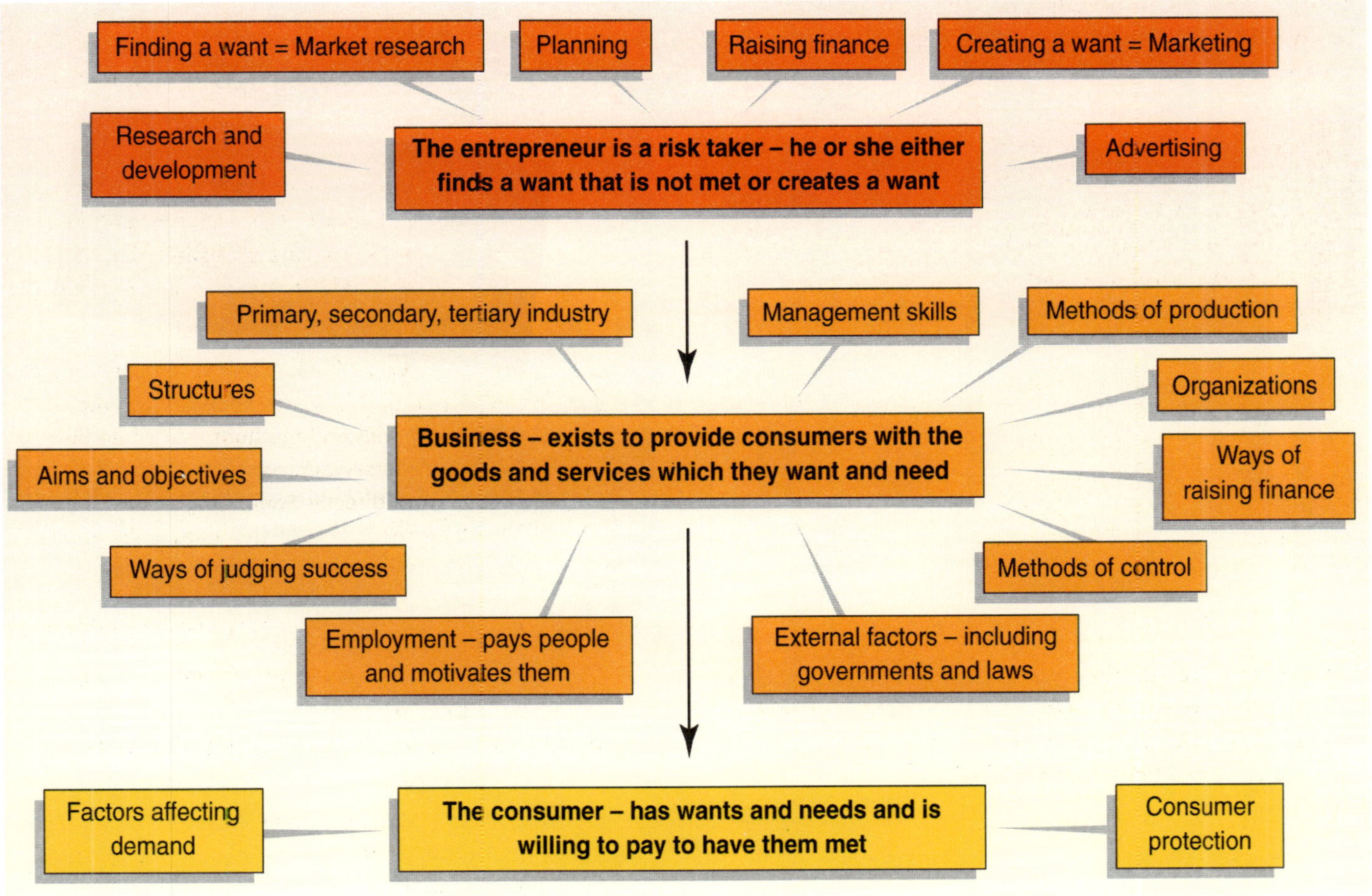

What is Business Studies?

In the industrialised western world, the majority of the population have little difficulty in meeting their basic **needs** and much production is given over to '**wants**'– goods and services that are not needed for survival. It is worth remembering that much of the world still exists at subsistence level – just surviving.

Did you know?

The richest 20% of the world's population own 80% of the wealth. The poorest 20% own less than 3% of the wealth.

Business Studies is the study of how businesses are set up, financed, organised and controlled, how people are employed, managed and paid, how goods are developed, produced and sold, how goods and services are priced, and of how local, national and international governments and organisations help or hinder business.

Activity

Choose a favourite possession of your own. Use a drawing package to construct a flowchart showing what stages the good has gone through before it reached you. Show how business was involved at each stage.

Codebreakers

Needs and wants: a need is something without which you could not survive, such as water, food and shelter. A want is anything over and above these basic needs.

Activity

Rich world, poor world

Here is a postcard issued by Christian Aid, a charity that is trying to help poor workers in the developing world and a newspaper article that shows the level of reward available for business success.

Report from *The Independent*:

Sales of Ferrari cars in the UK have recently reached an all-time high. The car, which costs around £240,000, is mostly bought by residents in the South East of England – successful business people who work in the City of London. The sort of people who bought a Ferrari, said Ferrari's sales director, were deciding between the car, a second house, a boat or a helicopter.

– October 1997

1 Use these two illustrations to explain the difference between a want and a need.

2 Explain what is meant by a subsistence economy.

3 Explain why you think that there is such inequality between the rich world and the poor world.

vi   What is Business Studies?

Unit 1
Sole traders

Businesses are either owned by private individuals – the private sector – or by public bodies such as central and local government. Private sector firms include sole traders, partnerships, limited companies and franchises.

Of all the businesses that are set up and run in the private sector in this country, the most common, by far, is the sole trader or **sole proprietor**. Of those businesses registered for VAT four out of every ten are sole traders. Many other sole traders will not reach the VAT threshold, meaning that an even greater proportion of businesses are actually sole traders. A trader is someone who carries on a trade, while a proprietor is one who owns a business. Tradespeople, such as plumbers, electricians, plasterers and builders; service providers such as driving instructors, hairdressers and bed and breakfast businesses; local shops, such as newsagents, butchers and bakers – all find that being a sole trader is the easiest, most convenient and straightforward way to start and run a business.

Any business has certain needs before it can begin trading. It needs somewhere to site the business – land; it needs someone to provide the workforce for the business – labour; it needs some money to buy equipment to get the business started – capital. Most importantly, it needs the ability to organise and the courage to take risks – someone with these abilities shows enterprise and is referred to as an **entrepreneur**. The business shown has a site – it is the houses that they will offer to work at; it has a workforce – the owner and anyone that the owner employs; it has capital – the ladders, buckets, leathers and van that are essential to the business. On top of this it has enterprise – as the owner has leafleted houses in the area, established that there is no other window cleaning service that is providing for these householders and has taken the risk of offering to provide such a service.

WHAT IS A SOLE TRADER?

A sole trader is a business that is both owned and controlled by one person. It is often referred to as a 'one-man business' but, as there are many women who run their own businesses, it should better be referred to as a 'one-person business'.

This means that a sole trader is:

- the single owner of the business
- the person who takes all the decisions
- the person who is responsible should anything go wrong.

Who owns the business?

The sole trader is the single owner and operator of the business. He or she must be identified as such by operating under the name of the owner (for example Joe Soap's Window Cleaning Service) or by displaying in an obvious place, the name and address of the owner (for example on the side of the van). They must also make sure that the name and address of the owner is printed on all letterheads, orders, stationery and demands for payment.

Activity

> One of the things a business has in order to give it an identity is headed notepaper. There are some examples shown here. Using a desktop publishing or word processing package, create your own headed notepaper.

You will need to decide how you want your notepaper to look – with your name and address to the left, the right, centred, or even at the bottom of the page.

You could then create a picture or design using drawing software, or import clipart or images to make your notepaper look really professional.

Who controls the business?

The sole trader makes all the decisions to do with the business. It does not matter whether these are decisions to do with the day-to-day running of the firm or to do with its long term plans and prospects. He or she may take advice from other people, but it is their responsibility to actually make the decisions. Major decisions such as where the business is to be sited, who is to be employed, what stock is to be kept and what money is to be borrowed are made as well as day-to-day decisions such as what hours the business will be open and what special offers may be given.

Where does the finance come from

Finance is needed by the owner of the business to start it up (*see start-up capital, Unit 21*) and to run the business. Because the amounts needed by a sole trader are generally small – it is likely that the rent or purchase of premises or the purchase of a vehicle will be the largest initial outlay – then usually the owner's personal funds are sufficient. These may be in the form of their own savings (often a lump sum of cash obtained as a result of redundancy) or loans from other members of the family. Banks may be approached for a bank loan or overdraft (however, banks will not provide more than half the capital needed).

There are also grants available from, for example, local or national government (economic development boards, for instance, or Training and Enterprise Councils).

Did you know? Training and Enterprise Councils (TECs) have been set up by the government to cover all areas of the UK. They are involved in making grants to small businesses, providing training and generally giving help to entrepreneurs.

How is the business established?

The sole trader is the easiest form of business to set up. All the sole trader needs is:

- Permission to trade in a particular area. This may have to be obtained from a local authority where a licence to trade is required or from a court if a particular licence (e.g. to sell alcohol or tobacco or to provide music or entertainment) is needed.

- Registration for the payment of value added tax (VAT) with Customs and Excise if the turnover of the business is likely to be over a certain amount.

Activity

Joe Soap has set up his window cleaning business as a sole trader. He has borrowed enough money in order to buy himself a van and the ladders and other equipment that he needs. He has found an area where there is no regular window cleaner and has offered his services.

1. Give three good reasons why Joe set up as a sole trader.
2. Think about the problems that Joe might have. Give three disadvantages that he might have as a sole trader.
3. Joe Soap's is only a small business. What problems might this give him that a large business would not have? Give reasons for your answer.
4. Outline the disadvantages a large business might have that a small business is not likely to have?

Handy hints: It is not worth quoting some figures in a book such as the level of turnover needed for VAT registration, as by the time you read it, the figure is likely to be out of date as it is constantly changing. It is worth you finding out what the current figure actually is!

- Profit and loss accounts and a balance sheet (*see Units 26 and 27*) so that they can be assessed for income tax and national insurance contributions.
- A knowledge of health and safety laws and a willingness to make sure that rules are kept.

Who is responsible for the debts of the business?

The owner of the business is completely responsible for all the debts of the business – up to the limits of his or her personal wealth. This last part is important as it means that the owner's responsibility for the debts of their business is unlimited. The responsibility for debts is called liability, and the fact that this liability is unlimited means that sole traders are said to have **unlimited liability**.

Did you know? The word 'bankrupt' is used to mean that you cannot pay your debts. It comes from the days when banking first started in Italy. A 'banco' was the bench which bankers lent money from. When they could not pay their debts their 'banco' was broken or ruptured 'rupto' hence bankrupt.

Unlimited liability means that the business person can lose all their personal wealth and possessions in order to pay off the debts of their business. This is what could happen:

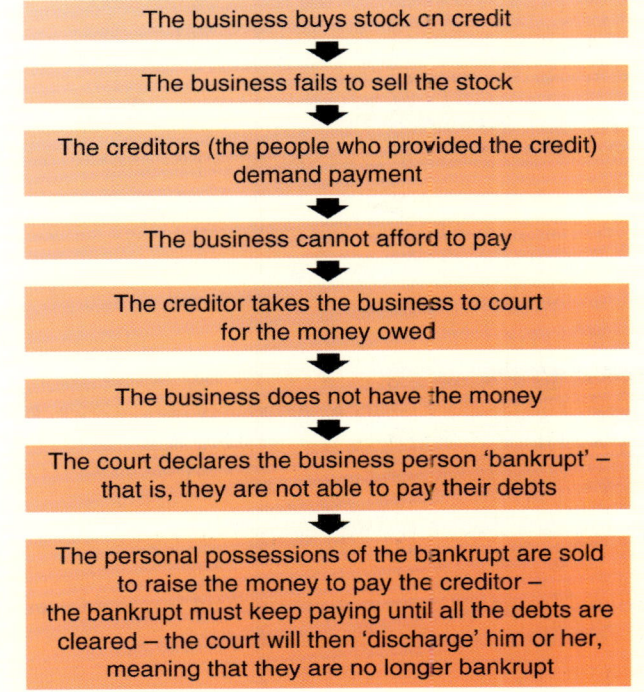

Who keeps the profits?

The owner of the business, the sole proprietor, keeps all the profits from the business. He or she does not have to share them with anyone else. However, this also applies to the losses of the business. It is the sole responsibility of the owner to pay off debts and cover losses.

What taxes have to be paid?

The business owner has to pay income tax on the profits that the business is making. For this reason he or she has to provide the tax authorities with a full account of the profit that the business has made and the expenses that went into the business. This means that both a profit and loss account and a balance sheet have to be provided for tax purposes. Sole traders also have to pay VAT if turnover is large enough and they reach the **VAT threshold**.

Handy hints: VAT stands for value added tax. It is the tax that is charged at each stage of production as the production process adds value to raw materials or parts. Producers of a good can offset the VAT they pay on raw materials, components or stock against that paid on sales so that they are only paying tax on the value that they have added. It is currently 17.5% on most items and services.

Activity

One of the NEAB's approved coursework titles is 'Why do small businesses continue to survive in spite of competition?' You could study a particular small business locally and see how many of the following contribute to its size. You could also look at Unit 7 on Business size.

Businesses may be small because:

- every business starts somewhere, most start small
- businesses may want to be small because it is easier to manage them
- businesses may be providing a personal or local service – a national chain of newspaper delivery boys and girls would not be viable, aromatherapists and manicurists need to be local
- many businesses need to be flexible and able to respond quickly to changes in demand. Businesses may need to be local (for example, a taxi service)
- businesses may have small markets
- there may be lack of other employment.

National Insurance contributions are paid but at a lower rate than if the business were a company and the sole trader an employee of that company. On earnings of £20 000, about £800 is saved by not having to pay employers' contributions on your own earnings.

What are the main aims of the business?

While most businesses may be said to be aiming to make a profit, this is often not the primary aim of a sole trader. Many sole traders continue to trade because they like to be self-employed – being 'your own boss' can outweigh many disadvantages. Rather than making as much profit as possible, many businesses just aim to survive, to keep trading to provide an income. Many others will be pleased to be providing a service or enjoying the status that goes with being a 'businessman' or 'businesswoman'.

Some businesses will want to grow larger, to expand, and many famous large businesses have started off in a small way as one-person concerns. Richard Branson, F. W. Woolworth and Rupert Murdoch all started off as small businesses. Branson owns the Virgin group of companies, Woolworths is a well-known high street store chain and

Activity

1. Look at the business pages of your local telephone directory and find ten examples of sole traders.
2. Put your examples into three columns, one for those in the primary sector, one for those in the secondary sector and one for those in the tertiary sector.
3. Which of your columns has the most businesses in it? Explain why you think this is so?
4. Looking at the business names you have collected locally, what sort of business do you think is missing in your area? Explain how you would set about starting up this business.
5. If you did not have the money to get the business started and could not obtain it from friends or family, where else could you get it from. Explain which would be the best source (no bank robberies, please!)

Sole traders

Murdoch owns The News Corporation Limited (*The Times* and *The Sun* newspapers, and BSkyB, the satellite broadcasting company, amongst others).

What are the main advantages?

The main advantages of the sole trader lie in the ease with which the business is set up and the control that they enjoy. The sole trader:

- makes all the decisions
- keeps all the profits
- has total control of the business
- can start with only a little capital
- can keep a simple management structure
- can keep the business flexible – things like hours worked or goods stocked can be altered easily and, apart from the information that has to be provided for the tax authorities, can keep business affairs private.

What are the main disadvantages?

- The biggest single drawback is the unlimited liability for the debts of the business that the sole trader has. They are always at risk of losing their personal wealth if the business fails.
- The lack of capital means that there are limited opportunities for expansion – few firms get to grow to be massive companies (and few sole traders want them to!)
- Because businesses tend to be small, they may not be able to get the advantages that big firms can. For example, they may not be able to keep prices down by buying in bulk, they may not be able to gain the benefits of specialisation and division of labour.

Codebreakers

Sole proprietor: a one person business, the same as a sole trader or sole owner.

Entrepreneur: a risk-taker; profit is said to be the reward that the entrepreneur gets for being enterprising.

Unlimited liability: responsibility for the debts of the business extends to a person's personal wealth.

Specialisation: concentrating on a particular task or job, being expert at it.

Division of labour: splitting up the labour force into different specialisms so that each carries out his or her own specialism with greater efficiency.

VAT threshold: the level of turnover at which the firm has to start paying value added tax.

Activity

> Copy the diagram below and fill in the information. Keep this as a revision guide.

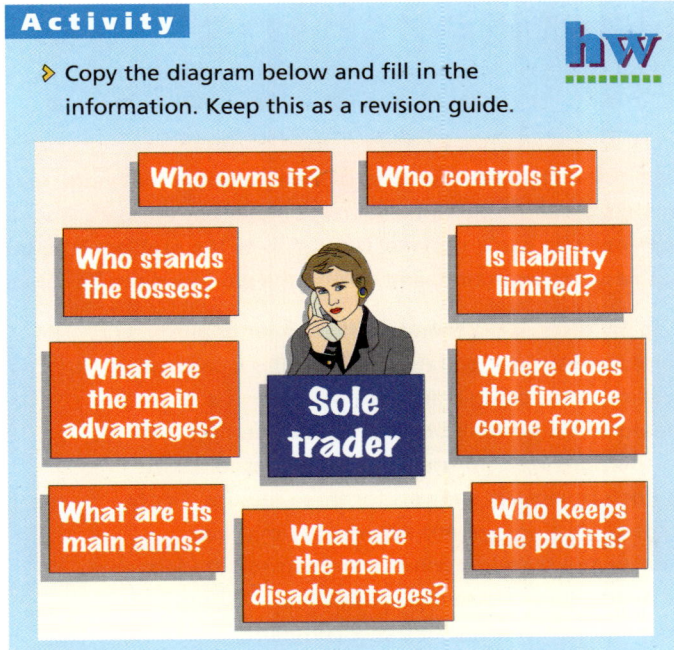

- A small businessman or woman, with few employees, will find themselves having to do a number of different jobs rather than specialising in what they are best at.
- The pressure of all the responsibility can be a disadvantage – although the sole trader can always take advice from others, it is always they that must make final decisions.
- Finally, there is a lack of continuity in the business – the sole trader *is* the business, therefore if they should fall ill, stop trading or die, the business is likely to die with them. While a son or daughter might take over the assets and continue trading, this would be as a new business.

SUMMARY

Eight points to remember:

1. Sole trader, sole proprietor or sole owner are all referring to the same thing.
2. The sole trader is often referred to as a 'one person business'.
3. Sole traders are the most common form of business organisation.
4. A sole tradership is the easiest form of business to set up.
5. Sole traders are owned and controlled by one person.
6. That person makes all the decisions and keeps all the profits.
7. That person must also stand all the losses – their liability for these is unlimited.
8. Most sole traders are not trying to make massive profits or become large firms.

Sole traders

Unit 2
Partnerships

One of the biggest drawbacks of being a sole trader is the pressure of having to take all the decisions yourself. As well as this, there is the difficulty of taking any holidays or time off. Also, there may well be expert skills needed by your business that someone else could provide. A solution to the problem is to take on a partner so that decisions can be shared, the risks of the business can be shared, and so that the workload can be spread out. Almost a third of all UK businesses are partnerships.

In many cases, it is a friend of the owner or an employee that will be taken on board as a partner. In some firms, being made into a partner is a measure of a person's progress within the firm. Partnerships are common amongst professions such as doctors, lawyers and vets for three reasons. Firstly, some professions are not allowed to limit their liability and therefore must operate as sole traders or partnerships. These include doctors, solicitors and accountants. Secondly, so that a continuity of service can be provided – the practice does not have to close down just because one of the partners is ill, or on holiday. Thirdly, so that all areas of specialism can be covered by the one business. For this reason there are also many partnerships in the building trade (a plasterer, a bricklayer and an electrician, for example, could team up to provide a comprehensive building service) or any trade where the sharing of skills is of benefit.

WHAT MAKES A PARTNERSHIP?

A partnership is an agreement between two or more people to take joint responsibility for the running of a business, to share in the profits and to share the risks.

A partnership means:
- shared ownership
- shared decision making
- a shared workload
- shared profit
- shared liability for debts.

Who owns the business?

The business is owned by the partners equally, unless this is stated as otherwise in the partnership agreement. There has to be a minimum of two partners and, in most cases, a maximum of twenty. In partnerships which involve banking, this number is limited to ten. For partnerships of accountants, solicitors and firms involved with the buying and selling of shares on the stock exchange, more than twenty partners is allowed. Some of the advantages and disadvantages of partnerships are magnified by there being a large number of partners.

Who controls the business?

The partners share the control of the business equally unless the partnership agreement says otherwise. In many partnerships there is a certain amount of **delegation** – meaning that particular partners are made responsible for particular jobs. If you have a partner who is trained in accountancy it would be foolish to have them responsible for personnel rather than for the financial records of the business.

Where does the finance come from?

The sources of finance are similar to those of the sole trader – partners will use their own resources, those of friends and family, bank loans and overdrafts and government grants where available. The partnership has a greater supply of funds as there are at least two people bringing their personal resources to the business. It is also likely that the partnership will find it a lot easier to borrow money from a bank as the bank will see less risk attached to two or more people going into business than if the business is relying on just one person.

Did you know?

The government has set up several bodies to help small businesses such as sole traders and partnerships to get established. They have set up a Small Firms Service and an Enterprise Allowance Scheme as well as a number of schemes to help with finance. To find out more about these schemes contact the Department of Trade and Industry or write to your local MP.

How is the business established?

A partnership is almost as easy to establish as a sole proprietor. If no formal agreement is drawn up, then the rules of the partnership are as laid down in the 1890 Partnership Act. Basically, this means that everything, including decision making, responsibility and profit, is

Deed of Partnership

between
Name James Formby
Name Wai-yan Li
Name Marianne Evans

The name of the business will be Formby, Evans and Li, Builders

The business will
provide a building and repair service using the skills of James Formby, bricklayer and Wai-Yan Li, plasterer.

Each partner agrees to provide the sum of
£5000 which will be used initially to purchase a van, tools, stationery and advertising.

The duties of the partners will be as follows
Marianne Evans, accountant, will advertise the business, manage the accounts, issue quotes and invoices and prepare annual profit and loss statements and balance sheets. She will arrange for all necessary insurances and for the payment of tax and National Insurance as it is due.
James Formby, bricklayer, will estimate costs and prepare quotes for jobs and will use his bricklaying skills in carrying jobs out.
Wai-Yan Li will assist in preparing quotes and will be responsible for all purchases of materials and tools as necessary. He will use his plastering skills in carrying jobs out.

Employment
If any workers are to be employed by the business then the decision as to who to take on and what to pay them will be made by all three partners.

The bank account will be
in the name of Formby, Evans and Li, Builders. Two signatures will be required for all banking, one of which must be that of Marianne Evans.

Voting
Each partner will have equal voting rights.

Profits
Each partner will have an equal share of the profits.

Wages
Each partner will be able to draw a wage as decided by Marianne Evans, but to be no less than £100 per week.

Leaving the partnership
Should any of the partners retire, die or otherwise wish to cease being a partner then they agree to the following:
all outstanding debts to the business will be paid off by the partner or their estate; the partner or their estate will be entitled to draw his or her share of that year's profit.

Signed ....
Witnessed ....

Handy hints

The Deed of Partnership is one of a number of business forms that you will need to learn something about. It is always easier to remember what should be included and why such forms are drawn up if you can get hold of a genuine copy. Visit your local Citizen's Advice Bureau who should be able to help you with examples of how to draw up agreements such as this.

Activity

1. Look at the Deed of Partnership Agreement illustrated here. What other details do you think could have been included on this deed?
2. Why have the partners decided that there must be two signatures for any banking?
3. Why do you think that one of those signatures should always be Marianne Evans?

split equally between the partners. If two or more people are running a business together then they are a partnership, even if no official agreement has been drawn up. It is, however, wise for the partners to draw up a special document, the **Deed of Partnership** Agreement, which outlines, in detail:

- how profits and losses are to be shared, if this is not to be equally
- how much money each partner is expected to put into the business
- how much money and what share of the profit each partner may take out of the business
- the working arrangements of the partnership – for example, who has responsibility for which part of the business
- arrangements for removing a partner or adding a partner to a business
- arrangements for ending the partnership and the distribution of assets once the partnership is dissolved.

Activity

Copy the diagram on page 5 replacing 'sole trader' with 'partnership'. Now fill in the information. Keep this as a revision guide.

Did you know?

Adding or removing a partner to or from a partnership can be very difficult. The agreement of all partners is required if another partner is to be allowed to join the partnership. A partner can only be forced to leave if a court order is made against them.

Who is responsible for the debts of the business?

The partners each have unlimited liability – a responsibility for the debts of the business up to the limits of their personal wealth. Each partner is responsible for the entire debts of the partnership, whether they have caused the debt themselves or not.

Activity

Read the passage and answer the questions. The people involved drew up the Deed of Partnership on page 7.

Wai-Yan Li saw a special offer at his local builders' yard. If he bought twenty bags of plaster, he could get a special discount. He knew that Marianne was negotiating a big plastering job on a new estate so went ahead and bought forty bags on the partnership's account. Later that day, they discovered that they had not got the contract. James was furious. He told Marianne that it was her job to get the contracts and that if she didn't she shouldn't have any of the profits. He told Wai-Yan that he could pay for the plaster they didn't need out of his own pocket.

1. Can James stop Marianne taking her share of the profit? Explain your answer.
2. Can James make Wai-Yan pay for the plaster himself? Explain your answer.
3. How would you suggest that the partners resolve this situation?
4. What future problems can you see arising in this partnership?

Who keeps the profits?

According to the 1890 Partnership Act profits are shared equally. A partnership deed is able to vary this. All the profits go to the owners – the partners.

Activity

One coursework title involves the comparison of the objectives of different businesses. A partnership is likely to have different objectives to a big public limited company but is likely to share many objectives with sole traders or other partnerships. By arranging to interview the partners in a firm, you could find out what their short-term and long-term objectives are and how they hope to reach them. This should then be compared with a different partnership or other business. Remember that many objectives may well be the same, so you need to explain why you think that this is so as well as why you think some objectives are different.

Activity

1. In class, get into groups of three or four and decide what sort of business your group could operate as a partnership. List the skills and expertise that each of you has to help you make a decision.
2. Draw up a list of what you would need to begin trading.
3. Find out the costs of the materials, tools, stock, etc. that your partnership would need to buy. This might mean looking in catalogues, ringing suppliers or asking parents or other adults.
4. Compare the lists that you have made and draw up a common list. How much do you need to start your business?
5. If you took on more partners, up to a maximum of 10, what extra benefits do you think that this would bring? What extra problems do you think that this would cause?

What taxes have to be paid?

Partners are classed as being self-employed, in the same way as the sole trader. Thus they pay national insurance contributions at the self-employed rate, income tax on the profits of the business (for this to be assessed, they must provide the tax authorities with a balance sheet and profit and loss accounts) and VAT, if turnover is high enough.

What are the main aims of the business?

The main aims of the business are likely to be similar to those of the sole trader. Profit will be one of those aims, but so will survival and stability. The partnership may well have been established in order to expand the business, in which case further expansion could be an

At the doctor's – most partnerships are happy to provide a stable business and continuity of service

> **Activity**
>
> 1. Use a word processing package to draw up a standard blank form that could be used for a partnership agreement. Think carefully about what headings should go into it and how it should be laid out. Make it attractive by using italics, emboldening and underlining.
> 2. Print out copies of the form and fill in the details about your group of three or four.
> 3. Fill the details in with the word processing package.
> 4. Print out the finished Deed.
> 5. Look at each other's Deeds – is there anything that has been missed out? Add in anything that needs adding and then save and print the form again.
>
> This task partially fulfils the requirements of the Word Processing Unit of the NEAB Certificate of Achievement in IT.

aim. A partnership will find it easier to expand than the sole trader because of the involvement of more than one person, meaning more than one source of personal finance. However, in most cases, expansion is limited by the number of partners allowed.

What are the main advantages?

- The partnership is easy to set up and possible future arguments can be avoided if a Partnership Agreement is properly drawn up.
- The business can gain professional help through taking on an experienced or qualified partner. This may cover an area of expertise that would otherwise be lacking. Often an accountant or a solicitor may be the ideal partner.
- The partners will not only bring extra expertise, but also extra capital.
- The responsibility of running the firm is shared. Shared decision making and a shared workload will make running the business much less stressful.

> **Codebreakers**
>
> **Delegation:** giving jobs to other people, in a partnership this means that people use their skills where they will have the most effect.
>
> **Deed of Partnership:** a legal document that outlines how responsibilities, profits and workload are to be shared.
>
> **Lack of continuity:** because the partners make up the partnership, if one of them leaves, then the partnership is dissolved. The partnership cannot be passed on or sold.

- Apart from information that has to be provided for tax purposes, the finances of the partnership are kept private.
- Division of labour means that the owners can specialise in what they are best at.

What are the main disadvantages?

- The partnership not only has unlimited liability, meaning that the partners could lose all their personal wealth to pay the debts of the business, but each partner is liable for all the debts of the business even if the debt was not caused by them.
- The partnership has a **lack of continuity**. For example, should one of the partners die, resign or be declared bankrupt, then the partnership is automatically dissolved and would have to be reformed.
- Partners can take decisions without consulting other partners and one partner's decision, whether the others agreed with it or not, is binding on all partners.
- Even with the addition of extra sources of finance, there is still a lack of capital.
- Disagreements between the partners are possible and this could make decision making more difficult.

Sleeping partner

A sleeping partner, sometimes also called a silent partner, puts capital into the business and will be entitled to a share of the profits but takes no part in the actual running of the business. They are allowed to limit their liability to the amount of money that they have invested.

SUMMARY

Five points to remember:

1. A partnership is where two or more people agree to run a business together.
2. Partnerships are common amongst some professions, such as doctors and accountants, and some trades, such as builders.
3. In a partnership, the key things are shared – these include decision making, workload, profits, losses and liability.
4. A Deed of Partnership sets out the aims of the business, the duties of the partners and how responsibilities are to be shared.
5. A Deed of Partnership should prevent disagreements.

Unit 3
Limited companies

Sole traders and partnerships who wish to expand are often held back by a lack of capital. In the case of the partnership there is also a legal limit on the number of partners who can belong to the firm. The other major drawback is the fact that both types of business ownership have unlimited liability. This means that taking risks on new developments, new processes or new markets can result in personal loss and bankruptcy.

A solution to the problem of lack of capital and to the risk that is associated with unlimited liability, is to form a **limited liability** company. This involves asking investors to put money into your company in the hope that they will get a return. These companies may be either public – the shares are on sale to the general public – a public limited company or 'plc', or private, where shares are held by a few individuals. The illustration shows the front cover of the offer of shares to the public in a plc – Somerfield – by a merchant bank – Kleinwort Benson – that is a private limited company (Ltd). Both types of company are still in the private sector of business ownership as they are owned by private individuals.

WHAT IS A LIMITED COMPANY?

A limited company is also known as a joint stock company, because its shares or stock are held jointly by a number of people. In America, stocks are more commonly known as securities. It is an enterprise that is established with a **separate legal identity** from its owners and with limited liability.

This means that a limited company:
- is owned jointly by shareholders
- has a separate legal identity
- has limited liability.

Handy hints: Don't forget that liability means the responsibility for the debts of the business. If you are liable for something it means that you are answerable or accountable for it. Limited liability means that your responsibility for the debts of the business is limited to the amount of money you invested.

Private and public limited companies

A private limited company is different from a public limited company in only one significant way. The shares are not offered for sale to the general public. Apart from this, the minimum number of shareholders in a private limited company is two, in a public limited company, seven (although recent changes in European law may alter this). There are slightly fewer steps to follow in setting up a private limited company as shares are not offered for sale to the public.

Did you know? Under a European Union Directive regarding Company Law, adopted by the UK in 1992, under special circumstances a single member private limited company may be formed. This means that the company would have only one shareholder. Such companies are extremely rare in the UK.

Who owns the business?

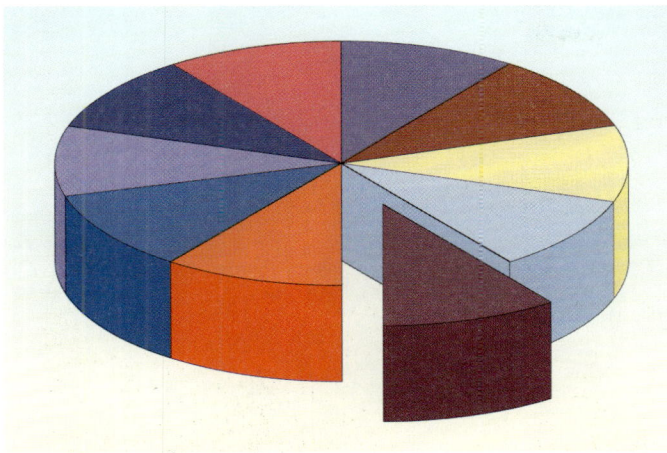

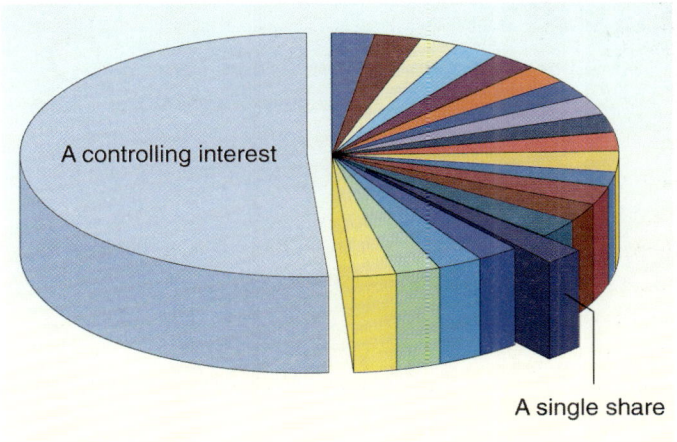

When a firm decides to issue shares, it is as if it is sharing out everything to do with the business – each share gets an equal slice of ownership and thus an equal slice of the profits and an equal say in the control of the company. The main groups that buy shares in private limited companies are family members, partners and employees. The three main groups that buy shares in public limited companies are insurance companies, pension funds and the general public. Members of the public who buy shares in a number of different companies are said to have a **portfolio** of shares.

Activity

> 1 If you had £10 000 to spend on shares, would you spend it on one company or on a number of companies? Give reasons for your answer.
> 2 Which particular company or companies would you choose to buy shares in? Outline your reasons.

Who controls the business?

Each share has an equal amount of control. There is one vote with each share meaning that the owners of the business share the control equally. However, if there are 10 000 shares, there could be 10 000 shareholders. In the case of the offer for sale of Somerfield, there are 300 000 000 shares on offer!

Because so many shareholders would find it impossible to meet and agree on the day-to-day running of the company, they meet once a year to elect a **board of directors** to take the decisions for them; this meeting is called the annual general meeting or **AGM**.

Shareholders do not, as a rule, buy single shares in a company, but buy them in blocks of hundreds or thousands. It must be remembered that while every share has an equal amount of ownership and an equal amount of control – one vote – anyone who holds more than one share therefore has more votes and more control.

Anyone who owns more than half of a company's shares therefore has total control over a company. If the other shares are divided up between a number of people, then even if they all join together, their vote is not big enough to out vote the major shareholder with a **controlling interest**.

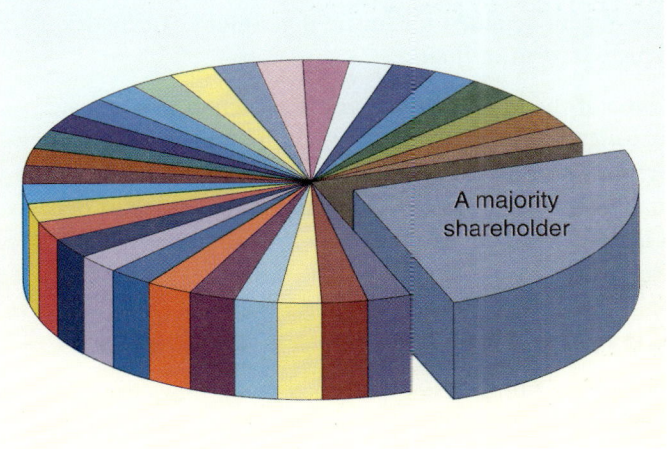

In many companies, the shares are spread around so many people that the ownership of just a few per cent of the shares could be enough to give control of a company. This puts control in the hands of the **majority shareholder** as organising the other shareholders to all vote in a different direction is extremely difficult. Directors are elected by shareholders (and are likely to be major shareholders themselves and so will vote for themselves) and take the management decisions for the company on behalf of shareholders. Shareholders keep the ownership of the company, but directors have control. This is called the **divorce of ownership from control**. If someone manages to buy enough shares in the company from other shareholders then there is always the possibility that the original owners could lose control.

Activity

> **1** Choose any three pages at random from your local Yellow Pages Directory and list the number of private limited companies (Ltds) and public limited companies (plcs). How many of each can you find?
>
> **2** Give reasons why you think there are so many or so few of each that you have found.

Where does the finance come from?

The finance for setting up or expanding a limited company comes from selling shares in the company. The money that comes from the sale of shares never has to be repaid to the shareholders. Shareholders can sell their shares on to other people but the company does not have to buy them back. Their duty is to try to make a profit so that shareholders can share in it. Sometimes special types of share are issued; debentures, for example, are like shares but with a guaranteed return and payment of the original loan. The return is not always in the form of money; some debentures guarantee seats at sporting events, for example. Sometimes profits are not given back to the shareholders but may be retained for future investment or expansion. This is a form of finance.

Some of the assets of the company, such as machinery, factories, plant, patents, etc. could be sold to raise money, or companies could borrow – either in the form of a bank loan or by using a factor. **Factoring** is the selling of debt to a third party. The details of how this works are in Unit 21, page 100.

How is the business established?

Setting up a limited company is a much more complex process than establishing a sole trader or a partnership. The benefits of limited liability are great enough, however, that there are around one million private limited companies and many hundreds of public limited companies. The steps to forming a limited company are as follows:

1. Register with the Registrar of Companies at Companies House in Cardiff.
2. Draw up a **Memorandum of Association**. This must include:
   - your name
   - whether you intend to be a private limited company (Ltd) or a public limited company (plc) plus a statement that declares that the liability of shareholders will be limited

Companies House, Cardiff

- the registered address
- for what purpose the company is established
- what capital it hopes to raise
- the name and address of at least one director
- the name of the company secretary.

Codebreakers

Limited liability: responsibility for debt is limited to the amount of money put in.

Separate legal identity: the company can now, for example, be sued in its own name.

Portfolio: a collection of shares in different companies.

Board of directors: appointed by shareholders to decide policy and run the company.

AGM: the meeting which must be held once a year for all shareholders.

Controlling interest: more than 50% of the shares held.

Majority shareholder: more shares held than any other single shareholder (this does not have to be a controlling interest).

Divorce of ownership from control: the shareholders are the owners but they no longer have day-to-day control of the business; it is the directors who do.

Factoring: selling debt to a third party, the factor, who will receive payments for the service provided.

Memorandum of Association: the document which outlines the external information about the company.

Articles of Association: the document which outlines the internal rules of the company.

> **Handy hints**
> The company secretary is not a typist or receptionist but the person who keeps all the company records, including financial records, the names and addresses of shareholders and all official documents.

3. Draw up the **Articles of Association** – these are the internal rules of the company and list such things as the other directors' names, voting rights, the rights of shareholders, when and how shareholders and directors are to meet and how profits are to be divided. These articles can later be changed by shareholders as long as the changes do not disagree with the Memorandum.

4. Obtain a Certificate of Incorporation from the Companies' Registrar – it is at this point that the company becomes a separate legal entity from its owners.

5. The company can then start trading.

There are three further steps if the company wishes to become a plc:

- they must issue a prospectus which details the company's finances, personnel, business aims, etc. and offers shares for sale
- when the shares are sold, the company must issue share certificates to purchasers
- the Companies' Registrar issues a Certificate of Trading to allow the company to start trading.

Who is responsible for the debts of the business?

The directors and shareholders are held responsible but, because of the limited liability, only up to the extent of the money they invested into the company.

> **Handy hints**
> Don't confuse creditors with debtors. Creditors have given a company credit, so the company owes them money. A debtor is in debt to the company, so owes money to the company.

Who keeps the profits?

The profits are either retained by the company for future investment or expansion – a decision that has to be agreed at the AGM by the shareholders – or paid out to the shareholders. As profits are divided equally amongst the shareholders, this is called a dividend.

What taxes have to be paid?

Corporation tax is like income tax for companies. Just as individuals are taxed on their earnings, so companies are taxed on their profits. Dividend payments are counted as part of the income of shareholders and are therefore taxed as income. If shareholders buy shares at a low price and sell them at a higher one, then they have made a 'capital gain' and must pay capital gains tax.

> **Did you know?**
> There is some debate over the use of the word 'investment' when referring to the buying of shares. Of course, the value of a share can fall as well as rise and people are warned of this in prospectuses and on advertisements for share issues. From the point of view of the shareholder, the money spent is 'speculation' – a gamble to try and make more money. From the point of view of the company, the money will be spent on the plans outlined in the prospectus and is therefore investment.

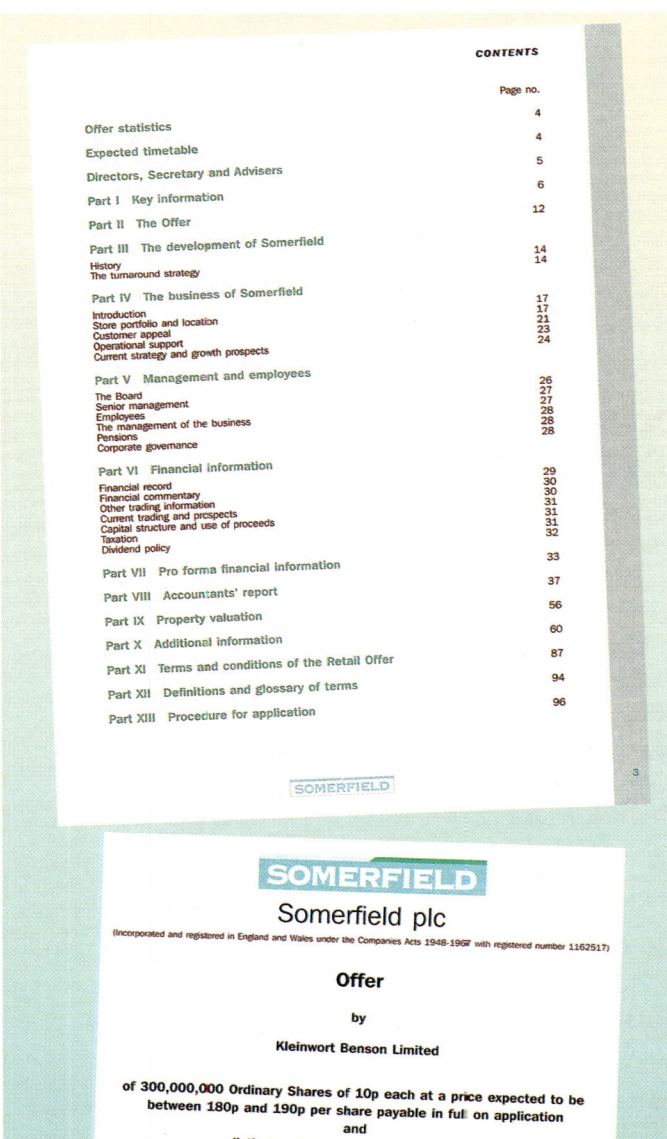

Contents of a prospectus and offer for sale

Limited companies 13

What are the main aims of the business?

The main aims are likely to be the maximisation of profit in order to maximise returns for shareholders, the maximisation of market share and the growth of the business. Sometimes a firm will aim to make sufficient returns to keep shareholders happy and also provide for future investment. Many large companies now also include charters or contracts in their aims. Many firms also have 'mission statements' or 'visions'. These charters and statements outline what they will aim for in terms of customer satisfaction (95% of our trains will run on time, 99% of deliveries will reach you by the next working day) or in the area of environmental concerns (we will only use recycled produce, we will not exploit cheap foreign labour, we will not use animal testing in our products) even if these may cut profits. In the long term, the reputation of the firm may be more important than current profits.

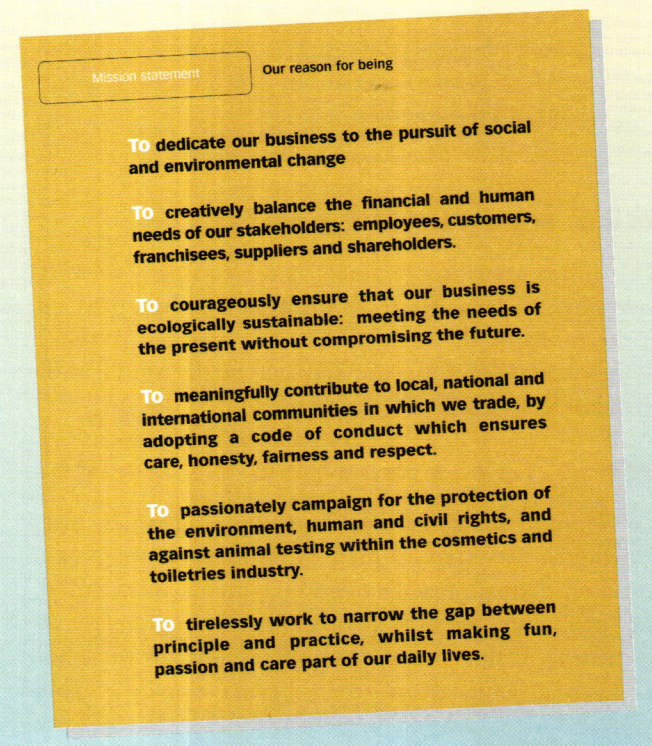

Body Shop Charter

Did you know? In autumn 1997 the Mercedes-Benz Company put all the weight of its reputation behind the launch of a new, family car – the Baby Benz. In November, before a single car had been sold in the UK, the company had to recall all the cars it had sold in Europe due to a design flaw which meant that the car tended to fall over when cornering. The damage to the reputation of Mercedes-Benz is likely to be much greater than the damage to its profits.

Winding up the business

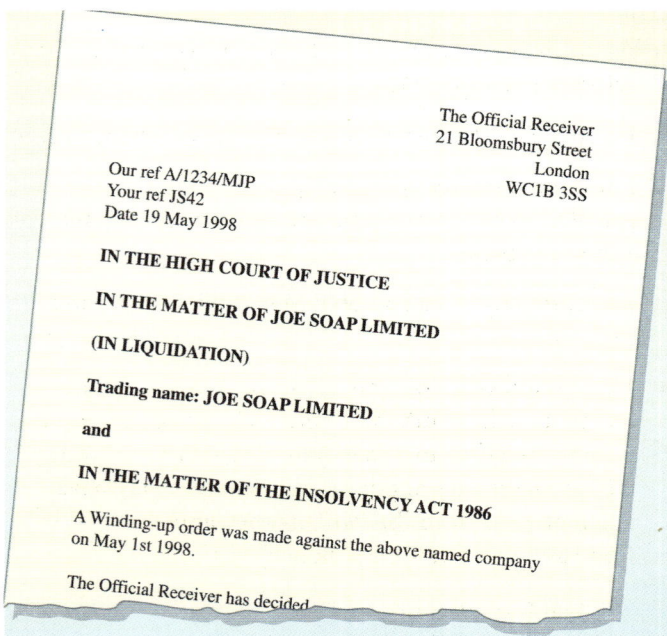

When a limited company ceases trading its affairs are 'wound up' and its assets are sold to turn them into money. Money is the most 'liquid' form of an asset (in other words, it is easily transferred and easily divided) so the process is called **liquidation**. The money is then distributed, firstly to pay off any outstanding taxes and wages and then to pay off other debts of the company. Finally, the remaining money (if there is any) is distributed to shareholders.

The winding up may be compulsory – brought about because the firm hasn't started trading, cannot pay its debts or has failed in its legal duties, for example has produced no report or accounts or has held no shareholders' meetings. A creditor, a shareholder or the **Official Receiver** may apply for a compulsory winding up order. Alternatively, the winding up may be voluntary – when the shareholders of a company decide that the company will cease trading.

What are the main advantages?

- Each shareholder enjoys limited liability – they are not risking personal bankruptcy.
- The business has continuity; because it has a separate legal existence to its owners, the business can be bought and sold like any other commodity; the death or retirement of shareholders does not affect it.
- Large amounts of capital can be raised in relatively short time periods.
- It is easier for the business to borrow money.

14 Limited companies

What are the main disadvantages?

- There are legal formalities which must be carried out before the company can be set up.
- There are legal constraints on how the company is run.
- The company must produce accounts which are available to the public – business affairs are not allowed to be kept private.
- The company is accountable to its shareholders and creditors.
- There is a divorce of ownership from control – the owners may have different aims from the directors they appoint; the directors may have different aims from the managers they appoint; the managers may have different aims from the workers they appoint. This can lead to no-one achieving their aims.
- A complex management structure may be needed, leading to difficulties in communication.
- The performance of the company may not be reflected in its share price. A company that is doing well could find itself seriously undervalued on the Stock Exchange if shareholders have decided to sell shares for other reasons.
- Companies are liable to take-overs by other companies or the original owners could lose control of the company.

Activity

1. Draw up a diagram like the one on page 5 and fill in the details for a private and a public limited company.
2. What other details do you think should be added to make this more helpful for your revision?

Activity

Joe Soap, through his experience in window cleaning, has developed a 'magic sponge' which cleans windows in half the time it takes with a traditional window leather. He persuaded the bank to lend him some money to manufacture and market the sponges and sales have gone well. The problem is that he is having to pay the bank loan back, including interest on it, and would like to raise money from another source. He needs around £40 000 for his plans.

Mrs Edna Soap (Joe's mum, retired accountant) 5000 shares
Albert Fletcher (Margaret's brother, Joe's brother-in-law) 2500 shares
Mrs Margaret Soap (Joe's wife, designer) 2500 shares
James Walker (senior manager) 10000 shares
Joe Soap 10000 shares
Basharat Hussain (senior manager) 10000 shares

He has £10 000 of his own and decides that he will offer shares in Joe Soap Ltd in order to raise the other £30 000 he needs. He offers the 30 000 £1 shares to members of his family and to his two senior managers, who agree to buy the shares shown below left:

1. What part of the name of the firm now has to change?
2. What benefits do each of the shareholders get as a result of buying their shares?
3. How else could Joe Soap have raised the money he needed?
4. Draw up the Memorandum of Association for the company using the information above.
5. How could Joe Soap and his family lose control of their company?
6. Suggest which of the shareholders should be a) the company secretary b) the chairman or woman, c) the directors.
   Give reasons for your answer.
7. Which method of raising the additional money would you recommend to Joe Soap? Give reasons for your answer.

Limited companies 15

Did you know? Sometimes the assets of a company – which may be such things as brand names and logos as well as machinery, equipment and factories – may be worth more than the company. Sometimes people will buy a company in order to make money by selling off its assets; this is called asset-stripping.

Activity
> Look at the 10 steps below that explain how to become an instant millionaire. Which of the 10 steps shown do you think are the hardest? Give reasons for your answer.

How to become an instant millionaire

Method 1 – Win the Lottery

Method 2 – Ten steps to success

1. Come up with an absolutely brilliant and unbeatable idea (don't forget to protect it with a patent).
2. Draw up a Memorandum of Association which, amongst other things, states that your company will have £2 000 000 of capital divided into ordinary shares of £1 each.
3. Draw up the Articles of Association and state that you have met all the legal requirements of the Companies Act.
4. Get your Certificate of Incorporation from the Companies' Registrar.
5. Issue a prospectus that proves how brilliant your idea is.
6. Offer £1 000 000 worth of shares for sale at £1 each.
7. Keep the other 1 000 000 shares for yourself.
8. Sell the £1 000 000 worth of shares.
9. Whatever price they start trading at, your own shares could now be sold for that amount.
10. As long as it's £1 or above, congratulations, you're a millionaire!

Note Some of these steps are much harder than others!

Codebreakers

Liquidation: the nearer an asset is to conversion into cash (stock is easier to sell than machinery, machinery easier to sell than buildings) the more liquid it is said to be. Cash is the most liquid form an asset can take and liquidation means turning all assets into cash.

Official Receiver: a court appointed official who will oversee the selling of a company's assets and the payments to its creditors.

Activity
> One possible coursework assignment is specifically designed for people who have an interest in this area, or who would find it difficult to go out and collect primary data. It is to send for the annual report and accounts of two public limited companies and compare them to see which company is doing better. Any public company will send you their latest report and accounts if you request them and they will contain a great deal of information about the company. There are some specific things to look for and you will find many of them outlined in Unit 28.

THE STOCK EXCHANGE

Once shares in a public company have been issued, they are traded on the stock exchange; this now takes place 24 hours a day in the main trading centres of the world. It is often said that 'as one market closes, another opens'. The markets of America, the principal one being New York's Wall Street market, are opening as London and other European markets close. The important markets of the Far East (Hong Kong and Japan) open as American markets close and European markets are opening as Eastern markets close. To buy shares in a company you would normally approach a bank or a stockbroker who will act as your agent. While many people only buy shares in a company because they want to share in the profits, there are also those who make money out of buying and selling shares.

SUMMARY

Ten points to remember:

1. A limited company has limited liability.
2. Limited liability means that the responsibility for the debts of the firm is limited to the amount invested.
3. Limited companies may be private or public.
4. Public limited companies offer shares to the public.
5. Companies must warn people that they have limited liability by putting either Ltd for private limited companies, or plc for public limited companies, after their name.
6. Profits and control are shared equally by the shareholders.
7. There can be a divorce of ownership from control.
8. Setting up the business involves legal processes.
9. The business has a separate legal identity from its owners.
10. The business can be compulsorily wound up.

Unit 4
Franchises

For many people, the prospect of starting up a business from scratch – finding a market, developing a product, risking their life savings – is far too daunting. Businesses which are started often find it difficult to survive, with over half of small businesses failing within the first two years of operation, many within the first six months. In contrast, less than one in fifteen franchise outlets actually ceases trading in any one year, with over nine out of ten reported as being profitable.

Perhaps one of the best known franchise operations in the world, certainly in America and the UK, is the McDonald's fast food group. This is the largest fast food company in the world and has franchises worldwide. Ray Kroc obtained a franchise in 1954 and the right to license more franchises from the McDonald brothers who founded the firm (the famous McDonald M is a representation of the arches over their first hamburger restaurant). By 1960 Kroc had bought out the brothers, by 1968 there were 1 000 franchised restaurants and more than 10 000 by 1990. The largest McDonald's in the world opened in Moscow in 1990 and within a year was serving over 27 000 customers a day.

WHAT IS A FRANCHISE?

A franchise is when a company allows someone to sell its goods or services using its trade marks, brand name, image and system of operation. A fee will be charged for this.

A franchise is a way for the franchisee to start a business with:

- reduced outlay
- reduced risk
- an established name, format and product.

At the same time it provides a way for the franchiser:

- to expand
- with limited costs
- whilst retaining control.

Handy hints: An employer is someone who employs, an employee is someone who is employed. If you remember this use of the -er and -ee endings then you will remember that the franchiser is the one who sells the franchise and the franchisee is the one who has bought it.

Who owns the business?

The franchiser owns the business idea and the successful product or service. They may themselves be owned by a larger company or corporation. There are over 400 franchise operators offering franchises in the UK, many of them in fast food, high street retail outlets and petrol station forecourt operations. Many franchisers also own their own outlets and rent or lease premises to franchisees. McDonald's, for instance, owns all of its outlets. The franchisee could be a sole trader, a partnership or a limited company. Providing they can satisfy the requirements of the franchiser as to their suitability to finance and operate the franchise, the form of business organisation they decide to take is unimportant.

> **Did you know?**
>
> Burger King is owned by Diageo, which was formed by the merger of Grand Metropolitan and Guinness.

Who controls the business?

A large degree of control is kept by the franchiser. Product lines, packaging, the use of the company's logos, slogans and brand names is strictly controlled. In a fast food operation, for example, the franchiser will provide equipment, food stock, menus, uniforms, point-of-sale material, colour schemes, portion sizes, instructions on ingredients, cooking times and methods (each food item, from whichever franchise, should be identical). In addition, they will provide training and may also provide such things as incentive schemes, loans and insurance.

The franchiser may also provide national advertising, marketing and promotion schemes that the individual franchisee would never be able to afford.

> **Activity**
>
> Look at the logos of franchisers on the previous page.
>
> 1. Make a list of them under three columns headed 'Fast food', 'Retail' and 'Services'.
> 2. Which is the largest sector? Why do you think this is so?
> 3. Look in a telephone or business directory and list which of these firms are located in your area. Choose one of the businesses that you have listed. Is there any independent competition locally? Why do you think that this is so?

> **Activity**
>
> As research for the coursework title 'Is there scope for a new business in the local area?' you could find out what opportunities exist for a franchise operation.
>
> 1. List the franchises that are already operating. As it is likely that these will have been given exclusive areas, you would not be able to open a similar franchise.
> 2. Identify what you think is missing – a gap in the market. This can be done through observation and consumer questionnaires.
> 3. Obtain a directory of franchise opportunities. Which of them would fill the gap found by your research?
> 4. Look at the financial requirements of the franchiser. How could you raise the money?
> 5. Evaluate whether you think the business would be a success, giving your reasons as to why.

The franchisee generally has a certain amount of limited day-to-day control of the business. In some franchises this may extend to operating their own working hours or even introducing their own varieties of product.

Where does the finance come from?

Sources of finance for the franchisee will be similar to those of other independent business operators – the franchisee's own funds, bank loans and overdrafts or, in the case of a limited company, money raised through the sale of shares. Banks tend to look more favourably on a franchise operation when considering loans as, because they are operating established business lines, they are much less of a risk.

How is the business established?

A successful business operation decides that it would like to expand. It can either open another branch (and there are many operations where this is the case) or it can sell the right for someone else to open and operate another branch. Essentially, it is selling its successful business idea or format. The company will advertise the availability of the franchise (there are specialist publications for this, such as the *UK Franchise Directory* and *Franchise World Directory*) and will set a fee for the initial purchase or **lease** of the franchise (this could be anything from a few hundred pounds to several hundred thousand pounds) and a further charge – a **royalty** – which is set as a percentage of the franchise's turnover.

The company will carefully consider the applicants, as there are generally many more applicants than there are franchise opportunities, The Body Shop, for example, receives over 10 000 applications each year, most of which will be rejected. Once an applicant has been chosen, the company provides some or all of the following: stock, training, premises, insurance, loans, advertising, legal advice, design and shopfitting, tools, an exclusive geographical area, computer software and even, in some cases, customers.

The franchisee pays the royalty on the year's turnover and keeps any further profit; if there are losses, the royalty on turnover is still paid and the losses have to be covered by the franchisee.

> **Handy hints**
> Using the correct terms is always important. Don't get turnover mixed up with profit. If I buy 10 chocolate bars for 10p each but can only sell them for 8p each then my sales turnover is measured by my sales revenue – 10 bars @ 8p = 80p. My costs were 10 @ 10p = £1, so I've made a loss – £1 - 80p = 20p. If I was a franchisee, my royalty payment would still be due on my turnover.

Who is responsible for the debts of the business?

Franchisees must cover any losses and are responsible for their own debts – if they have unlimited liability as a sole trader or partnership, then personal wealth is at risk; as a limited company, responsibility for debt would be limited to the amount invested in the company.

Who keeps the profits?

The franchisee keeps the profits they make from the operation. These can, however, be limited by the price restrictions enforced on them by the franchiser and by the fact that they may be forced to buy their stock from the franchiser – even though it could be available more cheaply elsewhere. Franchisees are also likely to be restricted to the range of stock supplied by the franchiser. The franchiser takes a share in the form of royalties. The higher turnover is, the greater the amount that the franchisee will have to pay, as royalties are calculated as a percentage of turnover.

> **Did you know?**
> Channel 3 commercial television stations in the UK are also franchises – companies who wish to run a station must bid for a franchise that will last for a limited number of years and then re-bid if they wish to keep the station. Thames TV, Central TV, Yorkshire TV, etc. are all franchisees to the franchiser – the Independent Broadcasting Association.

What are the main aims of the business?

For the franchiser, the main aim is to expand the business without having to take on the debt that this usually means. For the franchisee, the aim will be to start a successful business by using a tried and tested business idea. The franchiser is likely to have profit maximisation or taking a maximum market share as major aims. For the franchisee, a successful business and a reasonable income are likely to be the targets.

Activity

Read the passage and answer the questions that follow.

Brothers Steve and Jon did some market research while they were on a surfing holiday in Cornwall and found that there was a real demand for brightly coloured boards painted in designs of the customer's own choosing. When they got back to Manchester, they pooled their resources and rented a workshop for six months. They both really enjoyed making the boards but neither of them particularly wanted to be involved in selling them. At the end of the six months they had a good supply of boards but could not afford to rent the workshop any more. The fibreglass that they had bought on credit had to be paid for. They had nowhere to store their boards. Their business had failed.

1. Give three reasons why you think that Steve and Jon's business failed.
2. If they had been able to buy a surfboard making franchise, the business might have been a success. Give three reasons why.
3. Of the reasons that you have given, which do you think is the single most usual reason for business failure? Explain why.
4. Which do you think is the single most usual reason for the success of a franchise? Explain why.
5. What extra costs would the brothers have had to pay if they bought a franchise?
6. The brothers have come to you as a business adviser. Outline what advice you would give them.

What are the main advantages?

The main advantages to the franchiser are:
- expansion without the burden of debt
- a regular income
- a much smaller workforce than if a branch operation was established
- a much less complex management structure than if there were branches
- control over franchise operations.

The main advantages to the franchisee are:
- the low risk involved in franchising
- selling a product or service that is established and successful
- the use of the brand image of a successful business
- the provision of an exclusive area
- the provision of help, advice and training
- the national advertising and promotion that they could not themselves afford.

What are the main disadvantages?

The major disadvantage lies in the amount of control which the franchiser has over the franchisee. Restrictions placed on the franchisee may make them feel more like managers than independent owners. However, unlike most managers, successful franchisees are entitled to much of the profit from their operation and this can be a powerful incentive.

Codebreakers

Franchise: the right to trade under an established name.

Franchisee: the person or organisation buying the right.

Franchiser: the person or organisation selling the right.

Lease: to hire or borrow for a fixed amount of time.

Royalty: a payment made on earnings, payable as a proportion or percentage of earnings.

Activity

Jon and Steve have entered a franchise agreement with Surfin' Style, a large surf shop company. They are allowed to sell three types of board – the Chunky Baby (a beginner's board), the South Sea Islander (a better and faster board) and The Ultimate (a professional quality board).

The Chunky costs £90 to them and sells at £125. In the first year they sold 17.

The Islander costs £150 to them and sells at £175. In the first year they sold 15.

The Ultimate costs £200 to them and sells at £300. In the first year they sold 14.

The brothers bought twenty of each board, the minimum allowed under the franchise.

The franchiser takes a royalty of 5% on turnover.

1. Draw up a spreadsheet that shows whether the brothers made a profit or not.
2. Show what effect there would be if the royalty were reduced to 2%.
3. Demonstrate, using the figures in your spreadsheet, why the franchiser charges royalties on turnover and not on profit.

This task partially fulfils the requirements of the Spreadsheet Unit of the NEAB Certificate of Achievement in IT.

SUMMARY

Eight points to remember:

1. A franchise is the right to trade using a successful company's products and image.
2. The franchiser offers the franchise.
3. The franchisee buys or leases the franchise.
4. The franchiser expands their business without the burden of debt.
5. The franchisee can establish a low risk operation.
6. Payment of a fee and royalties is made to the franchiser by the franchisee.
7. Franchisers maintain control over many aspects of franchisee operations.
8. Franchisees are generally better motivated because of the profits they will receive.

Unit 5
Co-operatives

If a group of producers can set up a market of their own instead of sending their goods down the chain of distribution via wholesaler and retailer to the final consumer then two things are likely to happen. Firstly, prices are likely to be lower to the consumer; secondly, profits are likely to be higher for the producer. This would be a **producer co-operative**.

If a group of consumers were to band together in order to buy goods in bulk and shared the profits amongst themselves, this would be a **consumer co-operative**.

When a group of workers decide to own the business that they work in jointly and share decision making and profits equally, this is a **worker co-operative**.

With much produce, the traditional way to sell was directly to the consumer via a market, and indeed many producers still organise their own consumer sales. The well-known brand 'Sunkist', for example, is the trading name of the California Fruit Growers' Association – a producers' co-operative of the orange, lemon and grapefruit growers of California. Workers may also form co-operatives to share in an organisation's ownership and decision making or to share the benefits of bulk purchasing and independent pricing.

The museum in Rochdale dedicated to the co-operative movement.

ALL KINDS OF CO-OPERATIVES

A co-operative enterprise is any one where a group of people have come together to work, or to buy or sell goods or services, for the group's shared benefit.

A co-operative can be one of the following kinds:

- a worker co-operative
- a producer co-operative
- a consumer co-operative.

Worker co-operatives

The recession of the late 1980s and early 1990s meant that many businesses found that they could no longer operate. Rather than become unemployed, many workers actually took the option of buying out their firm with their **redundancy** money and becoming co-operatives. This had the double advantage of keeping them in work and giving them a share in the profits of the firm. The major features of worker co-operatives are shared decision making, shared risk and shared profit. A democratic decision making process means that everyone is involved in decision making, each with one vote. As a firm becomes bigger, of course, this becomes much less workable. While a meeting of sixteen workers might be possible, and each would be able to speak, a meeting of 160 or 1 600 workers is obviously extremely difficult. Each worker puts in an equal amount of money and takes an equal share of the profit, thus sharing equally in the success or failure of the firm.

> **Did you know?**
> Worker co-operatives do not have to be established by workers being made redundant. In many European countries, successful co-operatives have operated for many years. This is particularly true of the Scandinavian countries where the co-operative movement has been called the 'middle way' between capitalism and communism.

Advantages and disadvantages of worker co-operatives

The worker co-operative:

- has less chance of industrial relations problems than an owner/worker system; as the workers are the owners then there should be no conflict of objectives
- produces better motivation in the workers; as they are working for themselves, they will be encouraged to work better and harder
- is aware of its responsibilities to the local community from which the workforce is drawn.

On the other hand:

- there is little chance of successful expansion – raising extra capital is difficult and more workers make decision making harder
- ambitious workers will find that promotion or wage increases are hard to come by
- members get to speak and vote on decisions even if they have no knowledge or experience of the area being discussed
- there is a reluctance to employ outside experts, which could lead to poor management, weak financial control and ineffective marketing.

The Industrial Common Ownership Movement will give help and advice to worker co-operatives.

> **Handy hints**
> One of the biggest benefits of worker co-operatives is that they are generally set up as limited liability companies. Remember that this safeguards members' personal wealth. Only the money that they have invested is at risk.

Producer co-operatives

Producers who join together in order to share resources and marketing are becoming increasingly common. In South America, for example, small producers of coffee have banded together to co-operate in the marketing of their produce. As a group, they have more power over the sales value of their commodity. Café Direct, the name of one group, is able to ensure that the coffee is marketed at a fair price and without the farmers being exploited.

Another way in which such groups co-operate may be in the purchase of large and expensive items of plant or

Activity

By choosing a co-operative enterprise and a competitor firm in the same business you could tackle the question to 'Compare the objectives of two different businesses'.

1. Outline what the objectives of a co-operative are likely to be.
2. Outline what the general objectives of the co-operative that you have chosen are.
3. Interview the owner/workers and see if they agree with the objectives – do any of their objectives conflict with each other, or with the firm?
4. Outline the type of ownership of the competitor firm.
5. Describe what its general and specific objectives are.
6. Compare the two (or more!) sets of objectives.
7. Which firm has the clearest idea of what its goals are and why?
8. Which firm is most likely to achieve its goals and why?

Activity

1. Visit a local store or supermarket and see if they stock produce from either Café Direct or Sunkist.
2. Read the labels. What information is given about the co-operative?
3. Explain what you think happens to the profits made from the sale of these goods.

Activity

Read the passage and answer the questions.

Raminder Singh is the owner of a small textile manufacturing business, making woollen jumpers and cardigans. Recently, he has found that demand has fallen to a level where he feels that the business is no longer making enough profit; he would like to retire anyway. He has decided to close down the business and has offered to pay his 20 workers redundancy money. They have met together and decided that they would like to use the money to buy the business from Mr Singh. He is willing to accept their offer and has even said that he will manage the firm for them for the first six months until they 'get on their feet'.

The workers held a meeting and elected a committee of five of the most senior workers to make the most important decisions. The first decision they made was to lower the prices of their products.

1. Outline the main benefits that the workers would gain from forming a co-operative.
2. Outline the main problems that the workers are likely to face
   a) now
   b) in six months time.
3. Explain how you think that the co-operative can afford to charge lower prices.
4. What other forms of ownership could the workers have chosen? Which would you recommend and why?

machinery. A machine that would be too expensive for one farmer and only used some of the time, may be bought by several farmers who then share in its use. A preparation or packaging plant may be jointly owned by a number of producers where no single one would be able to afford it.

Consumer co-operatives

In the 19th century it was the practice of mill owners in the UK to have their own shops for mill workers to buy from. Sometimes workers were not paid in money, but in tokens for these shops. Further to this, the produce sold was often over priced and impure. Adding chalk dust to bulk out flour or giving less weight than had been paid for were common practices.

In 1844, a group of workers in Rochdale, Lancashire, set up their own grocery store. They formed the Rochdale Society of Equitable Pioneers, with each member contributing £1 from their savings to set up the business and buy stock. The store sold basic commodities at fair prices. Profits were divided (a '**dividend**' paid) according to the amount that had been spent in the shop. The store that was set up was so successful that it is now preserved as a museum of the co-operative movement. The Rochdale Pioneers, as they became known, were the fore-runners of a co-operative retail movement which now has a turnover of more than £8 000 million and nearly 5 000 shops nationwide.

The principles laid down by the Rochdale Pioneers have been adopted by modern co-operative movements. The three main principles are:

- each member has only one vote, regardless of the number of shares held
- anyone may buy a share and become a member, regardless of race, creed or religion
- goods and services are sold at reasonable prices. After business expenses have been paid, the profits are returned to the members in proportion to the amount that they have spent.

Co-operative union

Twenty-five years after the founding of the Rochdale Co-op, the Co-operative Union was formed. This is a body that helps and advises on the formation of new co-operative enterprises. It now forms an umbrella body linking the Co-operative Retail Societies (CRS), Co-operative Wholesale Society (CWS), and other co-operative enterprises such as the Co-operative Insurance Society, the Co-operative Press and the Co-operative Bank.

Mutual societies

Where a group of people come together to provide them with a benefit, this is often in the form of mutual societies. In the UK these have developed into two groups: insurance companies and building societies. Insurance companies share risk – the **premiums** that people pay are held centrally and can be paid out to anyone who has a misfortune. Forms of marine insurance have been around since Roman times, fire insurance grew rapidly after the Great Fire of London in 1666 and car insurance is now an enormous market. Assurance societies are similar to insurance societies in that each member contributes a premium. Their payments, however, are not based on events that *might* happen, but on events that *will*. Thus early assurance societies were to provide pensions and funeral expenses (you *were* going to retire, you *were* going to die). Assurance policies still pay out on the death of the assured.

Building societies are institutions that accept deposits from members and then lend the accumulated money to other members so they can buy their own houses.

Building society conversions

Building societies are mutual societies that now provide many other benefits such as current accounts, credit cards and personal loans. As a result of this, a number of building societies have converted to being banks. As a bank is a profit making institution, rather than an institution that exists for the benefit of its members, this meant that they had to ask their membership, through a vote, for permission to cease being a mutual society and instead become a company. Because the societies offered shares in the new companies to members, many were happy to vote for the change and a number of building

Activity

1. Using a drawing package, design a label for the goods of a producer co-operative. You may choose an existing co-operative, like Café Direct or Sunkist, or use a co-operative of your own making. The label must clearly state the goods that are being produced, the nature of the co-operative and the reasons behind the co-operation.
2. Produce three different versions of the label, in different shapes, colouring and lettering.

This task partially fulfils the requirements of the Graphics Unit of the NEAB Certificate of Achievement in IT.

societies became public limited companies. Many of the shares were sold by those who received them, who then spent this windfall, giving a boost to many parts of the economy. Other people were sad to see the mutual and co-operative principles on which the societies were founded being replaced by the profit motive.

Activity

Look at the logos of the various building societies illustrated.

1. Name any other building societies you know. Ask at home for those you can't name now.
2. Which of these converted to plcs? (Remember, they will now be quoted on the stock exchange.)

SUMMARY

Eight points to remember:

1. Co-operatives are where groups of people come together for shared benefits.
2. The three main sorts are producer, consumer and worker co-operatives.
3. Worker co-operatives are often set up as a result of business failure.
4. Their main advantage is the motivation which self-ownership gives.
5. Their main disadvantages are the difficulty of raising capital and the reluctance to involve outside help.
6. Producer co-operatives are often based on agriculture.
7. Consumer co-operatives were the starting point for the co-operative movement.
8. Mutual societies are another form of co-operative.

Codebreakers

Producer co-operative: a group of producers who join together to share plant, equipment or marketing.

Consumer co-operative or retail co-operative: a co-operative enterprise aimed at bringing fair priced goods and services to consumers and giving them returns on their spending.

Worker co-operative: a group of workers who share ownership and control.

Redundancy: when a job is no longer required to be done, the worker is no longer needed, they are therefore redundant.

Dividend: a share of profits given to members (shareholders).

Premiums: small sums of money that are paid regularly to a company to provide insurance.

Unit 6
Public sector organisations

Some organisations are either so big, so expensive to run, or so important to a country's safety or economy, that they are owned and controlled by the government of the country. They are paid for out of the money that citizens pay in taxation to the government.

The Royal Yacht Britannia, pictured here, was recently decommissioned (that is, taken out of service) and is to become a floating museum. It was actually a naval vessel that was used as a 'floating embassy' for the Queen and other government officials on visits abroad. It was, however, owned by the government, crewed by the Royal Navy and paid for by the taxpayer, not the Queen. During conflicts it has been used as a hospital and supply ship, underlining its role as part of the defence forces of the United Kingdom. All parts of the Royal Navy, the Royal Air Force and the Army are actually owned and controlled by the government and paid for by the taxpayer. Brittania was thus part of the **public sector**.

WHAT IS THE PUBLIC SECTOR?

The public sector is any organisation owned and controlled by government on behalf of the public.

Handy hints: Be careful not to mix up the public sector and public limited companies. The public sector is those corporations or parts of the economy that are owned or controlled by government on behalf of the public. Public limited companies are those where the public can directly buy shares in the company. Think of it as all taxpayers sharing in ownership of businesses in the public sector, but only those who have bought shares, share in the ownership of public limited companies.

This means that the public sector consists of:

- central essential services – defence, the Health Service, the Royal Mint
- government departments providing services – the Stationery Office, the Central Office of Information, the Office for National Statistics
- public corporations – the BBC, the Bank of England, the Post Office
- nationalised industries
- local government and the services it provides
- QUANGOs (see page 30) – English Nature, the Environment Agency, Training and Enterprise Councils.

Did you know? Most of these organisations are known just by their initials – COI, ONS etc. It is worth learning what the most important ones stand for. If the organisation has 'Her Majesty' in it, this doesn't mean that it belongs to the Queen. In general the 'HM' means that the organisation is a direct office of government for example, HMI, which stands for Her Majesty's Inspector (of schools).

Central services

The defence and safety of the nation is so important that this is a direct function of government, through the Ministry of Defence. It would be dangerous and is illegal for people to raise their own armed forces. The sums of money involved in the development and purchase of warships, aeroplanes and weapons are generally far too large for any commercial organisation to afford and can only be paid out of government tax receipts. Many weapons and arms manufacturing contracts, however, are won by private firms.

The National Health Service (NHS) is funded from **national insurance contributions**, a form of taxation paid by both employer and employee to ensure that unemployment benefits, health and pension care are available to all. The Health Service in the UK is paid for by taxpayers rather than being paid for at the point where it is used. (In the United States, for example, health insurance is taken out in case medical attention is needed and all treatments have to be paid for.) Recent changes to the way that the Health Service has been organised and funded mean that all treatment is not now prepaid by national insurance contributions. There is a charge for medical prescriptions and for dental and eye check-ups.

Many general practitioners (GPs – the family doctor) have become 'fund-holders' and have to run their own finances rather than being funded centrally. Regionally, NHS Trusts that sell services to hospitals and doctors have been established. Local health authorities control their own finances and are made to compete with each other in what is called the 'internal market'. Many hospitals have also become self-governing trusts, in charge of their own finances.

Administrator: 'Health authorities and doctors are much more efficient if they look after their own finances. That's better for everyone.'

Patient: 'I've been turned down for an operation by my hospital because it says it's too expensive at my age. If I lived in the next health authority I could have it free.'

Activity

1. Look at the statements in the cartoon above. Write or act out with a partner a conversation between the hospital administrator and an elderly patient needing treatment.
2. Outline what benefits the introduction of business competition practices could bring to the Health Service.
3. Outline what problems such competition might bring.

Activity

Many people think that the introduction of charges for dental and eye check-ups was a backward step. Find out:
1. what the charges are
2. in what circumstances eye and dental tests are still free
3. why people might think that the introduction of charges is not a good idea.

Some other services are necessarily provided by government, such as the printing and issuing of notes and coin by the Royal Mint.

Government departments

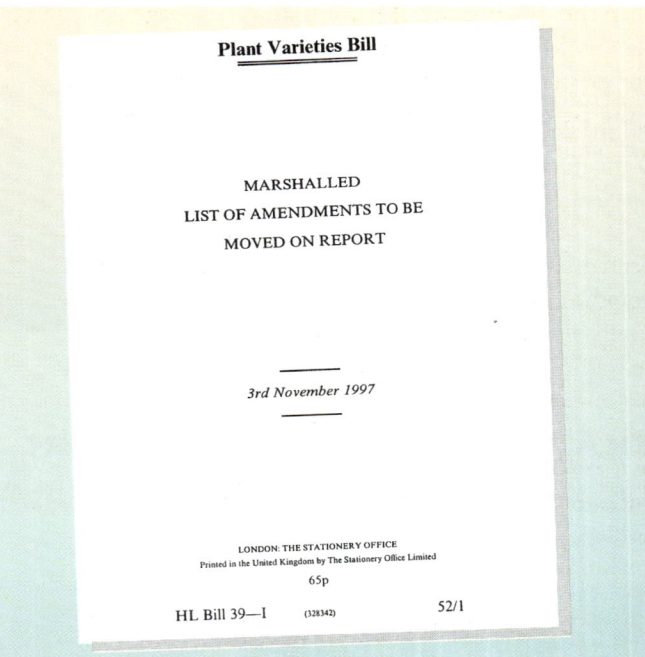

Apart from information, statistics and publications (The Stationery Office publishes all government Bills, statements and Acts of Parliament, ONS compile, collect and publish all government statistics) all government departments have

Handy hints

If you have a question about any aspect of government or government announcements you can write to your MP for further information. This can be a useful source of information for coursework. All MPs can be contacted at The House of Commons, Westminster, London SW1A 0AA. White Papers (proposals for Acts), Bills and other publications can be obtained from The Stationery Office Ltd, PO Box 276, London SW8 5DT. Tel. 0171 873 9090. MPs are duty bound to reply to enquiries from constituents regardless of whether they are government or opposition members.

a duty to provide advice and information to the public either directly or via a Member of Parliament.

Ministries may also be directly involved in providing services. Major highways are the responsibility of government while The Department for Culture, Media and Sport, for example, is responsible for the distribution of National Lottery money to the 'good causes'.

Public corporations

These are limited liability companies that are under the direct control and ownership of government. Not all corporations have the word 'corporation' in their title. The Post Office doesn't, the Bank of England doesn't and many of the nationalised industries were referred to as 'Boards' (the National Coal Board, the Gas Board, the Electricity Board) but this did not stop them being corporations. Since the programme of privatisation (see page 28) there are now few public corporations left. Corporations come into existence either by being created by government (such as the BBC) or by being taken into public ownership (nationalised).

Local government

Elected locally, your local council is responsible, by law, for providing certain services. This is either because they would be unprofitable to provide privately or because they are services that must be available to everyone. Legally, they must provide education, refuse collection, fire and police services. Most councils also provide other services such as leisure and recreation facilities and housing. Look at the diagram above right that shows the areas in which Kirklees Council, a large metropolitan council in Yorkshire, spent money in 1997/8.

The money is raised through:

- **Revenue support grant:** an amount directly set by central government according to the level that it thinks spending should be. The Standard Spending Assessment gives a figure that the council should set as its spending. A further higher figure is supplied to allow for some

Codebreakers

Public sector: ownership and control is by national or local government.

National insurance contributions: a tax used to provide sickness, unemployment and pensions benefits and to fund the NHS.

Corporation: a business that has been 'incorporated': given a separate legal identity and limited liability status.

Metropolitan council: a council that is mostly based on built up areas.

Service:	1997/1998 Gross (£m)	Net (£m)
Education	186.7	157.5
Social Services	74.0	58.1
Leisure and Recreation	24.3	17.8
Housing	127.3	10.8
Highways	23.8	19.8
Planning and Economic Development	6.8	4.9
Environmental Health	4.0	3.4
Refuse Collection and Disposal	11.3	9.1
Other Kirklees Services	49.9	18.2
Joint Committees	5.4	2.4
Contingency and Capital Charges	−11.2	−11.2
Total Kirklees Expenditure	**502.3**	**290.8**
Less: Balances used	3.0	3.0
	499.3	287.8
West Yorkshire Passenger Transport Authority	9.4	9.4
Peak Park Planning Board	0.1	0.1
Environment Agency	1.1	1.1
	509.9	298.4
Plus: Parish Council Precepts	0.2	0.2
	510.1	298.6

overspending but, above that figure, local authorities are 'capped'. This means that any spending above this level will result in the reduction of the revenue support grant.

- **Business rates:** a uniform business rate, linked to rateable value of the property where the business operates, is levied on local businesses.

- **Council tax:** this is an amount linked 50% to the value of a property (the property element) and 50% to the number of adults living in the property (the personal element). For the property element, different 'bands' are given different values. The lowest band, band A, is properties valued at less than £40 000, the highest band (band H) is properties valued at more than £320 000. Each band pays a different proportion of the council tax. If council tax were set at £400, for example, band A properties pay 6/9ths of the amount (£266), band D 9/9ths (£400) and band H 18/9ths (£800).

Where Kirklees Council will get its money from in 1997/8.

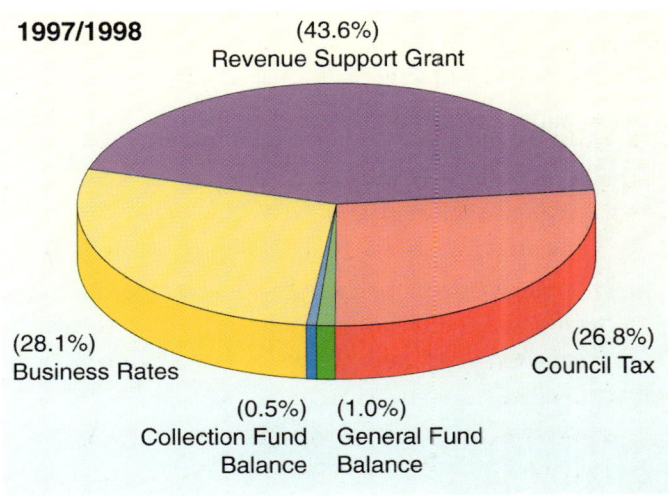

Public sector organisations 27

Nationalisation

A number of large or important industries were taken into government ownership at various times. At its largest, the nationalised industry sector of public ownership extended to the coal industry, shipbuilding, iron and steel, the railways, electricity, gas and water services, telecommunications and London Transport plus many smaller undertakings.

The main reasons why businesses were taken into public ownership were:

- **Economic:** the performance of large industries, particularly in the primary sector, is important to the performance of the economy as a whole. Their size means that they can be used as tools for economic planning. Wage limits, for example, could be imposed on the public sector and the private sector would be encouraged to follow suit. Government could also control the monopoly powers of these industries. Many of them are what are termed 'natural' monopolies – that is, their most efficient form of organisation is as a monopoly organisation. Railways, for example, cannot really compete with each other unless new lines and track are built at enormous cost.

- **Financial:** capital investment in many industries is extremely expensive. While the initial building of the railways was financed by shareholders, once new lines or new rolling stock is needed, there is a reluctance to invest more private money. Also, in some industries, the capital investment became too large for individual businesses to afford (building a new steel plant, for example).

- **Social:** governments could ensure that unprofitable industries stayed viable by giving them subsidies. Many of these were for social reasons, such as keeping unemployment down in an area, or providing affordable rail services to remote communities. The government could also control the pricing of essential services such as water and power to make sure that everyone could afford them.

- **Political:** Some services are seen as too important to leave in private hands – the space programme, nuclear waste disposal and chemical weapons research are examples. Profits could be shared amongst all of the population rather than just the wealthy few who owned the industries. Some nationalisation was to ensure the continuity of fuel supplies in a time of crisis, British Petroleum (BP) for example, or used to make sure that the government had a share in the industries involved in new technology (so-called 'sunrise' industries). Governments committed to nationalisation believed in state ownership as a way of having more control over the economy.

Privatisation

The Conservative government that came to power in 1979 promised to reduce the size of the public sector as they had decided that it had become too expensive. Also, many of the original reasons for nationalising industries no longer applied. They also said that the nationalised industries had become self-satisfied and inefficient and believed that competition would lead to greater efficiency.

Privatisation has three main forms. Firstly, selling public corporations into the private sector by offering shares to the public and then quoting those shares on the stock exchange. This also includes private sales (such as Sealink, part of British Rail, to a commercial buyer and the National Freight Corporation to its own workforce). At local level it has included the selling of council houses to the people who were renting them from the council.

The second form of privatisation has been to allow and encourage competition in areas where before there was none ('deregulation' and 'internal markets'). The third form has been the introduction of charges, such as for prescriptions and tests (see above).

The main privatisations were firstly in those industries where the reasons for public ownership were no longer present – BP was the first to be sold in 1979. Only Cable and Wireless was also sold before the Conservative election victory in 1983. This victory, resulting from popularity gained during the Falklands conflict, gave the government the confidence to go ahead with larger privatisations. Some (such as British Telecom) were sold in parts, so that the government still kept control and in others, the

Activity

When civil servants have to prepare information for governments, they often have to provide two summaries – one pointing out all the good points and one pointing out all the bad points. Imagine that you are the senior civil servant who has been given the job of preparing the information about the privatisation of state schools. Imagine that it has been proposed that state schools must become private institutions, with students paying fees and schools competing for students.

1. List the main points for and against these privatisation proposals.
2. Write two summaries, one in favour and one against privatisation.
3. Decide which one you agree with and write the speech you would make as a politician to persuade people to your point of view.
4. Hold a debate in your class or group and take a vote at the end on whether your group thinks that privatisation is a good or bad thing.

government kept a so-called 'golden share' with which they could outvote shareholders if necessary.

Since 1983 gas, electricity, water, coal, steel, British Airways, the National Bus Company and British Rail have all been privatised.

> **Did you know?**
> Plans to privatise the Post Office were shelved in 1994. Many MPs for rural constituencies were afraid that privatisation would mean the loss of a local service (for the cashing of pensions and paying of bills, for example) as private industry would not have been interested in providing such a service. They pressurised the government into dropping the plans.

The table below sets out the reasons for and against privatisation.

Privatisation

Reasons for	Reasons against
Putting the control of industry into private hands	Monopolies are created which can charge what they like
Encouraging more people to own shares	Private industry is not interested in providing non-profitable services that may bring social benefits (rural railway lines and post offices, for example)
Increasing efficiency by introducing competition	
Reducing the burden of government subsidies	
Political – state control is not desirable in business	Private companies may not be able to afford the levels of investment needed
Private sector decision making is much faster than government	Competition is wasteful and inefficient as resources are duplicated
	Profits go only to the wealthy few who can afford shares
	More efficiency often means greater job losses (the coal and steel industries, for example, are much smaller than when they were government owned)

> **Did you know?**
> Wider share ownership did not develop as the government had hoped it would as most people immediately sold any shares they had bought to make a profit. Most privatisations resulted in shares being sold at well below the market value of the company so that they immediately rose in price when trading started. It is worth remembering that the major shareholders are actually insurance companies and other financial institutions.

New jobs for old? The Meadowhall Centre now stands where the giant Tinsley steelworks used to be.

Internal markets

These have been introduced in many areas, not just the Health Service. The idea is that departments within corporations and councils have to compete with each other to provide the best service at the lowest rate. For example, council refuse collection services have had to compete against private companies for contracts to collect refuse. In many cases, this is done by competitive tender and councils accept the lowest priced offer. Criticism of this system centres on whether cheap services will necessarily be good services.

In education also, schools have been given control over their own budgets since 1994, on the assumption that they will know better where to target the money than will a Local Education Authority. A school's budget is directly linked to the number of pupils it can attract, meaning that good schools should attract more pupils and therefore more money. The criticism of this system is that schools

> **Activity**
> ▶ Make a list of the types of local service that could be lost if they were not provided by central or local government. Underline those you think will affect you personally during your lifetime.

Public sector organisations 29

with poor or deprived catchment areas actually need more money than schools in wealthy areas in order to maintain and improve the service they provide.

Private finance initiative

Capital projects such as the building of schools, bridges, roads and hospitals have traditionally been provided by central government hiring construction companies to do the work and then paying them in stages. In 1992 the government introduced the Private Finance Initiative, which meant that companies wanting to build major projects would have to provide much of the finance themselves and agree to maintain the building or project until the government repaid the finance. This means that:

- government needs to borrow less money
- private sector management and skills are used
- contractors have more incentive to complete work properly and on time.

QUANGOs

Quasi Autonomous Non-Governmental Organisations (QUANGOs) are partly independent organisations that are, nevertheless, government funded. There are hundreds of these bodies ranging from National Park Planning Boards to the Environment Agency, the British Waterways Board, the University Grants Committee, the British Tourist Board, the National Rivers Authority and Training and Enterprise Councils. Appointments are made by government (and often seen as political) and there is much criticism of the way in which QUANGOs operate.

Codebreakers

Nationalisation: taking a private business into public ownership.

Monopoly: a single firm controlling the majority or all of a market.

Subsidies: amounts granted to businesses by government to allow them to keep trading or to keep prices down (many local councils still subsidise local transport).

Privatisation: putting government owned businesses into private hands.

Deregulation: removing rules or regulations (generally in order to increase competition).

Activity

Look at the figures for Kirklees Council on page 27.

1. Enter the figures into a spreadsheet in appropriately headed columns.
2. Enter a formula into a third column which will give you the amounts of revenue Kirklees gets from each of the services it provides.
3. Use the graphics software in the spreadsheet to create a pie chart of the services.
4. Which area has the greatest percentage of expenditure? Which the smallest?

This task partially fulfils the requirements of the Spreadsheet Unit of the NEAB Certificate of Achievement in IT.

SUMMARY

Ten points to remember:

1. The public sector consists of any organisation owned and controlled by government.
2. The public sector has no public companies in it; they are in the private sector.
3. Public sector provision includes central services, public corporations and local government.
4. National government raises money through general taxation and borrowing.
5. Local government raises money through council tax, business rates and borrowing and receives a grant from central government.
6. Nationalisation is the taking into public ownership of private businesses.
7. Reasons for nationalisation are economic, financial, social and political.
8. Privatisation is the selling of government owned corporations into the private sector.
9. Reasons for privatisation are economic, financial, social and political.
10. Privatisation has also introduced competition into a number of areas.

Unit 7
Business size

The News Corporation Limited is, without doubt, a large firm. It operates in many different countries and owns or operates satellite and terrestrial television channels, newspapers and magazines, movie and television programme making facilities and book publishers. It has had an enormous influence on sport in its quest for sponsorship deals, creating the Rugby League Super League amongst other things.

Amongst The News Corporation's holdings are Sky TV and various newspapers, including *The Times, The News of the World* and *The Sun* in the UK. The shops that provide the delivery service for these newspapers are almost all small businesses, yet each type of business is equally viable. The News Corporation Limited could not afford the vast investment it needed to launch such things as satellite channels if it was smaller; newsagents would not be able to provide the local service which they do if they were bigger. So, how do we measure the size of firms and why are some firms larger than others?

WHAT IS BUSINESS SIZE?

Business size is *how* and *why* businesses measure size. It can be measured as:

- the size of market share the business has
- the turnover of the business
- the number of employees in the business
- the value of the business measured in stock market valuation or assets
- the number of countries the business operates in.

What is a big business?

What makes The News Corporation Limited a large business? There is no absolute measurement whereby we can say that a business is 'big' or 'medium' or 'small'. A business which only employs a few people may actually be a big business if these people control and operate large amounts of expensive machinery. In general, firms are measured by being compared with other firms in the same business.

Handy hints: Remember that a 'big' business is only likely to be big in terms of its competitors in the same market. A dairy farm in Devon may be big in terms of the market for milk in Devon but small in terms of its impact on the market for milk nationally.

There are a number of measurements that can be used:

- **The size of market share:** any company with a big enough market share to be able to affect the price in the market is large. This also depends on the overall size of the market – a 'large' company in a small market may be quite a small company by other measures. BSkyB is the only major satellite television provider in the UK.

- **The turnover of the company:** The News Corporation's total revenue in 1995 was over £5 billion, making it undoubtedly large. A turnover of over £8 million is considered to be a large firm in the UK. Less than £2 million is a small firm. £2 million – £8 million is medium sized.

Business size 31

- **The number of employees in the business:** The News Corporation Limited employs thousands of people in its various operations throughout the world. BSkyB alone has 4 580 employees with a wage bill of over £100 million. Any firm with more than 250 employees is considered large, with less than 50, small.

- **Stock market valuation:** this is worked out by taking the price of a share on the stock exchange and multiplying it by the number of shares issued. The value of BSkyB could be estimated by this measurement. When 20% of the stock was sold in 1994, it raised £3.6 billion.

- **Assets:** the value of BSkyB's assets (buildings, businesses, trade marks, stock, plant and equipment) was put in 1995 at around £13 billion. Any UK company with assets exceeding £3 million is said to be large, less than £1 million, small.

News International plc

THE TIMES LITERARY SUPPLEMENT

THE TIMES EDUCATIONAL SUPPLEMENT

Some of The News Corporation's most valued assets are its newspaper titles

Did you know? A billion is different in America and the UK? In the UK it usually means a million million – 1 000 000 000 000, In the US, it means a thousand million – 1 000 000 000. Increasingly, to avoid global confusion, the American billion is being used and all figures stated here refer to a billion as a thousand million.

- **The number of countries in which the business operates:** The News Corporation Limited has businesses in the UK, Australia, the United States, Latin America, India and the Far East.

Activity

> Draw up a table with column headings like the one illustrated here. Fill in the different criteria that show what size a firm is said to be. The first line has been completed for you.

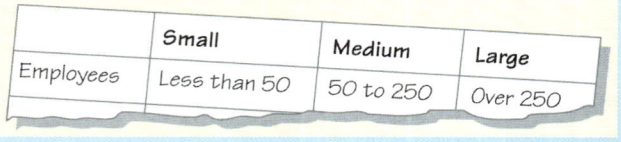

	Small	Medium	Large
Employees	Less than 50	50 to 250	Over 250

Activity

In October 1997, a scheme called Social Accountability 8 000 was launched by the American based Council on Economic Priorities. It is aimed at making sure that large firms do not exploit labour in developing countries by underpaying them, by using child labour or by using forced labour. It requires that proper health and safety standards are set and that trade unions are recognised. Companies must be open to inspection to make sure that standards are being kept.

Winners of the Council's 'Corporate Conscience Award' in 1997 included Kellogg's, Sainsbury's, the Co-op Bank and Toys 'Я' Us. Amongst those listed in their 'Campaign for Cleaner Corporations' as companies not meeting these standards were Exxon, Occidental Petroleum, (both multinational oil companies) and Formosa Plastics. The SA 8 000 standard will only be awarded to those firms who can show that they are sticking to the guidelines.

1. Why do some companies take some parts of their production to foreign countries?
2. Outline the possible advantages and disadvantages to the countries concerned.
3. What advantages do you think can be gained by companies that say they do not exploit labour, or animals, or the environment (that is, those companies who are said to take a 'public ethical stance')?
4. The Disney Corporation was accused in October 1997 of failing to uphold its own code of conduct in its Mexican factories. How might bad news like this affect the size of the company in terms of its value?

Why might a business need to be big?

Some businesses require large amounts of capital investment, for example, satellite broadcasting, oil exploration and drilling or aircraft construction. It is often necessary for a business to be big in order to either generate the amount of money that is needed or to have a high enough credit rating to be able to borrow the necessary money. Some businesses need to produce large amounts in order to be efficient. In the case of newspaper and magazine production, for example, the longer the print run (in other words, the higher the number of copies printed) the lower is the unit price.

Innovators, that is, firms with new ideas, may need to be big enough to withstand what may be early losses in order to gain profits later on. Satellite broadcasting began by making what seemed like huge losses from 1989 to 1991 (the group reported a loss of £163 million in 1991) but, due to the size of the operation, it moved into profit and is now a major contributor to the profits of The News Corporation Limited.

> **Handy hints**
> Capital investment isn't money. It is the plant, machinery, buildings, equipment etc. that has been bought with the money. The 'capital' of a business is measured in terms of the value of such assets.

Why do small firms survive?

Small firms form the backbone of the UK economy. Most stay small for one or more of the following main reasons:

- They may want to stay small – the bigger a firm is, the harder it is to manage and to maintain a personal overview.
- They may be providing a personal service – hairdressing, for instance, is not something that lends itself to a mass market approach.
- They may be providing a local service – taxis, for instance.
- They may be selling to a small market, in many instances because they are selling specialised goods or services.
- They may be providing component parts or materials for larger firms. In this case the size of the firm will be limited by the demands from business customers.
- They may have only just started up.

Economies of scale

Large firms are able to gain economies of scale. These mean that, in certain cases, things become cheaper as a firm grows larger. Economies may take the form of:

- **Financial economies:** large firms find it easier and often cheaper to borrow money. They can also gain by being able to purchase goods in bulk, thus lowering the unit price.

- **Technical economies:** mass production means that unit costs are lower. It also means that a firm can use plant and machinery that would otherwise be too expensive or underused by a small firm.

Activity

1. Collect the company reports of the companies mentioned in the Activity on page 32, plus those of other companies who either claim an environmental approach (The Body Shop for example) or who might be in a position to exploit labour in the developing world.

2. Think of what might be produced in the developing world – check labels on foodstuffs and clothes and look to see where magazines and journals have actually been printed.

   You can then use this information as the basis for a study of companies which declare that they are taking an environmental approach and those which don't.

3. Select two companies from the evidence that you have collected and then evaluate their approach to labour.

4. Decide whether you would award them SA 8000, and why.

Business size 33

- **Risk bearing economies:** firms can afford to take risks on new products because other parts of the business are still profitable.
- **Marketing economies:** advertising and marketing can be carried out extensively. Channels such as national TV advertising are no use to small firms.
- **Managerial economies:** top managers can be employed; they can only be attracted with top salaries.

> **Did you know?**
> Sam Chisholm, BSkyB's chief executive earned £18 714 a day (or £780 an hour, or £13 a minute) for every day of the year according to BSkyB's annual report published in the autumn of 1997, making him the highest paid UK director of a publicly quoted company. The package consisted of a basic salary plus share options and profit related pay, giving an annual salary of over £6.5 million.

Diseconomies of scale

Large firms can also suffer diseconomies from being big. They may take the form of:

- **Decision making diseconomies:** decision making can be slow, so that responses to changes take a long time. As firms grow, the record keeping and bureaucracy grow with them.
- **Managerial diseconomies:** there may be too many middle managers so that it becomes unclear as to who is in charge of what. Lines of communication can become blurred and broken.
- **Diseconomies of diversification:** the firm may be trying to do too many things at once, and going in too many directions for anyone to have an overall grasp of its affairs.
- **Geographical diseconomies:** head office and branch offices may be so far away from each other that branches could be pulling in a different direction from the centre.
- **Staff diseconomies:** employees may feel remote from a large organisation, leading to lower morale and to them being less loyal than they would be to a smaller firm.

Multinationals

Firms operating in more than one country are called multinational or transnational firms. They include many of the biggest companies in the world, such as Shell, Ford and Sony. Often they are criticised for manufacturing or producing in developing countries where labour is cheap but selling products at top prices in the developed world. Some are also criticised for being insensitive to local needs or issues, particularly with regard to the environment. On the positive side, multinationals often provide employment where there would otherwise be none, train the local workforce and create wealth in the countries in which they are established.

Monopolies

These are firms who are of a size where they can control the market or markets that they are in. BSkyB has a monopoly of satellite broadcasting in the UK, for example. A **perfect monopoly** is when there is only one producer in a particular market, so that they *are* the industry. This allows them to set high prices, offer a substandard or inefficient service, or create shortages in the market. In practice, such monopolies can only exist if the product in question is necessary and has no substitute. Satellite broadcasting is only part of the entertainment market. If the market is extended to include all broadcasting, then they have only a part of the market; if the market definition is extended even further to include all entertainment, then their part is even smaller.

Monopolies can also have good points. They can spend money on research and development so that consumers receive better products in the long run and they are able to set lower prices because of the economies of scale that they gain.

> **Activity**
>
> Read the information on page 31 about The News Corporation Limited.
>
> 1. What are the main economies of scale enjoyed by The News Corporation?
> 2. What do you think are the main diseconomies that the Corporation might suffer?
> 3. Outline the steps you think that management could take in order to remove the diseconomies.
> 4. Find out and describe what is meant by 'internal' and 'external' economies and diseconomies.

Activity

A large, multinational organisation will need to use global communications methods.

> **1** Explain what methods The News Corporation could use to gather data about its world-wide operations. What applications could they use?

> **2** Outline three benefits and three disadvantages that they might have from being able to use such communications methods.

> **3** The News Corporation could use public and private networks. Give one example of each.
>
> Outline the use that The News Corporation could make of the Internet, including a description of at least two facilities provided by the Net.

> **4** Find out what data communications standards might be used and why it might be of benefit to use them.

This task partially fulfils the requirements of the Communications Unit of the NEAB Certificate of Achievement in IT.

Codebreakers

Revenue: money received from sales: remember that this is not profit. Costs have to be taken off before profit can be calculated.

Credit rating: a measure of how credit worthy a business is – the better the credit rating, the more likely banks and financial institutions are to lend money, as a higher credit rating means lower risk of repayments not being made.

Economies of scale: cost savings that arise through a firm growing larger.

Bureaucracy: often called 'red tape': the record keeping and filing and the rules and regulations that grow ever more complex as firms expand.

Perfect monopoly: where there is only one firm in an industry and they therefore have total control of the market. A monopoly has some control.

Monopolies and mergers commission

This has existed in one form or another since 1948. It looks at the growth of firms to see if such growth is against the public interest and reports to the Office of Fair Trading who may decide to take action to prevent such growth under UK or, increasingly, European law. See Unit 8 for a more detailed discussion of its operations.

SUMMARY

Seven points to remember:

1. Business size can be measured in a number of ways – there is no absolute measurement.

2. Measurements used include those of size – market share, employees, geographical spread and those of value – stock market valuation, assets, turnover.

3. Some businesses need to be big because of large capital investment, economies of scale or to fund innovations.

4. Small firms have good reasons for staying small.

5. Large firms can gain economies of scale.

6. These may be financial, technical, risk bearing, marketing or managerial.

7. Large firms can also suffer diseconomies of scale. These may particularly affect communication and decision making.

Unit 8
Business growth

There is always news of businesses trying to get larger but why should they wish to grow? Recent reports include Guinness joining with Grand Metropolitan, Freeman's home shopping catalogue merging with Littlewoods, plans for some of the biggest six accountancy firms to join forces, the Halifax planning to take over another firm in the financial services sector and many others. Reckitt & Colman, some of whose brands are shown here, is reported to have paid £96 million to S. C. Johnson and Son for just four brand names: Spray 'n Wash, Vivid, Glass Plus and Yes.

There are hundreds of mergers, take-overs and purchases in any year. How do businesses grow and what are the attractions of growth?

Businesses are trying to grow by gaining more orders, by buying rival businesses or by taking a larger share of the market. They may do this by merging with other businesses, by taking them over, or simply by being more efficient or more competitive – driving competitor businesses out of their market.

THE IMPORTANCE OF BUSINESS GROWTH

Business growth means that a firm becomes larger in one or more of a number of ways. This could be by gaining a larger market, employing a larger workforce or achieving a greater value, either in assets or through the value of its shares. Look at Unit 7 to see how a firm measures its size – an increase in any one of these measurements means that the firm has grown.

Business growth is:
- a greater market share for the business
- a higher turnover
- a greater number of employees in the business
- a greater value to the business measured in stock market valuation or assets
- more geographically widespread operations.

Why do businesses grow?

Sole traders and partnerships start out small, as do many franchise operations. Remember that McDonald's started from a single burger bar; the giant Virgin Corporation started with a single record shop and Sainsbury's began with a single retail outlet. There are many other examples. There are also many examples of firms that started out small and stayed that way. Look at the reasons for the existence of small firms in Unit 7.

Businesses grow for a number of reasons:
- To expand into other types of good or service, in order to increase their **share of the market**, so that they have greater control over the market (and therefore over prices in the market). This may also have the benefit of spreading risk (*see diversification, page 38*).
- To put rival firms out of business, giving them more control over the market.
- To protect themselves from rivals in the market in order to survive.

- To gain economies of scale (see Unit 7) so that their unit costs can be lowered – profits are therefore increased.
- All these are with the aim of increasing the profit that they can make so that the owners – either individuals in private companies or the shareholders in public companies – can benefit.

Rate of growth

The rate of growth of a business is measured by seeing how fast its turnover, or its assets, or the value of its shares are growing. If the rate of growth is too high then it may be that the organisational changes that are needed for the running of a larger company do not keep up with the rate of growth, resulting in problems of management and poor communication. A too rapid rate of growth can mean that a company finds its resources 'too thinly spread'; in other words, it does not have the depth of management skill or worker expertise that it needs. This can make it vulnerable to take-over.

Internal growth

Businesses may grow internally – that is, without involving any competitor businesses, by expanding markets through aggressive marketing, increased sales, a better product range or through technological change. For example, the first firm in a market to adopt a new process or new machinery successfully will have an edge on its rivals. Firms may use aggressive pricing or other practices to gain a greater share of the market. If this is done unfairly, there are laws to protect other firms.

Multi-millionaire Richard Branson, founder of the Virgin Corporation

Activity

Read the passage and answer the questions.

> Richard Branson, head of the airline Virgin Atlantic said that he expected the European Commission to uphold his complaint against the sales tactics used by British Airways. He claims that BA's special discounts for some companies and extra commission for travel agents broke the competition rules laid down by the European Union.
> Mr Branson said that BA were using their power in the market unfairly. The Commission has the power to fine BA up to a tenth of its turnover if Mr. Branson is proved right. Autumn 1997.
>
> – Autumn 1997

1. How, according to Virgin, is BA acting unfairly?
2. Explain why you think that BA has the power to do this, but not Virgin Atlantic.
3. Explain why you think the Commission has been given the power to make such a heavy fine.

External growth – integration

> ### Volkswagen and Volvo – a marriage made in heaven?
>
> Volkswagen is the largest car maker in Europe. Volvo is a Swedish based company making cars and lorries. Both have excellent reputations. Volkswagen for its reliability – VW, Audi and Seat are its main brands – Volvo for its safety. Volvo's truck division is particularly strong. The announcement of a possible move by Volkswagen to take over Volvo is not surprising. VW particularly wants to expand its luxury car range and to move into truck making.
>
> – Autumn 1997

If a firm takes over another firm, or merges with it, then there will be a relationship between the products or services that the two businesses produce. Sometimes this is a very close relationship, sometimes it is a very distant one.

The report above is about Volkswagen and Volvo, two car manufacturers, and states that Volkswagen wants to enter

Handy hints: There is a difference between a merger and a take-over. A merger generally means that the two firms want to join together (although often there is a junior partner and a senior partner). A take-over generally means that the firm being taken over does not want to be. Firms can also grow by simply buying other firms or parts of them.

Business growth 37

the truck market (where Volvo is very strong). The easiest way to do it is by buying or joining with a firm that already has the expertise. This is a form of **integration**:

- **Horizontal integration:** is where a business joins with another at the same level of production. Volkswagen cars and Volvo cars is an example of horizontal integration.

- **Vertical integration:** is where a business joins with another which is at a different stage of production. This can be either forward, to a later stage in the chain of production, or backward, to an earlier stage.

Volkswagen (a manufacturer) joining with a raw material producer (a tyre or rubber manufacturer, for instance) would be an example of backward vertical integration.

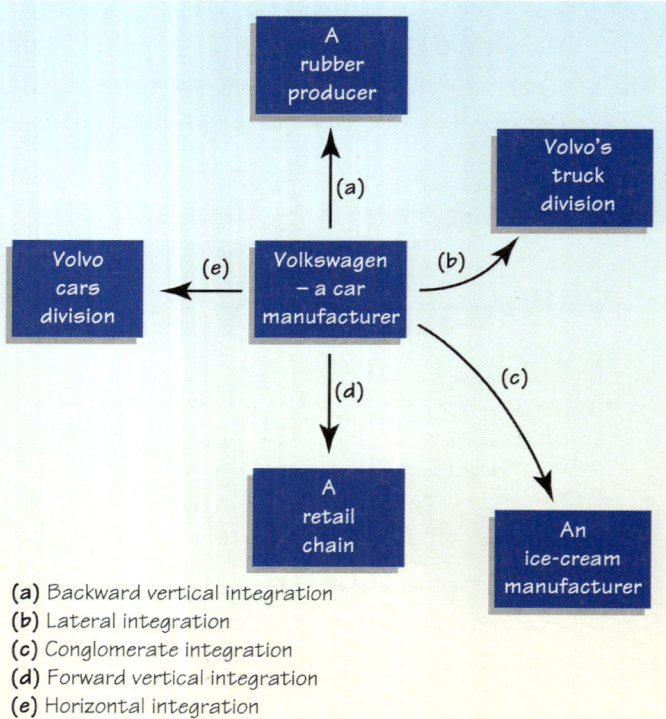

(a) Backward vertical integration
(b) Lateral integration
(c) Conglomerate integration
(d) Forward vertical integration
(e) Horizontal integration

Volkswagen (a manufacturer) joining with a chain of car showrooms (retailers) would be an example of forward vertical integration.

- **Lateral integration:** is when the products are related, but not the same. Volkswagen cars and Volvo trucks would be an example of lateral integration. Much of the technology and engineering know-how will be common to both producers who can benefit from each other's expertise, but a car is not a substitute for a lorry.

- **Conglomerate integration** or **diversification:** is when a company buys into something with which it has no connection – Volkswagen cars and ice-cream, for example!

Handy hints

You will find that types of integration follow the chain of production and distribution. The chain is the stages that a good passes through in production from raw materials to manufacturer to wholesaler to retailer to consumer. Vertical integration means moving up or down the chain, while horizontal means moving to the same stage in another chain.

Diversification

Many companies have grown by diversifying. This means moving into other areas of production or sales. In many cases, this is as a result of a threat to a particular market. Cigarette manufacturers, for example, have long been threatened with bans of one sort or another. Imperial Tobacco (Embassy cigarettes and Ogden's tobacco) diversified into paper and packaging (Mardon), breweries (Courage), seafood (Young's) and tomato ketchup (Daddy's), amongst other things.

The world's leading supplier of tomato ketchup is H. J. Heinz. They are also the major suppliers of prepared food to cafés, etc., in particular single portions of sauces and mayonnaise (known as foodservice products) whilst also producing baby food, condiments, pet foods, and tuna. Brands include Heinz, Quaker and Weightwatcher. A company operating in a number of different markets is called a **conglomerate**.

Did you know?

Thirty-one of Heinz' product lines sell at or near $100 000 000 worth of sales a year, with 26 of these selling over $100 000 000 worth. Many are the leading brands in their particular market, in whatever part of the world they are being sold.

Heinz Company report 1996

Activity

When a firm is thinking of taking over another, it needs as much information about that firm as it can find. Sometimes firms even use industrial espionage – spies – to find out the secrets of rivals!

1. Use a word processing package to outline how you could keep your data secure from such people.
2. Explain what other dangers your data might be subject to and how you would protect it from them.
3. Outline both physical and software methods of securing stored data.

This task partially fulfils the requirements of the Security of Data Unit of the NEAB Certificate of Achievement in IT.

Activity

▸ Choose a particular product in your household. It might be a food product like Heinz soup, an electrical product like a Sony Walkman or a larger product like an Electrolux washing machine or Mitsubishi car.

List the other products you can think of, made by the same firm. Is the firm you have chosen, in your view, a conglomerate? State your reasons.

Monopolies and mergers commission

The job of this organisation is to look into possible mergers and recommend to the government whether or not the merger will be 'in the public interest'. If it looks as if a merger will create a monopoly or a company that might misuse the power that it would gain over a market, then the companies involved may be refused permission to go ahead with it. The European Commission also has powers to block mergers that may not be in the interest of trade in Europe.

Codebreakers

Share of the market: how much of a particular market a firm controls – this may be in a particular area, country or world-wide.

Unit costs: the cost to produce each individual portion of the good or service.

Integration: the joining together of two businesses.

Diversification: the joining together of two businesses who operate in different markets

Conglomerate: a business that operates in many different markets.

Demerger: the opposite of merger – a business deciding to split into two or more separate businesses.

Getting smaller

Some firms grow to such a size that they find it is in their interest to actually get smaller. This may take the form of selling companies or divisions that they no longer feel are central to their business. For example, Volkswagen could merge with Volvo and find that Volvo has a manufacturing plant in Germany that is no longer of any use to the new firm. The plant could then be sold. Or it may be that a whole business is no longer needed. Volkswagen could keep the truck manufacturing side of the business and decide to sell Volvo cars.

In extreme cases, a **demerger** might happen. This means that two companies who have been together decide to separate. Imperial Chemical Industries grew into what were seen as two distinct businesses, one dealing in paints (including the Dulux brand), plastics and industrial chemicals, and the other dealing in fertiliser, pesticides, inks and dyes. After the announcement of a loss in 1993 they decided to split into two groups, ICI to concentrate on the traditional chemicals side of the business and Zeneca to concentrate on fertilisers and dyes, so that they could better compete in two different markets. The new company, Zeneca, took over the Huddersfield based former headquarters of ICI.

Activity

One of the approved NEAB titles for coursework is concerned with why a firm has decided to grow, or not to grow. You could choose a national business that is involved in a take-over or merger and follow the progress of the integration.

1. Write to the two businesses concerned to see if you can find out their reasons for wanting to grow.
2. Study newspaper reports to see what other reasons are put forward.

You might have a local business that has been involved in expansion.

3. See if you can talk to a manager to find out why they have grown.

   Businesses around you that have not grown have made a decision to stay the same size.

4. Interview the owners and managers of such a business – why are they not expanding?
5. Interview the customers of the business. Would they like to see the firm expand.

It might help you if you looked again at the reasons for the survival of small firms.

Business growth

Activity

Look at the two newspaper stories below:

Hiccup for Booze Crews!

The European Commission is set to block the merger of Grand Metropolitan with Guinness. They say that it will create monopolies in at least six EU countries. The merged company would control the markets for Scotch whisky, gin and vodka in the six countries. The Commission is expected to agree to the merger if the companies agree to sell off some of their brands, such as Johnnie Walker and J&B Whisky. European competitor firms have argued strongly against the merger.

– September 1997

A cold winter for Sear's?

The Government, on the advice of the Monopolies and Mergers Commission, has stopped the merger of Freeman's home shopping catalogue with Littlewood's home shopping catalogue. The merger would have meant that the two major players in the home catalogue sales market, Littlewood's and Great Universal Stores, would have controlled over 80% of the market. The Government said this was unacceptable as over 20 million people used mail order catalogues and around two-thirds of those were lower income families. Freeman's is currently owned by Sear's, who have sold 23 businesses recently in an attempt to boost their share price. Shares in Sear's have fallen from a high of over £1.30 in spring 1994 to less than 55p in the winter of 1997.

– November 1997

1. Outline the role of the Monopolies and Mergers Commission and of the European Commission.
2. Explain under what circumstances the European Commission might let the merger of Grand Metropolitan and Guinness go ahead.
3. Explain why the Monopolies and Mergers Commission will not let Littlewood's buy Freeman's.
4. Explain why the government should be concerned about this merger.
5. What good points could you see coming out of either of the mergers if they were allowed to go ahead?

SUMMARY

Ten points to remember:

1. Not all firms want to grow.
2. Those who do, measure their growth by turnover, value or market share.
3. Increased market share gives increased market power.
4. Businesses may grow internally through good marketing and sales techniques or by being first to use new technology.
5. External growth is by merger or take-over or purchase.
6. Such growth is called integration and can be vertical, horizontal, lateral or conglomerate.
7. Conglomerate integration is also known as diversification.
8. The type of integration is determined by the chain of production.
9. The Monopolies and Mergers Commission and the European Commission will prevent mergers that are against the public interest.
10. Sometimes firms decide to get smaller.

Unit 9
Business objectives

What are the aims of most firms? In its 1996 company report, the Coca-Cola Company speaks of 'infinite growth', returns on capital invested and increasing profits. Marks and Spencer's states that 'first class customer service remains our priority wherever we trade' while First Direct, the telephone banking arm of Midland Bank, 'strives to create harmony between the services it provides and the way people live their lives with simple, straightforward products'.

These are all aims as stated in company reports for three different public limited companies. Are the aims of small traders likely to be a great deal different from these? And is it true to say that there is one overriding aim behind all of these statements – the aim of making as much profit as possible?

HOW CAN WE DEFINE A FIRM'S BUSINESS OBJECTIVES?

Business objectives are the stated or attempted aims of firms and organisations.

Some business objectives need to be measurable in order for a firm to know whether or not it has reached them. Others may be stated as:

- general targets
- mission statements
- financial objectives
- long term aims.

Did you know?

A 'mission statement' is a short phrase used to state the general targets of a firm. Philips Electronics, for example, states its aims as a brief list – 'to delight customers, to value people as our greatest resource, to deliver quality and excellence in all actions, to achieve premium return on equity and to encourage entrepreneurial behaviour at all levels'.

Kodak has a corporate vision – to be the 'world leader in imaging', a mission statement and a quality policy; these three provide it with its general aims.

Business objectives 41

Maximisation

Maximisation means to make the most of something; to make the most possible profit is to maximise profit, while to sell as many goods as possible is to maximise sales. It is often assumed that the first and primary aim of the majority of businesses is to maximise profit, that is, to get the difference between costs and revenues to as high a level as possible. Maximum profit, however, may mean that other things are sacrificed, such as customer satisfaction or employee welfare.

Firms may prefer to:

- **Maximise efficiency:** this means the most efficient use of resources – eggs, for example, will not be packed in boxes made from oak or mahogany, but in much more efficient cardboard or plastic, giving just enough protection for the job that needs doing. The efficient use of resources will keep unit costs at their lowest level.

- **Maximise turnover:** this is the number of sales, times the price at which goods are sold. A higher turnover may lead to the more efficient use of resources – such as machinery and equipment. An aircraft, for example, is losing money as long as it is on the ground, so the faster it can be taking off again with a cargo or fare paying passengers, the greater will be the turnover of the company operating it.

- **Maximise their market share:** the greater the market share, the more power the firm will have to set prices or to control production. A market leader may have the power to set prices. The price of coffee, world-wide, is set by Brazil, as they produce more coffee than all other coffee producing nations. Other countries have to accept the price that Brazil decides. This makes Brazil into a **price maker** and the other countries into **price takers**. Maximum market penetration could also be a target under this heading. This could mean entering as many different markets as possible – an expansionist aim – or producing as many different products for the same market as possible. The spirits market, for example, is dominated by Diageo, with the leading brands of Johnnie Walker whisky, Smirnoff vodka and Gordon's gin.

Did you know? The Diageo group also own: Burger King, Guinness and the Green Giant and Old El Paso brands through ownership of Pillsbury. It was formed by the merger of Grand Metropolitan and Guinness mentioned on page 40.

Diageo's domination of the world spirits market based on 1996 sales revenues.

%	Company	Country
5%	American Brands	United States
5%	Brown Forman	United States
5%	Remy Cointreau	France
5%	Pernod Ricard	France
7%	Moet Hennessey	France
8%	Bacardi	Bermuda
13%	Seagram	Canada
16%	Allied Domecq	UK
36%	Diageo	UK

- **Maximise their return on capital invested:** this means getting the most back for shareholders, the return on **equity capital** or the most back for the firm's own investments in new plant, processes, equipment or brands for example.

Handy hints: Sometimes an objective may be to minimise, rather than to maximise something. A firm may have the aim of minimising labour turnover, for example. The three terms involved are maximising – making the most of, minimising – making the least of, and satisficing – being satisfied with a particular level of. Remember that you gain marks in both examinations and coursework for the correct use of terminology.

Activity

1. Your school or college may well have a 'mission statement' or something similar. Look at a copy of your school or college prospectus to find out what it is. Do you think that it is effective?

2. If you find that they haven't got one, then write one for them. Remember that the key points for an educational institution will probably include words and phrases such as 'excellence', 'good results' and 'high standards of dress and behaviour'.

Business objectives

Activity

Choose two different firms. It is often best to choose those firms with which you are familiar (a part-time job, a parent's employment, work experience).

1. See if they have any overall targets, perhaps expressed as mission statements or as general targets.
2. If they have no stated targets, interview the owner or a senior manager to see what personal objectives they have set for their business.
3. Interview a worker at the firm to see what their targets are.
4. Draw up a table of the various targets that you collect through your research and interviews. Split them into maximising, minimising and satisficing targets. Which are short term, which are long term?
5. You then need to contrast the two sets of targets – why do you think that some of them are the same? Why do you think that some of them are different?
6. You must also evaluate the evidence that you collected – which do you think was the most useful? Which the least?
7. Come to a conclusion regarding the objectives that you have found out. How sensible or attainable do you think the targets are? What other targets would you recommend?

For many of the above, the aim may not be to achieve the maximum possible immediately, but instead to achieve a steady and sustainable growth in these areas. This is particularly true of turnover, market penetration, market share and profitability. A firm showing growth in these areas is generally said to be healthy. Any slow down in growth (a 'down turn'), even if the firm is still doing well, would immediately ring alarm bells with management.

Satisficing

H. A. Simon, an American writer on business behaviour, introduced the idea of 'satisficing' in an article written in 1959. He said that firms do not, in fact, try to maximise, but instead set targets that are within reach and are then satisfied when such targets are reached. In this way, managers and owners are always setting themselves further goals, but they are reachable goals, meaning that the pleasure of achieving a target keeps spirits high.

For smaller firms, in particular sole traders and partnerships, maximisation of market share, turnover or profit may not be possible, but the achievement of a reasonable income, or of a certain lifestyle may be a high enough goal for satisfaction.

Survival

In 1989, after the political and social changes in the Eastern bloc countries, the Czech government began to look for an international partner for Skoda in order to ensure the firm's survival and bring it back to international competitiveness.

The goal of survival may be the major objective of many businesses, including ones much smaller than car manufacturers. For sole proprietors and partnerships, with unlimited liability, reaching and bettering break-even (the point where costs equal revenues and the business moves from loss into profit) and thus surviving in their chosen market place, is often the only objective. Further targets, such as expansion, can only be thought of once this survival point is reached.

> **Handy hints**
>
> Limited liability companies are easily spotted by the fact that they carry a warning to those that would trade with them. The warning is to be found in the letters Ltd or plc after the company's name. Companies with limited liability may still be struggling for survival, but shareholders are not likely to lose as much as sole proprietors or partners.

Independence and flexibility

Small businesses, in particular, may prize targets of independence and flexibility above others. For many small businesses, the target may well be to be self-employed, and to not have to work for someone else. This means that the business may have flexibility in terms of hours worked,

INDEPENDENCE MAY BE AN IMPORTANT GOAL

Business objectives

holidays taken or jobs tackled. Many senior executives have 'down shifted' to less stressful occupations which, while they may not offer the highest financial benefits, will offer the advantages of self employment.

> **Did you know?**
> Self-employed traders – sole proprietors and partnerships in particular – actually work for much longer hours than they would do if they were working for an employer. This is because they are actually working for themselves and can keep any benefits or rewards that they get for their labours for themselves.

Less obvious targets

Many firms aim for less obvious targets that cannot necessarily be easily measured. These include such things as:

- **Customer satisfaction:** attempts to measure this may be made. The Automobile Association (AA), for example, carries out regular surveys of members and collects customers' views of service performance. It asks customers to complete satisfaction questionnaires so that it can act on the findings. This may then be measurable in terms of targets set – every phone call will be answered within three rings, all breakdowns will be reached within a certain amount of time, for example. A mail order service may aim for a minimum number of returns.

- **Reputation:** many businesses rely on getting trade by building up a good reputation. A garage mechanic or the maker of a wedding dress, for instance, may be particularly skilful. They will gain more trade by keeping an excellent reputation as people recommend them to others.

- **Repeat trade:** the success of a business may be measured by the number of times customers return. This is particularly true of service industries, where such things as loyalty to a particular hairdresser are extremely important to the success of that business.

> **Codebreakers**
>
> **Maximisation:** making the most of something.
>
> **Price maker:** the dominant producer in a market who has the power to set prices.
>
> **Price takers:** the other businesses in a market who are too small to affect price and must accept what is set.
>
> **Equity capital:** equity capital is the term used for the money that shareholders have put into the business through their purchase of shares.
>
> **Satisficing:** setting a target and then being satisfied when it is reached. The word is derived from 'satisfaction'.
>
> **Subsidies:** extra amounts paid to companies by an organisation (usually local, national or international government agencies) in order to keep prices as low as possible.

> **Activity**
>
> Choose an appropriate package to complete the following task.
>
> > 1. Write a mission statement for your school or college, or for another organisation that you are connected with. It should be reasonably short, but contain the main points you wish to make.
> > 2. Put the heading 'Mission statement for ...' in bold letters and centred, use a fancy font if you wish.
> > 3. Use bullet points, underlining and italics to bring out the main points of your statement.
> > 4. Put a border around it to make it look attractive.
> > 5. Save it and print it for display.
>
> You should save and print your work at each stage.
>
> This task partially fulfils the requirements of the Word Processing and Software Applications Unit of the NEAB Certificate of Achievement in IT.

The public sector

44 Business objectives

The public sector is not expected to maximise profits, but to provide a level of product and service that maximises the benefit to the whole community, nationally or locally. This is especially true for local government where **subsidies** are still provided to ensure that services are available to all sections of the community. The West Yorkshire Passenger Transport Authority (WYPTA), for example, has lower fares for pensioners, children and the unemployed. It also subsidises buses, like the Metro bus shown, so that there is a service in the early morning, late evening and on Sundays as well as providing comprehensive timetable information and bus and train shelters. The WYPTA receives its money from Bradford, Calderdale, Kirklees, Leeds and Wakefield councils.

Many services are provided free at the point of use, although paid for by either national or local taxation. For organisations such as the police and fire services, which could not possibly be run with the aim of making a profit, different aims are provided. Public satisfaction, speed of response and efficient use of resources are the main ones.

Activity

Coca-Cola's philosophy of growth is stated in its company report as being in three parts. 'State expectations, meet or exceed expectations, repeat' is how the management sees the company growing and succeeding (an expectation can be thought of as a target). The third part of this, they claim, is always the hardest part. A sole proprietor might adopt the same approach but have very different targets in mind.

1. Outline what you think might be Coca Cola's five main targets.
2. Outline what you think might be a sole proprietor's three main targets.
3. What would you suggest as a possible long-term objective for a sole proprietor?
4. Why do you think that sole proprietors' and partners' objectives may be less ambitious than companies?
5. Explain the difference between maximising and satisficing. Choose one example of each from the targets you have written down for 1 and 2 above.

Mutuals and co-operatives

These aim to obtain the maximum possible benefit for their membership, although this may not be stated in terms of any sort of maximisation. Early building societies, for example, would have the goal of ensuring that each of their members could buy a house. Once this target was reached, they had then reached their goal, and closed down. Worker co-operatives are more likely to be aiming at survival and satisficing than at any kind of maximisation.

SUMMARY

Ten points to remember:

1. Business objectives fall into two categories – those that can be measured and maximised and those that cannot.
2. Targets that are difficult to measure include customer satisfaction, reliability and reputation.
3. Measurable objectives include profit, efficiency, turnover, market share and returns on capital.
4. Firms may aim for growth in any of these, or for maximisation.
5. Maximisation is getting the most possible of something.
6. Satisficing means setting reachable targets and being satisfied when they are reached.
7. The major aim of many businesses, particularly small ones, is survival.
8. Small businesses may also aim for independence and flexibility.
9. The public sector's target is to produce the greatest benefit for a whole community.
10. Some organisations exist purely for the benefit of their members.

Unit 10
Stakeholders' objectives

The stakeholders in a business are those people who have an interest in how well the business performs. They include customers, owners, managers, employees and suppliers. SmithKline Beecham is a major health company, whose brands include Beecham's, Hedex, Night Nurse and Andrews as well as Aquafresh and McLean's and the drinks Lucozade, Horlicks and Ribena. A part of their mission statement outlines who they think are their stakeholders; 'At SmithKline Beecham we are people with a purpose, working together to make the lives of people everywhere better, striving in everything we do to become The "Simply Better" Healthcare Company as judged by all those we serve: customers, shareholders, employees and the global community.'

Not every business claims such a wide number of stakeholders, but most will have more than one group, whose objectives may be different from each other. There are three theories of the behaviour of firms; one says that the firm has the single aim of profit maximisation; one says that firms are composed of two groups, managers and shareholders, with different objectives; the third that the firm is composed of many different groups, all with different aims and objectives. Conflicts can arise when the objectives of any one group of stakeholders is different from another.

WHO ARE THE STAKEHOLDERS IN A BUSINESS?

Stakeholders are the groups of people who have a stake or interest in the performance of a business. They can be split into a number of groups who may have differing objectives:

- customers – the people who buy from the business
- owners – the people who own the business
- managers – the people who manage the business
- employees – the people who work for the business
- suppliers – the people who sell to the business.

Activity

1. List the stakeholders in your school or college.
2. Outline the main objectives of each stakeholder.
3. Outline how these objectives may come into conflict with each other.

Customers

Above all, customers want value for money. If a good or service falls outside the price range a customer is willing to pay, then the business will soon find itself struggling. A 'reasonable' price for a ticket to a football match might be seen as £15 – £20 with half price for children. Below that level, it is seen as being cheap but better value for money. Above that level it may be seen as being too expensive. During the Euro '96 football tournament, for example, some international matches were extremely poorly attended as a result of over-priced tickets – in most cases these were matches between countries where there was little UK interest.

Did you know? Sometimes businesses can price themselves out of a market by dropping prices too far. Would you have a haircut priced at 25p, for instance, or would you decide that, at that price, it could not possibly be any good? It would fall outside your range of what you considered a reasonable price for the service offered.

What's a reasonable price for a ticket?

Customers also seek other objectives, for example they want reliability, quality and speed of service, as well as value.

Owners

The owners of a business may be a small group of people, in the case of a co-operative, or a partnership or a single person in the case of a sole trader. For a joint stock company, the shareholders will be the owners.

In small companies, the owners are likely to be aiming for survival, personal satisfaction and for other **satisficing** targets such as enough money to live on and a certain standing in the community. In joint stock companies, the shareholders, as the owners of the firm, are likely to want the company to aim for **maximising** objectives – in particular, the maximisation of return for the money that they have spent on shares.

Directors, as major shareholders, might also see the aim of maximising profit as important, but they are also likely to have other objectives, such as the growth of the company, in order to give them more power or prestige.

> **Handy hints**
>
> A joint stock company is one where the stock, or shares, is held jointly, that is, by a number of people. It is therefore a term which just means a firm with shareholders.

Managers

The managers of a company are appointed by directors acting on behalf of shareholders or by owners directly. It might therefore be thought that they should share in the same objectives as owners. Managers, however, are likely to be salaried and therefore extra profit will not give them any extra benefits. They may be more interested in the status benefits that they can collect such as a large company car, a privileged parking spot or an office on the top floor.

There is also the possibility that different managers may have different objectives, so that while one is trying to cut costs, another is increasing spending. Businesses recognise these problems and try to solve them through such things as good communication. In an attempt to make sure that managers' objectives are the same as those of the owners, many businesses run profit sharing schemes for certain managers, or bonus schemes linked to the value of shares.

Employees

The cartoon shows the different opinions employees may have of their own worth, compared to that of the employer. The employer, at one extreme, assumes that all workers want is the maximum amount of wages for the minimum amount of work. The employee, at the other extreme, assumes that all the employer wants is the maximum amount of work for the minimum amount of money. In reality, there is probably an element of both, but not at either of the extremes. Workers obviously like to receive higher wages, while employers are reluctant to pay higher wages.

Stakeholders' objectives

Suppliers

Suppliers want regular repeat orders (and will offer special terms for those businesses that trade with them on a regular basis, as this helps them to manage stock). They also want businesses who are going to be reliable in paying in full and on time. Again, there are generally special discounts for those who pay early. Of course, suppliers will also want to sell as much as possible at the highest price they can get.

Conflicts

> **Activity**
>
> > There are a number of organisations that exist with the main purpose of solving conflicts that might arise between different groups in business. Using your library, or other resources such as CD-ROM, find out the name and purpose of three such organisations.

Problems arise when two or more groups within an organisation actually have conflicting objectives. There are five examples of possibly serious conflicts shown below.

- **Profit vs. service:** the owner of a business may have the objective of maximising profit. To do this they need to cut down on costs, and one of the ways of cutting down on costs is to open for fewer hours. The customers of the business may use it mainly for its convenient opening hours. If they are cut back, they will no longer use the business.

> **Activity**
>
> One possible conflict that arises in an organisation is between those who wish to introduce new technology and those who see their jobs being threatened by it.
> > 1 Give at least four examples of how IT is now used to carry out jobs that used to be carried out manually.
> > 2 Outline at least three issues that this might give rise to in a business situation.
> > 3 Outline how you would go about solving the problems that arise.
> > 4 Choose appropriate software with which to present your work.
>
> This task partially fulfils the requirements of the Software Applications Unit of the NEAB Certificate of Achievement in IT, as well as the Information and its Effects on Society Unit.

- **Shareholder vs. worker:** when the economy in the UK was going through a phase of high inflation, the causes were said to be one of two things – greedy workers wanted more money but weren't prepared to work any harder for it, pushing up wage levels, or greedy shareholders wanted more money from their shares and therefore pushed prices up in order to gain more profit. Different political parties had different viewpoints.

- **Owner vs. management:** the owner of a medium sized business wants to see it expand so that it has a greater share of the market. The managers of the business do not want the extra responsibility that expansion would bring and are afraid an extra layer of management might be put in above them.

- **Pension fund vs. employment:** pension funds and insurance companies are major shareholders in many firms. Their main objective is to move workers' pension money around company shares and investments in order to get the best return possible. A firm that is struggling, may find that this is reflected in their share price. The pension fund may decide to sell its shares. In so doing it could force a firm to close, thus causing redundancies.

- **Employer vs. worker:** the employer wants greater efficiency from the workers and will pay them what they claim is a reasonable rate and all the business can afford. The employee wants more money, for better living standards, but does not want to have to work harder for it. They see the results of their hard work in the profits of the firm being shared amongst shareholders who they don't recognise as having made a contribution.

Activity

Look at the five conflicts outlined on page 48.

1 Write a short paragraph to suggest how you could solve each of these. Make sure that you take the views of both sides of the argument into account.

2 SmithKline Beecham mentions an even wider range of stakeholders. Outline how you think each of these has an interest in the organisation.

3 Suggest three other possible conflicts that could arise between any of the groups mentioned.

Because conflicts are so likely to arise between employers and employees there are formal ways in which to solve disputes and large organisations on both sides (Trade Unions and Employers' Associations) that are involved in industrial relations (*see Unit 19*).

Codebreakers

Stakeholders: the groups of people who have an interest in the success of a business.

Satisficing: reaching targets that are satisfactory, not necessarily the highest possible.

Maximising: reaching the highest possible targets.

Inflation: a general increase in price levels.

Activity

Choose two different firms.

1 Decide what the stakeholders are for each firm – owners, customers, managers, etc.

2 Find out, by interviewing representatives from each group, what the main objectives of each group are.

3 Collect literature from the firms; what aims are stated in it?

4 Draw up a table of the various objectives that you collect through your research and interviews.

5 What sort of conflicts can you see happening? Which firm is most likely to achieve most of its stakeholders' objectives?

6 What advice could you offer to the firms to suggest how they might avoid conflicts?

You must also evaluate the evidence you collected.

7 Which do you think was the most useful? Which the least?

SUMMARY

Five points to remember:

1 Stakeholders are any group with a stake in a business's success.

2 Stakeholders may have different objectives.

3 When this happens, there can be conflicts that affect the performance of a business.

4 Conflicts can be solved through effective communication.

5 Conflicts can be solved by formal means, using outside bodies.

Unit 11
Internal organisation

When a firm has more than one worker involved in producing the final good or service, some form of **organisational structure** is necessary. This is so that the people who work for the firm, or who have contact with the firm, know who makes the decisions, what sort of decisions they can make, who can allow others the authority to make decisions and how such decisions are communicated to others in the organisation. Even in a small, one-person business, there are many different decisions that have to be made. Decisions regarding finance, production, pricing, staffing, insurance etc. must all be made. As the business grows, the decisions become more complex and it is necessary to divide the decision making between different people. This means that they must each know what decisions are being made by the others so a form of organisation becomes necessary.

In the world of films and television, a single production can become a business in itself. The Star Wars film trilogy, although first produced over 20 years ago, still has a huge market for 'spin-offs'. This would not be possible without a great deal of organisation. One area where such organisation is made obvious is in the actual production of the movie. At the end of the film, all the specialised jobs that have had to be carried out are listed. At the very end come the most important jobs. There is the director, the person who makes all the major decisions – such as who plays which part – and who can give **authority** to others (like the art director or the director of photography) to make decisions. There is also the producer. This is the person who arranged for the financing of the production and who has overall responsibility for the budget.

Here is a list of many of the people that might be involved in the making of a movie and underneath we have drawn a structure into which they might be organised.

Activity
> Try to fit the jobs shown left into an organisational structure like the one shown below.

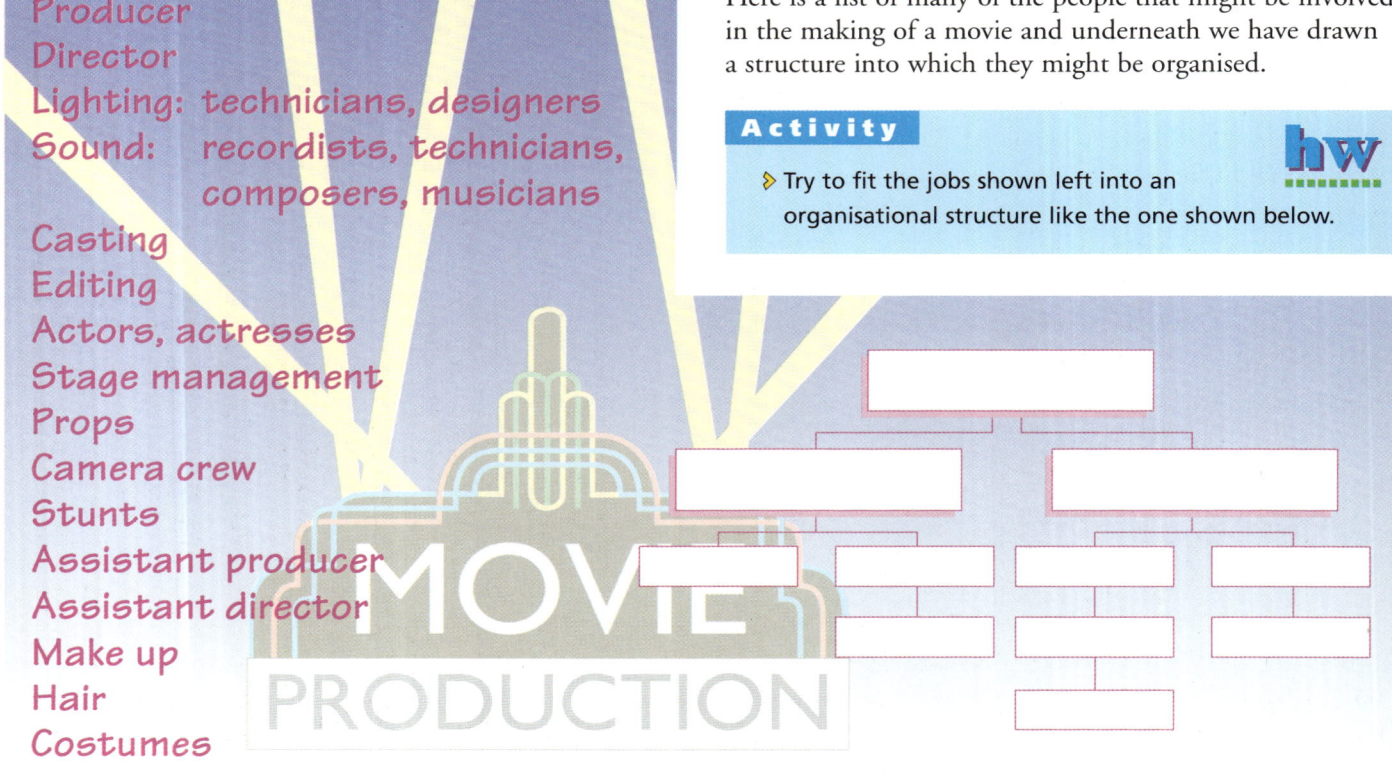

Producer
Director
Lighting: technicians, designers
Sound: recordists, technicians, composers, musicians
Casting
Editing
Actors, actresses
Stage management
Props
Camera crew
Stunts
Assistant producer
Assistant director
Make up
Hair
Costumes

HOW AND WHY BUSINESSES ORGANISE THEMSELVES

Internal organisation is how a business is structured for decision making and communication. This means that to a firm, internal organisation is:

- how the firm is structured
- who has what responsibilities
- what communications channels are used.

Why organise?

Imagine your school or college with nobody bothering to organise. You would all turn up on the first day of term (if anyone had told you when it was) but would not know which classes to go to. Your teachers would have no idea which room they were supposed to be in. A stock of books and equipment would not exist. You may not even be able to get into the building if caretaking staff have not been informed of the start date! Without organisation your school or college's service – which is education – could not be provided. Whenever a group of people are brought together to complete a task, organisation is needed. A school or college is organised to produce education. A film or television crew and actors are organised to produce a programme. A business is organised to produce a good or service.

Formal or informal?

In most businesses there are two forms of organisation in place. The formal organisation is the one that says what jobs people have, what responsibilities and how much power or authority. It will lay down channels and methods of communication. In other words, it will say who can tell who what and how they are supposed to pass on the message. The informal organisation of the workplace will be based on a totally different set of rules. It is based on the social groupings of workers and will include groups such as:

- **Common interest groups:** for example, supporters of a team, players of a sport (the staff football side, the ladies' keep-fit group), people who like films.
- **Friendship groups:** school friends and work colleagues for example.
- **Semi-formal groups:** some groups that have a common goal have to be put together in a semi-formal way. For example, a group of people who decide to join a lottery or football pools syndicate may have to agree how they are going to collect money and how they are going to spend the winnings when they come.

Informal groups can often have a powerful influence on formal decision making as, to many people, they can be more important than the formal organisation.

Hierarchical pyramids

Most organisations have a few people at the top of the structure and many more at the bottom. This leads to the organisation having a structure that looks like a pyramid or triangle – narrow at the top and wide at the bottom.

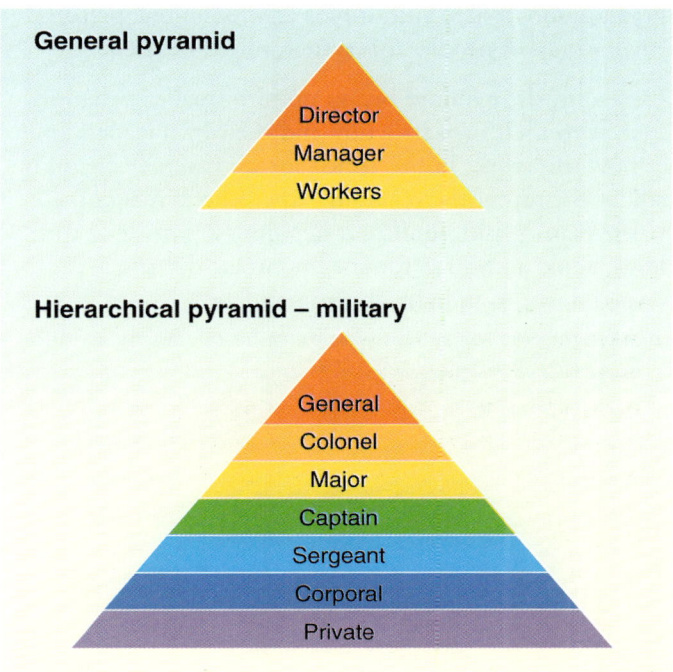

If the pyramid is also hierarchical, this means that it is organised into grades or classes stacked one above the other. In a hierarchy, the particular grade interacts only with the grade above and the grade below, accepting orders and instructions from the one above, giving orders and instructions to the one below. This is a very rigid structure, used particularly in military organisation.

Internal organisation

In the example shown here, the general decides that he wants the fence painting; he tells the colonel; he tells the major; he tells the captain; he tells the sergeant; he tells the corporal; the corporal tells the private – and the private paints the fence! Many organisations would find this too inflexible for their needs. However, in organisations where authority is centred in one person or a small group of people, this system might be used.

Generally, the pyramid breaks up into smaller pyramids, each with their own structure and their own leader. Look at how this works in the armed forces. Overall control is still at the top of the pyramid – the general makes the battle plans – and significant decisions are made at this level. Some authority, for less important decisions, is passed down to individual commanders.

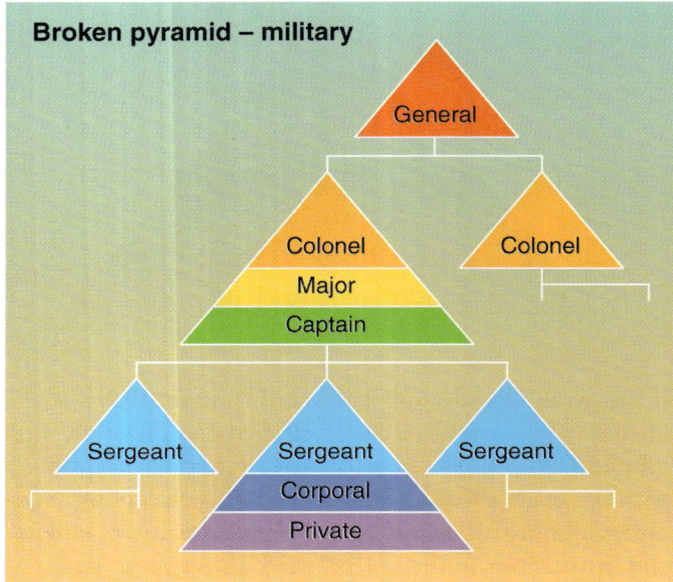

Delegation

Passing authority down to lower levels like this is called delegation. A delegate is given limited powers by someone at a higher level. Sometimes powers are delegated on a permanent basis. An assistant film director has all the powers of the director and can make many major decisions. However, because this power is delegated, the director can always overrule any decisions that he or she does not agree with. Also, the director has the power to remove the delegated powers from the assistant director.

In a typical organisational structure for a firm, a director may delegate powers to a manager. The manager will then make all the day-to-day decisions with the same authority as the director. It is therefore essential that the person delegating the authority has trust in the person – the subordinate – who is given authority.

Chain of command

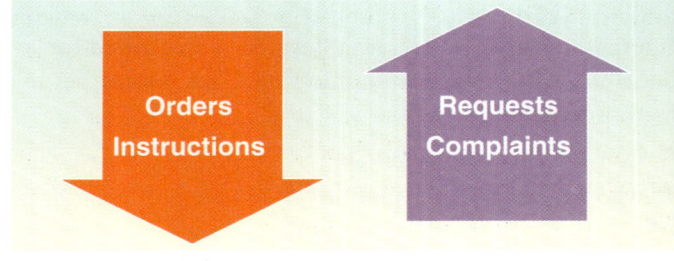

The military pyramid below left shows how a chain of command works. It means that you only pass instructions on to the next person in the chain, and they then pass them on to the people below them. If there are questions to be asked, or if people are unhappy with a situation, they take it up with the layer immediately above them. Coming down the pyramid are instructions and orders, going up are requests and complaints. In an organisation, the longer the chain of command, the more likely it is that orders will not be properly carried out.

> **Did you know?** This is where the term 'going over someone's head' comes from. It is used to refer to those times when someone appeals not to the person directly above them, but to someone even higher up in the organisation. Generally, this causes great resentment and problems.

Span of control

The span of control refers to the number of people over whom a person has direct authority. A narrow span of control means that the person has authority over only two or three people. A wide span of control means that the person has authority over a large number of people. In the film production example, the cameraman has a narrow span of control – over the camera crew; the director has a wide span of control, with responsibility for many different aspects of the film.

Centralised or decentralised?

In the production of a movie it is the director's interpretation of the script that is all important. The organisation is a highly centralised one, where anyone's decisions can be changed by the director.

A decentralised organisation will delegate decisions to people further down the hierarchy. This has the advantage that, as responsibility is increased, so is a person's willingness to work. Responsibility is a motivating factor.

One of the modern practices in business is to restructure by cutting out layers of middle management so that more people have responsibility. In car production, for example, teams are set up at the production level with their own team managers. These team managers may well link straight to directors. This process of **delayering** – removing layers of management – was introduced to this country by the Japanese. It increases responsibility and cuts down the number of stages in communication, leading to a better understanding of the shop floor by the directors and of the directors by the shop floor. On the down side, team leaders may not have the expertise or training that is required and it may also increase the workload of team members.

Drawing organisational charts

Most organisational structures can be shown as a chart. This makes it easier to see how the organisation is put together and how various parts of it interact with each other. It makes it easy to see who is in charge of what and can also help managers to see where problems might happen.

There are three main ways of drawing the structure:

- the hierarchical pyramid, as shown for the army below.

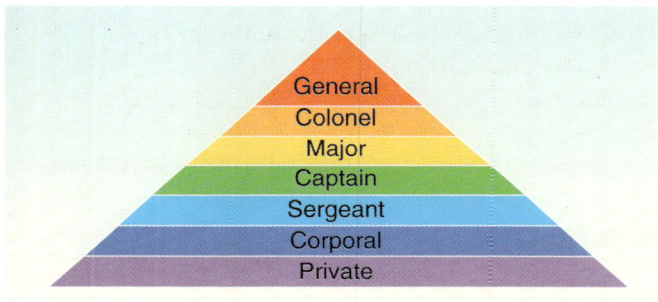

- the family tree type structure, showing branches and sub-branches. Below we see how this can be applied to a firm. (Look at page 50, for the film production team. A family tree type structure has been used for this.)

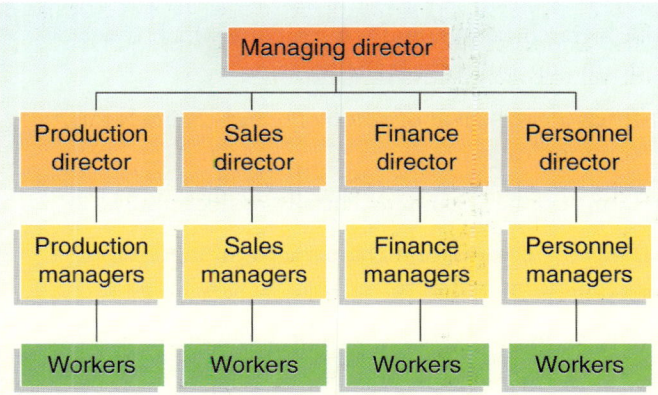

- a circular organisation chart, showing the director at the centre and the various layers as circles. Power and authority decreases as you move further away from the centre of the circle and nearer to the edge.

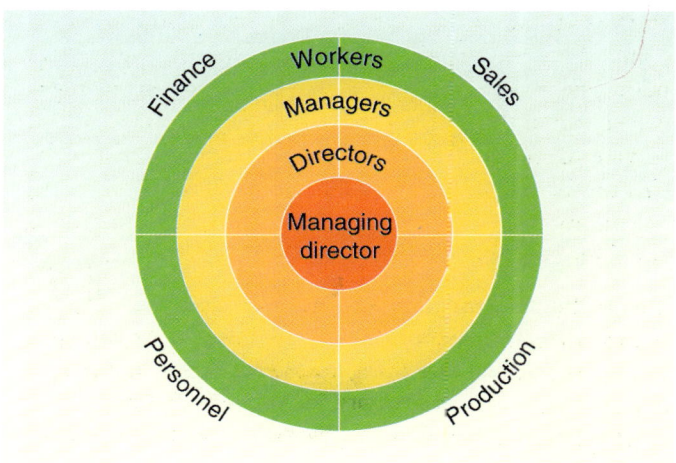

Structuring by what?

The way in which the business is actually divided can also vary. The most common structures are division by function, division by product or geographical division. A typical company is used as an example:

- **Division by function:** this is when the firm is divided up by the jobs that people do. The sales department has a sales director, sales managers and salespeople; the production department has a production director, managers, foremen/women and workers.

Activity

When you have the opportunity to work inside a firm, and therefore can make contact with a number of its employees, is a really good time to do a piece of coursework. Your work experience placement could be an ideal opportunity. You could look at the internal structure of the firm that you are working for and at its lines of communication. Note where problems tend to happen and then write a report for your work experience supervisor suggesting ways that the organisation could be improved. You could include their response to show that your work has been evaluated and appreciated.

Codebreakers

Organisational structure: the way in which a firm is organised.

Authority: the influence that a supervisor or manager has.

Delegation: the right or ability to give others authority.

Span of control: the number of people or departments that a person has under their command.

Delayering: removing layers of management.

Internal organisation 53

Handy hints: Organisational charts are a lot easier to understand if you make sure that every job in the firm is clearly shown. This is much simpler than trying to show what every person does, as many people may do the same job.

Activity

1. Choose a program with which to draw the jobs in your school in separate boxes. Once you have done this, move them around the screen to make an organisational structure for your school. Don't forget people like the office staff, caretakers and dinnertime employees, who are important as well!
2. Say why you chose the program you did.

This task partially fulfils the requirements of the Software Applications Unit of the NEAB Certificate of Achievement in IT.

- **Division by product:** this is when the firm is divided up by the type of product that is being made. A separate department deals with each product or family of products.

- **Geographical division:** this is when the firm is divided up by geographical area. This might be local – as in a branch system; regional – meaning that each division is based in a certain part of the country, or international – a firm with divisions in many countries. Increasingly, as the European Union becomes more important, organisations find it necessary to have a European division.

Did you know? A multinational firm is one that has production facilities and bases in many countries; some of the biggest have a turnover that is bigger than that of many small nations. Because their operations cross national borders, they are now often known as transnational companies.

Activity

Cute alien saves cute whale from undersea volcano II

Produced by . . . .
Directed by . . . .
Written by . . . .
From an original idea by . . . .
Assistant Producer . . . .
Assistant Director etc . . . .

1. Using the idea above – or coming up with a film title of your own – design a poster advertising a movie. Include as many jobs as possible on it.
2. Watch the credits at the end of a film – tape them and slow them down if this helps. How many jobs did you miss? Write down the jobs you missed and those you don't understand (what do you think a 'best boy' or a 'rostrum cameraman' do?).
3. Put your list of jobs into an organisation chart – use a family tree type.
4. Now change the format and put them into a circular chart.
5. Which chart do you think is the most effective, and why?

SUMMARY

Eight points to remember:

1. Good organisation is essential to the smooth running of a firm.
2. Both formal and informal structures will exist side by side.
3. The informal structures are often stronger.
4. A hierarchical pyramid is a structure which is narrow at the top and wide at the bottom.
5. It has a clear chain of command and channels for communication.
6. Firms can be organised centrally or decentrally.
7. Drawing organisation charts helps to understand organisation structures.
8. Firms can be divided according to different patterns.

Unit 12
Managers and management

In a small firm it is quite likely that one person would carry out all the management duties. When a firm grows to a level where it needs a formal organisation structure it will also need managers to carry out management functions.

The ice-cream seller in the picture will carry out his own management. He will set his own targets and communicate them to his assistants verbally. He will not delegate any authority for the running of the business. As the business grows (for instance, a second and third van might be bought) he needs to delegate some authority for some decision making to his assistants who will, in effect, be managing their own vans and their own areas.

In a large ice-cream producing company, like Wall's or Lyons Maid, there will be a number of layers of management, each with some authority for the levels below them.

THE IMPORTANCE OF MANAGERS

Managers are the intermediate layer in a company's structure. They are responsible to the directors and owners of the firm and have responsibilities for the levels and employees below them. Management is the art of managing – setting targets, making decisions, delegating authority, and motivating employees. This means that, to a firm, managers are:

- responsible
- salaried
- trustworthy
- motivated
- decision makers.

Payment of managers

Managers will be paid an annual salary by the firm. Unlike a wage earner, this means that managers will not be paid overtime and will often be expected, because of their position, to work longer hours than other employees. Managers may also be entitled to a number of 'perks' although some of these extras are becoming more and more commonplace for all workers. These 'perks' might fall into any of the following categories:

- travel – a company car, an interest free season ticket loan, specially designated parking
- health – private health insurance provided free or at reduced rates
- financial – share options, profit sharing schemes, **performance linked payments**
- social – tickets or seats made available for sporting occasions, concerts, etc.

> **Did you know?**
> 'Perks' is the shortened form of the word 'perquisites' which was used as the term for any extra money a feudal lord managed to take from his people over and above what was due to him. It has come to mean 'extras'.

Management functions

The directors have decided that they would like to increase their market share in the UK by introducing a new brand that has been successful in America. The job of the management is to look at the general target – the successful introduction of a new brand – and decide on a strategy that will achieve it. This strategy then needs to be communicated to subordinates who will be given particular jobs to do – that is, they must be organised and responsibility must be delegated. Management must then co-ordinate and control the process by which the brand is to be introduced. In monitoring its progress, managers must be prepared to motivate staff, give praise and encouragement for jobs well done, reprimands where there is inefficiency or laziness. Finally, it is their job to report back to the directors of the organisation. The functions can be summarised as below:

set target – plan strategy – communicate strategy – organise – delegate responsibility – co-ordinate and control – monitor – motivate – achieve – report – set new target (and start the process again)

> **Did you know?**
> The management approach that mixes rewards with reprimands is called the 'carrot and stick' approach. There are two ways of getting a donkey to move forward – to encourage it or to hit it!

Management – vertical links

Managers provide the link in a large organisation between the directors of the company and its employees. They receive information and instructions from directors or policy makers that they must then turn into action plans for their subordinates. The wishes of the directors are communicated to employees through managers. Communication also takes place in the opposite direction with employees passing opinions and ideas to directors via management.

Management – horizontal links

Managers will also have horizontal links with other managers at the same level. They may need to consult either formally or informally with other management to find out if their own targets, or their suggested method of achieving them, will cause a conflict.

For example, there could be an increase in raw material prices (butter fat for ice-cream) but the managing director and board have decided that prices to the consumer must not rise, otherwise the firm will lose market share. Savings must therefore be made somewhere. The senior personnel manager might decide that they can be achieved by letting experienced staff retire early and replacing them with less experienced, cheaper staff. The senior production manager may decide that savings can be achieved by giving more responsibility to senior staff to make decisions thus increasing efficiency and productivity. This conflict would need to be solved at a senior management or directorial level. Of course, a meeting of senior managers might also produce other solutions.

Management responsibilities – employers

Managers obviously have major responsibilities to their employers to try to achieve targets in the shortest and most efficient ways possible. Some companies that have been experiencing difficulties have decided to sell themselves to their own management. These **management buy-outs** tend to be successful because the managers have a much better knowledge of the workings of the company than the directors. In other cases management is brought in to replace the management layers in a failing organisation. Replacing management because an organisation is failing shows where owners and directors see the main responsibility for success or failure lying. A school or college that is seen to be failing may have its management replaced. Most famously, and most often, managers of football clubs are the people who have to take responsibility for the failure of their team.

England football manager Graham Taylor, famously depicted as a turnip by The Sun newspaper, had to take responsibility for England's poor performances.

Handy hints

Using real life examples to make a point in your work will always help you to explain the point more clearly. Using real life examples in coursework assignments is even more essential.

Activity

Read the passage and answer the questions below.

> Icicles Ltd is a firm that produces and sells special richly flavoured ice-creams. Directors have decided that they will no longer produce their own ice-cream but will instead licence production to small companies in Europe who can produce it more cheaply. This will mean some redundancies in the UK but the creation of a new senior management position to oversee European affairs. Some junior management will be asked to move from the UK to France and Belgium.

1. Outline the vertical links that a middle production manager will have in an organisation like Icicles.
2. Outline the horizontal links that a middle production manager will have in the organisation.
3. Suggest how a senior manager might be able to persuade a colleague to move abroad. Mention both salary and non salary based benefits.
4. Write a script between the middle personnel manager who has to sack a worker and the worker being sacked.
5. Role play the sacking in front of the rest of your group. The group could respond by marking your performance as a manager!

Management responsibilities – employees

They also have major responsibilities to employees. Many of these are outlined in European Union directives which became law on 1 January 1993. Prior to this, responsibilities had been outlined in the 1974 Health and Safety at Work Act which itself was based on earlier laws. The new law requires managers to be responsible for:

- the health and safety of employees in the workplace
- the safety and suitability of tools and equipment
- the safe handling of dangerous, heavy or awkward loads where these have to be moved by hand
- a safe, comfortable, clean and well-maintained workplace
- the provision of protective clothing and equipment where necessary
- the provision of the highest quality and lowest risk VDUs to reduce risk or discomfort to users.

Employers are also responsible for ensuring that there is no discrimination in the workplace, whether on grounds of gender, race, culture or disability (*see Units 15 and 20*).

Activity

> Create three notices that could be displayed in a workplace to reinforce any of the points above using an appropriate IT package. These can then be displayed in your classroom.

Managers and management 57

Management expectations

Management has a right to expect a certain level of commitment from employees. It can reasonably expect them to be on time, to put in a fair day's work, to follow instructions and regulations, to dress appropriately for the job and to be courteous, polite and not use offensive language. Employees should ensure that they tell managers if they cannot come to work and should treat the employer's property with care and respect. In return, employees should expect fair pay, fair treatment, training where appropriate and the upholding of health and safety regulations as above.

Levels of management

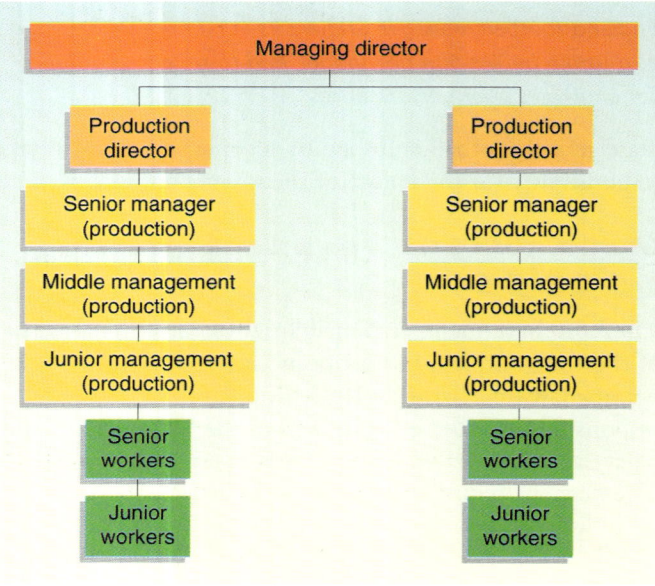

There are a number of different levels of management in a large firm. The structure of an ice-cream manufacturer's production organisation might look like this:

- **The managing director:** in overall charge of strategy, long-term targets and efficiency and ultimately responsible to the shareholders of the company. It is the managing director that is seen as responsible for the success or failure of the company. He or she will receive a top salary and it is likely that share options and bonus payments will be triggered if the company reaches or exceeds its targets.

- **The senior manager:** reports to the director with responsibility for his or her area. The senior manager must break down the general targets, as set by the managing director and board of directors, into individual targets for each of the areas under his or her control. In this organisation, the senior production manager is in overall charge of four plants producing different types or brands of ice-cream.

- **The plant manager:** a middle manager in this organisation, taking the targets as issued by the senior manager and working out how the plant can be made more efficient in order to reach them. He or she will set a target for the plant and individual targets for parts of the plant.

- **The line manager:** a junior manager, on the first step of the management ladder. They may be a recent college graduate or an experienced foreman who has been promoted to a management position. It is their job to ensure that their particular production line or section reaches the targets that have been set for it by middle management.

Management communication

The higher up the organisational structure the manager is, the less day-to-day 'hands-on' type decision making they are likely to make. At senior levels, managers have a general overview – they see the 'larger picture' and set general targets accordingly. At junior levels of management, managers are much more closely in touch with the workforce and more likely to know what is or is not possible or desirable. Senior managers will be much more successful if they take notice of the more detailed knowledge of junior managers. Good communication between senior and junior levels of management is therefore crucial to the success of a firm.

Styles of management

Authoritarian type management

Managers and management

There are a number of different styles of management that can be identified. Each has its advantages and disadvantages. In some, there is a definite leadership style, where the manager makes the decisions and then either tells subordinates what they are or tries to persuade them to his or her viewpoint. In others, the leadership style is less obvious and decisions may well be left to subordinates to make.

- **Authoritarian type management:** means that all the decision making is centralised. The major advantage of this is that it is always clear exactly what is wanted and tasks are very precisely defined. The major disadvantage is that subordinates are not allowed to be innovative or to suggest alternative strategies. This means that their motivation and enthusiasm are likely to be low.

- **The 'laissez-faire' approach:** the opposite of authoritarian management. *Laissez-faire* is French for 'let it be'. This style of management lays down very general guidelines and targets and then gives subordinates the freedom to achieve targets in their own way. The main advantage is that it allows for innovation and new ideas and is highly motivating. The major disadvantage is that subordinates are not always clear what they are supposed to be doing, or are allowed to do, and conflicts can easily arise.

Democratic type management

- **Democratic type management:** means that junior managers and even employees are involved in the decision making process. This sort of participation in management can be highly motivating – employees who see their own suggestions taken up and acted on have an increased loyalty to the firm. However, the democracy is not always genuine. Sometimes managers have already made decisions and use a consultation exercise as a way of justifying them. In this process employees often feel that their opinions or ideas have not been given sufficient weight. Managers may also use a persuasive approach to try and bring employees round to their way of thinking. The danger in this is if they do not succeed, their authority will be undermined. The main advantage of the democratic approach is that it can be highly motivating. The main disadvantage is that it can undermine the authority of management.

- **Bureaucratic type management:** similar to authoritarian management in that there is no room for individual innovation or opinion. It means that management is carried out by the rules and regulations that are laid down. It is thus an extremely inflexible system. The main advantage is that of certainty – employees will always know how decisions will be made. The main disadvantage is that it is highly inflexible and allows for no new ideas or suggestions.

- **'Hands on' management:** some senior managers insist on being involved in the organisation at many levels and as much as possible. They will visit production facilities and offices to check on progress

Activity

One of the approved coursework titles looks at the assessment of the effect of a business development of your choice on the local community. Managers will have had a great deal of influence over a lot of the decision making. By interviewing managers involved in the new development (this could be the opening of a new firm, the building of a new resource, the closure of a firm) you could find out:

1 What decisions they thought had been important.
2 Who had made those decisions.
3 What evidence had been used to help them come to a decision.

You could also find out about the communication involved with the development:

4 Did managers find that they had the information that they needed?
5 Were decisions taken higher up properly communicated?
6 Did managers feel that they had passed their decisions (and those made higher up) on effectively?

and efficiency and may even join in the production process in a plant or a meeting at a lower level – leading by example. The success or failure of this approach depends very much on the personality of the manager involved. The main advantage is that the manager experiences problems and difficulties at first hand and has a much better knowledge of the workings of the organisation. The main disadvantage is if the visits are seen as a threat or as interference in the normal running of the organisation

The advantages and disadvantages of these styles are summarised in the table on the right.

Downsizing

Management positions in the nineties are not as secure as they always have been in the past. At one time, once a manager had reached the first step on the management ladder, he or she could guarantee promotion and a 'job for life' providing that they made no major mistakes and that the company remained successful. Now organisations may delayer by shedding various levels of management and managers will have to retrain for positions in other firms. Companies may also be 'downsized' – broken up into smaller units, with less management – for greater efficiency.

Style of Management	Advantages	Disadvantages
Authoritarian	Clear exactly what is wanted, tasks are clearly defined	Subordinates are not allowed to be innovative, motivation is low
Laissez-faire	Allows for innovation and new ideas, highly motivating	Subordinates are not always clear what they are supposed to be doing
Democratic	Can be highly motivating	Can undermine the authority of management
Bureaucratic	Subordinates will always know how decisions will be made	Highly inflexible, allows for no new ideas or suggestions
Hands on	Manager sees problems first hand, has a much better knowledge of the organisation	Could be seen as interference

Codebreakers

Salary: the annual amount (usually paid in 12 monthly instalments) that a person is paid; salaried staff do not get paid for overtime.

Performance linked payments: bonuses or extra pay tied to the success of the firm.

Productivity: a measure of a worker's efficiency.

Management buy-out: when a firm is bought by its existing management.

Consultation exercise: asking for the opinions of workers on changes that might be introduced.

SUMMARY

Five points to remember:

1 Managers are the task setters in an organisation.

2 Managers provide the link between decision makers and the workforce.

3 Managers have responsibilities to directors and employees.

4 Managers will be employed at all levels in a firm – from managing director to junior managers.

5 There are different management styles – some more effective than others.

Unit 13
Business decision making

A firm is faced with decision making on a daily basis. They must make both short-term decisions, that will affect how they will operate in the next few days or weeks, and medium-term decisions, that will affect how they will operate for the next few months. They must also make long-term decisions, that affect how they will operate, survive or expand over the next few years. In all cases, the firm will be faced with a number of alternatives, or choices, only one of which will be the best course of action. Choices must be carefully considered and costed before a decision is made.

In the autumn of 1997 the brewery company Morland bought a rival brewers, Ruddles, from a large international brewing firm, Grolsch. The £4.8 million purchase has involved a number of decisions and will lead to more being made. The decision by Morland to buy their competitor is a strategic, or long-term, decision, taken at the highest management level. The decision by Grolsch to off-load Ruddles is a tactical decision. Grolsch management has decided that the small brewery is a resource that does not fit efficiently with their company's other products. Ruddles will face tactical decisions by their new owners, including the possibility of plant closures and staff redundancies. These are likely to lead to operational decisions making changes at the lowest level of decision making.

CHOOSING BETWEEN ALTERNATIVES

Business decision making is the way in which managers of businesses choose between alternatives in order to reach targets that they have set for their business. These decisions then have to be communicated to the people who will carry them out. This means that to a firm, business decision making is:

- setting targets or objectives
- collecting evidence and opinion
- making hypotheses
- deciding between alternatives
- communicating decisions.

Sole traders and small firms

The whole nature of a sole trader, or one-person business, means that only one person will be involved in the decision making process. This does not mean that decisions have to be made without any expert help. Sole traders will rely on expert advice from professionals such as accountants, lawyers and independent financial advisers, much of which is free. They will also be able to get help by using the experiences of other businessmen and women both informally – through business networking – and formally, through organisations such as local Chambers of Trade or Commerce. Local councils will also provide advice and most banks now have a small business advisory service. Partnerships, of course, may use the same services, but also have the advantage of being able to rely on the expertise of the partners.

Sole trader – one person makes all the decisions.

Business decision making 61

Handy hints: More in depth information about organisations like TECs and Chambers of Commerce can be obtained by telephoning them. The numbers can be found in Yellow Pages. Usually the information is free.

Did you know? Training and Enterprise Councils have been set up by the government and cover most areas of the country. They are responsible for organising training programmes for local needs and will also provide advice. The Prince's Youth Business Trust (PYBT) is specifically set up to help young people (aged 18–29) in business.

Franchises

Franchisees have much of the decision making for their business taken out of their hands as decisions are made by the franchiser. Take, for example, a franchise operation such as McDonald's; decisions on national advertising, wages for employees, product lines, prices and suppliers are all made centrally. Branch decisions are limited, even some day-to-day operational decisions such as hours of opening may be taken by Head Office.

Who makes the decisions?

In a larger organisation it will be necessary for a particular department or person to be responsible for decisions. These may be limited to the decisions in the area where that person has expertise – finance, or production, for example – or may be more general. It is important that whoever takes the decisions also takes the responsibility for those decisions!

Did you know? There is a Spanish proverb about 'the donkey who died' that illustrates the importance of decision making. The donkey in the story is given two identical carrots, placed at exactly equal distance from its nose and invited to choose between them. It eventually starves to death due to its inability to come to a decision!.

Decision making may be centralised or decentralised (*see Unit 12 on management styles, page 60*). Centralised decision making means that the managing director (MD) or chief executive officer (CEO) makes all the important decisions. This has the benefit that he or she will have an overall picture of how the company is operating and decisions can be made and communicated rapidly. In removing responsibility from lower levels of management, however, centralised decision making can be demotivating.

Handy hints: In both business and information technology there are a lot of 'acronyms' used. An acronym is where initial letters are used instead of the whole word or phrase. Common acronyms include PC, TV, MP, PIN, EC. In business you will come across acronyms such as CEO, MD, TEC, DTI. It is a good idea to make a dictionary of these to help you remember them.

Decentralised decision making can be slow and decisions in one department may come into conflict with another. This means that communication is extremely important. However, it has the benefit that decisions are taken by specialists who are likely to be more in touch with what is required. In most organisations, a combination of centralised and localised decision making is used.

Did you know? Taking responsibility for actions is important. American president Harry S. Truman kept a sign on his desk that read 'The buck stops here' to show that he took final responsibility for all the decisions made by his government.

Types of decision making

- **Logical** or **Scientific decision making:** uses a formal structure to make decisions. It is widely used in America and is designed to make sure that decisions are only made on the evidence presented. Both its strength and its weakness lie in the fact that it does not have any room for emotion or opinion. This is a strength, because it means that one persuasive person does not have the opportunity to get their own way and decisions are based on evidence. It is a weakness because it does not leave room for views and opinions that might be important. Typically it consists of five stages:
  - target setting
  - collection of information
  - making theories and projecting possibilities
  - testing
  - reviewing.

Look at this example of baking a cake.

Stage 1: Target setting – bake a chocolate sponge

Stage 2: Collect information – find various recipes

Stage 3: Theories and projections – decide which are the best two or three recipes

Stage 4: Test possibilities – make two or three different cakes

Stage 5: Review – taste and choose the best.

You can see from this that, while you might get an excellent chocolate cake, there is no room for flair or innovation!

The effectiveness of a decision may well depend on factors outside the control of the business. In this case, the use of a decision tree may help the decision maker. A decision tree looks at the likely response of, for example, competitors, and tries to give them a numerical probability. This is very difficult to do with accuracy.

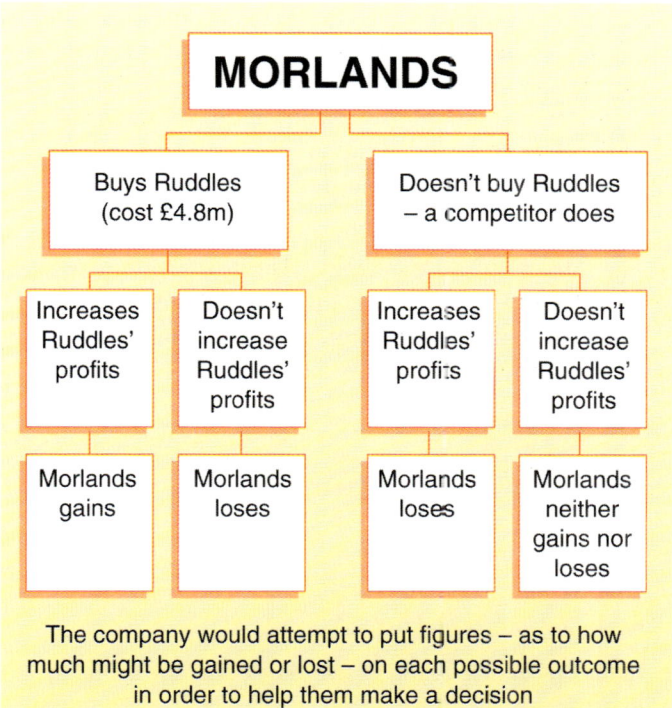

The company would attempt to put figures – as to how much might be gained or lost – on each possible outcome in order to help them make a decision

Above is a simplified decision tree for Morland's purchase of Ruddles. Figures for the most probable outcomes would be added at level two and each outcome at level three would then have a money value. Complex trees can be drawn to try to see the effect of, for instance, plant closures or redundancies. The real problem with decision trees is that most of the figures – especially the probabilities, are just guesses.

- **Cost benefit analysis:** this is the way in which an economist might look at the effects of a decision. Costs would be measured as **external costs** and **internal costs**. Internal costs could include redundancy payments, changes in production costs, wage bills and so on. External costs are those costs of an action that affect society in general, such as pollution, noise and litter.

Activity

Collect newspaper cuttings and other relevant information relating to the decision of a local business to either expand, or to stay the same. You could link this with your work experience placement. Collect information over a period of time and then use it as the basis for an investigation.

1. What decisions were made?
2. What types of decisions were they?
3. How were the decisions communicated to the people that would be affected?
4. Explain why you think it was the right/wrong decision for the business.

Business decision making

Social costs measure the whole cost to society of an action – internal costs plus external costs. It is difficult to measure these costs. The effect on a person's enjoyment of life of increased pollution, for example, is difficult to measure, although often changes in house prices are used as an indicator.

Benefits can be measured internally and externally in the same way and the firm makes its decision based on the evidence. Usually it is up to governments to make sure, through laws and regulations, that businesses take external costs seriously (*see Unit 23*).

> ### Activity
>
> Joshua Smith is managing director of Josh's Brewery Ltd. He says:
>
> 'The brewery needs to expand its product base. We can do it by launching a new product or by acquiring an existing strong brand name.'
>
> He has called a meeting of the directors of the company in order to come to a decision as to which course to take. These are the comments of some of the directors:
>
> 'We are almost at full capacity and couldn't launch our own brand without extra production facilities.' – Production Director
>
> 'An existing brand will be very expensive to acquire.' – Financial Director
>
> 'It will be difficult to market an existing brand under our company name.' – Marketing Director
>
> 'Dealing with an existing brand means extra transport will be needed.' – Transport Director
>
> 'We have a new brand ready for testing.' – Research and Development Director
>
> 'We would need to provide more overtime in order to produce another brand.' – Personnel Director
>
> 1. Outline what types of decision making are involved with each of the comments above.
> 2. Outline the good and bad points for each possible decision.
> 3. Draw a decision tree to help the managing director make a decision.
>
> The managing director has decided that Josh's Brewery Ltd will buy an existing strong brand. This means redundancies in research and development but more overtime in transport.
>
> 4. Explain how this decision would be communicated to:
>   - the directors
>   - the shareholders
>   - the workers in each department.
> 5. Do you think that the managing director's decision is the right one? Explain your reasoning.

Types of decision

- **Operational decision making:** also known as 'day-to-day' decision making. It involves managers making decisions about the running of their own departments and concerns the day-to-day working of a plant or office. Decisions such as holiday rotas, ordering new stock and deciding on loss-leaders are operational.

- **Tactical decision making:** the taking of medium-term decisions by senior or middle management. In general they will concern the efficient use of the business's resources in order to meet targets that have been set at a higher level. In a large firm, such as Grolsch, this may involve changing product lines, upgrading transport or modifying production. In a smaller firm, decisions such as whether to have loss leaders, to increase the number of staff or to change suppliers would be tactical.

- **Strategic decision making:** the taking of long-term decisions at the highest management level. The decision to buy another firm (as with Morland's and Ruddles) comes into this category. They are decisions that concern the overall direction of the firm and its long-term targets. In a small business they could be decisions such as whether to change a form of ownership (sole trader to private limited company or private to public limited company for example) or whether and how to raise extra finance.

The type of decision is more to do with the effects that it will have on a firm than with its costs. A strategic decision will have a large and long-term effect on a firm; an operational decision is essential in order for the business to keep functioning.

Communication

sender   medium   message   receiver
          (noise)   (I want my tea)

Communicating decisions accurately to those who are to carry them out is as important as the actual decision making. Communications involves four stages:

- a **sender** or **transmitter**
- a **medium** (a way to pass the message)
- a **message**
- a **receiver**.

Sender	Medium	Message	Receiver
Speaking	Voice – face-to-face	Speech	Listening
Speaking	Telephone	Speech	Listening
Writing	Letter/Fax	Written	Reading

Communication can break down if any one of the four parts is not operating efficiently. The sender may not be directing the message at the right **receiver**. The message may be in a **medium** or format which the receiver can't use or understand. The receiver may not be receiving. With advances in technology, much communication both within firms and to other firms now takes place electronically. This means that the speed and accuracy of information is greater today than it has ever been. There are still, however, important skills that must be used to pass non-electronic messages. Look at the table above and remember – the skills on the right are just as important as those on the left!

Activity

▶ Draw up a table of your own and add other communication skills to it.

External communication

Businesses often need to get particular information either to their customers, suppliers or to other businesses. The speed and accuracy of this external communication is essential to the efficiency of the firm. Sometimes it is necessary to have a record of the communication, in which case written messages are more useful than spoken ones. Increasingly, telephone calls are recorded by firms so that misunderstandings at a later date are avoided but this, of course, means that businesses cannot rely on calls always being private.

Other external communications range from things such as advertisements – getting a message across to consumers to buy a good – or standard information such as opening hours or timetables so that consumers know when a service is available. It is important that firms use the right message and the right medium and that it is appropriate and understood by the sender and receiver. Messages that fail to reach or be understood by the receiver are an expensive waste of time!

Activity

This exercise requires networked computers. Communication across a network is becoming an increasingly important way for businesses to pass messages internally. Much information is transmitted electronically.

▶ **1** Look at the words below.

Computer   Modem   Telephone line   Satellite

Explain how these devices could be used to send financial information from Britain to America. Show what different media could be used to carry the message – fibre optic cable, radio waves, etc.

▶ **2** If you were in America and wanted details of what money was in your account in Britain, how would you find out? Explain the process that takes place.

▶ **3** Send a message describing the Internet and some of the facilities it provides to a different computer on your network. Ask for an explanation of the difference between the private network you are using and the Internet in return.

This task partially fulfils the requirements of the Communications Unit of the NEAB Certificate of Achievement in IT.

Business decision making

Internal communication

USING THE WRONG MEDIUM FOR A MESSAGE

Internal communication involves sending messages within a business. It is used to pass on both decisions and information. The nature of the message will decide which method of communication is to be used. Some methods are seen as formal, some as informal.

	Formal	Informal
Verbal	Meetings Interviews Reviews	Face-to-face Intercom Telephone
Written	Memo Letters Reports	Noticeboard Suggestion box Newsletter
Advantages	Records kept Agendas Minutes	Easy Cheap Efficient
Disadvantages	Expensive Time consuming	No records kept Public

Codebreakers

Hypothesis: forming a theory often in the form of asking the question 'if. . . then. . .' 'If we do such and such, then such and such will happen'. The plural is hypotheses.

Networking: being in touch with other local business people, suppliers etc. through informal links such as knowing someone from school or being members of a charity organisation like the Round Table or Lions.

External costs: those costs over which the business has no control.

Internal costs: those costs that the business is able to control.

Operational decision making: the 'day to day' decision making essential for a business to operate.

Tactical decision making: the taking of medium-term decisions by senior or middle management.

Strategic decision making: the taking of long-term and far-reaching decisions at the highest level of management.

Sender or transmitter: the person sending a message.

Receiver: the person the message is intended for.

Medium: the device used to carry a message.

Activity

Information that is passed verbally often gets garbled or misunderstood.

1 Form a circle with seven or eight other students and whisper a message round the circle (Chinese Whispers is the name of the game).
- What happened to your message?
- Write down a different way in which the message could have been sent.
- What are the advantages of this over 'Chinese Whispers'?

2 Think of all the ways that messages can be sent.
- Write them down under three columns – transmitter, medium and receiver.
- In a fourth column, put one major advantage and one major disadvantage of each method.

3 Divide into groups of six or more. Your teacher (kind person) has given each group a bar of chocolate.
- Hold a formal meeting to decide who will get the chocolate (you will need to draw up an Agenda, elect a Chair and take Minutes).
- Write down the problems that you encountered in coming to a decision.
- If you made a decision, write down how you did it.
- If you didn't, what steps would you now take to ensure that the decision is made?

Privacy and security

Sometimes the most important consideration for the message sender is whether the message can be kept private and secure. Morland wants Grolsch to know that they are interested in buying Ruddles – they do not want Ruddles to know as they wish to avoid a reaction from Ruddles' management. Security between Morland and Grolsch will therefore be essential. Messages may be sent by courier, written down and carried from one firm to the other, by fax, in person in meetings or by e-mail. Even so, security can be breached by those determined to do so. There is a whole industry that supplies 'bugs' and undertakes to discover secret information so that they can benefit financially. This is called industrial espionage.

SUMMARY

Ten points to remember:

1 Businesses have to make decisions all the time. This involves choosing between alternatives to try to reach targets.

2 Small businesses can get help from experts and special organisations.

3 Decisions that are taken at the highest level and have major long-term effects are called – strategic decisions.

4 Those taken by middle management with medium-term effects are – tactical decisions.

5 Those taken by junior managers on a day-to-day basis are – operational decisions.

6 Businesses may try to use scientific methods to make decisions, putting figures on possible outcomes.

7 Good communication of decisions is essential – the four parts to communication are the sender, the medium, the message and the receiver.

8 External communication is outside the firm, internal is within the firm. Different methods are appropriate.

9 Formal communication is used where records need to be kept or important decisions made.

10 It is essential to choose the correct medium for your message.

Unit 14
Motivation

A firm, as we know, needs land (a site), capital (factories, machinery, tools) and labour (workers) before it can produce anything. The most important of these factors is often quoted as being labour – the **human resources** that are needed for a business to be able to produce a good or service. Human resources (workers) need to be paid, to feel secure, to be valued, to be praised, to be promoted. Businesses that have workers who work not just for money but because they enjoy their work and feel valued are likely to be much more efficient than other businesses. **Absenteeism** will be lower as will lateness and illness.

An example of this can be found at Marks and Spencer, the high street clothing and food retail chain. The philosophy here is that the firm will look after employees for life. They provide canteen and coffee break facilities as well as little luxuries such as a hairdresser's on the premises or, because employees spend most of the day on their feet, a chiropody service. When employees retire, they are still part of the Marks and Spencer 'family' and have outings, trips and other benefits. In return, Marks and Spencer has a loyal and hard-working workforce who feel that they are valued and appreciated.

Activity

> Think about what you would want out of a job. Write out a list of at least five things that you would want and then arrange them in order of preference. Compare your list with a partner. Do you want different things? The same things? Why do you think this is so?

GETTING MOTIVATED

Motivation is the way in which workers can be encouraged to do a good job. It involves much more than just pay. This means that to a firm, motivation is:

- finding ways to get workers to work harder or more efficiently by
- showing that they value workers
- providing ways for workers to succeed
- providing a structure for promotion.

Why work?

The main reason why many people work is for money, but there are many other reasons. While a top footballer will work hard at his job in a team in order to earn his wage, he will also want other things. He needs to be valued and appreciated (imagine top sides like Barcelona or Real Madrid playing to empty stadiums), he needs success and he needs security – for a footballer this may be a pension fund or it may be a benefit match! People also work because they don't want to stay at home, but want to meet other people. Some people work because they have skills, or time, or knowledge that they want to use for the benefit of others. Voluntary work in charity shops or volunteering for work overseas falls into this category.

Did you know?

Voluntary work in underdeveloped nations or with organisations such as the Red Cross or Scouting movement is work that is extremely poorly paid, sometimes not paid at all – and yet people are still motivated to do it. Why do you think that this is so?

Motivators

What makes people work harder, or more efficiently? Marks and Spencer have discovered that many incentives may be used and while good levels of pay are a common motivator, other methods work just as well. Many firms now use a whole range of tactics and benefits, from Japanese systems of having **single status workforces** (Nissan), German and Swedish systems of team working (Volkswagen, Volvo), American systems of lifetime training (IBM, Ford) to British systems of profit sharing (John Lewis Partnership, the Co-operative movement). Anything that encourages people to work better or harder for the firm is a motivator.

Motivational theories

There are several theories as to what it is that makes people work harder. The best known are those of Maslow, McGregor and Herzberg.

Maslow's Theory

A. H. Maslow (1908–70) was an American psychologist who said that people worked in order to gain certain things. Firstly, they need to satisfy their survival needs; this means that they must either grow their own food or earn sufficient money to be able to buy the basic necessities of food, clothing and shelter. Secondly, once these needs are met, people will want to be safe and secure, so the next level of needs was for security. Once people feel safe, they then look for friends and social activities; they want to be part of a group or family. People have social needs. Higher

The higher layers cannot be put on until the lower layers are complete. The wall is finished off with a coping stone – this is like ambition fulfilled.

order needs can then be met. The first of these is for status – a certain standing in the community or what we might call a good reputation. People need to feel that they are respected both for who they are and for what they do. Finally, there is what Maslow called self-actualisation needs. We might think of it better as ambition. People will set themselves targets and attempt to reach them. On the whole, such needs are never fully met as people generally want to be better off than they are; they therefore set themselves further targets once they have achieved those originally set.

> **Handy hints**
> Remember that many societies in the world (see the Introduction) only just survive with the basic necessities. These are people who are living at what is called subsistence level – just enough to keep them alive.

This succession of different needs is called a 'hierarchy of needs'. It is a hierarchy because each higher level can only be achieved if the level below is built first.

How would a firm like Marks and Spencer fulfil these needs?

- **Survival:** Marks and Spencer provide a pay structure where people can earn a good rate for the job, allowing them to meet their survival needs. Pay is thus an important motivator and, for many, may be the most motivating factor.
- **Security:** a firm like Marks and Spencer provides a 'safety net' for employees who fall sick, are injured or retire with such things as good pension schemes. This is backed up by a government system that allows for sick pay, benefits for those unable to work and a state pension.
- **Social:** social and sports clubs, outings and special occasions such as Christmas dinners are all part of the general social structure provided by most large firms. Even the ceremony by which someone leaves a firm –

Activity — IT

Twins Ltd is a firm specialising in selling matching pairs of vases, paintings and antiques. Sales executives for Twins Ltd receive £500 per month plus 10% commission on sales up to £5 000 and 15% commission on sales above £5 000. Claudia Markham has made the following sales in the first three months of the year:

January: Sales = £4 800 February: Sales = £6 400.
March: Sales = £8 400

1. Use a spreadsheet package to show how much Claudia would earn in each of the three months shown.
2. Put formulas in to work out the commission she would receive.
3. If this three months were typical for the year, how much would her annual salary be?
4. If she paid income tax of 25%, what would her salary then be?

This task partially fulfils the requirements of the Spreadsheet Unit of the NEAB Certificate of Achievement in IT.

Motivation

the leaving party and the presentation – is designed to let the leaver know that they are leaving the 'family' and to let those that remain know that they are still part of a social team.

- **Status:** the opportunity to take decisions or to improve education or skills can be seen as meeting status or success needs. Many large firms provide training as part of a general package to improve the skills of their workforce. Marks and Spencer can provide status through promotion, perhaps gained through their own management training schemes.

- **Self-actualisation:** Marks and Spencer provide opportunities for people to be promoted and to achieve targets. This is no different from many firms where workers may become supervisors, supervisors may become managers and so on.

Activity

> Look at the 'Five Ss' above. Describe how you think a small business such as a sole trader could fulfil this hierarchy of needs.

Handy hints

You can remember Maslow's Hierarchy of Needs by remembering the Five S's – survival, security, social, status and self-actualisation.

McGregor's Theory

D. McGregor looked at the way that employers and employees traditionally viewed work – the employer paid the money, supervised the worker and gave instructions; the worker did the job, didn't ask questions and took the money. This traditional way of working he called Theory X. This he balanced with Theory Y, which was that most people actually enjoyed working and would readily take on responsibility.

A believer in Theory X or Theory Y would say:

McGregor believed that the Theory Y worker was the more typical example and that, if people were treated as if they were Theory Y type people, then firms would be more efficient and better managed. He believed that people could be as well motivated by the sense of a job well done or by being given trust and responsibility as by money.

Herzburg's Theory

F. Herzburg came to similar conclusions to Maslow and McGregor. He asked workers what motivated them and found out that the main things were a job well done, a feeling of being appreciated, trust, responsibility and promotion. One of the major factors that demotivated people was if a job was boring. Some conditions, which Herzburg called 'hygiene' factors, were discovered to make people unhappy at work, to demotivate them if they were missing or poor. Pay and working conditions are two of the main ones. This means that good pay or good working conditions are not necessarily motivators, but bad pay or working conditions are demotivators. These are called hygiene factors as, just like a clean shop, people don't notice when they are there. If they are missing, however, (as in a dirty shop) people do notice.

Activity

Look at the table below. You need to get an important order out quickly, by the end of the week.

> 1 Outline how you would put this to the workers if you believed in Theory X.
> 2 Outline how you would put this to the workers if you believed in Theory Y.
> 3 What are the three main differences in the two approaches?
> 4 Which theory would you personally support? State your reasons as fully as possible.

Theory X Workers....	Theory Y Workers....
don't like working	enjoy their work
do as little as they can get away with	will work hard to gain rewards
don't like things to change	want to see new things happening
need to be told what to do	will work independently
can't be trusted to make a decision	can be trusted to make a decision
are only interested in money	are motivated by things other than money
must be closely watched	can work unsupervised
can't be trusted or relied on	are trustworthy and reliable

Pay

It may therefore not be a good idea to use pay as a motivator – a good rate of pay for a job may be only one of the factors that a worker needs in order to do a good job. The amount of money that people earn in their jobs can be adjusted to try to make them work harder. There are different ways of paying people:

- **Time rate:** this means that they are paid for the amount of time taken to complete the job; this is not very motivating as it is unlikely to encourage anyone to work faster. In fact, it may well lead to people working more slowly if they are being paid by the number of hours it takes them to do a job. (The longer it takes, the more hours they will be paid for.)

- **Overtime rate:** this is paid when a job cannot be completed in the time allowed for it, so an extra rate has to be paid (usually 'time and a half' or 'double time' – half as much again on the usual rate or double the usual rate). The opportunity to work overtime is a motivating factor.

- **Piece rate:** this means that people are paid for how many good 'pieces' (of whatever is being produced) they finish. It is used to encourage people to work faster in order to earn more but has the disadvantage that, by encouraging speed, it may well lead to more sub-standard products than would otherwise be the case.

- **Bonus payments:** these can be made to encourage people to complete a job on time. 'Finish this by Friday and you've earned a bonus' is obviously a motivation to work more quickly. Bonuses may be built into a firm's pay structure so that they are automatically awarded if anyone works particularly well.

Perks

One of the most common ways of motivating salaried staff is through fringe benefits or 'perks'. These are extras, other than money, that the person may have in addition to his or her actual pay. The most popular and most common perk is a company car. Even when the tax system was changed in 1995 so that having a company car led to a larger tax bill (with more expensive cars taxed at a higher rate than cheaper cars) business people wanted to keep their cars due to the status that it gave them. Other perks include health insurance schemes, subsidised travel or accommodation, cheap mortgages and store discounts. Many jobs are advertised with a salary and 'benefits' meaning a package of perks such as cheap travel or interest free loans. In general, such packages would nowadays include health insurance and a company car or substantial mileage allowance (or both).

Incentives

Another way of motivating people is through the use of **incentives**. The most commonly used of these is in sales, where a salesman or woman is offered a basic wage plus **commission** – a percentage of the value of every item sold after the basic wage has been earned. In this way, salespeople are encouraged to sell more and more of a good. In many firms there are also other bonuses or prizes to be earned by being the best salesperson for a particular period of time. The salesman/woman of the month might earn money, a trophy, even a holiday for his or her efforts.

Performance related pay is linked to the achieving of targets. Should a worker or manager exceed the target, then an extra bonus is earned. The biggest weakness of this system is that it relies on the personal judgement of

Activity

> Look in your local paper on the evening when management jobs are being advertised. Make a list of the jobs that you can find where more than just a basic salary is offered. What sort of extras are offered?

someone. Teachers in schools, for example, can earn extra money for being a 'good' teacher.

Profit related pay is another way of providing an incentive. If the workers in a firm all work hard enough to improve its profitability then they should share in part of that profit. The John Lewis Partnership is an excellent example of this approach. Share options are one of the ways in which directors of companies can earn substantial rewards for improving the performance of a firm. If the firm's profits are increased by a certain amount then directors may receive extra shares in the company.

Personnel function

People who work for a firm are called personnel or human resources. The personnel department or human resources department of a firm deals with all aspects of employment from interviews and appointments through to discipline and dismissal. In smaller companies it may be a single person, a personnel officer, rather than a department that deals with these issues. In a sole tradership, it is the sole trader. The personnel department will try to ensure that employees are motivated by making sure that people receive the rewards for a 'job well done' and that systems are in place to pick up on problems before they get out of hand. Some of these systems are discussed in detail in the next unit.

Appreciation

There are a number of formal ways in which employers can try to show their appreciation and concern for their employees. Involving them in decision making is only one way. Other schemes include Investors in People, quality circles and annual reviews, evaluations and appraisals. These are discussed in more detail in Units 17 and 34.

Codebreakers

Human resources: the term used to mean not just workers, but the abilities of those workers.

Absenteeism: deliberate absence from work when not really ill, usually caused by elements such as stress or overwork.

Single status workforce: all workers, managers, directors are treated the same, for example, they all use the same canteen or washroom facilities.

Demotivate: the opposite of motivate, making workers want to work less hard.

Incentives: extra benefits are awarded when targets are reached.

Commission: a payment based on a percentage value of sales. A salesman on 10% commission who sells a £5 000 car would receive £500.

Activity

What makes a good teacher?

Look at the cartoon. Is Mr Jones a good teacher or not?

1. Write down what you think.
2. Write down who you think should make the decision.
3. Give reasons for your answers.

SUMMARY

Ten points to remember:

1. The most important of the production factors is labour.
2. Firms want people to work harder or more efficiently.
3. To do this they can offer rewards or motivators.
4. People work for more than just money.
5. People like to be appreciated and valued.
6. Maslow describes a hierarchy of needs – survival, security, social, status and self-actualisation.
7. McGregor thought that workers are 'naturally' motivated – Theory Y not Theory X.
8. Herzburg sees some factors as basic to motivation. These he called 'hygiene' factors.
9. People can be motivated by 'perks' such as extra pay, bonuses, rewards and other incentives.
10. The personnel department in a large firm deals with employees.

Unit 15
Labour requirements

A firm needs all four factors of production before it can produce a good or service. The most important of these is often quoted as being labour. Labour does not just mean manual labour but includes any work whether by hand or brain. An office worker or a professor or a lawyer are just as much 'labour' as a factory or manual worker.

The pattern of work used to be what was called '50, 50, 50'. This meant that most people worked for 50 hours a week for 50 weeks of the year for 50 years of their life – leaving school at 15 and retiring at 65. The pattern is changing towards '40, 40, 40'. The working week has been reduced to below 40 hours, the working year for most is now 47 weeks and, while students tend to leave full-time education much later, early retirement is possible in many industries. Working practices are also changing to try and give labour a greater say in what happens in a firm and to ensure that **labour turnover** is kept down.

An example of this is the Blue Circle Cement Company. Their old way of working was similar to that of many other firms. Decisions were made by the top managers and directors of the firm and passed, through several layers, to the workers (*see Unit 11 for examples of this 'hierarchical' approach*). The emphasis today is on a teamwork approach – Blue Circle decided that work was best carried out by teams of workers, with wide responsibilities. While it meant the reduction of the working week (sixty hours had been common) and no overtime, it also meant increased basic pay and the opportunity for workers to gain greater skills. At the Cauldon Works in Staffordshire, these new practices led to a reduction in employees of 237 between 1980 and 1990 (almost half the workforce) but an increase in **productivity** – cement production rose by 300 000 tonnes (almost half as much again). By 1996, the labour force had reduced by a further 90 with no loss in production. In fact, workers were earning more but working shorter hours. Blue Circle has created workers with the power to make decisions (see the flow diagram on page 76) and to work in teams and has collected a number of awards for this new way of working.

HOW DO FIRMS WORK OUT THEIR LABOUR REQUIREMENTS?

Labour requirements are not only the number and type of workers that a firm needs, but also the training and team working skills needed.

This means that to a firm, labour requirements are:
- the number of people they need to employ
- the skill levels they need
- the ability of workers to adapt and be flexible
- the team working skills of employees.

Labour turnover

Labour turnover is measured as the number of employees leaving a firm over a period of time. A high labour turnover means that staff are not staying with a firm. This leads to extra costs for recruitment and the training of new staff. Turnover is measured by a simple formula that gives a percentage. The higher the percentage, the more people are leaving. The way to work out the yearly turnover is:

$$\frac{\text{Number of staff leaving in the year}}{\text{Average number of staff employed}} \times 100$$

Turnover is kept down by keeping workers interested and motivated and by ensuring that they are as well paid as the competition. Firms that see a high rate of labour turnover will need to identify why this has happened (for example, the job is boring, there is no prospect of improvement, the pay is poor) and try to change things so that they are not always having to advertise for new staff.

> **Handy hints**
>
> There is a difference between an occupation and a job. A worker might stay in the same occupation (a sales assistant for example) but have several different jobs, working for different firms. Changing jobs but keeping the same occupation is usually quite easy. Changing occupation generally means that some form of retraining is necessary.

> **Activity**
>
> ▹ Look at the job advertisements in your local paper over a period of a few weeks. Identify firms where there always seem to be vacancies. Why do you think that this is so?

Labour mobility

There are two types of labour mobility, occupational mobility and geographical mobility:

- **Occupational mobility:** means the ability of labour to move between different jobs. Not many years ago, a worker could expect to be in the same occupation, sometimes the same job, for life. Now it is likely that a worker will need to retrain for two, three or even more different occupations before they retire. This makes the learning of *transferable skills* particularly important. Skills and expertise that can be taken from one occupation and used in another make labour much more mobile – and therefore much more likely to stay in employment. One of the most important transferable skills is the ability to use a computer as this can be used in many different occupations and is becoming increasingly important for almost all areas of work.

- **Geographical mobility:** means the ability of labour to move around the country in order to take a job. Workers are generally more geographically mobile when younger or unmarried as they may have no family ties to the area that they are in. As workers get older, marry and have children, they become much less geographically mobile – children may need to change schools, partners may have jobs, houses may be bought and so on.

With some firms, geographical mobility does not just mean within a country, but can be world-wide. A multinational company may wish to post workers to any of its offices or plants anywhere in the world.

Keeping labour

> **Activity**
>
> Read the passage and answer the questions that follow.
>
> Bessie's Bakery is a small firm producing bread and cakes. The firm employs mainly part-time, female staff and allows them to work flexible hours to fit in with childcare and school requirements. Workers do not have to be particularly skilful, as basic training is given and all specialist jobs are left to management or the three full-time employees. The bakery does not pay very high wages but it does have a high labour turnover.
>
> ▹ 1 Give three reasons why the labour turnover for this firm may be high.
> ▹ 2 Make three suggestions as to how Bessie's Bakery could lower labour turnover.
> ▹▹ 3 What extra costs have to be paid by Bessie's Bakery if there is a high labour turnover?
> ▹▹▹ 4 Suggest ways in which Bessie's Bakery could increase the productivity of its workforce.

One way for a firm to keep labour turnover low is to introduce schemes to make the job more interesting or to give the worker more responsibility. The main ways to do this are through schemes such as HRM and Kaizen, (*see Unit 34*), or through one of the following:

- **Job enrichment:** giving the worker greater responsibility. Production line workers in an assembly plant who used to see only the small part of the job that they worked on, will work better as part of a group that sees the whole production process through to the finished product.
- **Rotating jobs:** this means getting people to do a number of different jobs. Workers in a large supermarket, for instance, will not just be shelf-stackers or checkout operators, but will move from one job to another at regular intervals.
- **Job enlargement:** this means making the range of responsibilities wider.

> **Handy hints**
>
> Wages are the price of labour. Just like the price of a good or service, wages are set by the levels of Demand and Supply for labour. A shortage in supply (a skilled footballer, a good musician, a highly trained brain surgeon) leads to a high price (high wages) as long as the skills or talents are demanded. High demand for a particular type of labour will also push wages up. If there is low demand for a type of labour then wages tend to be low, even more so if there is a high level of supply – untrained manual labour, for example. Look at Unit 38 on how prices are determined and see how that theory can be related to labour.

Losing labour

The three main ways in which labour is lost to a firm are:

- **Retirement:** the official retirement age for men is 65 and for women 60 although there are moves to bring these in line with each other. In many jobs, people retire earlier, often as early as 50. In some cases, people never retire and continue to work well into old age because they enjoy the job or the benefits it brings. Natural wastage is when workers retire or leave the firm and are not replaced.
- **Redundancy:** this is where the job no longer exists. Some jobs are no longer necessary due to new technology or just because the world moves on! There is now no need for people to be employed lighting gas street lamps and, while employment opportunities for blacksmiths have fallen, those for motor mechanics have risen. Voluntary redundancy is when a firm has to reduce its workforce and workers volunteer to leave, usually in return for money. Compulsory redundancy is when the firm is forced to make workers redundant and has to give them compensation.

- **Dismissal:** 'getting the sack', 'being fired', 'getting the boot' are all used to describe being dismissed from employment. The main reasons for dismissal are poor quality work, bad time-keeping or dangerous or illegal behaviour. In some cases (such as time-keeping) a number of warnings must be given to the worker. In other cases summary dismissal may happen. This means that the worker is immediately dismissed, with no notice period. If, for example, a bank clerk was found stealing from a till or a lorry driver arrives to work drunk, then they could be summarily dismissed.

Labour rights

Labour has certain rights in the workplace that all employers are bound to give their workforce. These include a safe and healthy working environment, fair and equal treatment, sick pay, maternity benefit and the right to a reasonable amount of time off for specific things such as holidays, funerals and trade union duties.

Labour laws

Workers are protected against employers taking advantage of them by various laws. The most important of these are:

- The Trade Union Reform and Employment Rights Act
- The Health and Safety at Work Act
- The Sex Discrimination Act
- The Race Relations Act

> **Activity**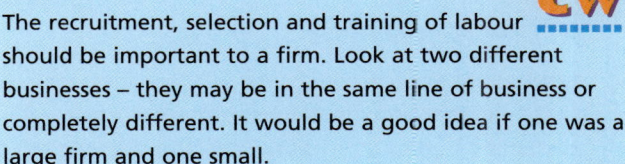
>
> The recruitment, selection and training of labour should be important to a firm. Look at two different businesses – they may be in the same line of business or completely different. It would be a good idea if one was a large firm and one small.
>
> 1. Look at the ways in which they recruit staff – collect job advertisements for the firms and compare them for coverage (how many people are they likely to reach) and effectiveness.
> 2. What processes do job applicants have to go through?
> 3. Compare the application forms that have to be filled in. (A small firm may not use one – why not?)
> 4. Look at how interviews are conducted – are they formal or informal? Is it a professional interviewer or someone from the firm? Sit in on an interview if you can get permission.
> 5. Find out what induction and training is offered by the firm.
> 6. Evaluate the processes in the two firms – which is most effective, and why?

Labour requirements

- The Disability Discrimination Act
- The Equal Pay Act.

These Acts are dealt with in detail in Unit 20.

> **Activity**
>
> Look at the titles of these Acts and decide what you think they are about. Then look them up in your library. What are the main points of each of them?

Did you know? Some jobs are seen as a 'calling' or vocation. This means that people have a particular wish to do a job, such as nursing, teaching, working with old people, working with children, making music, being a priest, because they want to help others or for other, personal, reasons. In this case, the wage is usually of little or no importance to the worker.

European laws

As a member of the European Union, Britain has to agree to laws that are passed in Europe. The most important recent laws are contained in what is called the Social Chapter. This is aimed at giving workers increased protection, guaranteeing that all get reasonable holidays and reasonable pay (a **minimum wage**) and increasing workers' part in decision making at all levels of a firm.

Codebreakers

Labour turnover: the number of employees leaving a firm over a period of time.

Productivity: a measure of the efficiency or work-rate of the workforce; a more productive worker puts in the same hours as other workers, but produces more.

Transferable skills: skills and expertise that can be taken from one occupation and used in another.

Natural wastage: reductions in the workforce through retirement, promotion, people seeking jobs elsewhere.

Summary dismissal: the worker is dismissed immediately, with no notice period.

Minimum wage: the least that an employer can legally pay a worker.

Performance related pay: the better the worker, the more they are paid.

Human resources

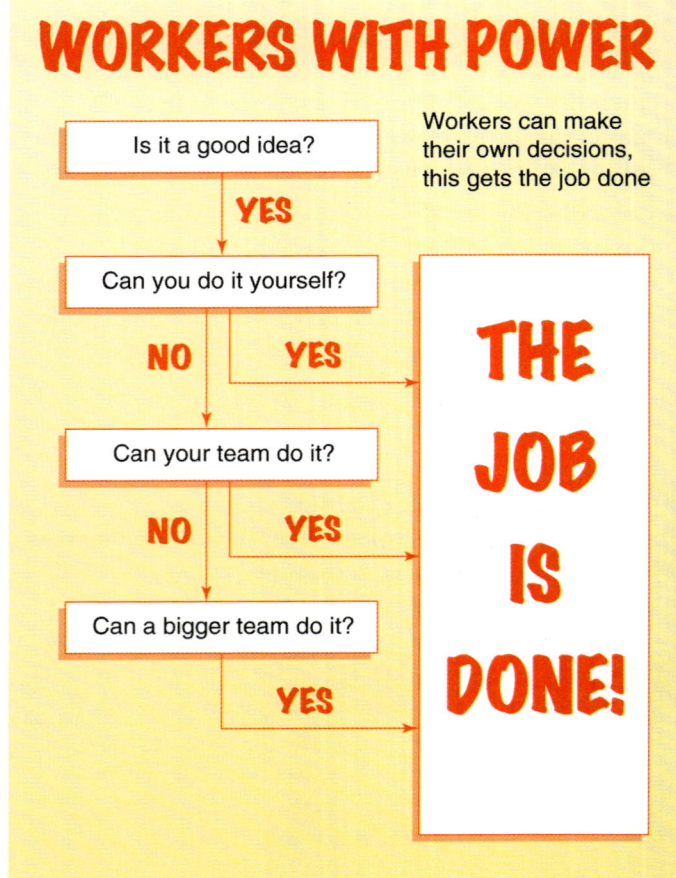

Labour is also thought of as 'human resources' and the management of a labour force can be referred to as 'human resource management'. In many firms this is handled by the Personnel Department. The job of the Personnel Department is to find the staff the firm needs, interview and appoint them, train them, discipline them if rules are broken and end their employment as necessary. In some firms a total human resource management approach is used. This is not just a way of dealing with employees, but a whole system of labour management. There is no longer a Personnel Department but the treatment of employees becomes a central part of the whole firm. Firms practising this approach include Marks and Spencer, IBM Computers and McDonald's. There are three main parts to 'HRM'. They are:

- employee involvement – workers are involved in decision making and their ideas are listened to
- **performance related pay** – the better the worker, the more they are paid
- good selection and training procedures.

Activity

> Select an appropriate program to draw up an exciting job advertisement for the following post. You can create a logo for Magic Motors to use in the advertisement.

> Full-time team manager at Magic Motors. £30 000 p.a. plus benefits. In charge of a team of 12 highly skilled engineers. Team working and leadership skills essential. Good promotion opportunities. Degree in engineering essential. Recent experience in engineering production desirable.
>
> Apply: Personnel Manager, Magic Motors, Appletree Lane, Wigton. WG1 2AP
>
> We are an equal opportunities employer on a non-smoking site.

Once you have completed and printed the advertisement, write a brief explanation of why you chose the particular package that you did.

This task partially fulfils the requirements of the Software Applications Unit of the NEAB Certificate of Achievement in IT.

SUMMARY

Eight points to remember:

1 Labour is the human element needed to produce a good or service.

2 Whether hand or brain is used, it is still labour.

3 Labour turnover is the rate at which workers leave a firm.

4 Geographical labour mobility is the ability of labour to move to a different location to work.

5 Occupational labour mobility is the ability of labour to move to a different occupation.

6 Labour is lost through redundancy, retirement or dismissal.

7 Labour is protected against unfair or unsafe practices by law.

8 More modern employer-employee relations are based on trust and teamworking.

Unit 16
Recruitment and selection

Only in the smallest of firms will there be no need for the **recruitment** of additional staff. Even in a classic, one person business, it is still likely that the owner will need to employ some people – even if they are only in a part-time capacity. In a large firm it is essential that the right people are recruited to do the jobs that the firm needs doing. Advertising for new staff and the process of recruitment and selection can be an expensive activity so a firm needs to try to make sure that they get it right.

The advertisement below appeared in *The Guardian* newspaper on 25 October 1997. It was placed in the 'IT & T' (Information Technology & Telecommunications) section of the paper's Saturday 'Jobs and Money' supplement. It is looking to recruit computer specialists for computer development, software engineering and as account managers. The company involved, called Zuken-Redac is one that designs printed circuit boards using computer assisted design (CAD) packages. This company is not a household name in this country and therefore needs to introduce itself in its advertising before stating what it wants.

Activity

1. How effective do you think that this advertisement would be in reaching the people it wants to recruit?
2. What do you think Tony Knowles' job is?
3. What 'extras' are offered by this company as part of the employment package?
4. Why do you think that there are no salary levels mentioned in the advertisement?
5. Design a job advertisement for Zuken-Redac that you think would be more effective.

78 Recruitment and selection

HOW DO FIRMS SELECT THEIR EMPLOYEES?

Recruitment and selection is the process of finding and choosing, from the widest possible selection of applicants, the best people to meet the needs of the organisation. This means that to a firm, recruitment and selection is:

- advertising for staff in the right places
- providing the right information for **jobseekers**
- asking for the right information from jobseekers
- considering the responses thoroughly
- long listing and short listing
- assessing candidates through interview or other appropriate means
- making the right appointments.

Situations vacant

It is important to the jobseeker that they are looking in the right place and to the employer that they are advertising in the right place. A small firm might advertise vacancies in a newsagent's shop window or in the local paper. A larger firm might use the local paper or advertise in a job centre. Some employers may also advertise on television if a cheap enough slot is provided or put their vacancies on to the Internet.

> **Did you know?**
> Yorkshire Television provide for employers to contact applicants through a programme called 'Jobfinder'. This is a one hour slot in the early morning (4.30 to 5.30) where employers can advertise vacancies.

Job Centres are provided by the Department for Education and Employment, and aim to reduce unemployment. Employers advertise vacancies on standard cards and under particular categories. Jobseekers can then easily find out if there are any local vacancies in their own field of employment.

National newspapers are a major way for large firms and organisations to recruit. It is important that jobseekers know which newspapers to look in and on which days. When looking for a job in marketing, for example, it could be Monday's speciality in one newspaper, Thursday's in another and not appear as a category at all in another.

There are also specialist publications that are aimed at people seeking jobs in particular fields. *The Times Educational Supplement*, for example, advertises teaching jobs and jobs in education generally, while *The Times Higher Education Supplement* concentrates on university jobs.

Activity

1. Explain why Rightway employs mainly part-time staff.
2. Rightway needs to advertise for part-time staff. Explain, giving reasons, the most effective ways to advertise the vacancies.
3. Explain what would be the most effective ways for Rightway to select from the applicants for the part-time vacancies.

(This question is adapted from the NEAB's Business Studies Paper 2, 1996.)

> **Activity**
>
> ▷ Imagine you are seeking a job in the Information Technology field. Look in your local newsagent's, or in a major newsagent's in a town centre, and list the specialist publications where you think you would find jobs advertised. Where else could you look for jobs of this type?

Agencies

The Bahrain Bugle
Business Editor/Writers

The Bahrain Bugle is a new and exciting publication which has as its focus the national and international business community in the Middle East. An experienced financial writer/journalist with specialist economic and business knowledge in the Middle East is required to join our go-ahead team. A person of the right quality would be considered for the post of Business Editor.

Send CV and letter to:
MidEast Consultants
47 Stead Street
LONDON EC14 3EC

Some large organisations do not use their own company to recruit staff but give the work to specialist **recruitment agencies** or consultants. This is often the case with companies from other countries who wish to recruit in the UK. The advertisement shown here is an example of an agency being used by a foreign newspaper. There are also general agencies such as Manpower and Reed International who provide a link between prospective employers and jobseekers by keeping jobseekers' details and making them available to employers. There is usually a charge to register with such agencies and many specialise in a particular type of work (office work, for example).

Government help

It is in the interests of government to try to make sure that people seeking jobs are put in touch with employers in order to keep unemployment down. As well as Job Centres, the government has set up job clubs, where advice on filling out application forms, writing letters and composing **CVs** is available and equipment, such as typewriters and computers, is provided. In certain cases such things as postage costs for applications and travel expenses to interviews may be given, or even grants or loans for interview clothes.

The Jobseekers' Allowance replaced Unemployment Benefit in 1996. People claiming benefit must prove that they are actively looking for a job. They must:

- be available for work
- sign a Jobseekers' Agreement saying that they are seeking work
- keep a record of the jobs that they have applied for
- go to regular review meetings to show that they are looking for work.

Other routes

> **Activity**
>
> ▷ Look up the word 'nepotism' in a dictionary – what does it mean? Why do you think that this practice is not well liked in firms?

Not every vacancy is filled by a process that starts with advertising. Many jobs are never advertised at all. These fall into four main categories – internal appointments, personal inquiry, personal recommendation and 'head hunting':

- **Internal appointments:** often a vacancy that needs filling can best be filled from the staff that are already working at a firm. The post may be advertised

80 Recruitment and selection

internally – through a company newsletter or bulletin board, in which case there will be a process of selection – or it may not be advertised at all.

- **Personal inquiry:** where a jobseeker has sent their details to a firm or has called in to a firm on the chance that there may be a job available. In many cases there may not be a job immediately, but the firm could keep the details and then contact the jobseeker when a vacancy does arise. This obviously saves them money but is only effective if they are really sure that they are getting the right person.

- **Recommendation:** where a person is recommended for a post, either by someone who already works there or through a family or social connection. Again, this saves the firm the expense of going through a full advertising and recruitment procedure.

- **Head-hunting:** this is where a firm decides who they want for a particular job and then sets about enticing them away from another company. In general this is done with senior positions in large companies. The recruiter will offer better pay or conditions or additional extras (such as a 'Golden Hello') to the person that they are trying to get to work for them.

Job analysis and person specification

Job analysis is the breaking down of a job into its component parts in order to identify exactly what the job requires. This means that a company can then advertise for staff who exactly match the detailed job requirements. The analysis will be used to draw up a detailed description of the job. In the advertisement at the start of this unit the job of Software Engineering is mentioned. A job analysis for this might look something like this:

Tasks	Skills	Qualifications	Additional
Designing software	Programming	Good degree in ...	CAD experience
Installing software	Design	Computer science	PCB experience
Testing software	Communication	Mathematics or	Problem-solving skills
Writing guides for clients		Electronic engineering	Knowledge of certain programming languages
Launching software			

This analysis would then be used to draw up what used to be called a job description. This would contain basic information about the job. In this case it might be:

Information	Description
Job title	Software engineer
Purpose of job	To develop software to solve clients' problems
Duties	Research, designing, installing, testing and launching software. Writing software guides
Line management	Senior software engineer, Research director
Location	Tewkesbury
Hours	35 per week

These two pieces of information could be used to write a job specification, now more usually referred to as a **person specification**. This is the detailed description of the person that you want to fit the job. It will contain

It is important to be able to break down some jobs into component parts – like the parts of an engine.

> **Codebreakers**
>
> **Recruitment:** the process of finding someone to fill a vacancy.
>
> **Jobseeker:** someone looking for a job.
>
> **Recruitment agencies:** specialist firms that deal with recruitment.
>
> **CV – curriculum vitae:** the 'story of your life'.
>
> **Golden Hello:** a sum of money paid to a new employee as an introduction to a firm or an enticement to join a firm.
>
> **Job analysis:** breaking a job down into its component parts.
>
> **Person specification:** description of the person that fits the job.

Recruitment and selection

additional skills or qualities which the employer particularly wants to see and is usually drawn up in two parts:

- the essential qualities needed
- the non-essential but desirable qualities.

Some employers add a third heading of additional qualities that they feel might be particularly useful. The person specification for the software engineer could look something like this:

Essential	Desirable	Additional
Good degree	Experience in a similar field	Sense of humour
Wide knowledge of programming languages	Good communications skills – written and verbal	Non-smoker
Programming skills	Experience of dealing directly with clients	
Ability to work in a team		
Problem-solving skills		

Activity

1. Write out a job analysis for the following jobs: airline pilot, schoolteacher, nurse, professional sports player, car salesman.
2. Choose one of the job analyses that you have created and write the person specification that goes with it.
3. Look at the additional qualities you have chosen. What additional qualities do you think might be asked for in those jobs that you have not written a person specification for?

Qualifications

One of the major things on both the job analysis and person specification is the level and type of qualifications. Senior posts in many companies require a university degree. Other companies prefer to take on trainees who have A-levels and pay for their university education. In return, the company will gain a loyal member of staff trained to the company's requirements. Other firms will

Did you know?
There is a range of qualifications that are vocational – linked to a job or occupation – rather than academic. These include NVQs and Modern Apprenticeships. The table above right shows how these compare with 'academic' qualifications.

Academic qualifications	Vocational qualifications	
	NVQs provide training in specific areas such as IT or Agriculture	GNVQs are broader based than NVQs
Doctorate		
Masters degree	NVQ Management = Professional qualification	
University Honours Degree First Upper second (2.1) Lower second (2.2) Third		GNVQ Higher = Degree level
Ordinary degree (not honours)	NVQ Higher Technician = Higher education	
GCE (A-level) A B C D E	NVQ Technician = 2 A-levels	GNVQ Advanced = 2 A-levels
GCSE A* A B C D E F G	NVQ Craft = 4 GCSEs at A–C NVQ Foundation = 4 GCSEs at D–E	GNVQ Intermediate = 4 GCSEs at D–E GNVQ Foundation = 4 GCSEs at D–E

prefer jobseekers with **vocational qualifications**. The illustration here shows equivalent qualifications. Many jobs have a 'qualifications ladder' which can be drawn to show what qualifications are needed and how long it could take to gain them. For example, a software engineer will have needed to pass enough A–C grade GCSEs to study for A-levels, enough A-levels to get on a degree course and then a good enough degree to be accepted into employment.

How to apply

There are a number of different ways in which an employer will ask you to apply for a job. For a small company or a sole trader or partnership, they may just ask jobseekers to telephone them or to call in at their premises. In a large organisation, it is likely that a much more structured approach needs to be taken. Firms will want application by some, or all of:

- **Forms:** application forms are designed to give a firm a quick reference to applicants' qualifications and details. They will include headings that ask for name, address, current job, employment history (jobs held in the past), education, training and qualifications, and general health. There will also be a section for additional information, where candidates can write a letter of application.

- **Letter of application:** this may be part of the application form or a separate letter may be requested. This is the candidate's opportunity to say, in more detail, what makes him or her the ideal candidate for the post. They can explain what experience they have had and what qualities they could bring to the job.

- **Curriculum Vitae:** this is the 'story of your life', sometimes referred to (especially in America) as a 'résumé' but more commonly just referred to by its initials as 'CV'. A CV contains personal details such as name, address, age and date of birth. It lists educational establishments attended and qualifications gained. It shows what job you are currently working at and what jobs you have had in the past. It also gives you the opportunity to show what special skills and talents you have.

> **Activity**
>
> ▷ Using the following headings, draw up a starter CV for yourself:
>
> Name, address, date of birth, education (secondary schools attended, with dates), qualifications expected, IT skills, work experience, hobbies and interests, awards received, additional information

> **Handy hints**
>
> It is important to keep your CV up to date. As you gain qualifications, these need to be added on. This does not just apply to 'academic' qualifications. When you pass your driving test, for example, this should be added in. Some qualifications become less important as higher qualifications are gained. Somebody with a Master's degree, for example, is not likely to still be listing their GCSE passes; somebody who has worked full-time for a firm for a length of time is unlikely to be listing teenage jobs such as baby sitting or paper rounds.

Selection

Once the closing date for applications has passed, the firm will look at all the CVs, forms and letters of application it has asked for. The first stage is to **long list**. This is the process of weeding out all the obviously unsuitable applicants. Initially, many applications may be rejected because they have failed to follow instructions – black ink may have been requested so that forms can be photocopied, applicants may have been asked to write in capital letters, or to typewrite the form. Those not following instructions are likely to be rejected immediately. Applications that are untidy, illegible or messy will also be rejected.

From the remaining applications, the employer will draw up a **short list** – those candidates that are worth further attention, and from this list will select the candidates for interview. For many jobs there will be hundreds of applicants, dozens on the long list and yet less than ten invited for interview.

> **Handy hints**
>
> If you are invited to interview, you should use it as a learning experience. Even if you do not get the job, it is good practice for further interviews. Many employers will be happy to give you feedback on your interview performance and why you didn't get the job. You can use this information to improve your chances at future interviews.

> **Activity**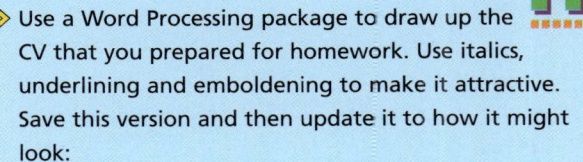
>
> ▷ Use a Word Processing package to draw up the CV that you prepared for homework. Use italics, underlining and emboldening to make it attractive. Save this version and then update it to how it might look:
>
> - in five years time
> - in ten years time.
>
> Take out those things that will no longer be important and add in those things that you hope to achieve.
>
> This task partially fulfils the requirements of the Word Processing Unit of the NEAB Certificate of Achievement in IT.

Interviews

Final selection will usually take place through an interview. The candidate will be invited to answer questions put to them by a panel of interviewers or a single person. A panel for a large firm could consist of the Personnel Officer, the Head of Department and the Line Manager. In a small firm it might just be the owner. In a firm that has employed a specialist recruitment company, the specialists will lead the interview.

Interviews are not always the best way to make sure that the best candidate is chosen – interviewers are often not trained and may appoint people for the wrong reasons. Because this weakness has been recognised, many firms now use other methods in order to make appointments.

Handy hints

There are some important Do's and Don'ts associated with the interview:

DO be on time, dress smartly, try to answer questions fully and clearly.

DON'T smoke, chew, swear, dress casually, sit down before being asked.

Other tests

Sometimes simple tests are given to see if a candidate can do the maths involved in the job, or can work at speed, or can speak the languages that they claim to speak. Sometimes candidates are asked to give a presentation on a particular subject, or to say how they would react in a

Activity

1. Look at the CV and application form filled in by Jon Letterman for the post of software engineer. By using this information and that contained in the advertisement on page 78, write his letter of application.

2. Using the information, design a better application form for the company.

3. Sometimes employers ask for parts of the application form or letter to be hand-written, sometimes they may ask for it to be typewritten. What reasons can you give for these requests?

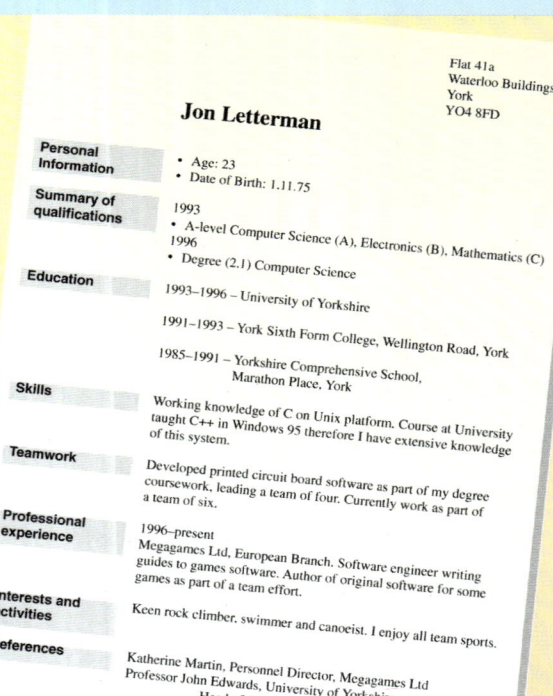

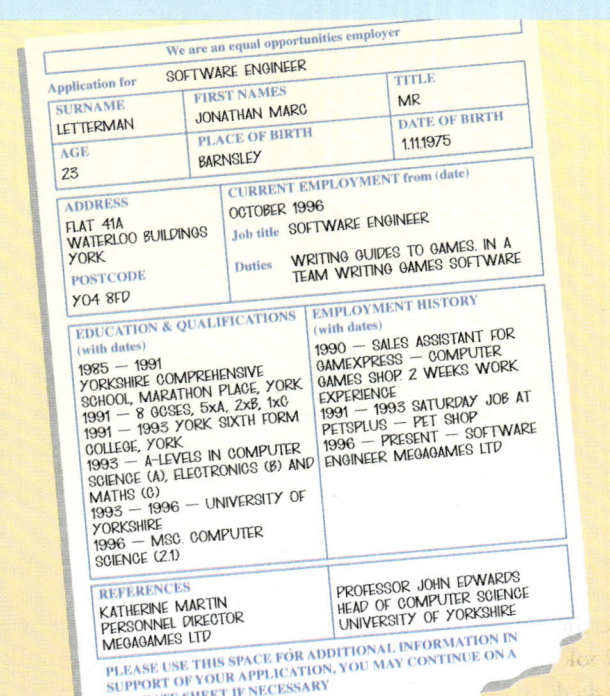

84 Recruitment and selection

particular situation that might come up (situational interviewing). Their solutions can then be checked against the solutions of those with experience at the job. Some companies go to great lengths in their recruitment exercises using such things as Army assault courses and Outward Bound Schools in order to assess leadership qualities and problem-solving abilities.

Modern skills for a modern age. You could be tested on your IT abilities.

Did you know? There is now a range of Modern Apprenticeships that are mainly for 16 and 17-year-old school and college leavers. There is no set age for beginning. Apprentices study in a particular field (engineering, for example) and work towards NVQ Technician Level (Level 3). The apprenticeship is a mixture of 'on the job' training and college.

Contract of employment

Once the employer formally offers the job and the candidate accepts it, then a Contract of Employment needs to be drawn up. This will include the

- job title and starting date
- rate and regularity of pay (weekly, monthly)

Codebreakers

Vocational qualifications: qualifications linked to particular jobs.

Long list: those candidates not discarded after an initial look at applications.

Short list: those candidates invited to interview.

Line manager: the worker's immediate superior.

Situational interviewing: putting interview candidates into situations that might occur and asking them what decisions they would make.

- hours of work, holiday entitlement and sickness benefits
- place of work
- disciplinary procedures and how problems are to be dealt with
- Trade Union agreements
- period of notice that needs to be given to end employment
- pension rights and contributions.

Details of each of these are to be found in Unit 18.

Activity

Choose two businesses that you have a connection with. You might work part-time for a business or have completed your work experience there. You might have a member of your family or a friend who works there.

1. How do they advertise their vacancies?
2. Do they use different methods or different outlets for different types of job?
3. Why do you think that this is?
4. What recruitment process do they follow? You can look in detail at how they long list and short list, how they interview, what other tests or methods they use.
5. How effective are their methods of recruiting and selecting staff?
6. Which firm do you think has the most effective methods, and why?

SUMMARY

Ten points to remember:

1. Recruitment is how a firm finds the staff it needs.
2. Most jobs are advertised.
3. Employers must advertise in the right place.
4. Jobseekers must know where to look.
5. Application is how jobseekers apply for jobs.
6. Forms, letters and CVs are all used.
7. Selection is how employers choose between applicants.
8. The selection process is usually long listing, short listing and interview.
9. Some firms use methods other than interview.
10. Once appointed, a Contract of Employment must be made.

Recruitment and selection

Unit 17
Training and development

When a firm has recruited new staff, when it reviews problems with its work-force, and when it is working positively towards human resource management, training and development will play an important part. Training and development of the workforce may have a number of purposes, from introducing new staff to the company, to showing existing staff how to operate new machinery and to the complete retraining of workers with redundant skills. A number of methods may be used, but broadly they can be either on or off the job. While most training will have benefits to both employee and employer, there are also possible costs to both. Training and development is also vital to the improvement of the UK economy.

Remploy is a national company which was set up to employ large numbers of disabled people. It employs over 12 000 people on 96 sites in the UK. Over 10 000 of these employees are registered disabled. One of the factories is at Ashington, in Northumberland, with 105 shopfloor employees – all people with disabilities. The company operates a general induction programme for all new employees, covering health and safety training in addition to information on the company, company history and all the rules, regulations and benefits offered by Remploy. Once this is complete, any specific skill training is delivered in the factory. Remploy uses what they call the 'buddy system' where a skilled operator is teamed up with the trainee. All training is to NVQ Level 2 in Manufacturing, Assembling and Processing skills so that all employees achieve a formal qualification. As Remploy states, 'All employees will be helped and encouraged to attain their highest level of ability and a multi-skilled work-force will emerge fully motivated and rewarded'.

THE PURPOSES OF TRAINING

- Some training is used to introduce new employees to the firm, its workplace and the job.
- A lot of training will be aiming to increase the efficiency of the workers. Virtually all firms are keen to increase the output obtained from their workers, and training may help to achieve this. In the modern workplace, there is a greater need for workers to be able to do a variety of tasks. The process of achieving this is called 'multi-skilling' and it allows workers to be used flexibly.
- When new technology is introduced into a firm, many employees will need training both in how to use it and how to repair and maintain it. This is often referred to as 'upgrading skills' and is particularly important now as Information Technology is being used increasingly in the workplace.
- As laws change and as everybody becomes more aware of the dangers in a workplace, firms are increasingly expected to provide training in health and safety procedures.
- Many people believe that appropriate training is a way to motivate workers.
- Training may help some workers to gain promotion, either inside or outside the firm that employs them. This is often referred to as 'staff development'.
- For an increasing number of employees in an increasing number of industries, retraining is vital so that they can move into new jobs as their old ones disappear.

TYPES OF TRAINING

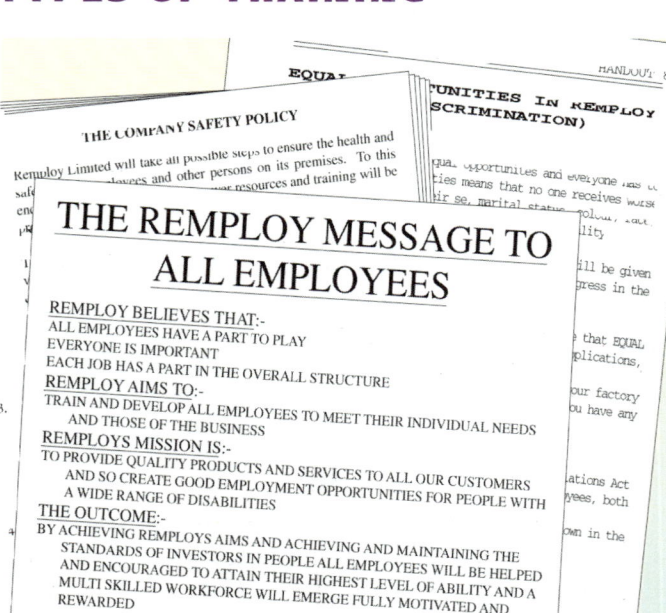

86 Training and development

Induction

Where **induction training** is used, a firm usually introduces new workers to the firm, the workplace and the job. A lot of information will be given to the new workers about the company and its products, the company regulations and important health and safety considerations. If the job is in a large building, workers may be given a tour and shown the layout of all the facilities. They will be introduced to the people they will be working with, and will be told about the other key personnel. The firm may also take time to identify the particular needs of the new worker. This information may then be used to help plan the more specific types of training needed.

On the job

This type of training takes place within the firm and on the 'production line'. **On the job training** often means working with an experienced employee who will show you how to use any machinery and will check your progress. Some firms try to improve on this by using specialist instructors. In general, you are 'learning by doing' and you will be making the product or providing some sort of service. So, the firm receives some direct benefit from this training, although new employees may create a lot of waste while they learn the job.

Off the job

Off the job training takes place away from the 'production line'. The trainee will not be making goods or providing services that can be sold. Larger firms may have their own training centres staffed by specialist instructors, while smaller firms are more likely to use Colleges of Further or Higher Education to provide specialist courses. In this case, the trainee will be released from the workplace. This could be for one day a week or perhaps for a whole block of time. It is quite likely that such training will lead to an external award or qualification; and in some cases the firm may want trainees to receive a broader training rather than something that would just help them directly in the workplace.

Activity

It is quite a useful exercise to think of the costs and benefits of training, both to the worker and to the firm. Some of the possible costs and benefits are given below.

Improving company image	The cost of courses
Better quality products	Higher production
Wage rates may rise	Lost production
Wasteful	Improved worker motivation
Workers are more skilled	Improved promotion prospects

1. Look back at the information on the purposes and types of training. See if you can identify any more possible costs and benefits of training.
2. a) Decide whether they are costs to the firm or the employee.
   b) Decide whether they are benefits to the firm or the employee.
   c) Create a grid to record your decisions.

Did you know? In 1995, The World Competitiveness Report ranked the UK 24/48 in a world skills league. It was ranked 40th in a willingness to train league. These are very worrying results for the government because they suggest that the UK will struggle to compete with its major industrial rivals. No wonder, then, that both the previous and the present governments have put a new emphasis on improving training.

GOVERNMENT AND TRAINING

Most people know of government training schemes such as Youth Training (YT) and Employment Training (ET) for older unemployed people. Most of these schemes are now managed and promoted by Training and Enterprise Councils (TECs) at a local level. Nationally, the Training, Enterprise and Education Directorate (TEED) has been created to promote training. Targets have been set with these organisations aiming to train half of the unemployed workforce to NVQ Level Three standard, or the equivalent, by the year 2000.

INVESTORS IN PEOPLE

The TECs are also expected to promote training for existing workers. They work with local colleges or specific training organisations to fund and provide courses. One of the best known schemes is the Investors In People (IIP) Award. Any organisation working towards IIP must work through a series of steps, setting itself some goals and making a plan to achieve them. The staff must then be fully involved in these plans and staff training needs identified to achieve the goals. Training must then take place, ending up with a thorough evaluation to see how far the investment has been a success. Organisations that successfully work through the steps may then display the IIP award at their premises and on their headed paper.

Governments hope that improved training and development for all employed and unemployed people will help British firms to be more competitive with foreign companies. The work-force should be better skilled and more flexible. Productivity should rise and quality should improve, leading to higher sales of British goods and services. This should then help unemployment and improve the standard of living of the British people.

SUMMARY

Four points to remember:

1 New, existing and unemployed workers will all require training at some points in their lives.

2 Both employers and employees may benefit from the training given to the work-force and a number of methods may be used.

3 Training will certainly involve a cost to the employer and possibly to the employee, so any scheme should carefully weigh the costs against the benefits.

4 Governments are keen to create a better trained UK work-force through a number of schemes.

Codebreakers

Induction training: for new staff, an introduction to the company, its organisation, its rules and regulations and to the job.

On the job training: methods of training that involve workers learning the job as they work on the actual production line.

Off the job training: methods of training that take place away from the production line so that the trainee is not involved in producing the good or providing the service.

Unit 18
Employment contract and pay and conditions

When a firm hires a new employee, it must issue a written contract. In addition, a worker must be given a written statement of terms and conditions. Part of this statement will be details of the worker's pay. There are several pay systems that may be used depending on the type of work and product that the employee is involved with. Some pay systems may also include non-monetary rewards for the employee. All workers need to remember that there will be a number of deductions from pay so that take-home pay will be less than gross pay.

It is quite difficult to find an example of an organisation that has all the payment systems explained below. One organisation that has quite a number is a school. All permanent teachers will be on an annual **salary**. Secretaries are likely to be salaried although they are often on part-time contracts. Those paid an hourly wage will certainly include supply teachers and possibly technicians. Both secretaries and technicians might be able to work overtime and this will certainly apply to caretakers. Some schools are responsible for the upkeep of the grounds, and so gardeners may find their wages are a mixture of an hourly rate and a productivity scheme for some jobs. It is unlikely, however, for a school to be paying any commission based pay or a profits related bonus. There also seem to be few **fringe benefits**!

CONTRACT OF EMPLOYMENT

Each employee hired by a firm must be given a written **contract of employment** within 13 weeks of starting work. In the eyes of the law, a contract exists once a person has agreed to work for an employer and the employer has offered to pay wages. The employer has made an offer which the employee has accepted and both are benefiting from the agreement. These conditions help to make the agreement – even though it may only be a verbal agreement – a legally binding contract.

Once the worker actually starts work, a written statement giving the terms and conditions must be issued within 13 weeks; but this statement is not a contract in itself. The main items of the written statement include:

Activity

> Create your own contract of employment as a shop assistant for Joe's Fruit an' Veg shop, working 17 hours a week at £3.10 per hour. Remember to put the name and address of the shop at the top of the contract.

CONTRACT OF EMPLOYMENT

Employer _____
Employee _____
Position of employee _____
Job title _____
Date employment commenced _____
Any other employment which counts towards this person's period of continuous employment _____
Hours of work _____
Rate of pay _____
Payable _____
Pension rights: The Social Security Pension Act 1975 contracting-out certificate is in force for this employment.
See Employee Handbook for Pension Fund details
Statutory Sick Pay of up to 28 weeks per 'period of entitlement'.
See Employee Handbook for details
Holiday entitlement. See Employee Handbook for details
A minimum of one week's notice of termination of employment for each year of continuous employment to a maximum of 12 weeks is required
Employee has the right to take part in trade union activities
Employee is permitted to complain to an industrial tribunal
Contractual amendments will be preceded by a consultation period and the employee will be notified in writing before they are implemented
Signed on behalf of the company _____ Employee's signature _____
Position _____ Date _____

PAYMENT SYSTEMS

There are several different systems for paying employees. A large manufacturing firm may use a mixture of these to pay particular groups of workers. Other firms may opt for a single system of payment. Whatever the system of pay used, it will need to be seen to be fair by the employee and to be in the interests of the employer.

Payment by time

There are two sorts of **time rates**:

- **Flat rate:** this is where workers are paid a fixed wage rate per hour for a set number of hours. It is often called 'basic pay' because it is the minimum workers would expect to receive in return for their time and effort.

- **Overtime:** if workers are asked to work more than the set number of hours agreed, then a higher rate of pay might be offered for these extra hours. 'Time and a half' or 'double time' would mean that employees would be paid at one and a half or twice the flat rate for each extra hour of overtime worked. A firm may find it cheaper to offer overtime rather than to take on extra employees.

Payment by results

The two sorts of **payment by results** are:

- **Piece rates:** under this system, workers are paid a rate per finished item. In this case, they can influence how much is actually earned by the speed of their work. The firm may also build in quality checks so that workers only get paid if the item meets a certain quality standard.

- **Commission:** this is a system of paying sales staff. For each sale made, they may be paid a percentage of the value of the good or service sold, particularly if the good is of a high value. Alternatively, the percentage could be based on the total value of sales at the end of each day or week. Some sales staff are paid totally on commission – so no sales equals no pay!

Other systems

Salaries: these are typically paid to non-manual employees. The pay is for performing a particular job and in many cases overtime is not available. This may mean that the number of hours an employee is expected to work is not laid down. Most people employed on a salary basis will be paid monthly rather than weekly.

Bonuses: a bonus is paid out as an additional reward or encouragement. It may be a reward to sales staff for a successful marketing campaign. It may be a reward to the manufacturing workers for exceeding expected productivity levels. Sometimes, it is a traditional reward to staff at special times of the year, such as Christmas. Many firms are linking bonuses to profits either through extra money in the pay or through the gift of shares in the company.

Fringe benefits: some groups of workers may receive perks or benefits which are not a direct part of any pay packet. Rail workers have received free rail travel in the past; sales staff have often been given company cars, complete with company name and logos; supermarket staff receive discount on goods bought; subsidised food in canteens has traditionally been offered in manufacturing companies. One of the fastest growing fringe benefits seems to be private health care schemes.

Handy hints

For the examination papers you need to be able to recall the basic items that would be included in a worker's terms and conditions. You should also be able to suggest and justify appropriate pay systems for different types of workers.

Activity

1. Decide which pay system might be appropriate for each of the following workers.

   Warehouse supervisor   Bank employee
   Lorry driver   Butcher
   Double glazing   Word processing
   salesperson   operator
   Cosmetic bag machinist Nurse
   Cleaner   Car assembler

2. Explain why you have made your suggestions for each worker.

WHICH PAYMENT SYSTEM IS BEST?

There is no definite answer to this question. A firm will need to weigh up the need to give a fair wage to all staff that motivates them while keeping wage costs under strict control. It will depend on the type of good being made or sold, on whether a service is being provided, on whether productivity can be easily measured, and on the type of job being carried out. The best system for a firm is not necessarily the best system for an employee.

Codebreakers

Salary: a system of pay based on an annual income, paid monthly or weekly that may not lay down the number of hours to be worked.

Fringe benefits: payment by goods or services rather than by money.

Contract of employment: a written document detailing an employee's terms and conditions of employment.

Time rates: any payment system that pays workers by the amount of time worked.

Payment by results: a payment system based on the quantity and perhaps quality of work completed.

Take-home pay: the net pay left to the worker after all the deductions have been taken away from the gross pay.

GROSS AND NET PAY

When discussing pay, students need to be careful to distinguish between gross and net pay. Gross pay is the total amount of money earned by an employee before any deductions are made. Net pay is the pay left to the employee after all deductions are made. It is sometimes called take-home pay. Most employees, if they earn enough, will have to pay income tax and national insurance contributions. Many employees will also contribute to a company pension scheme, so a further deduction called superannuation will be made. After that, you might decide to pay into a private pension scheme, to a savings scheme, to a trade union or even contribute directly to a charity.

SUMMARY

Three points to remember:

1. All workers should have a written contract of employment plus details of terms and conditions of employment.

2. There are several pay systems that firms may use, mainly based on time or results.

3. Workers will have several deductions made from their pay before they receive their take-home pay.

Employment contract and pay and conditions

Unit 19
Industrial relations

When a firm is operating it will have to manage a wide range of human relations issues. Many of these will be the day-to-day, individual staff matters such as lateness and illness. At certain times of year, the firm will have to deal with major industrial issues such as pay negotiations or health and safety concerns, which affect the whole work-force. All of these matters affect a firm's industrial relations with its workforce. In any negotiations on industrial relations, there may be three 'parties'.

The old image of trade unions simply pushing for ever higher wages for their members is changing. Trade unions are increasingly helping to improve their members' employment rights in the country's courts. Early in 1998 the High Court ruled that two female, casual workers who acted as tour guides at Blyth Power Station, in Northumberland, were entitled to full employment rights including holiday, sickness and maternity pay.

This court ruling came after a five year campaign by the GMB union and should ensure that casual workers throughout the country have full employment rights. Such a ruling will have an effect on employers, and National Power, who employed the two women at Blyth, are to appeal against the ruling to the House of Lords.

Blyth worker, Janet Leese after her landmark court victory

THE EMPLOYERS' SIDE

When they are negotiating on any issue with their workers, employers have to be careful to look after the interests of the company. For example, if the negotiations are about a pay deal, the employer will try to keep any agreement to a minimum so that its costs and, therefore, prices are not too badly affected. Negotiations on hours or working practices could also affect costs and a firm's competitiveness. Most employers will be keen to prevent disputes with the workers and their representatives and will want to promote good industrial relations. In large companies, many of the day-to-day concerns about industrial problems, such as disciplinary or grievance matters, will be carried out by the personnel department.

The most important issues will be left to the senior managers and even the board of directors.

Many employers have formed and joined groups to represent and protect their common interests. The best known is probably the Confederation of British Industry (CBI).

Such an organisation will represent employers in discussions with the government, with trade unions, with the European Union and with the media. It will give help and advice on a wide range of issues from training to tax, and from the environment to the law.

In some industries, an employers' association will bargain directly with a trade union on key matters such as minimum pay or holiday entitlements. Once these are set, each individual employer will then negotiate separate conditions and agreements at the workplace.

THE WORKERS' SIDE

What are trade unions?

They are a collection of workers who agree to negotiate with employers as a group, rather than as individual people. There are four types of union. Firstly, craft unions

represent workers in small, highly skilled trades. Secondly, the industrial unions tend to represent most workers in a particular industry. In the UK, unions such as the National Union of Mineworkers have declined in power as their industry has shrunk and other unions have grown. Thirdly, there are general unions representing workers in many different trades and industries. These are some of the biggest unions in the UK and typically represent unskilled and semi-skilled workers, although many skilled workers have also joined them. Finally, there are white collar unions typically representing office workers, nurses, banking staff and teachers.

What do unions do?

They exist to represent and protect the interests of their members, and to give advice and information on a whole range of issues. Such issues will include:

Pay	Pensions	Sick pay
Conditions	Holidays	Hours
Redundancies	Training	Health and safety
Changes in working practices		

The big advantage for a worker is that the union will take part in 'collective bargaining'. The union represents each worker and will negotiate with a small group representing the employer. Most unions are organised into branches with elected representatives. These representatives can then call in the professional advice of full-time officials where there are problems in the workplace that they cannot solve. Much of the work of the unions is involved in sorting out small scale problems which are nearly always solved by negotiation.

What is industrial action?

If negotiations break down on a big issue, such as a demand for a pay rise, a union may decide to ballot its members to see if they wish to take any industrial action. No industrial action may be taken unless a **secret ballot** (vote) has been taken and a majority of members voting agree on it. The ballot itself may put pressure on a firm if most workers say they are prepared to take action. Otherwise, the main forms of action are likely to be:

- **Overtime bans:** only working the set hours.
- **Work to rule:** keeping strictly to the rule book even if it is out of date.
- **Go-slows or non-cooperation:** slowing down production or refusing to do something that has not been officially agreed in the past.
- **Selective strikes:** pulling out key workers at key times to cause maximum disruption at minimum cost to the workers.
- **All out strikes:** all union members are supposed to withdraw their labour so that production stops. This may have to be enforced by official union picketing at the entrance to the workplace.

Obviously, industrial action will be costly both to the firm involved and to the union members. When a dispute continues for a long time, external agencies may be called in to help bring it to an end.

OUTSIDE AGENCIES

These 'third parties' in industrial relations will normally only get involved in any dispute or negotiation when the two main sides are unable to reach an agreement. The most important agency in the UK is The Advisory, Conciliation and Arbitration Service (ACAS). It has a number of roles in industrial relations issues. Firstly, it provides guidelines for employers and employees on good practice in such matters as dismissal. Secondly, it is legally obliged to try and resolve individual grievances before they reach industrial tribunals. Thirdly, its resources are used to give advice on a variety of industrial matters, such as training, to both sides of industry. Finally, it will get directly involved in industrial disputes between unions and employers. It does this in three main ways:

- **Conciliation:** an independent person will listen to both sides in an industrial dispute and will try to find a way of bringing them back around the negotiating table. The aim is that the two sides in dispute may then find their own solution to the problem.

- **Mediation:** an independent person again listens to both sides involved in the dispute and then proposes a way to settle it. The two sides do not have to accept the proposal so the dispute could continue.

Did you know?

A relatively modern form of industrial relations development is the Single Union Agreement. The employers only recognise and negotiate with one union. It certainly simplifies and speeds up negotiations for the employers, although the employees might prefer to be represented by their traditional union. Sometimes these agreements have been introduced alongside no-strike deals, where workers agree not to strike in return for compulsory arbitration when a dispute cannot be settled. Such a deal may be seen by workers as better than no recognition of any union by a company.

Codebreakers

Working practices: the expected way for workers to carry out a job possibly written down in formal rules and regulations.

Disciplinary matters: problems with workers who have broken the rules and need to be seen by the personnel department.

Grievance matters: possible disputes caused by workers having a grievance with the firm.

Collective bargaining: negotiations on industrial relations matters with all sides represented.

Secret ballot: voting on action and other issues by completing a voting slip in secret and posting it anonymously.

Handy hints

In an examination paper, you might be expected to explain how a firm could be affected by the actions of a union, especially any industrial action. You might be asked how any co-operation between unions and employers may be advantageous to both sides. This would certainly apply to new developments such as Single Union Agreements.

Activity

1. Explain how a firm processing frozen foods might be affected by the following forms of industrial action:
   a) overtime ban   b) work to rule
   c) selective strikes   d) all out strikes
2. How might this firm try to overcome the effects of each type of action?
3. How might ACAS be used to sort out these problems?

- **Arbitration:** both sides in the dispute agree beforehand to abide by the decision of the arbiters. Two or three independent people will listen to the points from both sides in the dispute and will then make their decisions.

SUMMARY

Three points to remember:

1. Industrial relations involves employers working with the representatives of employees to solve a whole range of problems.
2. When negotiations break down, trade unions may ballot their members to see if they want to take industrial action.
3. Long running industrial disputes may require the services of outside agencies like ACAS to solve the problems.

Unit 20
Employment and the law

When a firm is operating, it must expect to obey many laws. Two key legal areas in the employment of people are **health and safety** and equal opportunities. In both cases there are laws setting out regulations that firms must follow and the penalties that will result if they are broken. Many firms may choose to operate their own rules and regulations that protect the worker by more than that required by law.

In a message to its employees, Remploy states that it believes that:

'All employees have a part to play

Everyone is important

Each job has a part in the overall structure'.

They develop this in a number of policy statements, including their **equal opportunities policy**. Remploy states that, ' … all employees will be given encouragement and equal opportunities to progress in the organisation'. The company expects everyone to take the responsibility for making the policy happen and is particularly keen to promote it in job applications, interviews, training opportunities and promotion.

The company's safety policy is very detailed, involving risk assessment, safety committees, the use of advisory bodies, strict rules and regulations, safety officers and safety audits. These more than obey the various laws, but again Remploy emphasises the role of all workers when it states, 'All staff and employees have a duty to take personal care of themselves and other persons who may be affected by their acts or omissions.'

HEALTH AND SAFETY LAWS

There are a number of general laws covering health and safety in the workplace. In addition, in some industries – such as coal mining and chemicals – there are special health and safety codes. Some firms and industries add to this through their own voluntary regulations, often as a result of negotiations with trade unions.

The main general laws covering health and safety are:

- **The Factories Act, 1961.** This applies to most businesses that operate machinery whether the premises are a garage, building site or workshop. The Act covers such things as ventilation, heating, fire escapes, safety guards on machinery, toilet and washing facilities.

- **The Offices, Shops and Railways Premises Act, 1963.** Important regulations for shops and offices include ventilation, temperature, lighting, floorspace, toilet and washing facilities.

- **The Health and Safety at Work Act, 1974.** This stresses that both employer and employee have a responsibility to keep safe conditions at work. Employers must take all steps, where reasonably practicable, to ensure the health, safety and welfare of all employees. Employees are expected to take reasonable care to look after their own safety and the safety of others in the workplace. If the rules are not obeyed, the employer could be punished by a court of law. To check that the rules are being obeyed, the Health and Safety Executive have the right to inspect the premises and will enforce the Act.

- **Reporting of Injuries, Diseases and Dangerous Occurrences Regulations, 1985.** Any injury that results from an accident at work and causes an employee to be unable to work for three or more days, must be reported to the authorities. Listed diseases must be reported, as must any accident involving work equipment.

- **Control of Substances Hazardous to Health Regulations, 1988.** An employer must identify any task which is likely to be harmful. The risks have to be minimised and workers dealing with hazardous substances must be given both detailed information and appropriate training.

- **Noise at Work Regulations, 1989.** Employers are now expected to reduce the risk of hearing damage to employees. This might be greater noise insulation around machinery or, more simply, providing ear protectors.

WHAT EFFECT DO THESE LAWS HAVE ON FIRMS?

In the majority of firms, the workplace should now be a much safer place for employees. It may increase costs in some firms, although some of this ought to be offset if the number of accidents falls and therefore there is less disruption to the production process. Few firms are keen to risk the punishment and bad publicity that would result from a court case for infringing the regulations. In general, it has made both employer and employee more health and safety conscious, with all organisations employing five or more people having to produce a written safety policy. This policy:

- sets out who is responsible for workplace health and safety
- must set out all the arrangements made for health and safety in the workplace
- must be communicated to everyone in the workplace
- must be backed up by training of employees, by inspections of the workplace, and – in large organisations – by an active health and safety committee.

Did you know?

In the UK over 500 people die each year as a result of accident or injury in the workplace. Thousands more lose time at work through illness or injury. For some employees, the dangers are not realised until much later in life. For example, it is estimated that many thousands may have died as a result of inhaling dust from asbestos. In 1997, people began to win compensation for the injuries caused by vibrating machinery, while repetitive strain injury is recognised in all varieties of work from the digging of holes in the road to operating keyboards.

Activity

- All schools will have a health and safety policy. Many of these rules will be included on the notices in your classrooms. Identify the health and safety information that applies to you. Create posters to improve the way this is communicated to you, the students. Try to spot any health and safety matters that are not covered and write your own suggestions for sensible rules.

EQUAL OPPORTUNITIES IN THE WORKPLACE

A lot of people mistakenly believe that this is simply about making sure that females have a fairer chance of getting a job. Equal opportunities is much wider than this and aims to give all individuals identical rights and opportunities regardless of:

- gender
- racial group
- age
- physical characteristics
- sexual orientation
- other features.

From a firm's point of view, it ought to be in its interests to provide equal opportunities, since it should only gain from getting the best person for each job. For the employee, it should at least guarantee that he or she is treated in an identical way to everyone else.

EQUAL OPPORTUNITIES LAWS

- **The Sex Discrimination Act, 1975.** As the name suggests, this act tries to prevent any sex discrimination in the workplace. It is illegal for an employer to discriminate in:
    - selection procedures
    - employment terms
    - training and development opportunities
    - fringe benefits
    - selection for redundancy.

Under the terms of the Act, discrimination could be direct. For example, if one of the criteria used to judge the suitability of a manager was that he was male, then this would be direct discrimination. Another example would be stating that a post was only open to an unmarried person. Indirect discrimination is also illegal but is more difficult to prove. For example, the criteria for appointment might clearly state that the job is open to both sexes, but by the nature of the job it might have been traditionally filled by a male and fewer women feel able to apply for it.

- **The Race Relations Act, 1976.** Under this Act nobody should be discriminated against on the basis of their race.

- **The Equal Pay Act, 1970.** A man and a woman in a company or organisation, doing the same work or work of equal value, should be paid the same amount. To make a claim that you are not being paid an equal

> **Activity**
>
> ▷ Try to word laws that would prevent discrimination in the workplace on the basis of age. Display your main points on a card for display in the classroom and use this as a basis for discussion about the merits of such a law.

amount means you must be able to compare yourself with a person of the opposite sex who is doing exactly the same work. This is where the problems might occur, as it is often difficult to find someone who is directly comparable to you.

■ **The Disability Discrimination Act, 1995.** Past Acts have stated that employers of more than 20 people should employ 3% of the work-force who are disabled. Many employers do not meet this quota and few prosecutions have been made. This new law makes it unlawful for employers with 20 or more staff to discriminate against current or prospective employees because of a reason relating to their disability. They must not be discriminated against in recruitment and retention, in promotion and transfers, in training and development, and in the dismissal process. In some cases, employers must adapt the workplace for the disabled so that they are not disadvantaged.

You can see from this list of Acts that not all discrimination is illegal. For example, no law has yet been passed preventing discrimination by age. It might be quite difficult to word such an Act because the young, middle-aged, and the old might all claim that they have been discriminated against at some time or other.

> **Codebreakers**
>
> **Health and safety policy:** any policy introduced by a firm to meet the country's laws and its own regulations in ensuring the health and safety of its employees.
>
> **Equal opportunities policy:** a policy written by a firm to meet the law and to set its own rules so that all individuals have identical rights.

> **Handy hints**
>
> For the GCSE exam, you would not be expected to know the specific names and dates of each law. Instead you need to be able to explain the basic legal requirements for firms both in Health and Safety and in Equal Opportunities. You need to be able to explain how the work-force is protected by these requirements and how the firm might be affected. For example, one question we have used in the past is 'Why does this firm state that it is an equal opportunities employer?'

SUMMARY

Three points to remember:

1. When dealing with its work-force, a firm must obey laws that look after both the health and safety and the equal opportunities of its employees.

2. Many firms will create policies that protect workers by more than that required by the law.

3. Such policies may increase costs for a firm, but the many benefits to the firm will normally outweigh these costs and will certainly benefit the work-force.

Employment and the law

Unit 21

Sources and uses of finance

When a firm is being set up and then operated, the owners will need money. They might be able to provide some of this money themselves, but most firms will have to look for additional sources of finance. Many of these sources will involve some form of borrowing. Some types of finance might be available for short periods of time only, while others might be available for many years. Some types of finance will have very specific uses while others may have a variety. Large firms will find they have several sources of finance open to them while small firms usually find only a limited number available. As firms grow, they will find that their financial needs change.

Next was one of the success stories on the UK's high streets in the late 1980s and early 1990s. During this period, about one third of its finance was used for its everyday needs. This mainly came from trade creditors and bank overdrafts. Nearly half of its finance for capital investment came from retained profits and most of the rest was provided by shareholders. As a result, Next had to borrow very little in the form of medium- or short- term loans. This helped it to keep down interest payments and therefore helped its overall costs and profits.

TYPES OF FINANCE

These can be broken down into three broad categories.

Owners' funds: as the title suggests, **owners' funds** consist of money put or invested into the business by the owner. A sole trader or partners might decide to use personal savings or perhaps redundancy money to set up a business.

When a limited company is being set up, the owners are known as shareholders. They share in the ownership of the company and they share the responsibility of putting money into the business.

Owners' funds or capital is permanently invested in the business. It is not a loan so the owners will not earn any interest on this money. Instead, they will expect to share the profits made by the firm. When the business is a company, this share of the profits is usually called a 'dividend'. Instead of taking out all the profits earned, the owners might decide to retain some of the profits to reinvest in the business.

Sometimes, the owners might decide that they want their capital back. For a sole trader this will mean either selling the business to someone else or closing it down and selling off the assets, such as the premises. A partner wanting to leave a partnership could also try to sell to someone else but if no one is prepared to buy into the business it would probably close down and the assets then sold off.

For shareholders, the process is much easier. They just have to sell their shares in the business. The capital will stay in the company. The shareholder selling will receive payment for the shares from the shareholder buying.

Owners' capital can be increased. A sole trader might have further savings or might decide to find a partner. Partnerships might look for additional partners while companies can issue further sets of shares. The only problems from increasing the number of owners are that more people will share the profits and might want to share the running of the business.

> **Did you know?**
> Retained profit is the biggest source of finance for UK companies. How much profit is available will depend on how large the profit is after tax has been deducted. It will also depend on what share of the profits the owners will expect. No interest has to be paid out on this finance and it does not have to be paid back.

Borrowed funds: this is sometimes called debt finance as it will involve the firm in obtaining some form of credit or loan and therefore going into debt to someone. Any form of **borrowed funds** will probably involve an interest charge and will have to be repaid. Depending on the type of credit, money can be borrowed for just a few days or for several years. Most of these sources of credit are explained further on in this unit.

Grants: a wide range of **grants** are available to all sorts of firms. The amounts of money involved can vary from £50 per week for new, small starters up to many £millions for multinational companies. The grants might be targeted at firms providing certain goods or services or at those in a particular region. Providers of grants vary from the EU to local councils, and from the UK government to charitable trusts.

Activity

> What grants are available to firms in your locality?

In groups, you could write to a number of organisations to find out this information. Use directories such as Yellow Pages to discover addresses.

Who might provide information?

Local District or County Councils
Training and Enterprise Councils (TECs)
Your local MP
Local companies
The Board of Trade
Your Euro MP
English Partnerships
The EU
High street banks

WHY IS FINANCE NEEDED?

Businesses need money for all sorts of things. Some money will be needed before the firm is ready to open. More finance will be needed just to keep the business running on a daily basis. Once the firm has been operating for a while, it may need further capital to help it progress into the future. So, we can identify four broad categories of financial need.

Start-up: most new firms are small and will have limited amounts of money available from the owners themselves. Large sums of money may have to be borrowed to pay for all the start-up costs such as the premises, equipment and a first stock of materials. It may take several years for a new firm to become really successful and for the finance to be paid back.

Cash flow: a firm needs a steady supply of funds to pay the costs of producing more goods and services. Delays in receiving payment for goods sold may lead to cash shortages when wages have to be paid and materials bought. Finance must be available to cover any temporary cash shortage.

Renewal: most machinery and equipment, or 'plant' will have a certain expected life and at some stage will need replacing. So, finance will be required to help renew and maintain this plant. Some firms will find this a bigger need than others. It will depend on how much equipment there is, how expensive it is and how quickly it wears out.

Expansion: a firm might be quite successful and the owners might want it to grow. In many ways, expansion will be similar to start-up but the firm may no longer be small. It may have a good reputation and own valuable assets such as land and property. Large amounts of money might be needed for any expansion and it might take several years for the expansion to be really successful. As a result, it may not be possible to pay back any borrowed funds for several years.

Codebreakers

Owners' funds: money put into the business by the owner. This investment will be by the sole trader, partners or shareholders. The money will stay in the business as long as it continues to operate.

Borrowed funds: money that is borrowed in some way and will have to be repaid, often with an interest charge.

Grants: money given to a firm to help it to operate and expand. The sums given will vary according to the size of the firm receiving the grant, what it is to be used for and the organisation giving it.

Sources and uses of finance

A firm's financial needs are clearly varied. Some finance will be required for just a few days while other finance may be tied up in the firm for many years. There are, therefore, different sources of finance for these different time periods.

> **Handy hints:** Some textbooks and some financial institutions will suggest different lengths of time for these time periods. Use the following as a general guide – you do not have to be exact for the exam.

Short-term finance

Short-term finance can be given for any period between one day and three years and will take the form of:

- **Bank overdraft:** an agreement with a bank to overspend the business's account, up to a specified limit. The business will go into the 'red' and interest will be charged according to the amount overdrawn and the time involved. Many businesses arrange permanent overdraft facilities with the overdraft changing as money flows into and out of the business.

- **Short-term loan:** a specific sum of money is borrowed for a fixed time period. Interest will be charged on the full amount borrowed. The loan will be for a particular purpose, e.g. for a new van or a small machine. Most of these loans will be repaid monthly.

- **Hire purchase:** this is a method of buying equipment by paying for it in instalments. The full price paid is likely to include a charge for interest. The firm buying the equipment will not own it until the final payment has been made.

- **Trade credit:** arrangements with a supplier to postpone payments for goods and services received until an agreed date. In most cases this will be 30 days of credit but it depends on a firm's business reputation.

- **Factoring:** some firms deliberately delay payment of their bills for several months. This might leave a firm with a cash shortage while waiting for payment. The firm might approach a specialist factoring company who may offer an immediate payment of up to 80% of the amount owed. The remainder will be paid once the debt is settled. A fee will be charged for this service.

Medium-term finance

Medium-term finance is given for between three and ten years. It consists of:

- **Term loans:** these are similar to short-term loans but the banks often offer a wider range of conditions. Interest rates might be either fixed or variable. Repayment might be made in instalments at the end of each year or might be made at the end of the loan period. The loans might be for larger amounts.

- **Leasing:** the leasing company will buy the asset and then lease it to a business (the lessee). The leasing agreement will be for a fixed time period, after which it might be renewed or a new agreement reached for a more up-to-date piece of equipment. The lessee will pay a regular payment for the use of the asset. The leasing company may be responsible for repair costs but the lessee will not own the asset.

- **Instalment credit:** this is the same as hire purchase but will be arranged for longer time periods and probably for larger sums of money.

Long-term finance

Long-term finance is given for 10 years or more and can be in the form of:

- **Term loans:** the same as for medium-term loans but may be for as long as 20 years. Any lender would make sure that the borrower had sufficient security in case the loan could not be repaid.

- **Syndicated loans:** for very large loans, a group of banks or other financial institutions might jointly provide the money. This would spread out the risk of non-repayment.

- **Mortgage loans:** these are loans for the purchase of land and buildings. These may involve very large sums of money and so may be for between 20 and 35 years.

- **Sale and leaseback:** an asset, particularly land and buildings, may be sold to a company specialising in leasing. The seller then leases the property back from the buyer. This gives the selling firm a large sum of money, but it no longer owns the property and it will have to pay out a regular sum of money for its use.

- **Debentures:** large public limited companies can borrow through the City of London by issuing debentures (sometimes called stocks or bonds). These loans may be for as long as 25 years. The rates of interest may be fixed or they may be lower than for other loans if the borrowing company can offer sound, specific assets as security.

Activity

> Create a table of advantages and disadvantages for these seven types of finance.

Type	Advantage	Disadvantage
Overdraft		
Trade credit		
Hire purchase		
Leasing		
Term loans		
Retained profits		
'New' shares/new owners		

Activity

In groups:

> 1 Study the details of each firm below and its financial needs.
>
> 2 Make a short list of the possible types of finance for each firm.
>
> 1 As a class, discuss the advantages and disadvantages of each type of finance for each firm.
>
> 2 In your groups, decide the 'best' type of finance for each firm. Make a list of reasons in each case.
>
> 3 Display your decisions so that the whole class can compare with them.
>
> 4 Working individually, decide for each firm what further information you would like to help you make a 'better' decision on the best type of finance. Write up your conclusions.

Firm A Sandwich delivery Sole trader

The owner of a sandwich delivery business needs to replace his motorbike with a small van to transport a bigger quantity of sandwiches more hygienically.

Firm B Clothing manufacturer Public limited company

A very successful clothing manufacturer specialising in making female fashions for major high street chains requires finance to build an additional factory.

Handy hints

- Make sure you understand the three broad categories of finance and the four main needs for it. You must be able to describe the main types including any advantages and disadvantages and be aware of the time periods for each type.

- Exam questions often ask you to advise on the most suitable form of finance for a particular firm and its specific need. Think carefully about what the finance is needed for, how much is needed, the type and size of the firm, and any financial details given to you in the data. Remember, there might not be a clear 'best' type of finance for the firm in the case study: rather, the examiners are wanting you to show you can consider all the evidence and then give a logical, reasoned conclusion.

Codebreakers

Short-term finance: money that is borrowed for between one day and three years. It is mainly needed to help cash flow, to buy assets such as vehicles and to buy in additional stocks of materials.

Medium-term finance: money that is borrowed for between three and ten years. It may be used to buy assets such as machinery, to set up the business and to pay for small scale expansion.

Long-term finance: money that is borrowed for at least ten years. This will be used to start up larger businesses, to buy lifelong assets such as buildings and to pay for large scale expansion.

Sources and uses of finance

Activity continued

Firm C A medium-sized accountants' Partnership

This accountancy business is finding that its existing computers are expensive to maintain, are too slow in processing data and the software is out of date. It needs ten new computers, accessories, a network system and the latest software.

Firm D Gardener Sole trader

A gardener decides to take on a second employee to help tackle the bigger landscaping jobs she is taking on. She needs additional tools and equipment for this worker and heavier digging machinery for some of the larger jobs.

Firm E Plumbers' Partnership

Activity continued

The two partners have had an increase in the amount of subcontract work from local builders. As a result they now spend an average three days a week on this and only two days on the everyday jobs for individual customers. As most of the builders do not get paid until the end of their particular work, the plumbers are having to wait several weeks to be paid for this subcontract work. They therefore require finance for large quantities of materials and their other day-to-day running costs.

Firm F Farming business Private limited company

After the various problems with beef and dairy cattle, the owners have decided to concentrate on pig and sheep farming. They have also decided to expand by buying up the vacant farm bordering theirs to use it for crop growing. Finance is needed for this farm land and to buy further stock (pigs and sheep), pens for the pigs and additional farm machinery for the extra crop production.

SUMMARY

Three points to remember:

1 Firms need finance to start up, to maintain, to expand and to run their businesses.

2 Finance may be provided by the owners themselves, through grants from various organisations or may be borrowed in a variety of ways.

3 Money may be borrowed for short, medium or long periods of time according to the type and size of firm, the reason for borrowing the money, and the risk to the lender.

Sources and uses of finance

Unit 22
Business plans

When a firm is going to set up and when it is going to change or expand its operations, it usually needs a plan. In many cases, it will produce a formal, detailed business plan that sets targets, that includes a mass of data about the business, that allows progress to be checked and that helps the firm to obtain finance. The content of the plan will depend on the size and type of the firm, the good or service provided, and the reasons for producing a plan.

Ken opened his hairdressing business in Ashington in 1975. He trained at top salons in Newcastle, and after three years' further experience had saved £4 000 which he hoped to use in setting up his own business. He calculated his start up costs as £10 000 and approached his bank for a medium-term loan for the extra £6 000 he needed. The bank made Ken complete a detailed business plan using its standard forms. Extra advice was available for Ken from the local council's business advisors and they helped Ken to realise that he would need to borrow £8 000 to cover a number of running costs in the first few months of the business. They also helped Ken to set targets and to plan for problems. As a result, the bank were happy to lend Ken the £8 000 because the plan had been well thought out. In the first two years of the business, Ken built up a list of regular customers; he was able to check off his targets as he firstly broke even after four months and achieved a steady level of profit after 15 months.

Handy hints
Many candidates in exams are able to describe the basic contents of a business plan. They find it more difficult, however, to explain why a business plan is created and how it might be used by a firm. Make sure you pay particular attention to the first part of this unit which will help you to avoid this problem.

THE BUSINESS PLAN

Why will a firm produce a business plan and how will it be used?

The reasons for making a plan and the ways it might be used are closely linked. There are five main reasons:

- To make sure any business activity is successful, a firm will need a plan so that nothing is forgotten. Whether a new, small firm is being set up for the first time or whether a multinational company is about to build an additional factory, the owners and managers have to be sure that they have a plan that will work. Any mistakes could be both costly and risky.

- To run and control the business successfully, the business plan needs to include a checklist of key guidelines. The managers can check that they are following the plan and can use it to see how to correct any problems. For example, a new sole trader might have a list of tasks to do each day, while the distribution manager in a small company might have a set procedure to follow if a customer rings up to complain about a delivery problem. In other words, the plan is a working document and not just a glossy brochure.

- To help the owners and managers review progress, the plan can include a set of aims, objectives or targets. These can be set out in specific detail with key dates set out for their planned achievement. For new firms, these targets might be 'to break even by the end of the first nine months in business'. Established firms might be wanting their new production line 'to be fully operational within six months of starting the installation'. Profit levels, sales figures or the number of outlets could all be targets included in business plans.

- To help obtain loans and other forms of credit, particularly from banks and financial institutions, means that most business plans must be very detailed and well thought out. This will be necessary both when the firm is being set up and when any additional finance is required. Any lender will expect to see that the plan has been well thought out and that its risks when lending money are minimised.

- To show potential investors that the firm is worth the risk of investing capital in it means that a business plan can be used to attract additional partners or shareholders. A sole trader might use it to change the business into a partnership. Companies might use the plan as part of the documents needed to issue new sets of shares.

> **Did you know?**
>
> Starting a new business is very risky. Estimates suggest that nearly half of new businesses fail in the first 12 months of operation. Another 25% of those surviving the first year then go out of business in their second year. Those that survive are usually the firms that produce the most detailed, well thought out plans – though luck sometimes plays a big part in deciding between success and failure! Remember that business failure is surprisingly common – around 17 000 businesses will have failed in the UK in 1997.

What should be included in a business plan?

This partly depends on the type and size of firm and the reason for producing a plan. The contents shown here are the normal requirements when setting up a new, small firm. They are set out in a condensed format to show how a business plan might be laid out.

Name of business

Address

Telephone number

☐ Sole trader
☐ Partnership
☐ Franchise
☐ Limited Company

Target start up date

Type of business

Aims and Objectives
Your ultimate goal

What do you expect to achieve by the end of
Year 1
Year 2
Year 3

Your market
Describe the type, size and location of your market

Describe your customers

Activity

> - This task could be done by the whole class working on one business proposal, or separate groups could choose different business ideas with individual students then working on one section of the plan.
>
>   - As a class decide on a business idea that you might be able to turn into a business proposal.
>   - Organise yourselves into groups.
>   - Each group should select one of the sections of a business plan.
>   - Each group can start to plan what information is needed for the business proposal and suggest any early decisions that could be made for its section of the plan.
>   - Share these ideas with the whole class so that each group can use any information and decisions in its section.
>
> - As a class make any decisions you feel are necessary at this stage.
> - Back in your groups, start work on researching and writing up your sections of the plan.
> - Report back progress to the whole class and make any further decisions.
> - In your groups, finalise your sections of the plan.
> - Each group should present the final section to the whole class.
> - Try to evaluate the plan, identifying weaknesses and strengths, and suggesting further information needed.

Your product/service

Compare your product with two competitors using:

price
quality
availability
customers
staff skills
reputation
advertising
delivery
location
special offers
after-sales service

Why is your product/service special?

Why will it be better than your competitors'?

Pricing

Itemise your costs

Calculate your break even point

Financial matters

What business assets do you have and what are they worth? (e.g. equipment, vehicles)

What assets will you need to start up? and continue through your first year?

Give details of your premises e.g. lease, rent, rates, location, condition

What credit do you expect from your suppliers?

Promotion and selling

How do your competitors promote and sell their products/services?

How are you going to promote and sell your products/service?

Estimate the cost of doing this

Why are your promotional and selling methods appropriate?

Staff

Personal details of owners

Details of key staff to be hired

Number/job descriptions/cost of staff to be hired

Financial matters continued

Who will keep your financial records?

Give an estimated:
12 month cash flow forecast

12 month estimated profit and loss account forecast

What finance do you require and what are your proposed sources?
Grants
Own resources
Loans
Creditors

Business plans 105

How do banks decide if a business plan will work?

Banks and other lenders and investors will all want to be sure that the business proposal stands a good chance of success. They will not want to risk lending or investing money if the business might fail. The following questions can be used to assess a business plan.

1 Has the product/service been proven to work?

This will be particularly important if it is a new type of product.

2 How does the product/service compare with others already on the market?

This is important whether it is a really 'new' idea or if it is already a common one. The quality of the product/service might be an important consideration in some markets.

3 Does the management have the expertise and experience to achieve its objectives?

The owners of new, small businesses are unlikely to have all the necessary experience and skills themselves. The banks will be checking to see that the plan shows the sort of expert help that needs to be bought in.

4 Is there a market demand for the product/service?

5 Are the sales projections realistic?

Both of these need to be judged against the results of any market research. The quality of the market research needs to reviewed as well.

6 Is the planned sales and marketing strategy the right one?

Any such plan must be suitable for the product and the type of consumers.

7 Is the financial data calculated correctly and realistically?

Key calculations would have to be checked. The planners would have to show that the figures were likely to be achieved.

Activity

One of the approved coursework titles for the NEAB's GCSE courses is 'How will I plan my business proposal?' Look again at 'What should be included in a business plan?' You could use these details as the basis for your coursework assignment. Most banks provide booklets and forms to help write business plans and will usually give them to students if you explain what you are doing. Bank staff will also visit schools to give practical advice. So, if a group of you have decided to do this particular coursework title, why not contact the business advisory section of one of your local banks. Discuss this with your teacher first!

SUMMARY

Two points to remember:

1 A business plan is produced to organise the business proposal, to help run the firm, to check progress and to raise finance.

2 The main sections include the type of firm and its objectives, the type of product and its market, the marketing of the product, the management and manpower of the firm, and the financial details.

Unit 23
Costs and revenue in business

When a firm makes a product, sells goods or provides a service, it needs a wide range of resources. Whether these resources are premises, equipment, raw materials or workers the firm will have to pay for them. These payments are called costs of production. Selling goods or services will provide a firm with an income to meet these costs. This income is usually called sales revenue. As long as revenue is greater than the costs the firm will make a profit.

In Unit 22 you were introduced to Ken and his hairdressing business. When Ken was preparing his business plan, one of the first things he did was to make a list of his costs. He found a vacant shop premises for rent and planned how to decorate and equip it for hairdressing. Ken arranged for basic services such as electricity, water and telephones. He remembered that there would be a number of overheads such as rates and insurance and he decided to advertise for three weeks in the local newspaper. Finally, Ken arranged for some part-time help in the salon on Fridays and Saturdays. Having thought of all the costs, Ken then placed them in two lists. One list he called 'start up' and the other 'running'. He was quite surprised to see how many costs appeared in both. It certainly helped him to think about the 'right' prices to charge his customers. Ken's salon was located just off the main shopping centre, and he realised that he needed to build up a list of regular customers rather than relying on passers-by. He used discounts for both children and his elderly customers, and kept a tight control of costs so that he could keep all his prices competitive.

Handy hints: Do not mix up the terms 'price' and 'cost'. Examiners like to see you using terms correctly and you are more likely to gain marks if you do so. A 'price' is what you pay when you buy a good or service. The price will have to cover all of the producer's costs.

TYPES OF COSTS

A business often finds it useful to look at its costs by placing them into different groups.

One way of dividing up costs is into:

Fixed costs

These do not vary from week to week or month to month; so they are said to be **fixed costs**. They do not change if the firm produces more goods or sells less items. Fixed costs still have to be paid even if output is zero. Sometimes, they are called indirect costs or overheads.

Examples:
- rent on buildings
- interest on loans
- rates to the local councils
- insurance payments.

Variable costs

These costs change directly with output. If a firm increases its output of a good, its **variable costs** will rise. A firm serving fewer customers will find its variable costs will fall.

Examples:
- raw materials
- parts and components
- packaging
- food ingredients.

Fixed or variable costs

It is not always easy to divide up firms' costs neatly. Some costs will be a fixed cost for one firm but a variable for another. Look at the picture below, for example. The power used for heating and lighting this travel agency will be a fixed cost; but the electricity used by a dry cleaning business to clean clothes will be a variable cost. Other examples of costs that could be fixed or variable include:

- wages
- transport
- advertising.

Activity

> Can you think of any other costs that could be fixed or variable?

For new or expanding firms, a useful way to divide up costs is into:

Start-up costs

These have to be paid when setting up a new business or when an existing business decides to expand. Most of these costs will be paid out before the firm starts to trade.

Examples:

- refitting a shop
- buying in machinery
- decorating the premises.

Running costs

Once the business has started to trade, many costs will have to be paid out at regular intervals to keep the business running.

Examples:

- rent for the business
- postage and phone calls
- insurance premiums
- wages to employees.

Activity

Look at the photograph above.

> 1 Make a list of all the likely costs for a roadside restaurant, such as a Little Chef or Happy Eater.

>> 2 Create a four column table with the headings – fixed, variable, start-up, running costs. Place all the likely costs for a roadside restaurant in the most suitable columns.

>>> 3 Explain why some costs for the roadside restaurant could be placed in all four columns.

Start-up or running costs

Obviously, many costs will need to be paid out both before the business starts trading and once it is operating.

Examples:
- stocks of materials
- advertising.

CALCULATING COSTS

Whether a firm is just about to start up or whether it is already operating, it will need to calculate its costs of production. One set of calculations is shown in the table below.

Table of fixed, variable and total costs

Output units	Fixed costs	Variable costs	Total costs
0	3 000	0	3 000
100	3 000	150	3 150
200	3 000	280	3 280
300	3 000	430	3 430
400	3 000	580	3 580
500	3 000	750	3 750

This table can be turned into a diagram which will help you to understand the relationships between the costs and the level of output.

Diagram of fixed, variable and total costs

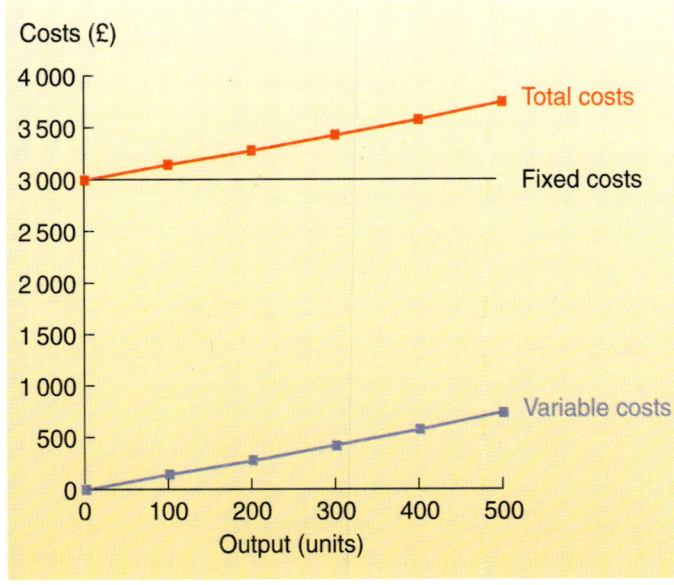

What does the table on the left tell us?

- £3 000 of fixed costs have to be paid even when nothing is produced.
- These fixed costs stay the same when output rises.
- No variable costs are paid until goods start to be produced.
- Variable costs rise directly with output.
- The total costs for any level of output can be found by adding fixed and variable costs together.

Average costs

Many firms refer to these **average costs** as unit costs because they will tell a firm how much it costs to produce each unit or item. Average costs can be calculated using the formula:

$$\text{Average cost per unit} = \frac{\text{Total costs}}{\text{Total output}}$$

By calculating average costs as output changes, a firm can measure how efficient it is. The lower the average costs, the more efficient the firm is in producing its product. If average costs are plotted on a diagram, the firm can easily see its best or optimum level of output. This can be seen in the diagram below.

A diagram of average costs may look like this

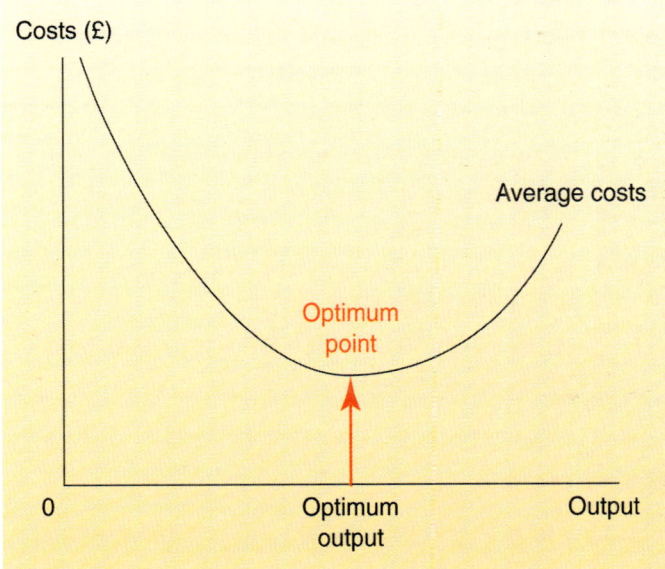

Costs and revenue in business

Activity

▶ This table shows an incomplete set of calculations for the production of picnic tables.

Q	FC	VC	TC	AC
0	4 000	0	4 000	–
10		500		450
20		960		
30		1 610		
40		2 200		
50		2 800		
60		4 400		

a) Create a spreadsheet to complete the calculations in the table

b) Use the spreadsheet to draw two separate sets of graphs. (Remember in each case to put costs on the vertical axis and output on the horizontal axis.)
   i) graphs for FC, VC and TC
   ii) a graph for AC.

Activity

As an alternative to using a computer to do the above IT Activity:

1. Write out the table for the costs of producing the picnic tables. Complete the missing gaps.

2. a) On graph paper, create two separate sets of graphs, one set on each side of the paper:
      i) TC, VC and FC curves
      ii) AC curve. Mark the optimum level of output.
   b) Describe what happened to average costs as output increased.

3. a) Explain the reasons for the change in the average cost curve.
   b) Why might a firm find it difficult to produce at its optimum level of output?

Revenue

This may be quite simply thought of as a firm's income from the sales of a product or service. It is often referred to as turnover or sales turnover and it is what is earned before any costs are taken away. To calculate total **revenue** use the following formula:

Total revenue = price of product x the number sold

So, the revenue earned will be influenced by the price charged and the number of items the firm can sell. Changing the price of its goods is therefore an important strategy for any firm.

Higher prices mean:
■ more revenue is gained from each item sold
■ but fewer goods might be sold so some revenue will be lost.

Lower prices mean:
■ less revenue is gained from each item sold
■ but more goods might be sold so gaining revenue.

Whether a firm loses revenue or gains revenue when changing price depends on how sensitive the customers are to that price change.

Profit

At this stage, think of **profit** as when a firm earns more revenue than it pays out in costs. It could always make a loss when its costs would be greater than its revenue.

Controlling costs

Did you know?

Price changes will affect a firm's revenue and therefore its profits. Changes in costs affect its profits too. A rise in fixed costs or a rise in variable costs will reduce profits and may mean that prices will have to be increased. This could make the business less competitive with other firms. It is essential, therefore, for a firm to keep all its costs under control.

Activity

1. Think about the goods and services bought in your home.
   a) Which sorts of goods will have sales that are sensitive to price changes?
   b) Which sorts of goods are likely to be insensitive to price changes?
   Explain why you believe this to be the case.
   Why might a firm find it useful to know if customers are sensitive to price changes?

2. Think of a local business near you.
   Which costs could that business most easily control?
   Which costs would it be almost impossible for that business to control?
   a) Which sorts of businesses seem to face the most competition on price?
   b) Suggest some reasons for this.

110 Costs and revenue in business

Handy hints

If you have not already done so, why not create your own dictionary of key terms using the Codebreakers? Start with this unit and work your way through the others.

Terms to define in this unit include:

Costs	Fixed costs	Variable costs
Total costs	Average costs	Price
Profit	Loss	Revenue

Codebreakers

Fixed costs: costs which do not change when output changes.

Variable costs: costs which change when a firm changes its output.

Average costs: how much it costs to produce a single unit or item.

Total costs: for any level of output fixed costs are added to variable costs.

Revenue: a firm's income before any costs are paid out.

Profit: when a firm's total revenue from sales is greater than its total costs.

SUMMARY

Five points to remember:

1 Payments for using resources in producing goods or services are called costs.

2 Costs may be split into different categories – fixed or variable, start-up or running.

3 Total and average costs may be calculated to help measure a firm's performance.

4 A firm earns revenue when it sells goods or services.

5 Setting the right price to sell the good or service and to cover the costs of production is vital if a firm is to make a profit.

Costs and revenue in business

Unit 24
Break even analysis

When a firm first starts up, one of its early objectives is to break even. Existing firms might also target this as an objective when they introduce a new range of products or when they change the production methods. Break even can be calculated using the contribution formula or it can be shown on a graph. A firm can use break even graphs to analyse the possible effects of changes in costs and changes in price. This analysis can then allow the firm to make decisions to help its performance.

In Ken's hairdressing business, he was able to break even after four months. This had been an important target for Ken as he felt it meant the business was more secure and would survive. He monitored the break even position each week. To do this he worked out the fixed costs for each week and calculated an average for the costs that varied with each customer. This depended on the amount of hair washing and drying and whether perms or dyes were being used. Finally, he worked out an average price per customer because this also depended on the type of style for each customer. By calculating the number of customers needed to break even each week, Ken knew how well the business was doing. It helped him to make decisions about changes to price and possible costs that could be cut, especially if there was an unexpected rise in costs such as electricity or rates.

THE BREAK EVEN POINT

What is the break even point for a firm?

Break even point is the level of sales where the total costs of making the items equals the total revenue received from selling them. Above this point, a profit may be achieved while below it a loss may be made. You can see from this how important a target it is for most small firms.

How is break even calculated?

The simplest way is to use the **contribution** method which has a two part formula.

1. Price per unit − variable cost per unit = contribution to fixed costs

2. $\dfrac{\text{Fixed costs}}{\text{contribution}}$ = break even level of sales

All the figures used must be for a certain length of time. This could be for a day, week, month or even a year.

For example: a firm sells small haversacks at £10 each. The variable costs of each haversack are £3. The firm's fixed costs per week amount to £35 000.

What is this firm's weekly break even point?

1. (Price per unit) − (variable cost per unit) = (contribution to fixed costs)
   £10 − £3 = £7

2. $\dfrac{\text{(Fixed costs)}}{\text{(contribution)}}$ $\dfrac{£35\,000}{£7}$ = 5 000 haversacks need to be sold each week to break even

Handy hints: Always show your workings for any calculation question – even if you have used a calculator. There may be as many as eight marks for calculating break even. The examiner marking your script would first of all look to see if you had the correct answer. If you had, you would be awarded eight marks immediately. If your answer was incorrect, the examiner would then look to see if any marks could be awarded for parts of the answer where you had followed the correct method. You can only get these marks if you show your working. Also, always remember to use a calculator as the examiners expect you to be able to handle complex numbers.

How can break even be plotted on a graph?

A firm can set out its actual cost figures in a chart. The figures in this chart can then be used to draw the break even graph. For example:

Break even table

Number of items sold	0	50	100	150	200	250
Fixed costs	2 000	2 000	2 000	2 000	2 000	2 000
Variable costs	0	200	400	600	800	1 000
Total costs	2 000	2 200	2 400	2 600	2 800	3 000
Total revenue	0	700	1 400	2 100	2 800	3 500

To plot this on a graph, label the vertical axis for costs and revenue and the horizontal axis for units sold. Separate lines can then be plotted for fixed costs, total costs and total revenue. The break even (BE) point is where total costs and total revenue cross. A line may be dropped from this point to the bottom axis to give the number of items that need to be sold to break even.

Break even graph

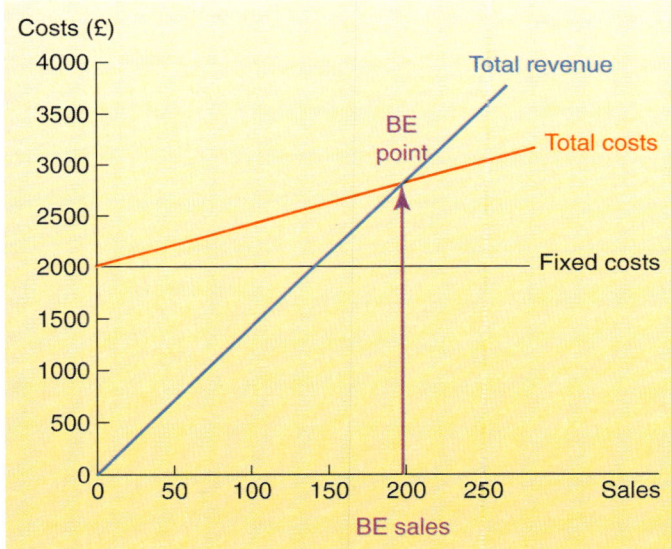

Why is it important for a firm to know the break even point?

- To show a firm how much has to be sold, over a certain period of time, for its costs to equal its revenue.
- This point will show a firm when it could start to make a profit and it will be an important target for new firms.

Activity

Cuddly Teddies Ltd makes and sells a small range of teddy bears.

It has worked out the following costs for its best selling bear 'Dozy Bear'.

Fixed costs   £20 150 per week
Variable costs   £5.50 per 'Dozy Bear'

1 a) If the price for a 'Dozy Bear' is £12, calculate how many Cuddly Teddies Ltd must sell each week to break even. Use the contribution formula and show all your working.

b) Using the same cost and price figures, draw up a break even chart (see the break even table left for the column headings). Calculate the figures for sales of 0, 500, 1 000, 1 500, 2 000, 2 500, 3 000 and 3 500 'Dozy Bears'.

c) Using the figures from this chart, draw the break even graph for 'Dozy Bears' (see the break even graph left to help you plan it).

d) Either on the same graph or on a new copy, plot the following changes:
- Fixed costs rise to £21 535
- Variable costs fall to £5.20 per 'Dozy Bear'
- A price of £12.50 per 'Dozy Bear'.

e) Explain the changes that have taken place to the break even point for 'Dozy Bears'.

f) Why might Cuddly Teddies Ltd need to be careful even though their break even point seems to have improved?

Break even analysis

Activity

- Parts a) to d) of the activity on page 113 could all be completed using a computer.
- For part b) create a spreadsheet and then use this to create the graphs for parts c) and d).
- How could you use the computer to calculate part a) and how could you prepare it to recalculate break even if the firm's costs or price changed?

- Producing a graph may not be the most accurate method of calculating break even, but it can help a firm to spot problems:
  - its fixed costs might be too high
  - its variable costs might be too high
  - its revenue might be too low.

- Spotting these problems may help the firm to take action that puts them right. This might mean a change in price, cutting costs or increasing sales.

- Sometimes, changes outside the firm may affect its costs or sales. A break even graph will help the firm to predict the results of such changes. The firm might be able to offset these changes. For example, an increase in rent and rates will increase a firm's fixed costs. The firm could see that this would increase its break even point. To offset this, the firm might try to cut other costs or consider increasing price. All of these ideas could be thought through using the break even graph.

Codebreakers

Break even point: the level of sales for a firm where the total costs of those sales equal the total revenue.

Contribution: the sales revenue of an item (its price) minus the variable cost of making and selling that item.

SUMMARY

Four points to remember:

1. Break even is an important business objective for many firms but especially for a new, small business.
2. The break even point shows a firm the level of sales at which total costs will equal total revenue.
3. A firm's break even point may be calculated using the contribution formula or drawn as a graph
4. Break even graphs help a firm to analyse the effects of changes in costs and revenue and to plan action to correct any problems that result.

Unit 25
Cash flow forecast

When a firm is operating, it will need to make sure that it has enough cash to pay its debts. It may appear to be quite a profitable business but it could still fail if it suffers a shortage of cash. To prevent this, a firm needs to prepare a budget that will predict its future flows of cash into and out of the business. This is usually known as a **cash flow forecast**. The actual flow of cash can be checked against this forecast so that the firm can take action both before and when it suffers any problems.

Cash management is vital to all firms, both small and large. Hanson plc is a leading building materials and equipment company in the UK and US and will develop its business there, in Europe and in Asia. Hanson has grown by buying, and sometimes selling, these companies and by encouraging them to expand their range of products. While Hanson expects profits to be made, it demands that all its companies are effective in controlling and managing cash. This is needed to keep production going and to make sure that investment plans can go ahead. Cash problems in one of the companies could have affected the success of the whole group. Hanson has had great success in the business world, partly due to its cash management policies.

MANAGING THE CASH FLOW

Inflows and outflows of cash

Even before a firm starts to operate, it will find large sums of money have to be paid out for all the setting up costs. At the same time, some money will flow into the firm as the owners put in their capital, as any grants are received and as money is borrowed. Once the firm is actually operating and selling its goods or services, revenue will begin to flow in from these sales. This **cash inflow** will help to pay for the **outflow** of cash as the firm starts to pay out its running costs.

The flow of cash in and and out of a firm

Will the inflow of cash equal the outflow?

The problem for both new and well-established firms is that the inflows of cash are unlikely to equal the outflows on any particular day, week or month. One week a firm may have a small **cash surplus** but the next week it may suffer a large shortage, or a **cash deficit**. Any shortage could stop a firm paying its immediate debts. This might make it difficult to obtain new stocks of materials, to pay power and phone bills, or even to pay wages to its workers. In extreme cases, a firm might have to stop trading.

How will a cash flow forecast help?

A cash flow forecast can help both new and existing firms in several ways:

- it will help a firm to plan its financial activities before problems arise

Cash flow forecast   115

Activity

John has been operating as a sole trader for six months. He makes and sells metal bar stools from his small workshop on an industrial estate. Together with a business adviser, John compares the actual cash flow with his forecast.

John's cashflow forecast compared with actual cashflow

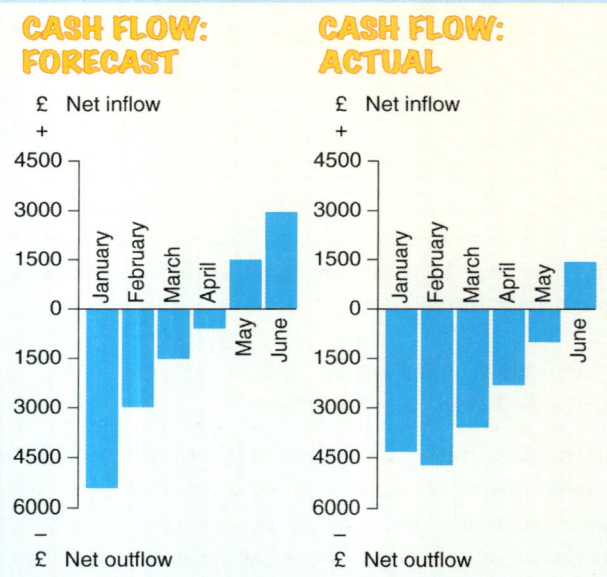

> **1** Explain what the graph of the cash flow forecast shows.
>
> How does the actual cash flow differ from John's forecast?
>
> **2** Why might John's actual cash flow have differed from his forecast?
>
> What problems might these differences have caused John?
>
> **3** How might John try to improve his cash flow?
>
> Explain why it is important for John to control his cash flow.

- it will help to predict when the firm might suffer from cash shortages
- this knowledge should help the firm to control its business and financial operations
- by comparing the forecast with the **actual cash flow** it can see when:
  – it needs to speed up the flow of cash into the business
  – it needs to slow down the flow of cash out of the business
  – it can afford to pay off some debts
  – it can afford to buy new stocks or equipment
  – it needs to increase its overdraft facilities.

How is a cash flow forecast set out in a chart?

There are several ways to do this, but the following plan shows the key parts and one useful layout. This can be made more detailed by including a list of different types of costs and by a list of different sources of revenue and other income. Total A shows the amount of cash with which the firm starts the week. Total E shows the cash remaining at the end of the week. Figures in brackets are minus figures or show that cash is paid out.

A cash flow forecast chart

Week	1	2	3
A Bank balance brought forward	£200	(£100)	(£200)
B Revenue from sales	£500	£650	£850
C Total cash available (A+B)	£700	£550	£650
D Total cash out	(£800)	(£750)	(£600)
E Bank balance carried forward (C–D)	(£100)	(£200)	£50

Codebreakers

Cash inflow: a flow of cash into the business.

Cash outflow: a flow of cash out of the business.

Cash flow forecast: a future prediction of how cash might flow into and out of a business. This may be set out in a chart or a graph.

Cash surplus: a situation when the cash inflow is greater than the cash outflow.

Cash deficit: a situation when a firm finds itself short of cash because the outflow is greater than the inflow.

Actual cash flow: this will be a statement of the actual cash flows which can be compared with the forecast.

Cash flow forecast

If a firm makes a very detailed cash flow chart it can check on trends in both costs and revenue. As new figures become available it can put these into the chart and update the forecast. To speed up the calculation process, most firms use a computer spreadsheet program to calculate the figures. The effects of various changes can then be quickly and easily analysed.

Activity

1. Draw up a cash flow forecast table for six months starting in March. You will need to create lines for:
   - balance brought forward
   - cash receipts (sales)
   - total cash available
   - expenses
     – wages
     – transport
     – rent and rates
     – advertising
     – stock
     – power
     – other
   - total payments
   - balance carried forward.

2. Use the following information to complete the cash flow forecast chart.

Brunt & Partners has two DIY shops. It sells the usual range of DIY products and has set out the following information for its cash flow forecast.

- At the start of March, Brunts had £3 500 cash available.
- In March, Brunts receives £29 000 in cash from its sales in February.
- Sales in March are estimated at £30 000. They are expected to rise by £2 000 each month. The actual cash from these sales is received 30 days later.

Activity continued

- Power bills amount to £1 500 a quarter with the next bill due in April.
- The wage bill each month is £16 000. A pay rise due in May should push that up to £17 000 a month.
- Van hire and related costs averages out at £500 a month.
- Rent and rates on the two shops totals £800 a month but Brunts expects this to rise by 10% in June
- Advertising amounts to £600 a month.
- Brunts has only been operating for 12 months and its suppliers do not allow it any trade credit. All stock must be paid for in cash when it is delivered. £10 000 worth of stock is received in March. To keep up with the rise in seasonal demand for DIY products, Brunts increases this order by £1 100 each month.
- Other expenses average out at £3 200 per month.

3. What problems does Brunts appear to have with this cash flow forecast?

4. How might they improve their cash flow situation?

Activity

- Students taking IT can do parts 1 and 2 of the previous activity using a spreadsheet program.
- You could also produce a graph of the forecast from the spreadsheet.
- One of the benefits of using a spreadsheet is that data can be easily changed and the results automatically computed. Try this for yourselves by increasing the cash receipts figures by 5% and each of the wages and stocks figures by 6%. How has this affected the cash flow forecast?

SUMMARY

Three points to remember:

1. A firm needs to control its flows of cash very carefully to avoid major business problems including possible closure.
2. A cash flow forecast can be used to predict a firm's future flows of cash.
3. This prediction can help the firm to spot possible problems so that it can act to prevent them.

Cash flow forecast

Unit 26

Profit and loss account

When a firm is set up, one of the usual objectives will be to make a profit. At a simple level, profit can be thought of as a situation when a firm's income is greater than its expenditure. Creating a profit and loss account to calculate the level of profit shows that this idea is too simple and that there are different measures of profit to consider. Also, as firms change from being a sole trader to a partnership and then to limited companies, more complicated accounts are required. Whatever it looks like, a profit and loss account will show a firm how well it has performed in the past.

The performance of major retailers seems to be constantly hitting the headlines in national newspapers. In November 1997, for example, Marks and Spencer announced plans for a three year, £2.1 billion expansion. Half of this will be spent in the UK with over 5 000 jobs being created. In particular, the company plans to expand its food business by opening bakeries in 50 branches and adding 60 butchers' counters to the existing 40. Extra stores will be opened, including 19 bought from Littlewoods in July 1997. Marks and Spencer is aiming to open 20 'neighbourhood stores' selling food and basic clothes such as shirts and underwear. It even plans a mail order clothes operation for 1998. The company felt it was able to do this because its six monthly profits to October 1997 were up £22 million to £452 million. This figure was achieved from a revenue figure of over £3 742 million. Total store space will rocket by a third over the three years – estimate how much profits might increase in that time!

Handy hints

This textbook is written for students aiming to sit a GCSE in Business Studies and not a qualification in Accountancy. You will need to know and understand the basic types of accounts used by firms, but to help your understanding, we have simplified some of the accounts and we would not expect you to know all the possible layouts. This unit will show you the only styles of layout which you will be expected to understand for the exam. In many exam papers, questions will be set on only a part of the profit and loss account.

HOW IS A PROFIT AND LOSS ACCOUNT LAID OUT?

In this unit, the profit and loss account will be set out as if it is for a limited company. This means that there are three parts to the account.

1 The trading account

This shows a summary of a firm's trading activities. The firm's revenue from the sales of its goods or services is set out and then the cost of those sales – raw materials, parts, components and ingredients – is taken away. The difference will give the firm its gross profit. So, in a very simple form the trading account would look like this:

Calculating gross profit

Sales revenue	£550 000
Cost of sales (–)	£314 000
Gross profit	£236 000

To arrive at the **cost of sales** figure, a firm needs to measure its **stocks**. It will need to measure its stock at the start of the trading period, record the purchases of its

stocks during the year, and then measure the stock remaining at the end of the trading period. The full **trading account** for a flower shop such as Glorious Flowers Ltd would therefore look like the one below.

Trading account for Glorious Flowers Ltd for the year ended 31.3.98

	£	£
Sales revenue		550 000
Less Cost of sales		
Opening stock	5 000	
Add Purchases	315 000	
	320 000	
Less Closing stock (–)	6 000	
		314 000
Gross profit		236 000

Obviously, flowers will perish quite quickly so the company is careful not to overstock and will depend on a regular flow of newly purchased stocks. The trading account shows this with only £5 000 worth of flowers in stock on the first day of the trading period and £6 000 on the last day. After £315 000 of flowers have been purchased, Glorious Flowers Ltd makes a gross profit of £236 000 from its revenue of £550 000 in the year ending on 31 March 1998.

Remember, **gross profit** is not the final amount of profit that a firm earns. It is simply the profit made from trading or from selling goods before other expenses are taken into consideration.

Did you know?

If this was an account for a manufacturing firm, cost of sales might include any wage costs directly involved with making the good. Any other wages and salaries, such as those for administrative staff, would be part of the firm's overheads and would be listed under expenses. These expenses would then be taken away from gross profit in the next section of the profit and loss account. For simplicity, do not include any wage costs in the cost of sales: put all wages down as an expense.

Codebreakers

Cost of sales: Calculated by taking opening stock *plus* purchases *less* closing stock.

Stocks: may be a mixture of raw materials, components, parts, ingredients and finished goods.

Trading account: a record of sales revenue and the cost of sales, showing how a firm's gross profit is achieved.

Gross profit: the difference between sales revenue and cost of sales.

2 The profit and loss account

Rather confusingly, this section of the account is called the profit and loss account.

It shows other income that the company might earn and all the other operating expenses or overheads paid out during the year.

Other possible sources of company income

- Rent from leasing out land or buildings to other companies
- **Profi**ts from selling unused assets such as land or buildings
- Dividends from investments in other companies
- Licence fees from other companies using a patented process or product.

Typical operating expenses or overheads

- Rent of premises
- Power – gas and electricity
- Interest on loans
- Advertising
- Vehicle expenses
- Business rates
- Cleaning
- Wages
- Insurance
- Administration
- Communications – telephone and postage
- Depreciation.

Once any additional income is added to gross profit and then expenses are taken away, the firm is left with its net profit. This can be shown in a shortened version for Glorious Flowers Ltd below.

Calculating net profit

	£
Gross profit	236 000
Add other income	5 000
	241 000
Less Expenses	172 000
Net profit	69 000

> **Activity**
>
> ▶ Public limited companies have to publish their accounts. These may be available from the head office of such companies. As a class, write to 10 companies asking for their annual reports and then compare the layouts used. Alternatively, your school may have 'The Times 100' CD-ROM which contains part of the annual reports for 100 top companies. You can access this to view the layouts of profit and loss accounts. A more detailed account would look like the one below.

Profit and loss account of Glorious Flowers Ltd for the year ended 31.3.98

	£	£
Gross profit		236 000
Add other income		
Rent received		5 000
		241 000
Less		
expenses		
Business rates	5 000	
Wages	86 000	
Interest paid	6 000	
Power	4 500	
Advertising	29 000	
Administration	11 000	
Depreciation	2 600	
Vehicle expenses	8 000	
Other	19 900	172 000
Net profit		69 000

What is depreciation?

The assets of any business will wear out over time. As a result, they will lose value. This may be because of simple wear and tear or because they become out of date and inefficient compared to new assets. Most businesses will 'write off' these assets over their expected life span. They do this by charging the annual loss in value as an expense on the profit and loss account.

One way of calculating the amount to charge on the profit and loss account is the straight-line or equal instalment method. It is calculated by:

$$\frac{\text{Initial cost of asset} - \text{Residual or scrap value}}{\text{Expected useful life of asset}}$$

For example, Glorious Flowers Ltd has bought assets worth £17 000. They expect the assets to last for five years when they have estimated that they might sell them for £4 000. Using the formula, Glorious Flowers Ltd needs to charge £2 600 to **expenses** each year, over a period of five years.

$$\frac{£17\,000 - £4\,000}{5 \text{ years}} = £2\,600 \text{ per year for five years}$$

3 The appropriation account

This final section shows what happens to the **net profit** made by the company. A portion of the net profit will be paid to the government in taxes. This is mainly Corporation Tax, a tax on company profits. Another portion of net profit will be distributed to shareholders with each share receiving a **dividend**. Finally, the company may decide to **retain** some of its **profit** to pay for new investment. The **appropriation account** for Glorious Flowers is shown below.

Appropriation account for Glorious Flowers Ltd for the year ended 31.3.98

	£
Net profit (before tax)	69 000
Taxation	15 000
Profit after tax	54 000
Dividends paid	26 000
Retained profit	28 000

Full profit and loss account

The full profit and loss account can be built up from the three separate sections. The table below shows the main figures for the account.

The profit and loss account for Glorious Flowers Ltd for the year ended 31.3.98

	£
Sales Revenue	550 000
Less Cost of Sales	314 000
Gross Profit	236 000
Add Other income	5 000
Less Expenses	172 000
Net profit	69 000
Less Tax	15 000
Profit after tax	54 000
Dividends paid	26 000
Retained profit	28 000

Handy hints

A sole trader will not need an appropriation account. Any net profit belongs to the owner and he or she can 'draw' out this money when it is required. For partnerships, the net profit will be split among the partners as set out in the partnership deed. Sole traders and partners will have to pay income tax on this profit. The partners could decide to retain some of their net profit instead of sharing it out; while the sole trader could decide to reinvest some of his or her profit. Most exam papers will not ask you questions on the appropriation account.

USES OF PROFIT AND LOSS ACCOUNTS

- The tax authorities will use profit and loss accounts to assess a company's tax.

- Other businesses may look at published accounts to compare their performance.

- The profit and loss account is an important record of the revenues and costs of a business over the past year. The figures may be compared to previous years and even to similar companies. The owners and managers may use the account to help make decisions about the future.

- Lenders, investors and shareholders will want to see how well the business is doing. They will want to assess the risk involved in keeping their money in the business.

Codebreakers

Expenses: all the other operating costs of a firm, sometimes called overheads.

Net profit: gross profit minus expenses.

Profit after tax: net profit minus tax paid to the government.

Dividends: a share of profits paid to shareholders.

Retained profits: profits kept back in the company for reinvestment.

Appropriation account: the section of the profit and loss account showing what happens to any net profit that is made.

Activity

Frostyfingers Ltd is a medium sized company selling frozen foods in several small towns in northern England. As part of its training programme, trainee managers have been given the task of preparing the company's annual trading and profit and loss accounts. Use the following data to:

a) Prepare the company's trading account for the year ended 31 May 1998.

b) Prepare the company's profit and loss account for the year ended 31 May 1998.

c) Prepare the whole trading and profit and loss account for the year ended 31 May 1998.

Sales revenue	£900 000	Opening stock	£60 000
Stock purchases	£400 000	Closing stock	£65 000
Wages	£150 000	Power	£50 000
Rent and rates	£65 000	Advertising	£90 000
Other expenses	£67 000		

Activity

a) Complete the above tasks using a spreadsheet program.

b) Create a new trading and profit and loss account but increase sales revenue by 10% and stock purchases by 15%. Compare the results.

SUMMARY

Three points to remember:

1 A profit and loss account shows a firm how it has performed in the past year.

2 The full account has three sections showing how gross and net profit are calculated and how the net profit is distributed.

3 Different types and size of business may produce their own special layout for a profit and loss account. GCSE Business Studies students will only be expected to know the versions shown in this unit.

Unit 27
Balance sheets

When a firm wants to know what it is worth now, it can use a balance sheet. This account shows a firm the value of what it owns, the value of what it owes and the value of the capital invested in the firm. Balance sheets will be set out in different ways according to the type and size of firm but this unit will keep to a standard layout. Whatever the layout, the balance sheet must always 'balance'.

It is always an interesting exercise to compare the balance sheets of what appear to be two very similar companies. For example, in 1995 Tesco plc had fixed assets worth £5 210 million while Sainsbury plc had £4 950 million. Tesco's stocks, however, were only worth £415 million while Sainsbury had stocks worth £508 million. Short-term debts amounted to £1 781 million for Tesco and £1 835 million for Sainsbury. There was a greater difference on long-term debts, with Tesco owing £921 million and Sainsbury only £669 million. The amount of capital and reserves in each business was quite similar with £3 113 million in Tesco and £3 289 million in Sainsbury. All of these figures show that, overall, the two companies are worth similar amounts. Why then, in 1995, did Tesco make £551 million profit on its ordinary activities before taxation, and Sainsbury make £809 million?

DEALING WITH THE BALANCE SHEET

What is a balance sheet?

The balance sheet is an account that gives a statement of a firm's wealth on a particular date. It is sometimes said to be like a 'snapshot' because it records the company's value at that moment in time, just as a photograph records people or events in an instant. By the next day, the value of the firm will have started to change. Normally, a balance sheet will be produced at the end of the firm's financial year. The balance sheet has three main parts:

- **Assets:** everything that a company owns and which has a money value
- **Liabilities:** everything that a company owes and which has a money value
- **Capital:** the different forms and sources of money invested in the firm.

How is a balance sheet set out?

There are several ways to set out a balance sheet. This depends on the type of firm, its size and even which accountancy firm it uses. The balance sheet opposite is for a limited company.

Balance sheet for Pringles – THE Opticians Ltd as at 31.3.1998.

	£ '000s	£ '000s	£ '000s
Fixed assets			
Land and buildings	120		
Equipment and vehicles	35		
Furniture and furnishings	10		
			165
Current assets			
Stocks	35		
Debtors	4		
Cash	2	41	
Less			
Current liabilities			
Creditors	15		
Bank overdraft	5		
		20	
Net current assets			21
(Working capital)			
Net assets employed			186
Financed by:			
Share capital			98
Retained profit			20
Bank loans			68
Capital employed			186

Handy hints

Any balance sheets used in the NEAB's GCSE Business Studies examination papers will be set out like the table on page 122 even though the firm in the case study might not be a limited company. This table is simplified but is the fullest form of balance sheet you will need to know. In many papers, you will find a shortened version is used.

Why do 'net assets employed' equal 'capital employed'?

The capital employed provides the funds for obtaining the company's assets. Therefore, the **capital employed** must equal the **assets employed** in the company.

Activity

1. What sort of fixed assets might Pringles – THE Opticians have?
2. What sort of stocks will Pringles have?
3. Who might be Pringles' debtors?
4. Who might be Pringles' creditors?
5. Why might Pringles have such a large figure for its stocks?
6. Why will it be important for Pringles to have a large enough figure for its net current assets (working capital)?

Activity

Use annual reports from public limited companies to investigate their layouts for balance sheets. Compare the balance sheets for the values of fixed assets, current assets and current liabilities. Find out how much capital is invested in the companies and the sources of this capital.

What is the purpose of a balance sheet?

- To show the wealth or value of the company at a moment in time.
- To show the value of assets employed, the value of liabilities owed and the capital at work in the company.
- To show the owners and managers how well the firm is doing:
  - it can help measure the profitability of the company
  - it can help to measure the firm's cash situation
  - it can allow comparisons to be made with previous years and even with other similar companies.
- Checking the performance of the company might help in key decision making.
- For many firms, and especially for limited companies, it is a legal requirement to produce one.

Codebreakers

Fixed assets: these are assets that are used to help production take place.

Current assets: these are assets that can be easily turned into cash, such as stocks of materials and finished goods.

Debtors: these are people or business organisations who have obtained goods or services from this firm but have not yet paid for them.

Current liabilities: these are debts which the firm has to repay within one year.

Creditors: these are people or business organisations who have supplied goods or services to the firm but have not yet been paid for them.

Net current assets: this is sometimes called working capital because it is the amount of money a firm has available to meet its day-to-day needs. It is calculated simply as current assets less current liabilities.

Net assets employed: this is calculated by adding the value of fixed assets to net current assets.

Share capital: this can be simply thought of as the value of the shares when they were first issued.

Retained profit: this is the profit left after all deductions are made and is added to the reserves on the balance sheet.

Capital employed: this is the total amount of capital put into the business and is calculated by adding share capital, retained profit and long-term liabilities together.

Balance sheets

Activity

> The following balance sheet is for Icyfoods plc, a retailer of frozen foods. The figures in the shortened account are for 1997. The account is a typical layout that has been used in exam questions.

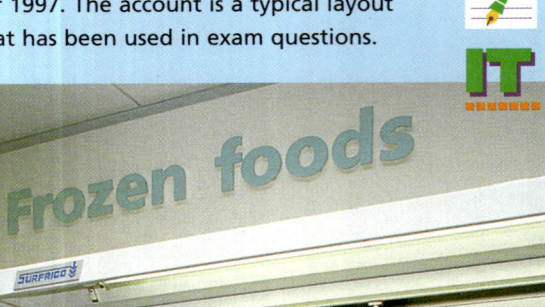

Extract from a balance sheet for Icyfoods plc as at 31.5.1997

	£ '000s	£ '000s	£ '000s
Fixed assets			25 000
Current assets			
Stock	800		
Debtors	100		
Cash	200		
		1 100	
Current liabilities			
Creditors	500		
Overdraft	200		
		700	
Net current assets			400
Net assets employed			25 400

Activity continued

> **1** Use the following figures to create an extract from a balance sheet for the same company as at 31.5.1998.
>
> Fixed Assets – £26 000 000
> Stock – £900 000
> Debtors – £200 000
> Cash – £200 000
> Creditors – £400 000
> Overdraft – £200 000.
>
> **2** Use the balance sheet for each year to compare Icyfoods plc's performance.

SUMMARY

Three points to remember:

1 A balance sheet shows the value of a firm at a point in time.

2 It shows the value of the assets owned, the liabilities owed and the capital at work in the firm.

3 Balance sheet figures can be compared to previous years and sometimes to other companies to help interested groups monitor progress and performance.

Unit 28
Business ratios

When a business wants to know how well it is doing, it can look at a number of measures. It can look at individual figures, both on its profit and loss account and on its balance sheet. It can look at trends in these figures and make comparisons, particularly to previous years. One of the most useful ways for a firm to assess business performance, however, is to use figures from these accounts in ratio analysis. For GCSE Business Studies, students need to know how to calculate and use profitability ratios and liquidity ratios.

ICI is one of the UK's best known companies making a whole host of famous brand names including Dulux paints. It is very aware that different groups or stakeholders share an interest in the success of the company Stakeholders include managers, customers, employees, the community, the government and the shareholder. In the last few years, ICI has tried to boost its efficiency and its profitability. It has aimed to achieve a return for shareholders of 20%. This would be a very high return for any company operating in such a sector. It has not quite reached its target, yet, but it is still working towards this by continual improvements in products and service and through increased productivity.

Registered trademark

WHO NEEDS TO KNOW HOW WELL A BUSINESS IS DOING?

- **Owners:** to see if they are getting a good return for risking their money in the firm.
- **Managers:** they have a responsibility to the owners to make the firm perform well. They will also want to build a good personal business reputation.
- **Employees:** will want to keep their jobs and will hope to receive the higher pay and rewards which a successful firm might bring.
- **Creditors:** any organisation that lends money to a firm will want to be sure that the money will be repaid, with interest. Successful firms will ensure this.
- **Customers:** a successful firm will continue to provide its customers with the quality goods and services required.
- **Governments:** the higher the profit, the more tax the government receives. More importantly, successful firms guarantee jobs and help the UK's trade with the rest of the world.

HOW DO YOU DECIDE IF A FIRM IS DOING WELL?

'Doing well' is rather vague, and it is much better to talk about measuring business performance. This may be done using costs, revenue, profit, or the value of assets, liabilities and capital. Such figures may be compared with previous years or even other companies if their figures are published. Simple totals or even changes in these totals do not always give the clearest picture of a firm's performance. Using these figures in ratios allows one total to be compared with another. Profitability ratios and liquidity ratios are two of the most important sets of ratio analysis that most firms will use.

> **Handy hints**
>
> This unit will show you how to calculate and use five ratios. These are the only business ratios you will need to know for the GCSE Business Studies exam papers. In each case, learn how to calculate the ratio, try to understand what the ratio is saying about the firm's performance and consider how the firm might try to improve the ratio.
>
> You will notice that sometimes the ratio can be set out and calculated as a simple ratio with the use of the ratio sign ':' in the middle of two figures. The ratio might also be calculated in a percentage format which is often more useful for making easy comparisons. Follow and learn the methods set out below – but always remember in the exam to show your working!

PROFITABILITY RATIOS

Gross profit to sales revenue

The figures for this ratio may be obtained from a firm's profit and loss account. This ratio shows what has happened to sales revenue in relation to the cost of sales. For example, Executive Cases Ltd makes a range of brief cases and carrying bags. Its sales revenue figure for 1995 was £750 000 while its gross profit was £487 500. Its gross profit to sales revenue ratio may be calculated in two ways.

i) Gross profit : Sales revenue
487 500 : 750 000
4 875 : 7 500
195 : 300
13 : 20

ii) $\frac{\text{Gross Profit} \times 100}{\text{Sales revenue}} = \%$

$\frac{487\,500 \times 100}{750\,000} = 65\%$

These figures tell the firm that it is making a gross profit of 65% on its revenue: or that for every £20 of revenue, £7 goes on its cost of sales, leaving a gross profit of £13. This is quite a useful way of thinking about the meaning of the actual ratio figure, but for comparisons it is easier to use the percentage figure.

For example, in 1996 Executive Cases Ltd found that its sales revenue was £815 000 while gross profit was £503 000. Clearly, gross profit has increased but so has sales revenue. Calculating by the percentage method shows:

$\frac{503\,000}{815\,000} \times 100 = 61.7\%$ – a small fall in profitability.

Using the same figures set out as a simple ratio:

503 000 : 815 000 may be reduced to
503 : 815 if whole numbers are maintained

Stating that for every £815 of revenue a gross profit of £503 is earned is clearly an awkward figure to compare with the 1995 figure.

Net profit to sales revenue

This shows how much net profit a business earns per £ of sales revenue. The higher the profit per £ of revenue – the higher the ratio – the more profitable a business is likely to be. A lower ratio suggests that a business is not as profitable as others. Falling ratio figures over two or three years show that a business is becoming less profitable.

Using figures for Executive Cases Ltd, in 1995 it made a net profit of £90 000 from its revenue of £ 750 000. As a percentage the ratio is:

$\frac{90\,000}{750\,000} \times 100 = 12\%$ while as a simple ratio it is
90 000 : 750 000
or 3 : 25

These figures show that in 1995 Executive Cases Ltd is earning 12% net profit on its sales revenue; or, that for every £25 of revenue, £22 is being spent on expenses and cost of sales, leaving a net profit of £3.

Activity

1. In 1996, Executive Cases Ltd made a net profit of £91 280 on its sales revenue of £815 000. Calculate the percentage of net profit to sales revenue.

2. Describe how the figure for 1996 compares to the figure for 1995.

3. In 1997, Executive Cases Ltd achieved a sales revenue figure of £825 000.

    Gross profit was £552 750. Net profit was £107 250.

    Calculate, showing workings;

    a) the 1997 ratio of gross profit to sales revenue

    b) the 1997 ratio of net profit to sales revenue.

4. Describe the changes in profitability that Executive Cases Ltd has experienced over the three years 1995, 1996 and 1997.

5. Why do you think these changes might have taken place?

Return on capital employed

The figures for this ratio may be obtained partly from a firm's balance sheet and partly from its profit and loss account. Return on the capital employed measures the profitability of a firm by comparing its profit with the amount of capital invested in it. A high return means a more profitable investment and therefore happier investors – especially the owners of the firm.

The formula for **return on capital employed** (ROCE) is quite simple:

$$\frac{\text{Net profit}}{\text{Total capital employed}} \times 100 = \text{ROCE \%}$$

For example, we already know that in 1995 Executive Cases Ltd earned a net profit of £90 000. The company's total capital employed at the end of that year was £1 125 000.

When these figures are put into the formula we can see that Executive Cases Ltd made an 8% return from the capital invested in it.

$$\frac{90\,000}{1\,125\,000} \times 100 = 8\%$$

This figure is telling the company that for every £100 invested, a profit of £8 is being earned. To decide whether this is a good return the company can compare the figure:

- to the ROCE for previous years
- to the ROCE earned by similar sized companies
- to the average ROCE earned by firms in the company's industry
- to the gross and net profit to revenue ratios
- to the typical rate of interest earned on savings accounts.

LIQUIDITY RATIOS

These look at a firm's ability to pay its debts. Any assets that are easily turned into cash are said to be 'liquid'. **Liquid assets** are therefore important in helping a firm to be able to meet immediate debts or liabilities. All figures for the two **liquidity ratios** can be found from the balance sheet. Executive Cases Ltd identified the following figures from its balance sheet at the end of 1995.

Current assets:	£400 000	– Stock	£250 000
		– Debtors	£130 000
		– Cash	£20 000
Current liabilities:	£160 000		

Handy hints

You might find it easier to think about how ROCE works by considering any savings accounts you might have with banks and building societies. If you received £10 interest on the money you put in your savings account last year, you had to decide if this was good or bad. You could not really say until you knew how much money you had in your account. If you had put in £20, the £10 interest payment would mean you were earning a staggering 50% rate of interest. If you had put £500 in the account, the £10 interest payment would have meant a more modest interest rate of just 2%. If the actual amount you had saved was £200, then in a sense your personal return on the capital you had saved or 'invested' would have been 5%. Any investors in a firm would want to earn two to three per cent more than the rate from a savings account to compensate them for the greater risks.

Current ratio

The **current ratio** shows how often its short-term debts can be paid out of its current assets. It is sometimes called the working capital ratio because it uses the two sets of figures that calculate a firm's working capital.

$$\text{The basic formula is:} \quad \frac{\text{Current assets}}{\text{Current liabilities}}$$

For Executive Cases, its current ratio in 1995 was

$$\frac{400\,000}{160\,000} = 2.5 : 1$$

This showed that Executive Cases Ltd could meet its short-term debts two and a half times over from its current assets. A typical ratio should be 1.5 : 1 or better although a ratio of more than 3 : 1 suggests that a company is not using its assets very profitably. A figure of less than 1.5 : 1 may mean that a firm might have trouble paying its immediate debts.

Acid test ratio

One problem with using the current ratio to measure a firm's ability to pay short-term debts is that it includes a figure for stocks. For example, Executive Cases Ltd might find it difficult to sell off stock quickly to pay for any immediate debts. In this case, a better measure of a firm's liquidity is the **acid test ratio** because it does not include a figure for any stocks.

$$\text{Acid test ratio} = \frac{\text{Current assets} - \text{stocks}}{\text{Current liabilities}}$$

For Executive Cases Ltd, its acid test ratio at the end of 1995 would have been:

$$\frac{400\,000 - 250\,000}{160\,000} = 0.94 : 1$$

This ratio suggests that Executive Cases Ltd would have much more trouble in meeting immediate debts, although it could probably sell off some stocks to help pay the bills. Generally, a healthy acid test ratio is said to be anywhere between 0.5 : 1 and 1 : 1.

Codebreakers

Profitability measures: ways of measuring how profitable a firm is so that its performance can be assessed.

Gross profit to sales revenue ratio: a comparison of the gross profit of a firm with its sales revenue once cost of sales have been deducted. It may be calculated as a simple ratio or as a percentage.

Net profit to sales revenue: this compares net profit with sales revenue once all costs have been deducted. It may also be calculated either as a simple ratio or as a percentage.

Return on capital employed: This measures the firm's ability to make a profit from the capital invested into it. It is always calculated as a percentage by dividing net profit by total capital employed and multiplying by 100.

Liquidity measures: these attempt to measure a firm's performance by assessing its ability to pay short-term debts using current assets.

Liquid assets: these are assets that can be easily turned into cash such as stocks and debtors.

Current ratio: this measures the firm's ability to pay short-term debts by comparing its current assets with its current liabilities.

Acid test ratio: this is a tougher measure of liquidity calculated by the ratio of current assets minus stock to current liabilities.

Activity

The following figures are taken from the balance sheets and profit and loss accounts of Icyfoods plc for the financial years 1997 and 1998.

	31.5.97	31.5.98
Net profit	£2 540 000	£2 937 000
Stock	£800 000	£900 000
Current assets	£1 100 000	£1 300 000
Current liabilities	£700 000	£600 000
Capital employed	£25 400 000	£26 700 000

1 Calculate for 1997:

   a) the return on capital employed (ROCE)

   b) the current ratio

   c) the acid test ratio.

2 Calculate the same ratios for 1998.

3 Compare the ratios and explain whether Icyfoods plc has improved its performance on profitability and liquidity.

SUMMARY

Four points to remember:

1 Businesses can measure their performance using liquidity and profitability ratios.

2 There are three ratios to measure profitability and two ratios to measure liquidity.

3 By comparing ratios to previous years, to expected levels and even to those of other companies, a firm can assess its performance.

4 Several different groups of people are interested in knowing and using these business performance figures.

Unit 29

Methods of improving profitability

When a firm has reviewed its profitability, it might decide that it needs to improve its performance. Strategies open to the firm include ways of reducing costs, methods to increase revenue, the introduction of new products or services and the expansion of the business. To choose the best strategy, a firm will have to weigh up the costs and benefits of each possible action. It might need to opt for a mixture of several actions. In extreme situations, if profits are too low, the firm might have to stop part of its production or even to consider closing down all together.

Retailing companies argue that their market is the toughest one to operate in. This means that there is a continual need to cut costs, to boost sales, to develop new products and markets, and to expand. Iceland is one well-known high street retailer that has grown despite all the competition. It has done this by concentrating on its core activity of selling frozen foods; by expanding through opening new stores and taking over the food halls of Littlewoods; and by introducing over 200 new products each year. In each store, all managers are expected to take a lot of responsibility with the control of costs an important target.

HOW TO CHOOSE THE RIGHT STRATEGY AND ACTION

Each action that a firm takes will give it an advantage or benefit. Almost certainly, each action will also have at least one disadvantage or cost. To choose the best actions for improving profitability, a firm ought to consider these costs and benefits. An action should only be chosen if the benefits clearly outweigh the costs.

Reducing costs

For many firms, reducing costs is the first option to consider when trying to increase profitability, especially when competition is fierce. Some firms may have more chances to reduce costs than others. If its costs are already cut down to a minimum, a firm will find it difficult to reduce costs further while still maintaining output and quality. Another firm may have a number of costs that could be reduced.

Manufacturing firms may have quite different sets of costs to those providing services, while retailing firms are likely to have different types of costs to those in agriculture and mining. Large scale firms, like those in the petrochemical industry, may find that a large proportion of costs are linked to buildings, plant and machinery. Retailing firms are likely to find that labour costs are a large proportion of total costs. Each firm will therefore have its own quite different opportunities to cut costs.

When firms look at ways to reduce costs of production, they are aiming to lower unit costs. One way to achieve this is to cut the actual costs involved in producing the product or service. A less obvious method that will achieve the same aim is to increase output while controlling costs.

In general, firms can identify a number of groups of costs that can be targeted. These include:

- property and land e.g. rent and rates
- labour costs e.g. wages and salaries, bonuses and commission, national insurance
- power and utilities e.g. electricity, gas, water
- equipment e.g. repairs, maintenance, replacement
- transport e.g. repairs, insurance, petrol, maintenance
- promotion e.g. advertising, sponsorship
- administration e.g. telephone, postage, paper
- finance e.g. interest, accountants
- stocks e.g. raw materials, components, parts, ingredients
- other e.g. insurance.

Increasing revenue

In simple terms, this may be achieved in two ways. Firstly, a price increase will bring in more revenue for each good or service that is sold. Secondly, an increase in the number of goods or services sold, while keeping prices fixed, will also increase a firm's revenue. Unfortunately, neither of these are quite as simple as they sound. They certainly have costs as well as benefits.

- **Changing price:** in most cases, an increase in the price of a good is likely to reduce sales. This means that the firm will gain extra revenue from each good sold but will also lose revenue for each item that is no longer sold. Alternatively, the firm could drop its price hoping that sales will increase. Higher sales will bring in more revenue from each unit sold, but will this outweigh the revenue lost from the lower price? To answer this question, the firm will need to know how sensitive consumers are to price changes. The firm will also need to consider how long special offers should last and whether pricing tactics like psychological pricing are of any use.

- **Increasing sales:** while a fall in price may do this, firms may believe that other marketing tactics will have a greater impact. Advertising and other forms of sales promotion, such as packaging, are frequently used by many firms to increase sales. The problem is, of course, that while extra sales might result, extra costs are being created. Will the extra revenue more than pay for the extra costs involved in advertising? Market research may be used to help answer this sort of question and to reduce the risks of such tactics. In the end, the consumer is the final decision-maker!

Introducing new products

This is another marketing tactic that firms frequently use to help improve profits. Sometimes, the 'new' products are simply re-packaged versions of the old product. This may help profits for a while but if consumers are 'tired' of the basic product, the firm will have to find a completely new idea. In many cases, a product or service may be extended by adding on extras. Most firms will try to extend the life of their existing products as a first tactic, before developing and introducing completely new product lines. New products may cost a great deal to research, to develop and to launch on to the market; and, of course, there is no guarantee that the product will be a profitable success.

> **Did you know?** There are many products available to consumers today that started out as much more basic models, but that have undergone considerable development. For example, when home video recorders were first launched on to the market, they were extremely basic with only key functions like play, record, rewind, fast forward and timer record. The first remote controls were in fact linked directly to the video through a lead. Later, infra-red remote controls were created, followed by more advanced functions such as freeze frames, picture search and digital stereo recording. Through this product development and expansion, consumer demand has been maintained and profitability kept within acceptable limits.

Activity

> Look around your home. Identify ten products or services that your family frequently use. Ask your relatives how these products have changed in the last five, ten and twenty years. You might be able to find out some idea of the original prices. Another source of information might be your local museum. An increasing number of museums and tourist attractions are creating displays of domestic goods from the 1950s onwards. Report back to your class on your findings. You may even be able to make a class display from your research. Why not start with home computers? Some people may still be able to show you the merits of the 'Sinclair Spectrum'!

Expanding the business

This is not simply making more of the same products, but looking towards different product markets. Expansion certainly includes increasing output with more factories or more outlets to sell the good or service. The business may need to diversify into markets or products that have no, or very little, link with the original business. In some cases this may require a firm taking over or merging with another one. Generally, the larger the firm, the more profitable it is likely to be.

Did you know?
In the 1990s, some large firms started to think that their profits would be helped if they sold off some of their business interests. For example, ICI has sold a number of its subsidiary businesses; while in February 1998 Waterstone's, the booksellers, was demerged from WH Smith.

Handy hints
Most exam papers have at least one question where you are asked to give advice about ways for a firm to increase its profits. Try to think of the possible costs and benefits of each method given. Think about how the firm might be affected. Finally, weigh up the costs and the benefits and advise the firm on the methods you think are best – but make sure you have given reasons. In most cases there is not a correct answer. The examiners are trying to assess your ability to analyse and reason logically, and are not necessarily concerned about which method you select – as long as you have justified it.

Activity

A small sandwich shop is keen to boost its profits. At the moment, the sole trader opens between 10.00 and 15.00, Monday to Friday, selling home-made sandwiches from her shop. This is located on a small side street off the main shopping centre. Sally has no employees and feels that she has her costs well under control.

1. Make a list of the possible ways that Sally could improve her profits.
2. Think and note the costs and benefits of each possible method to boost profits.
3. Advise Sally on the best way that she might be able to improve her profits.
4. Suggest further information you would find useful to help give more accurate advice.

SUMMARY

Three points to remember:

1. Profits may be improved through reducing costs, by making production more efficient, by increasing revenue, by introducing new products or services and by expanding the business.
2. Each possible method of improving profits is likely to have costs and benefits to the firm.
3. Before deciding which action to take, a firm needs to weigh up the costs and benefits of each.

Methods of improving profitability

Unit 30
Resources and the production chain

When a firm produces a good or service, it needs a wide variety of resources. Payments for these resources are the firm's costs of production. As a product is created, it passes though several stages along a chain of production. At each stage, the producing firm will be trying to add value until the product is sold to its final consumer.

The production of Kellogg's breakfast cereals is one good example of a production chain. It begins with the planting, ripening and harvesting of maize. This is imported into the UK where it arrives at Seaforth. After storage it is then milled to remove the parts that would harm freshness and taste. The milled 'grits' are taken by road to Manchester where they are flavoured, cooked and dried. At each stage they are checked for quality. The next stage is to roll the maize into flakes which are then toasted at high temperatures. At last, the cereal can be put into inner liners and then packed into cartons. The cartons are collected into cases for storage in the warehouse before being transported by road to the country's supermarkets and then on to consumers' breakfast tables.

1. Harvesting
2. Seaforth
3. Milling
4. Bulk transport
5. Flavouring
6. Cooking
7. Drying
8. Holding
9. Quality assurance
10. Flaking
11. Toasting
12. Filling
13. Packing
14. Case packing
15. Distribution

Activity

- Draw out the production chain for this breakfast cereal clearly showing each stage or link in the chain. Use the diagram in the left hand column of page 134 to help you. If you do this on the computer, illustrate each stage by selecting pictures from the clipart sections of your program.

WHAT IS PRODUCTION?

This is the process by which a product or service is created to meet the needs of consumers. At each stage of the process, the product will have **value added** until the final value is achieved and the good or service is sold to a customer. This is more easily demonstrated with a manufacturing company.

Value added in the pottery industry

Stage	Input	Output	Value added
Extract China clay	£0	£20 000	£20 000
Refine to potting clay	£20 000	£35 000	£15 000
Make coffee mugs	£35 000	£60 000	£25 000
Total			£60 000

In this case, coffee mugs have sold for a final value of £60 000. This has been created in three stages, with £20 000 added value when the China clay is washed out of a quarry; £15 000 added value when the china clay is refined into clay suitable for potting; and £25 000 added value when the mugs are shaped, fired and painted ready for sale to the final consumer.

> **Activity**
>
> ▸ Discuss in groups how value might be added in the following services:
> - Hairdressing
> - Serving a meal in a fast food restaurant
> - Building an extension to a house.

What resources are needed for production?

The resources needed for any production to take place may be grouped in a number of ways. The diagram below shows the **production resources** grouped under seven headings with the **entrepreneur** at the centre. This is because the entrepreneur is the person who organises all the necessary resources by buying in or hiring their services. The entrepreneur is said to be adding enterprise to the business and takes risks by putting money into the business. In return, the entrepreneur expects some profit from the enterprise and this, like all the rewards to the owners of the resources, is part of the firm's costs.

Production resources

The chain of production

Every product has a chain of production with each stage linked to the next. There might be a different number of stages but virtually every product will start back at the **primary production** stage. This is where the raw material is extracted. From here, the raw material will enter the **secondary production** stage where it is processed or manufactured into a finished product. Finally, the product will enter the tertiary stage where the product will be distributed to organisations prepared to sell it on to the final consumer. **Tertiary production** includes all types of services, such as the commercial services of banking and advertising, and the direct services of doctors and hairdressers.

Resources and the production chain

These stages of production are said to be part of a chain because they are linked together as illustrated in the diagram below. You should remember, of course, that various services will also be needed at each stage to help production take place. For example, the services of a bank will be needed by virtually every firm involved in the chain.

Chain of production for aluminium foil

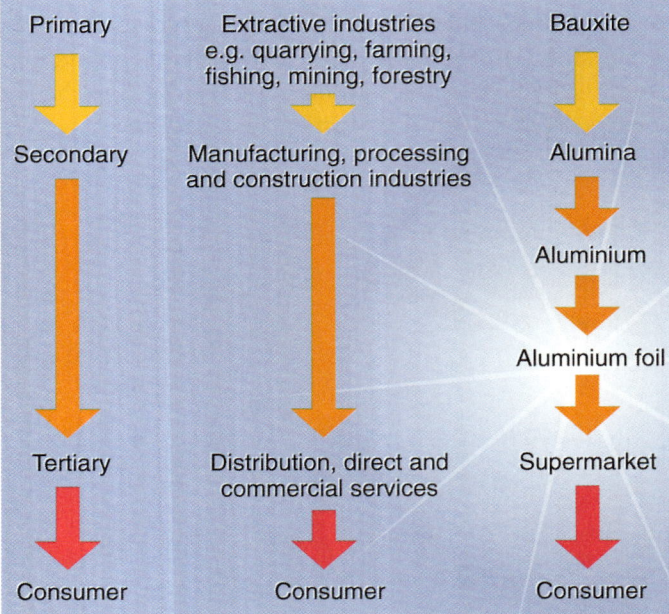

Activity

> Create production chains for everyday products or services that you buy.
>
> If you have access to any literature produced by large companies, you should be able to use these to help draw up the production chain for their products/services.

SUMMARY

Five points to remember:

1. Resources are needed for production to take place.
2. The entrepreneur is one of the most important resources because he or she organises the other resources.
3. Payments for the resources are a firm's costs of production.
4. Most products go through a chain of production from the primary stage through a secondary stage to the tertiary stage before reaching the final customer.
5. Value is added at each stage as the product is made.

Codebreakers

Value added: this is the difference between the value paid for the inputs used in production and the value of a firm's output.

Production resources: these are everything a firm needs in order to make a product or provide a service. These factors of production will include raw materials, buildings, equipment and workers. The payments for the resources are a firm's costs of production.

Entrepreneur: this is the person who takes the risk by investing money into the business, who organises all the resources so that production takes place, and who hopes to make a profit.

Primary production: a first stage of production where raw materials are extracted.

Secondary production: at this stage, raw materials are manufactured and processed into the final good.

Tertiary production: this is the provision of services of all kinds both to business and to the general public.

134 Resources and the production chain

Unit 31
Choosing the right scale

When a firm is setting up or when it has been operating for some time, it will have several decisions to make about the production of its goods or services. Many of these decisions will be organised by the production manager but taken in co-operation with other departments. Two of the key decisions will be what products to make and what scale or size the production should be.

For firms like Nissan and Ford, producing for a world-wide car market means that large scale production is extremely desirable. The advantages of large scale production are also vital to food manufacturers such as Heinz, not least in keeping unit costs to a minimum. Their current adverts emphasise that their products are produced and bought throughout the world and the adverts show images and music from different countries all united around the consumption of a Heinz product. While Heinz obviously benefits from an image of quality brands, the gains from large scale production allow it to market this so intensively.

Firms like ERF, who manufacture trucks in the UK, will not have this large scale market. Typically, they have 10% of the UK market but this means selling between 2 000 and 3 000 trucks a year. Consequently, they do not enjoy the benefits of large scale production which would result from producing, say, 100 000 trucks per year. ERF's unit costs are therefore much greater than they would be at this higher level of output. For companies like ERF, all decisions about the product and the production process and method are vital if costs are to be reduced and productivity increased. These decisions are explained below.

DECIDING WHAT TO PRODUCE

One of the earliest decisions for any new firm is deciding what to produce. From time to time, well-established firms will also have to make decisions about the products they make as demand for their existing products declines. To make these decisions, a firm has to study four main areas:

- **Supply:**
  - Are there similar products on the market?
  - Are there any gaps in the market?
  - How many competing firms are there?
- **The market:**
  - Do consumers prefer cheapness, reliability, quality, appearance, etc.?
- **The product:**
  - Will there be a need for skilled labour and new machinery?
  - What will the production costs be?
  - Will there be any production problems?
  - How much should be produced?
- **Profitability:**
  - Will the expected revenue pay for all the costs?
  - Will a profit be made?
  - Is the size of the profit worth the risk?

All of these questions will need a lot of information from different departments in the firm. Other units in the book will deal with much of the information, but this unit looks at the role of the production manager and the importance of choosing the right scale of production.

THE ROLE OF THE PRODUCTION MANAGER

In simple terms, the production manager is responsible for producing the goods in the best way possible. This hides the fact that a production manager has to do a number of complex tasks, most of which are described in detail in the remainder of this unit and the three units that follow this one. The main tasks are:

- to help choose the right scale of production
- to keep production flowing smoothly by detailed planning of the best production method and close control of the output of goods
- to produce goods on time, working to a production schedule and using appropriate production strategies
- to maintain or improve the quality of the products made
- to keep costs within the production budget so that production is as efficient as possible
- to predict and deal with production problems
- to co-operate and communicate with other departments.

CHOOSING THE RIGHT SCALE OF PRODUCTION

It is a fairly obvious statement to make that firms should only produce what they can sell. For many firms, this may mean remaining small. Small size can have its advantages. These include:

- the firm can offer personal service
- specialised products can be supplied
- the firm can be quite flexible in meeting changing demand for goods
- highly expensive, luxury products will not be in great demand, suiting supply by a small scale firm
- high transport costs make it too expensive to sell far from the producer so again benefiting lots of small local suppliers.

The main problem of remaining small is that unit costs may be higher than in large scale firms. This will then have an effect on price and therefore on sales. So, most firms have an incentive to increase the scale of production. There are many benefits for firms as they grow larger. In general, as they increase the size or scale of the output, the lower will be the unit (average) cost of production. These benefits of large scale production are called economies of scale.

Economies of scale

There are several categories of economies of scale. Some of the most important include:

Technical economies

Large firms can afford:

- teams of machines that work at different speeds rather than perhaps just one machine of each type, with output at the speed of the slowest
- conveyor belts and specialised machinery for producing in huge numbers
- to use larger equipment without a major increase in costs, e.g. a ten ton lorry, will not cost twice as much as a five ton lorry to buy and run but will carry twice as many goods

---

Did you know?

You may have already learned about the 'Four Ps' of marketing. There are 'Five Ps' of production decision making that you may also find useful to recall. They are:

Product: Will the product sell? Will the product design allow it to be made quickly and easily? What materials will be used and what will they cost?

Plant: What buildings and equipment will be needed and how should they be laid out?

Processes: Will the product be made as a 'one-off', in batches, on a continuous production line or in some other way?

Programmes: How will different strategies and functions be programmed to achieve an organised timetable of production?

People: What does the firm need to consider about the people involved in the production of a good or service?

Activity

1. Make a class list of as many firms as possible within three miles of your school.
2. Group those firms into small, medium and large. Explain how you have made those decisions.
3. Choose a typical example of a small firm.
   Try to decide what advantages it might have from being a small firm.
4. Choose a typical example of a large firm.
   Try to decide what advantages it might have from being a large firm.
5. Choose a typical example of a medium-sized firm.
   What advantages and disadvantages might this firm have compared to both small and large firms?

NB When you do this activity you need to decide whether to consider firms making the same type of goods and services or different ones.

- to carry out research and development into new products and new ways of making products.

Managerial economies
- specialist, highly skilled managers can be hired by large firms
- most managers could cope with higher output and sales without needing extra managerial staff.

Trading economies
- large firms may buy in bulk which reduces the costs of buying inputs
- specialist buyers and sales staff can be employed
- one advert can sell 10 000 items or 100 items – the cost is the same.

Financial economies
There are three main benefits for large firms:
- rates of interest on loans and overdrafts are likely to be lower
- there are more sources of finance available

Codebreakers

Economies of scale: these are the advantages of producing large quantities of output. The advantages should help the firm to reduce unit costs.

Diseconomies of scale: these disadvantages arise when a firm becomes too large to manage effectively. They will often result in a rise in unit costs.

- loans are larger because large firms can offer more security.

Risk-bearing economies
- large firms are able to produce a range of products and sell in different markets. If one product or market fails, the firm can keep trading with the others.

Welfare economies
- large firms are more able to look after the welfare of workers. For example, they can afford canteens, medical provision, and to sponsor sports teams.

Are there any disadvantages to being a large firm?

There can be. Some firms become too large and find that their unit costs start to rise rather than fall. They tend to find it difficult to control everything that is going on in the company. Communications may become a problem as a firm grows too large and sometimes the morale of the work-force falls as they feel distanced from the management. These are usually called **diseconomies of scale** and when they occur it has sometimes led to the breakup of large firms.

SUMMARY

Three points to remember:

1. A production manager will have to make many key decisions about how to produce the firm's products.
2. One way of remembering these key decisions is to use the 'Five Ps' of production.
3. Producing on a large scale may give a firm many benefits but in some markets there are advantages to producing on a small scale.

Choosing the right scale 137

Unit 32

Manufacturing methods and strategies

When a firm has to decide how to produce its goods and services, they will probably have to carry out a great deal of research and development. In particular, some scientific and technological research may be necessary. This will involve the product being developed from the original idea to an actual product that can be made. The best production method will have to be researched and tested along with production strategies to help manufacturing take place efficiently.

Many people associate production methods and strategies with manufacturing firms. Retailing companies, however, have always led the way in new storage and ordering techniques and many of these are then adopted by manufacturing companies. For example, Safeway – the supermarket group – announced in November 1997 that they are linking with suppliers through the Internet. Initially, Birds Eye Wall's and Walkers (the crisp firm) will be able to use the Internet to monitor sales of their products at Safeway stores. The manufacturers will be able to check when stocks need to be replaced at the retailer. This will help their own production planning while preventing Safeway running out of stocks. 1998 should see 20 more firms coming on line and Safeway hope to expand this to as many of the remaining 2 000 suppliers as possible.

METHODS OF PRODUCTION

There are four methods of manufacturing production that need to be highlighted. Although it is possible to show the differences between each method, some firms adapt methods for their production needs so that they combine the best features of two or more methods. In particular, many manufacturing firms combine **batch** and **flow/mass production** methods together. Sometimes, there may be a particular project that requires elements from job, batch and flow production.

Job production/jobbing

Job production means that a product is made individually from start to finish. Each product is likely to be different and designed to meet a customer's personal specifications. Many services involve jobbing while the range of products may vary from the very small to the very large. Examples include: road bridges, aeroplanes, house extensions, plumbing services, landscape gardening and haircuts.

Advantages
- high quality products/services
- skilled labour is used
- workers are highly motivated
- each item may be different

Disadvantages
- output may be expensive
- a lot of expensive labour is needed
- difficult to speed up production

Batch production

This involves making similar or identical items in batches. Production may be halted to make changes before the next batch is made. This may involve both small- and large-scale production. Good examples include: bakery products, sweets, wallpaper and clothing.

Advantages	Disadvantages
■ some variety of product	■ storage is necessary, raising costs
■ workers may be more specialised	■ jobs may be more repetitive
■ unit costs may be lower than jobbing	■ specialist machinery may need to be reset
■ more specialised machinery may be used	■ batches may have to be moved between sections – more costs

Mass/continuous flow

A product is made continuously along a production line. This will often mean the product passes through a large number of specialised operations, usually along a conveyor belt or assembly line system. Products made by a process may also be included under this type of method. Examples include: car production, canning factories, paper manufacturers, breweries and petrol refineries.

Advantages	Disadvantages
■ large output, low unit cost	■ huge cost of machinery
■ little lost production time	■ difficult to change the production line
■ very specialised workers	■ few labour skills/poor worker motivation possible
■ products should be a standard quality	■ products may be too similar
	■ breakdowns cause major problems

Project production

Project production is when a project has been planned that requires the bringing together of a number of skilled people and a wide variety of resources to complete a special product or event. It might be making a film, a TV outside broadcast such as the Cup Final, a rock music festival or even the building of the Millennium Dome at Greenwich. This final method of production helps to show that all methods may be linked together in some ways; and, that it is not always easy to categorise clearly the method of making every product or service.

Manufacturing methods and strategies

PRODUCTION STRATEGIES

Strategies that help a firm innovate and produce quality products efficiently are explained in Units 33 and 34. There is one strategy that needs to be linked into this unit and the four methods of production and that is a very special strategy for stock control.

Just-in-time (JIT) – lean production

JIT production techniques involve the raw materials, parts and components arriving at the factory's assembly line just in time for them to be used in the production process. This is increasingly being used by manufacturing firms as they take this idea from the Japanese and mirror firms like Nissan.

One of the best known examples in Nissan's Sunderland plant is the supply of car seats. A new Nissan Primera takes about three hours to make. As the car shell begins its journey down the production line, the company supplying seats – Ikeda Hoover – is just starting to make the seats for that car. Just under three hours into the production of the car, the seats must be delivered to the right station on the production line, less than 10 minutes before the car arrives for the seats to be fitted.

The big advantage for firms like Nissan is they do not have to store stocks of components such as seats, thus reducing costs. Any faults should be spotted quickly and the firm will not have stockpiled components with similar problems. The companies involved in this strategy must plan and work closely together but any problems in supplying the components could bring the production line to an almost immediate stop. JIT certainly puts pressure on all the companies involved and it is not appropriate for all types of production and all types of parts.

JIT is now seen as part of a larger strategy called lean production. The aim is to produce by using less of all resources such as materials, manpower, time, floorspace and capital. This should raise the productivity of each worker and reduce production costs while improving quality. The end result should be more reliable products, less waste, and substantial marketing advantages for the firm.

Activity

1. Use the information on the production methods to identify clearly the meaning of each method, the advantages and disadvantages, and typical examples.
2. Design a table that you can use to record this information in key notes. If you have access to a computer, design this using an appropriate program and add pictures from the clip art to illustrate the methods.
3. As a class, try to think of any types of product, production processes and stocks which would not be suitable for a strategy of just-in-time.
4. Write up these examples explaining why you believe they would not be suitable for JIT techniques.

Codebreakers

Job production: producing a single, 'one-off' product or service to meet the individual requirements of a customer.

Batch production: the production of a similar or identical good in batches with production stopped to allow for modifications before the next batch is made.

Flow or mass production: the manufacturing of identical goods in large numbers on a continuous production line.

Project production: the bringing together of production methods to make a special one-off project or event.

Just-in-time (JIT): a strategy involving the supply of stocks to the producer just-in-time for their use in the production process.

SUMMARY

Three points to remember:

1. There are four main types of manufacturing methods: job, batch, flow and project.
2. The production of many modern manufactured goods involves a mixture of methods.
3. A special form of stock control for both manufacturing and retailing is the Just-in-Time (JIT) strategy, and this is now part of a wider strategy known as lean production.

Unit 33
Efficiency and innovation

When a firm has started to produce its products, it will wish to operate as efficiently as possible. This will mean trying to produce as many high quality products as possible at the lowest possible cost. There are a number of ways of measuring the firm's efficiency and even more ways for it to improve on its performance. It will need to be efficient in order to compete effectively in the market place. One of the major ways to increase efficiency will involve innovation in new products and production processes.

Philips is one of the world's leading electronics companies making products such as electric shavers, light bulbs, video recorders, televisions and audio equipment. In the 1980s the market for consumer electronic products was increasing at the same time as major innovations were being rapidly created. New firms were entering the industry, particularly from Japan. Competition intensified and many European companies were knocked out of the market. Philips was strong enough to carry on, but by 1990 it was approaching a financial crisis. It took three main actions. Firstly, it targeted efficiency by restructuring the company and by cost cutting. In particular it cut staff by some 45 000 workers. Secondly, it attempted to introduce a need to change in all parts of the company with each section given specific targets to aim for. Finally, it set the principle that the customer had to come first. All of this was brought together in 1995 when Philips introduced its campaign 'Let's make things better', with part of that strategy aiming to make further improvements in productive efficiency.

HOW IS EFFICIENCY MEASURED?

It is probably easier to measure efficiency in a manufacturing firm where the output is an actual good than it is to measure efficiency in a firm providing a service. Some measures may be quite exact while others may require an evaluative judgement. Six possible ways of measuring the efficiency of production are suggested, together with any obvious problems in using the measurement and ways of increasing efficiency. It is unlikely that a firm would only use one way to measure its productive efficiency; rather, it will choose a mixture of measures to suit its product and production process.

Productivity

This involves measuring the quantity of goods produced in a certain period of time. This may be done in a number of ways, such as output per shift, output per person, output per man-hour or output per machine. For example, if 100 tons of coal were mined by 10 workers over 10 hours, the productivity would be 1 ton per man-hour. Measuring efficiency by productivity is very common, especially when a good is produced. Productivity might fall if machines break down or if there are problems with the workforce. Improvements to productivity might result, therefore, from introducing new machinery, from **changing work practices** and from **productivity deals** with the workforce.

Unit costs

This measures the cost of producing a single good or service (a unit). To calculate this, the firm needs to know its total costs from producing a certain quantity of goods. The formula can then be applied:

$$\text{Unit costs} = \frac{\text{Total costs}}{\text{Quantity produced}}$$

For example, if 500 units are produced at a total cost of £10 000, each unit on average has cost £20 to make. This is an important measure of efficiency for most firms since a rise in unit costs will mean falling profits, unless prices are increased. Rising unit costs indicate a fall in a firm's efficiency either because production costs have risen or because the quantity of goods made has fallen. To increase this measure of efficiency a firm must therefore try to increase output, especially if fixed costs are high, and reduce or at least control costs.

Idle resources

Occasionally, a firm may find that some of its resources are not actually working or are not working to their full capacity. For example, a machine may only need to be used for half the shift, or workers may have to wait for the previous section to finish its tasks before they can start their job. This sort of inefficiency may be identified by observation and by *work study methods*. The problems caused by idle resources are higher costs and lower output. Improvements may be achieved by changing work practices, by the greater use of part-time workers, and by more mechanisation.

Stock levels

Unit 32 explained the just-in-time (JIT) system of stock control. Under any system of stock control, a firm needs enough stocks – raw materials, components, semi-finished goods, finished goods – to keep production flowing smoothly and to meet customer demand. Too few stocks and production may stop and sales will be lost. Too many stocks and the firm may find it is left with stock that deteriorates, goes out of fashion and cannot be sold, causing major cash flow problems. A firm will need to monitor the actual levels of stocks and its *stock turnover* constantly. Systems such as JIT may be used by firms, although smaller firms may find they can manage by using observation and their business experience to keep efficient levels of stock.

Product quality

Poor quality products are wasteful, may lead to higher production costs and will often result in lost revenue when sales are lost. All of these indicate that a firm is acting inefficiently. To improve, the firm might need to give workers more and better training; or it might need to introduce more thorough quality control or better quality management systems. These are explained in Unit 34.

Resource management

Measuring and improving efficiency may involve the management of a company in developing whole strategies that link together different sections of the business. Productivity may be low, costs may be high, quality may be poor, sales may be falling and there may be a high turnover of labour. Facing this evidence of inefficient production, a firm may need to consider major re-organisation of the company. It might invest in management training and new ways of organising production, such as *teamworking* or *cell production*. The solutions chosen must always depend on the individual circumstances of each firm, but there is no doubt that inefficient firms quickly find themselves in trouble, operating in an increasingly competitive business world.

THE ROLE OF NEW TECHNOLOGY

New technology in manufacturing

One important way to improve efficiency in manufacturing firms is through innovation. This involves carrying out research and development into new products and new production processes. If a firm believes that these innovations will be commercially successful, it may decide to invest in these new technologies. In manufacturing firms much of the new technology centres around the use

Where are the workers?

of computers. In GCSE Design and Technology courses you may have come across some of the following terms which describe new manufacturing technologies. They include:

- CAM = Computer-aided-manufacturing meaning that computers help to control machinery
- CNC = Computer-numerically-controlled machines which perform very specific tasks
- CIM = Computer-integrated-manufacturing where the whole factory will be linked to and controlled by computers
- CAD = Computer-aided-design where the product is designed on a computer screen, with problems solved before any prototypes have to be made.

New technology in service industries

Again, much of the new technology in service industries centres around the use of computers, although the emphasis is on the role of the computer within information technology. Service industries are making increasing use of IT programs to store, handle, produce, present and retrieve information. This allows firms to reduce their use of paper, while allowing greater and faster communication in most operations.

The benefits of technological change

- New methods of production lead to greater efficiency with higher output and lower unit costs.
- In many cases there are fewer routine, boring jobs so workers should have greater job satisfaction.
- New and improved products ought to result as they are 'found' through research or as new technology allows those that have already been discovered to be commercially produced.
- Higher quality products should be achieved through better production methods and through better quality control methods.
- Better customer service should result; for example, efficient stock control should spot when new stocks have to be ordered.
- Better management of information and data should be achieved through the use of databases, spreadsheets, word processing and desk top publishing packages.

The costs of technological change

- Some new technology may be very expensive to introduce. The firm would need to produce and sell large quantities to make the investment profitable. There would be very high risks involved, therefore, in borrowing the finance to pay for the new technology.
- New technology is developing so rapidly that any new machine bought may become out of date very quickly, well before it wears out.
- The skills of many workers are becoming redundant, leading to unemployment and the need for regular retraining.
- There are many health and safety concerns with some new technology.
- As manufacturing industry appears to become more and more automated, many workers complain of lower job satisfaction, of lower morale, and of feeling dehumanised.

Fewer jobs? Different jobs?

Efficiency and innovation

Handy hints

For the exam, you need to know how firms might be able to measure efficiency and how they could improve it. You need to show that you understand the idea of new technology and innovation, but you must be able to discuss the possible advantages and disadvantages of introducing new technology. Try to adapt your knowledge to the particular case study in the exam paper so that your answers and suggestions are possible for that type of firm making that type of product or service.

Codebreakers

Changing work practices: the introduction of new technology will often mean that the original way of organising workers is out of date. Negotiations between workers and employers may be needed to change the way workers operate so that more efficient methods are introduced.

Productivity deals: any increase in wage rates is linked to an increase in output, so when the extra output is sold it more than pays for the extra wage costs.

Work study methods: these studies look at the way tasks are carried out. An observer might note that some tasks may be done in a different way or in a different order to increase output.

Stock turnover: no organisation wants its stock to be sitting on the shelves for too long. A firm may measure its stock turnover by calculating the average period of time an item is held before it is used or sold.

Teamworking/cell production: this involves a firm using production teams to make part or all of a specific product. The team members are likely to be given a lot of responsibility to make key decisions and to organise themselves. The term 'cell production' is sometimes used because a team will often organise the production layout in a rough circle and will be virtually self-sufficient. Other production cells will be at work in other parts of the factory.

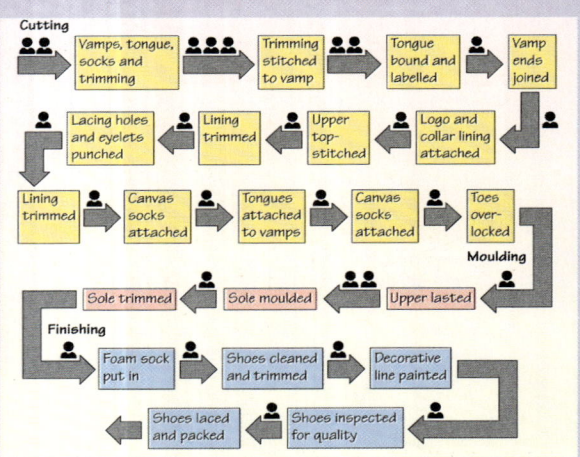

Activity

> In groups, write to firms in your local area asking them:
> - how they produce their products
> - how they measure efficiency in their company
> - how they have tried to improve efficiency in the last couple of years
> - how they try to ensure quality control in their company
> - how they have introduced new technology into the company
> - how they use information technology in the company.

One way to obtain this information is to ask a company representative to come in and talk to the class. Much of the information you collect will help you complete a coursework assignment on the production of goods or the provision of certain services.

Possible types of firms might include:

Supermarkets	DIY stores
Pharmaceutical companies	Garages
Bakeries	Clothing manufacturers

but the list is really endless and you might be quite surprised at what information local firms may be prepared to give you.

SUMMARY

Four points to remember:

1. Efficient production means making best use of all resources so that the highest number of quality items may be produced at least unit cost.

2. There are up to six ways to measure efficiency and individual firms will need to choose the best ways for their type of product and market.

3. Introducing new technology and investing in innovations will have major benefits for a firm's efficiency.

4. New technology may also create costs as well as benefits to the firm, its workers and society.

Unit 34
Quality management

When a firm produces a good, consumer law dictates that goods must be fit for their intended purpose. All goods produced should be of the same quality, so efficient and successful quality control is important. The firm may find some possible conflicts with this need. For some products, like clothes, design and appearance may sometimes be a more important consideration than quality. Other firms may have to concentrate on charging the 'right' price to attract customers rather than putting quality as a priority. All firms, therefore, have a number of decisions to make about how to manage the quality of their output.

In 1979, a group of A-level students visited Proctor and Gamble's Tyneside factory. One of the products being manufactured was Fairy Toilet Soap. There were two production lines using quite simple forms of machinery to press and shape bars of soap. There was virtually no waste because any bars with a defect could be put back in at the start of the process to form part of later output. There were about five workers on one production line and their pay was a mixture of time rate, piece rate and bonuses based on quality. Quality was measured at regular intervals by a quality contoller. Sample bars were extracted and checked for weight, blemishes, for the design of the baby logo, for shape and for overall smoothness. The workers could check part of the quality themselves simply by carrying out their own visual checks. Any poor quality bars could go back in to be restarted. As the A-level students commented, the quality control was quite simple and yet effective. More complicated products will involve much more complex quality control systems but this example shows that it is not always necessary to introduce complexity to be effective.

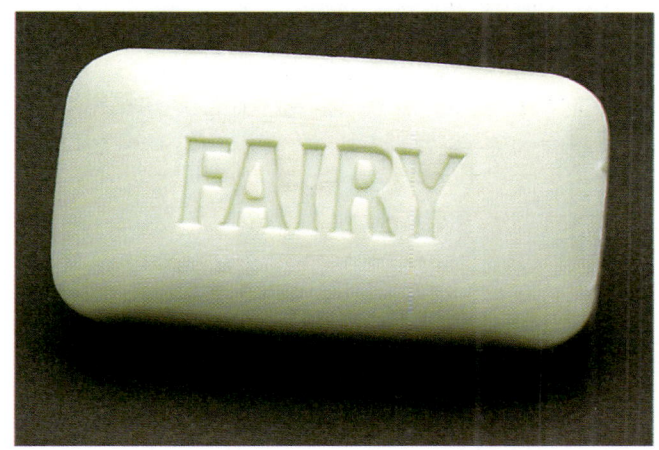

QUALITY MANAGEMENT DECISIONS

Every business has to decide what level of quality to aim for, whether it is producing a good or providing a service, and how to achieve this. There are five key decisions for a firm to take about its quality management:

- What is the minimum level of quality to meet the requirements of the law?
- What is the minimum level of quality acceptable to customers?
- What is the firm's desired level of quality? How much higher should it be than the minimum for the law and the consumer?
- Who in the business will be responsible for maintaining quality?
- How will the firm be organised to ensure quality at least cost?

TRADITIONAL METHODS OF QUALITY CONTROL

Imperfect products are spotted and extracted

Quality management **145**

In many ways the example of Fairy Soap is a typical example of a traditional method of **quality control**. Quality control checks are made on completed products by taking samples at regular intervals. The specialist quality controller will be responsible for checking the product against a list of measures. The main problem with this system is there could be a lot of waste if a fault was found in a finished item. The fault could be present in much of the output, and it is not always possible to put the fault right. Even in the case of Fairy Soap, there is waste in the sense that the bars have to be produced again, costing both time and money.

An extension of this system would involve checking a sample of raw materials or parts before they are used in the production process. Quality controllers might also carry out checks at each stage of the production process before the product was finished, as well as testing a sample of finished products. Sometimes, this type of system is referred to as **quality assurance** with teams of the work-force, rather than inspectors being responsible for quality.

Another A-level group of students witnessed this at what was Glaxo's factory at Cambois in Northumberland. This plant manufactured a basic form of penicillin that was then sent off to other plants for processing into various forms of medicines. Penicillin is grown from a very carefully controlled form of mould by feeding it with sugar, syrup and other key ingredients. Each of these ingredients is carefully tested for purity and as the penicillin grows and is transferred to bigger pots and kilns, it too is tested. A fault shown by the quality controls at any stage would mean the whole batch being dumped. For this type of product, the more traditional method of quality control would seem to be quite appropriate although Synpac, who has bought this plant, may now operate a different quality control system.

MODERN METHODS OF QUALITY CONTROL

Statistical process control

The Japanese first introduced statistical process control. It simply requires each machine operator to check at regular intervals during the shift that the machine is working correctly. Some final checks may still be made on the finished products but the machine checks should have eliminated much of the possible waste, and fewer specialist quality controllers need to be employed.

An operative checks his machine for correct settings

Total quality management

This system was also created in Japan, in the motor vehicle industry, although it is now copied and adapted throughout the world for all sorts of firms and products. **Total quality management** is likely to include a number of features:

- it involves every part of the organisation
- quality is the responsibility of every department
- quality is the responsibility of every worker
- machines should be checked regularly
- teams of workers should discuss how to improve quality.

Activity

Robertson and Tonge Ltd manufactures seat belts for use in the motor vehicle industry. It supplies three leading car assemblers who demand the highest quality standards in the seat belts. Robertson and Tonge has therefore made quality its number one priority.

1 Why will the car assemblers demand the highest quality standards in the seat belts?

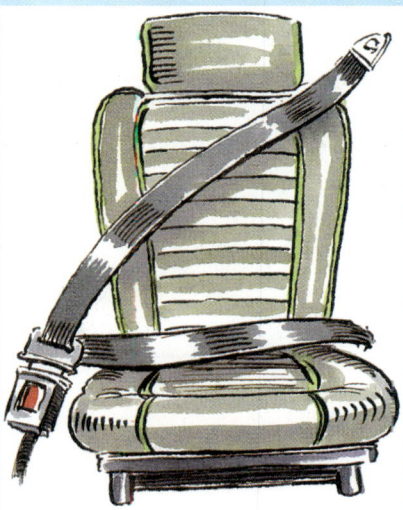

2 Explain how Robertson and Tonge Ltd could try to achieve high quality standards when producing its seats belts.

3 What problems might Robertson and Tonge experience if it does not achieve high quality seat belts?

4 Why might firms who manufacture furniture decide not to make high quality products their number one priority?

Codebreakers

Quality control: inspectors check the final products for defects. Those products that do not meet the set standard will be rejected, possibly resulting in a lot of waste.

Quality assurance: quality is checked both during and at the end of production. Teams of production workers are likely to be responsible for quality reaching the set standards.

Total quality management: everyone in the workplace is encouraged to be concerned about quality in everything they do. Customer satisfaction is the major aim.

- raw materials and components are checked for quality as they arrive although suppliers are expected to meet rigid quality standards
- the needs of the customers should be checked to see if they are satisfied: if they are not, the firm would expect to make changes.

The main idea of this system is that 'quality is built into the products' rather than being checked for once production has taken place.

Kaizen

Another Japanese concept – this time meaning literally 'continuous improvement'. It is really an extension of the total quality system because the idea is that the company and its workers are continuously trying to make the product and the production process better. Everyone in the company is encouraged to participate, some having a direct involvement while others play an indirect role. When it works at its best, the Kaizen principle means that potential sources of concern are dealt with before they become an actual problem.

SUMMARY

Three points to remember:

1. All firms by law must make sure that their products are fit for the purpose they were intended for and they must work when they are purchased.
2. Some firms may decide to provide goods that more than meet the minimum requirements.
3. Firms may use systems of quality control, quality assurance or total quality management to achieve the desired standards.

Unit 35
Locating the business

When a firm is planning to start up a new operation, one of the most important decisions it has to take is where to locate its business. Whether it is manufacturing a product or providing a service, and whether it is small, medium or large, a firm must consider a number of factors. Ideally, the location will keep costs to a minimum while helping to generate maximum revenue. Sometimes, decisions about location will be influenced by outside bodies such as the government, European Union, development agencies and local councils.

British Alcan has been smelting aluminium at Lynemouth in Northumberland since March 1972. It chose Lynemouth for a number of reasons. There was a suitable area of land available next to the coast. This enabled both the smelter and its own power station to be built. Smelting aluminium takes vast amounts of electricity and Alcan calculated that it was cheaper to provide this from its own power station using coal from the nearby Ellington Colliery, plus the North Sea could be used to cool the generators. Alumina could be imported to a port at Blyth just eight miles away and transported by rail to Lynemouth. Over 1 000 workers were needed and many of these came from the declining mining industry in Northumberland. A new road link was being planned, which meant that the aluminium ingots could be easily transported to other plants to manufacture hundreds of different aluminium products. Finally, Alcan received government grants for 25% of the investment costs because Lynemouth was in a region of high unemployment and was classed as an area requiring assistance to attract new industry and jobs.

WHAT FACTORS SHOULD A FIRM CONSIDER BEFORE DECIDING THE BEST LOCATION?

There are a wide variety of factors that ought to be considered. For some firms, only a few factors will be really important. Other firms may have to consider and balance a complex mixture of location factors. Possible location factors include:

Geographical factors

- Water supplies – this will be very important for firms using large quantities of water like paper manufacture, pharmaceuticals and electricity generation.

- Prevailing wind – for some firms that create smell, smoke or dust during the production process, it might be important for the usual wind direction to take these pollutants away from areas of population.

- Waste disposal – some firms create a good deal of waste during production. Various laws strictly control how

148 Locating the business

this should be disposed off safely. Firms like Alcan need a large area of suitable land for the 'ash lagoons' to hold the waste created in the production process.

- Safety – some firms make products that are dangerous or use production processes that are dangerous to the public. These firms will need a site well away from people's homes. Typical examples ought to include fireworks factories, nuclear plants, chemical processors and petrol refineries.

Cost of the site

- How long will the site be needed?
- Should it be rented or purchased?
- Will the site need to be drained and levelled?
- Is it a green field site, disused or on a well-developed industrial park?
- What is the level of rates payable to the local council?
- If there are extra risks with the site, will this raise the insurance premiums?
- Is there room for expansion?

Infrastructure

- Are there adequate transport systems for the site? – road, rail, air, river/canal, ports?
- Are there adequate communication systems, especially telephone facilities?
- Are there ancillary firms to help production take place? For example, are there firms to deal with waste disposal, to repair machinery, to transport the finished product and to supply computer services?

Labour

- Is there an adequate supply of workers?
- Do those potential workers have the right skills?
- Are there training facilities nearby if needed?
- Will the wage rates the firm feels able to pay attract enough workers? Firms may find they can pay lower wage rates in areas of high unemployment.

The nature of the product

- Will the product lose bulk or weight as it goes through the production process? For example, it takes four tons of bauxite to make two tons of alumina to make one ton of aluminium. To keep down transport costs, Alcan locates near the port of Blyth for the import of the alumina. Firms in similar situations should locate as near to the supply of raw material as possible.
- Will the product gain bulk or weight during the production process? If so, as with car production, transport costs may be kept down by locating near to the large centres of population that are going to buy the products in largest quantities.

Locating the business

Historical factors

- In the past, sources of power supplies were a very important consideration when locating a business. The early woollen mills located next to rivers so that water power could drive the early looms. Steam power generated by coal soon took over, thus leading to so many industries locating in the coalfield areas of the country. The creation of electricity and North Sea gas together with a national grid system for distribution has given most firms more flexibility when considering power supplies.

- For some industries, the original reasons for location have disappeared. For example, the centre of the pottery industry is in the Midlands but the reserves of China clay were exhausted long ago. The area now has other benefits that outweigh the extra costs of transporting in China clay. New firms will be attracted by the skilled labour force, by the firms experienced in dealing with the needs of the industry, and by the tradition of the area.

- Sometimes a firm locates at a particular site by chance. For example, many of our oldest firms became established in an area because the original owner happened to live there.

Did you know? Some firms spend a very long time researching the best possible site for their business operation. They may approach different areas of the country to see who can offer the best financial package of external help. Other firms, however, draw up a list of key factors and will look at only a short list of five or six sites. They may be quite indifferent as to where they locate. For some, being near to Head Office is more important than any other factor.

EXTERNAL HELP

Throughout the 20th century, there have been some regions in the UK with higher rates of unemployment than others. Within these problem regions there have often been small areas with very high rates of unemployment. It was not until after 1945 that governments began to use measures to help reduce unemployment in the problem regions. Most of these measures aimed to persuade firms to locate in the regions of high unemployment. Such regions were called **assisted areas** because financial assistance was available to many firms, either expanding in or relocating to those areas. Over the last 50 years, the types, amount and sources of assistance have changed and so have the regions identified as having unemployment problems.

The county of Northumberland provides an excellent case study of virtually every type of assistance available to firms, much of it involving the location of 'new' business projects. This map shows Northumberland's assisted areas.

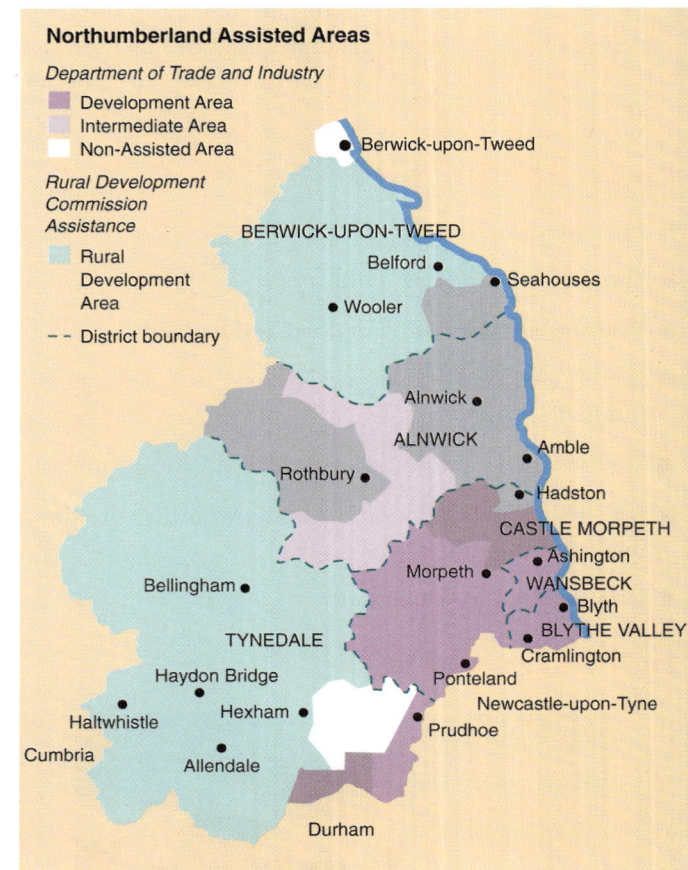

The major forms of assistance include:

Advice and information

- Northumberland County Council's Business Development Unit provides funding advice and practical assistance in assembling business plans for firms proposing to create or safeguard jobs.

- District Councils have economic development officers to give advice on local development issues and opportunities.

- Northumberland Training and Enterprise Council (NTEC) has subsidiary organisations giving information and counselling support to all types of business.

- The Rural Development Commission (RDC) supports firms with between 5 and 50 employees in manufacturing, service, tourism and some retailing. Support includes training courses on both rural skills and business skills.

150 Locating the business

Financial assistance

- British Coal Enterprises Ltd provides loans or investment capital for job-creation projects. The support is limited to 25% of the total funding package, or £5 000 per job created over three years.

- The Department of Trade and Industry (DTI) can provide various forms of financial help for firms in the assisted areas. Regional Selective Assistance for manufacturing and some service businesses of any size is available for investment projects. The level of grant is the minimum for the project to proceed and is linked to the number of jobs created or safeguarded. Regional Enterprise Grants may also be available in some parts of the assisted areas for small firms undertaking investment projects or innovation projects. There is special support for firms with up to 250 employees developing new products.

- NTEC can provide a mixture of grants and interest free loans to new firms.

- The RDC can offer top-up loans at fixed interest rates for projects in rural communities.

- There are a number of other organisations both in the private and public sectors who offer loans and grants. These include:
  - the commercial banks such as Barclays
  - Northern Enterprise Ltd
  - Northern Venture Managers Ltd
  - The Prince's Youth Trust
  - The Royal British Legion
  - some of the District Councils.

Premises

Northumberland's Business Development Unit keeps a register of all advance factories and industrial sites in the county. There are a wide variety of units available for purchase or on lease. These are provided by organisations in both the public and private sector including the County Council, the District Councils, English Partnerships and the RDC.

The availablility of suitable premises at the right cost will be a major influence on location

Locating the business 151

Business training

This form of help is often forgotten about and yet is very important. Again there are a number of organisations providing a wide range of training. Providers include NTEC, The Durham University Business School, The University of Northumbria at Newcastle, and Entrust.

Help from the European Union

Parts of Northumberland are able to receive financial assistance from the EU. Details of this help are included in Unit 47.

> **Activity**
>
> ▷ The above details give some of the major forms of help to firms operating and locating in just one county of England. The help in the area where you live may be similar but may be either more limited or more extensive. There may be several different sources of help. With your teacher's guidance, find out what help is available in your local area. Start by making a list of the organisations mentioned above and use the Yellow Pages to see which ones operate in your area. Plan how to contact some of the organisations. Decide how to record the information. Those of you familiar with computers may use a database to record your findings.

OTHER FORMS OF HELP

There is one other way in which the government tries to influence the location of industry, that is not available in Northumberland. This is through the creation of *Enterprise Zones*. These are quite small areas which often have pockets of particularly high unemployment. The area may have suffered from the decline of a major industry and it may have a number of derelict business properties or industrial estates. The idea is to make them like 'mini-Hong Kongs': in other words to encourage a lot of new enterprise so that as the area becomes more prosperous, the benefits spread out to surrounding neighbourhoods. Over 24 such zones have been created over many years. The major help that is available is:

- rates are free for up to 10 years
- there are tax advantages to locating in a zone
- there are easier planning controls on new premises so it should be quicker to build and get operating
- there may be other financial help available such as that indicated in the assisted areas in Northumberland, but this depends where the zone is located.

> **Activity**
>
> ▷ **1** For each of the following types of business, make a list of the possible factors that each one should take into account when deciding on the location of a new business. To help you, identify any similar businesses in your area and decide why they located where they did:
> - a supermarket
> - a DIY superstore or DIY and Garden Centre
> - a garage selling and servicing cars and small vans
> - a manufacturer of tinned foodstuffs.
>
> ▷▷ **2** In each case, decide which of the factors would be most important and which would be the least important by putting them in order of priority.
>
> ▷▷ **3** Give reasons for your order of priority.

SUMMARY

Four points to remember:

1. When any firm is deciding where to locate, there are many factors to consider.
2. Most firms will try to find a site that keeps costs to a minimum while helping to maximise sales revenue.
3. Some firms may be equally happy to locate at a number of sites or anywhere near the Head Office.
4. External help such as financial assistance, information, advice and training may persuade a firm to choose one site over another.

> **Codebreakers**
>
> **Infrastructure:** transport and communication networks.
>
> **Assisted areas:** large areas or parts of regions that have high unemployment and need help to keep and attract new business and industry. Created by the government.
>
> **Enterprise Zone:** a smaller area, usually with high unemployment, that is given special help to attract new business and industry to locate there. Created by the government.

Unit 36
Analysing the market

When a firm has a product or service that is new, it is likely that it will only appeal to a certain type of consumer. It may be a particular age group, a particular gender or people earning a particular level of income. The firm will have to decide which group of consumers is their **target market**.

This means that they need to divide the market up into separate parts according to age, gender, income etc. These parts are called sections or **market segments**.

An example of this is the market for magazines. Britain has a large number of magazines and newspapers – just a few of the dozens on offer are shown in the photograph. Some are aimed at women, some at men, some at young people, some at teenagers, some at particular professions. The market has been divided and sub-divided many times in order to cater for every interest. A firm about to launch a new national magazine would first have to analyse the existing market for magazines to see whether there was a space in the market for a new title and to find out which segment it should target its advertising at.

WHAT DO WE MEAN WHEN WE TALK ABOUT ANALYSING THE MARKET?

Analysing the market is breaking down the whole demand for a good or service by splitting it into parts. These parts are called market segments. Consumers will usually appear in more than one market segment. You could, for example, be a boy (gender), aged 16 (age) who plays the guitar (hobby or pastime). Market analysis concerned with the supply of a good or service can also be used. (*See the section on SWOT analysis in Unit 38.*)

This means that, to a firm, analysing the market is breaking the market down into parts in order to:

- target advertising and promotion
- make the good or service more attractive to a particular segment
- maximise sales by targeting different goods or services, or variations of them, on different market segments.

A BREAK DOWN

The market for newspapers and magazines is a good example of how a market is segmented. The whole market is huge and no publisher would attempt to reach it all. The circulation of national daily newspapers alone is around 14 million with the two largest, the tabloids *The Sun* and *The Mirror* claiming almost six million readers. The Writers' Handbook lists over 600 magazines ranging from *Abraxas* and *Accountancy Age* to *Xenos*, *Yachting World* and *Zene* and covering every subject imaginable – pets, hobbies, sports, interests, professions, music, entertainment and so on. By

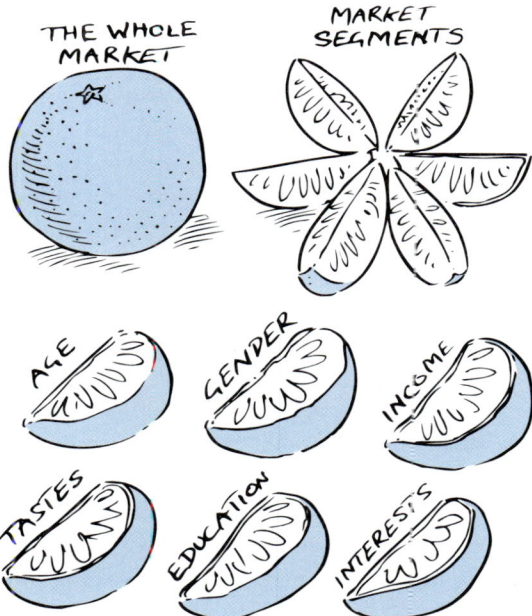

Analysing the market   153

looking at particular magazines we can see how this huge market is segmented by publishing firms into target markets defined by age, gender, race and religion, geography, interests and hobbies, education and income.

> **Handy hints**
>
> When you are answering an examination question it is always a good idea to use your own experience and to use examples to explain your points. For instance, think of the magazines that you or your friends and family actually read and use them to explain how a market can be analysed. Think of the advertisements that are in them: who are they aimed at? Which segments? It is always a good idea to use examples.

> **Activity**
>
> ▸ Think of the magazines that you might find in a doctor's waiting room – who do you think would buy these magazines? Think of the magazines that come into your house. Who are they are aimed at?

Age

Just 17, My Guy, The People's Friend, The Oldie – these are typical of magazines aimed at particular age groups. Look at the way in which these publications are described:

Just 17 – news, articles and fiction of interest to girls aged 12 to 18

My Guy – weekly teen magazine for boys and girls

The People's Friend – a good read for all the family

The Oldie – monthly humorous magazine for the older person.

In marketing terms there are various well-defined age groups. Publishers will have a definite age range that they are targeting. *Just 17* is, of course, aimed at as low as 12 year olds, the magazine *19* is aimed at 17 to 22 year olds.

Age groups

Some age groups are more important than others. These are the groups where there is a high level of **disposable income**:

- Between the ages of 25 and 45 is when many people reach their maximum earnings. It is also the age group that is getting married, bringing up families, taking holidays, buying convenience foods, buying cars, taking out pension plans and buying **consumer durables** such as fridges, video recorders, microwave ovens and washing machines.

> **Handy hints**
>
> In coursework, always use the correct, technical terms where you can and show that you know what they mean. For example, the first time you refer to 'disposable income' in your coursework, explain that this means the amount of income that a person has left to spend after normal outgoings have been spent and bills have been paid. From then on, you can use the technical term. There are specific marks for your correct use and understanding of terms.

- Between the ages of 45 to 55 is another important segment. Children may have grown up and left home and there is likely to be more money available to spend. Couples may well finish paying for major purchases such as the mortgage on a house or the finance on a car. This age group has different tastes and is likely to spend more on exotic holidays, restaurant meals and other luxury goods.

- After 55, people tend to be either retired or looking towards retirement. The amount of money available to spend may well fall and patterns of demand will again alter. Britain currently has an ageing population, which means that more and more people are in the older age groups. Many more goods and services are now targeted at these segments as they have grown in size.

Gender

Activity

1. Read the paragraph about marketing to different genders. Choose a different market to magazines, perhaps cars, or electrical goods. Write two advertising slogans which you could use to advertise in the market that you have chosen.
   a) to women
   b) to men
   c) to both.

2. Describe why you think the advertising would change if you were aiming at a male or female market.

Magazines like *Woman*, *Woman's Realm*, *Take a Break* and *Mizz* are aimed at women or girls. Men's general interest magazines are not very common, with the market being further segmented by sports, hobbies and pastimes. Women's magazines will have a different content depending on which age group they are aimed at. Many teenage magazines are aimed at girls and concentrate on music, love stories, fashion and boyfriends. For the older age groups there are competitions, recipes, 'true-life' stories, short stories and feature articles on the home and garden. Remember that everybody is in more than one market segment. For example, *Mizz* is a fortnightly magazine 'aimed at the 14 to 19 year old girl' – targeted by both age and gender.

Race and religion

Did you know?

Britain has around 30 newspapers that are national to England, Scotland and Wales. They fall into two main groups. Broadsheets are 'big' papers such as *The Guardian*, *The Independent*, and *The Telegraph*. These are aimed at higher income groups who have had higher education (Socio-economic groups A, B, C1). Tabloids are the easier to handle 'small' papers. These fall into two groups: papers such as *The Sun* and *The Mirror* are aimed at socio-economic groups C2, D and E while papers such as *The Mail* and *The Express* are aimed at C1 and C2.

Analysing the market

Some goods and services are aimed at particular racial or religious segments of the market. Specially prepared food such as Halal and Kosher meat are an obvious example. Magazines such as *Asian Times, Jewish Chronicle* and *The Voice* are aimed at Asian, Jewish and Afro-Caribbean communities.

Geography

Markets can be segmented by geographical area. Some tastes are local to particular areas – pie and peas in Yorkshire, jellied eels in London, haggis in Scotland! If the market segment that a firm wishes to target is a geographical one, then in Britain there is also the opportunity for firms to use regional television – YTV, for example, covers the Yorkshire and Humberside area, Granada Television is based in Manchester and the North West. There are also a large number of regional and local newspapers, – *The Yorkshire Post*, *The Liverpool Echo* and *The London Evening Standard* are examples. Geographical differences can be very important to some firms. Do

Did you know? Postcodes are extremely important to businesses who want to target a particular geographical area. The first two letters of the postcode are your town (NG is Nottingham, HD is Huddersfield, MK is Milton Keynes), the number then gives the area within the town, the following numbers and letters are your area and your street. Businesses can therefore be very accurate if they want to target an area.

Codebreakers

Target market: the group of consumers that a firm aims its product or service at.

Market segments: the separate parts into which the whole market is divided.

Disposable income: the money left for spending after essential spending, bills and so on have been paid.

Consumer durable: a good that can be used again and again without being 'used up', such as a vacuum cleaner, an electric drill, a car.

Socio-economic group: the groups into which the population is split according to the occupation of the head of the household.

Londoners buy more mobile phones? Do people in the North spend more on outdoor clothes? Many newspapers publish different editions for different areas of the country. To other firms, regional differences are unimportant – chocolate, for example, is likely to be eaten everywhere.

Interests and hobbies

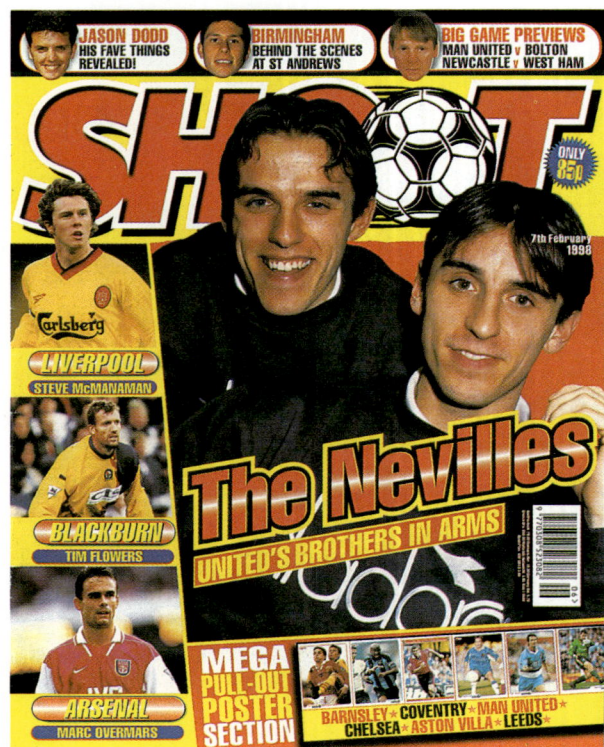

A market segment may be based on a particular hobby or pastime. *Horse and Hound*, *What Car*, *Shoot* and *Garden News* are examples. Again, remember that everyone is in more than one market segment. *Shoot*, for example, is aimed at 10 to 15 year olds (age) interested in soccer (interest).

156 Analysing the market

Activity

Using a database package to show how the market for magazines is segmented:

1. Create at least five appropriate fields, for example: title of magazine, cover price, age targeted, gender targeted, socio-economic group targeted.
2. Enter the data for at least 10 magazines. Your first entry might look like this:

Title	Price	Age	Gender	Group
Top of the Pops	£1.35	10 to 15	Girls	BC1C2

3. Save and print out the file.
4. Search the database for magazines aimed at your age group.
5. Delete the other records.
6. Add details for one more magazine of special interest to you.
7. Add a field, for example, *typical advertisements* and enter the data.
8. Save and print the amended database

This exercise partially fulfils the requirement of the Database Unit of the NEAB Certificate of Achievement in IT.

Socio-economic groups

These are very important market segments used by both the government and by firms. Socio-economic groups split the market up into parts based on the occupation and income of a person. The level of education that a person has had will also be used. People are put into five classes or groups!

- Class 1, Group A are professional people such as judges, doctors and top civil servants
- Class 2, Group B are people in management, technical and executive jobs and includes bank managers, teachers, company directors, solicitors, accountants
- Class 3 is usually split into two groups -
  – Group C1 are people in supervisory and clerical (non manual) jobs such as sales assistants, filing clerks and secretaries
  – Group C2 are skilled manual workers such as carpenters, plumbers and electricians
- Class 4, Group D are semi-skilled manual workers such as assembly line workers, packers and fitters
- Class 5, Group E are unskilled manual workers, the unemployed and other low income groups. This includes people such as single parents, state pensioners and those carrying out unskilled work such as cleaning.

Advertisements

Because magazines target particular segments, firms can use them to make sure that their advertisements reach their target market. Just by looking at the advertisements in a magazine, you can work out which sector of the population the magazine is aimed at. Is it advertising make-up, or fashion items, or CDs and bands, or holidays, or cola, or adventure parks or rocking chairs? Are the advertisements for expensive goods and services or relatively cheap ones? It is extremely important that firms know which newspapers or magazines to advertise in, otherwise they could be wasting a lot of money on advertisements that are not reaching their target market.

Activity

You are the marketing manager for a chocolate manufacturer that is planning a 'hearts and flowers' promotion for Valentine's Day. This consists of giving away a red rose with every box of luxury chocolates bought.

1. Which market segments would you target? Explain why.
2. How would your choice of market segment affect the price you charged?
3. Decide in what ways you could alter the promotion in order to appeal to a larger market segment.
4. Manufacturers do not always try to sell to as wide a segment as possible. Explain why you think this is the case.

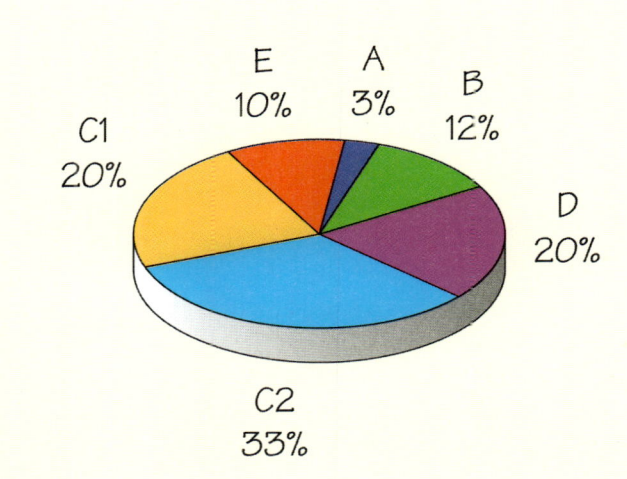

Percentage of the UK population in each socio-economic group

E 10%, A 3%, B 12%, C1 20%, D 20%, C2 33%

Analysing the market

Niche markets

You can see that markets can get more and more specialised as they become more and more segmented. Very small, specialist markets are called 'niche markets' (a niche is a small hole or cranny). An example of a niche market could be a firm supplying the equipment for a sport that not many people play. Octopush, for example, is a version of hockey played underwater, obviously needing specialised equipment. Customising cars to individual customers' requirements is another example. In this case the market segment has been reduced to a niche of one – an individual's choices.

Activity

Tim Hutchings paints traditional designs on canal barges. He is based at a boatyard in Chester.

He operates a scale of charges ranging from the painting of entire 70 foot (21 metre) barges, to the painting of individual boat names. A barge owner has come to ask Tim to design a particular style of lettering for her barge and to paint the name in this lettering.

> Explain what type of market Tim is operating in and why this type of market has become more important in recent years.

Activity

> **1** What would you really like to see on sale in the shops that isn't already there? A solar powered personal stereo? Self-tying shoelaces? Clothes that never need washing? Use one of these ideas or one of your own and show which market segment or segments you would target it at and why.

> **2** Describe whether you think it would be a success and why.

SUMMARY

Six points to remember:

1. Businesses break down the total market into separate parts.
2. The separate parts are called market segments.
3. The main segments are age, gender and socio-economic group.
4. Socio-economic groups break the population down by occupation and income.
5. Businesses target advertising and marketing at particular segments.
6. Niche markets are even smaller, specialised sections of market segments.

Unit 37
Researching the market

When a firm decides that it has a new product that can be sold, or an improvement on an old one, it not only looks at the market segment that can be targeted but also at its own position in the market and at the possible reactions of the consumers that it intends to target. There are three sources for this information:

1 The firm's own sales data, taken from till information.
2 Research aimed at the consumer – market research.
3 The firm's own analysis of where it stands in the market – a SWOT analysis.

An example of this is the new Oasis holiday village in the English Lake District. This is based on the concept of a traffic free holiday that is unaffected by the weather as there is always access to a central, 'sub tropical swimming paradise' in a covered dome. The concept was first introduced to the UK by Center Parcs, a Dutch firm which now operates three of these self-catering holiday centres. Oasis has placed its holiday centre much further to the North of the country than any of its competitors and in a recognised holiday area. To do this it must have collected enough information to be confident that the project would be a success.

WHAT IS RESEARCHING THE MARKET?

Researching the market is finding out as much information about your market as you can, from as many sources as possible.

This means that, to a firm, researching the market is:
- collecting information from its own records
- collecting information about competitor firms
- collecting information about the market in general
- collecting information about consumers
- bringing all this information together in order to make marketing decisions.

Market research

Market research is the collection of information from customers and potential customers and about customers and potential customers. It involves collecting both secondary data and primary data – material that has already been published and new, original material and information. The information that businesses need to collect includes:

- who will buy their product or service
- what will they be prepared to pay for it
- where is it best to sell it
- when can they best be persuaded to buy it
- what advertising will be most effective.

Desk research

Some research will already have been done and there will be no point in repeating it. Also, there will be published statistics and information collected for other purposes. It is called desk research because it is information that can be collected whilst sitting at a desk! Because it has already been collected by someone else it is also known as secondary data. The information may be held in published materials – books, magazines, newspapers, reports from the government, from business groups, companies, consumer groups, trade groups and local councils. It may be held as written material – books, papers, microfiche – or, increasingly, electronically on CD-ROMs.

There is now a huge source of secondary information on the Internet, much of which is freely available. Companies and organisations post information about themselves as do their rivals and competitors.

Internal factors

A firm has a great deal of information about itself on which it can draw. Some of it is published and measurable and some is unpublished and not really possible to measure.

Look at the half year profit and loss account for a major supermarket below. It shows turnover, staff costs, income, profit, earnings per share and dividends amongst other things and compares these with the two previous time periods. From its full accounts it has information such as profit ratios, turnover ratios, return on capital invested and so forth. This information is not only useful to Morrisons but also extremely useful to their competitor supermarkets.

Consolidated profit and loss account
half year ended 4 August 1996

	26 weeks ended 4 August 1996	26 weeks ended 30 July 1995	53 weeks ended 4 February 1996
	£m	£m	£m
Turnover	1,092.8	999.7	2,099.4
Change in stocks	(22.5)	(14.9)	0.5
Other operating income	7.6	5.5	11.7
	1,077.9	990.3	2,111.6
Raw materials and consumables	843.7	779.5	1,641.8
Staff costs	108.3	97.7	208.4
Depreciation of tangible fixed assets	22.5	19.9	41.7
Other operating charges	48.6	43.5	93.5
Operating profit	54.8	49.7	126.2
Loss on disposal of land and buildings	–	(0.1)	(0.7)
Net interest receivable	0.4	1.5	1.6
Profit before taxation	55.2	51.1	127.1
Taxation	21.0	19.0	47.9
Profit after taxation	34.2	32.1	79.2
Minority interest	(0.1)	–	–
Profit for the financial period	34.1	32.1	79.2
Non-equity dividends	0.7	0.8	1.6
Profit attributable to ordinary shareholders	33.4	31.3	77.6
Equity dividends	2.4	2.0	10.3
Profit retained	31.0	29.3	67.3
Earnings per share	4.52p	4.30p	10.67p
Fully diluted earnings per share	4.34p	4.09p	10.09p
Dividend per ordinary share	0.325p	0.275p	1.40p

Did you know? In the dispute between two protesters and the giant McDonald's Corporation which led to a three year court case (known as the McLibel case), all the details of the case were published on the Internet. This provided both McDonald's customers and competitors with an enormous amount of information about the firm.

Handy hints Firms' published accounts can be extremely useful when carrying out coursework. The information that the Annual Report and Accounts contains can be used in many ways. Publicly quoted companies will provide Annual Reports and Accounts free of charge. Many also produce a student pack specifically aimed at coursework.

Businesses can thus compare themselves with other firms' results and published figures and with their own previous years' performances. Even firms who do not have rivals with published accounts will be able to at least estimate how well competitors are doing and how well they themselves are doing in comparison. Center Parcs is a limited company (*see Unit 3*) and thus has to publish its accounts. Oasis will have gained much useful information from these.

Firms are constantly collecting current, up-to-date information on sales, returns, stock movement and so on. Most of this information is collected at the **'point of sale'**, a process that is made a lot easier with the new technology and bar code scanners. One major supermarket chain has introduced a system where shoppers can scan their shopping as they place it in a trolley in order to make the check-out process even more efficient. This also provides the supermarket with further information about customers and their purchases.

> **Did you know?**
> Bar codes are one of the ways a firm uses to trace its stock and to see what is selling well, which promotions have been successful and so on. The bar code contains the product name. When the product is scanned electronic contact is made with the central computer which contains current prices and special offers. This information is sent to the till so that the customer can be charged and a receipt printed. At the same time, the central computer updates its own stock records and, in the most advanced systems, will call stock up from a warehouse or order new stock when necessary.

Census information

One of the most important sources of secondary data is the Census. Every 10 years, on the year ending in '01 (1971, 1981, 1991 – next in 2001) the government hold a National Census of Population. This not only counts the population, it also collects a vast quantity of information about family size and structure, shopping habits, incomes, spending patterns and so on. There is a whole government office that collects and publishes this information. It is called the Office of Population Census and Surveys. (OPCS). When you are looking at secondary data, you will often see 'Source – OPCS' which shows that the information was collected through the Census. The information is highly accurate as it includes everyone who lives in Britain; it is against the law not to fill out the Census return.

> **Handy hints**
> Much research has already been carried out by the government. The Central Statistical Office is the government agency responsible for the collection of a wide range of official statistics for use by government, business and education. Many national and regional statistics are published each year, each quarter and each month. Some of these could be of great help with coursework tasks. The CSO will provide a guide to available products. They may be contacted on 0171 270 6081.

Problems with desk research

There may be problems with the collection and use of secondary data, for example:

- it may be difficult to find exactly the information that you need
- the data may not be accurate or complete
- information may well be out of date (this year's company report actually refers to last year's trading). Census information can take several years to reach publication because there is such a lot of it
- it may be expensive
- it may be in a format that is difficult to analyse.

Field research

The information obtained from secondary sources may, in many cases, be enough to enable firms to make a decision. Often, however, it is necessary for them to carry out 'field research'. This means information that is collected 'in the field' (not amongst the sheep and cows but by contacting consumers directly). Field research is used to gather primary data. Successful field research involves the business in a scientific approach to the collection and presentation of information. There are specialist firms that can be employed by companies to carry out field research.

The business must decide:

- what information it needs to find out
- which people it needs to ask, and how many
- how it wants to ask the questions
- how it wants to present the information.

What information?

The question 'Who is going to buy this and at what price?' may seem obvious, but much research can go to waste if firms are not certain of the information they want or if they ask the wrong groups of people. Research carried out on a weekday afternoon in a town centre to find out if a new teenage magazine would be a success is likely to be of little use. The potential market for the magazine – teenagers – will mostly be at school or college. This is a case of asking the right question but of the wrong people. Conducting a survey at a football match to ask 'Do you like sport?' will give a different result to asking the same question in a supermarket – asking the wrong question of the right people. Questions need to be carefully phrased and carefully targeted.

Who do we ask?

Businesses will try to target a particular market segment (*see Unit 36*). That is, they will try to aim their product or service at a defined section of the market, chosen by age, income, education, gender and so forth. Surveys or questionnaires can be targeted in a number of ways. Existing customers can be targeted by the use of guarantee cards. An example is shown here.

SoftwareEssentials

WARRANTY REGISTRATION CARD

To claim preferential service, complete and return this registration card now. The benefits of ***Software*Essentials** Extended Customer Service are available for one year from the date of purchase and commence when we receive this completed registration card.

Name Mr/Mrs/Miss/Ms ________

Comany (if applicable) ________

Address ________

Postcode ________ Telephone ________

Fax ________ Email ________

Product ________ Retailer ________

Serial No ________ Address ________

Purchase date ________

Please take a few moments answering these questions: your cooperation will help us give a better service.

How did you discover this product?
❑ Advertisement ❑ Magazine/newspaper article ❑ At an exhibition ❑ At the retailer

Please name the computer magazine you read most ________

What was the main purpose for which you bought this product?
❑ Games ❑ Music ❑ School ❑ College use ❑ Specialist training ❑ Business/presentations
❑ Computer product development ❑ Other ________

Thankyou for choosing ***Software*Essentials**

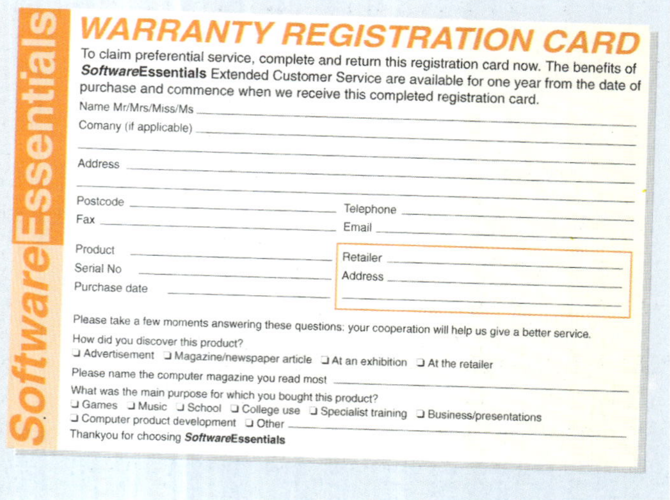

Guarantees or warranties are used for much more than providing a guarantee against faulty workmanship or break down. They are used to collect information about the type of customer buying the product, where they heard about the product (this gives feedback on the effectiveness of advertising) and who sold it to them.

Other information such as telephone number and date of birth may also be asked for. Firms may wish to contact you on or near your birthday when you reach a certain age or may telephone to try to sell you goods or services. (Tele-sales are increasingly popular.) In many cases, an incentive is offered to the consumer to get them to fill in the card – in this case it is a one year subscription to Extended Customer Service.

Thanks for buying this release – we hope you enjoy it! To keep you up to date with what's to come, join our free information service. All you need to do is enter you details below.

In return, we'll tell you in advance about the records we are releasing, and let you know about tours and special appearances by our artists. This service is free, exclusive and delivers to your door.

Which release did you find this card in?

Artist ________

Title ________

How did you hear about this record?
❑ At a club ❑ TV ❑ Radio ❑ Music Press ❑ Personal recommendation ❑ Mailing

If you also want to receive information on any of the following artists, please tick the box(es)
❑ Sasha ❑ Sleeper ❑ M People ❑ Nightcrawlers ❑ Notorious Big ❑ Morrissey ❑ TLC ❑ David Bowie

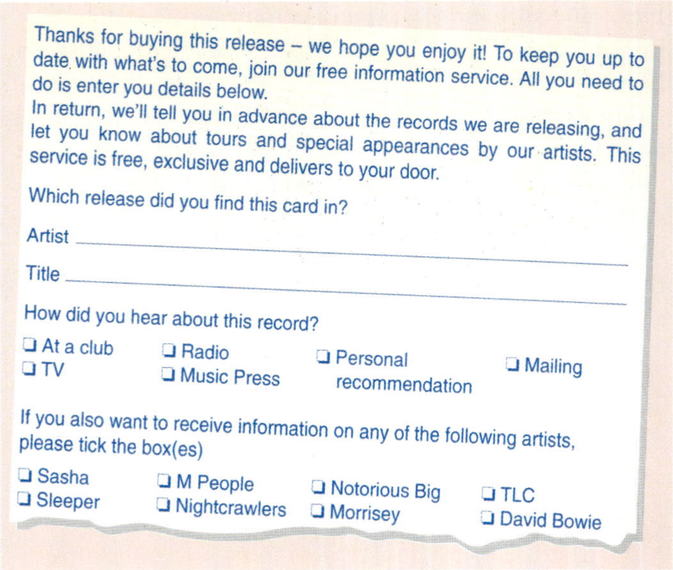

Questionnaires are also used. This one is to be found in a CD recording and collects information about CD buyers. In return, it offers to send information to you about the recording company's artists. The information collected will be held on a database and you can then be directly mailed by the company.

How many people do we ask?

It is obviously impossible to survey everyone in the population. Only the government has the resources to do this and they can only manage to do it every 10 years. Businesses therefore have to decide how they are going to survey a reasonable cross-section of their chosen target market. There are a number of ways in which they can do this:

- **A random sample:** A percentage of the population in a particular area is interviewed, with each person in the area having an equal chance of being approached. Such surveys are carefully constructed in order to gain the maximum amount of information. Such surveys can be expensive to carry out over a wide area and may be highly inaccurate unless a good percentage (5-10%) of the target group is approached.
- **A quota sample:** The population is split up into typical segments by age, occupation, income, etc. and a tightly controlled number of people are asked in each

When segments are chosen it is like taking a slice from a cake – it is likely that whatever the slice contains will fairly reflect what was in the rest of the cake

segment to reflect the make up of the population. If, for example, 20% of the population are in the 18–20 age group, then 20% of the survey would be conducted on 14–16 year olds. Surveys such as these are used by newspapers to predict how people will vote in elections. A survey of 1 500 to 2 000 people is generally very accurate.

If a random number of people in each segment are asked, this is called a stratified random sample.

- **A targeted sample:** a group may be targeted by geographical area, by occupation, by postcode or by purchases made, amongst other things. For example, sports shoe manufacturers will carry out surveys in running and athletics clubs. Often they will offer an incentive, such as entry in a prize draw or money-off vouchers, for completion of the survey.

What type of questions do we ask?

The business needs to decide whether it wants to collect qualitative or quantitative data. It also needs to decide whether it just wants information about its own products or whether it can use the same questions to gain information about competitors. The different kinds of questions it can ask are:

- **Open questions:** these are questions where no pre-set choice of answers is given. They are used for finding specific information (address, postcode, occupation) or where an opinion is wanted. 'What else could your local council do to ease traffic problems?' is an example. The answers given may provide a range and depth of information but are extremely difficult to analyse.

- **Closed questions:** these are questions where a set of possible answers is provided. They are easy to analyse but will only provide limited information according to the pre-set answers. Other, possibly equally good, answers are excluded.

- **Boolean questions:** these are questions where only one of two answers is possible. If you choose one answer, the other cannot be possible. The most obvious type of these is the Yes/No or Male/Female type of answer.

> **Did you know?** Boole was a mathematician who was involved in the development of computer science. He developed logic switches where a gate was either open or closed; in punched cards either there was a hole or there was not. All questions where this applies (like yes/no questions) are called Boolean questions.

- **Multiple choice questions:** a number of possible answers are provided and you may be asked to tick one or many of them. For example a question which asks 'What sort of music do you like?' and gives a lot of possibilities could have you ticking several boxes. This provides limited information but is extremely easy to analyse.

> **Handy hints:** When preparing multiple choice questions it is always a good idea to add a 'catch-all' answer at the end. Something like 'none of these' or 'none of the above' means that everyone questioned is able to give an answer.

- **Single choice questions:** sometimes a group of answers is provided in such a way that only one choice can be correct. If the question above asked, for example, which was your favourite type of music, then only one answer would be possible.

Researching the market 163

- **Preferences:** respondents may be asked to show an order of preference by numbering answers – by placing a 1 by their favourite, a 2 by their next favourite and so on. These questions are easy to analyse and produce accurate information.

- **Scales:** sometimes a scale is provided so that people have to think about where on the scale they would place themselves. An example is shown below. This gives an accurate picture of how a product is used but is extremely difficult to analyse.

Do you find Whizzo...

Brilliant   OK   Rubbish

Mark on the scale where you think your opinion is

> **Handy hints**
> Using questionnaires is often a good idea for collecting coursework information. Be careful that you use them in the right time and place and be extra careful that your questions are actually asking for the information you need!

How do we ask them?

The questions a market researcher asks may be better answered on a face-to-face basis with an interviewer, or by post, or by telephone. There are a number of methods used:

- **Face-to-face:** this is the oldest and still the most widely used form of questioning. An interviewer, with a printed sheet of prepared questions, approaches a member of the public in order to carry out a street interview. Generally this is used to collect quantitative data.

- **One on one:** these differ from face-to-face interviews in that the interviewer is not using a questionnaire. Instead a series of questions is asked in order to obtain in-depth reactions to a product or service. Instead of in the street, these interviews will take place in the comfortable surroundings of a home or office environment. Because of the time taken and the inconvenience to the respondent it is likely that they will be rewarded in some way. They may be directly paid for their time or offered discounts or vouchers.

- **Telephone:** this involves telephoning people and asking them a series of questions. This is not as effective as many of the other methods as people are less likely to want to answer questions over the telephone than face-to-face with a questioner. It is, however, a much cheaper and more convenient way of contacting a large number of people.

- **Post:** response rates tend to be very low for postal surveys and businesses will often try to improve the response rate by offering some sort of incentive to those who complete the questionnaire. This may be a special offer, a prize draw, or some other money back attraction. Postal surveys can be well targeted – geographically, by using postcodes, or by distributing the questionnaire in a particular way. A cat-food manufacturer, for example, might print a questionnaire on the inside of a cat-food tin label, knowing that only cat owners will fill it in.

- **Panels:** some market research is conducted by permanent panels of people. These people are given a reward by market research companies. Television viewing figures, for example, are taken from such panels who record which TV programmes they have watched. Some 'average' families are used as product testers for products such as washing powders and household cleaners.

- **Observing, tasting and testing:** the reaction of people to certain advertisements or to such things as changes in packaging can be judged by trained observers. Sometimes a small group of people will be invited into a hall or cinema and asked to give (in return for a small reward for their time) an opinion on an advertisement or on an aspect of marketing. Street or store sessions to taste or test a product or a rival's product may be set up in stores, supermarkets or on the street. 'Blind' tasting or testing is when the tester does not know the identity of the product. The results of such tests are analysed on a national basis to give a picture as to what people's views on the product or its rivals are.

How do we want to show the results?

It is no use a business thinking of this question after they have put their survey questions together! A firm must consider how they want to show their results – do they want quantitative information that can be easily graphed and charted, or qualitative information that is more accurate but more difficult to present? Look at the examples for the results of a simple quantitative question.

This has been presented as a 3-D pie chart; a bar chart with a key and a doughnut with percentages. Which do you think is the most effective?

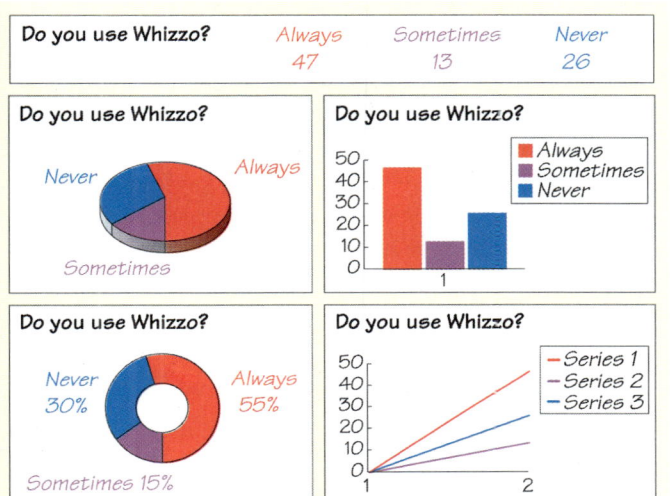

Activity

You could use a database program to show how a questionnaire could be used.

▷ 1   Design a form to ask the questions you want, making sure that you have used some yes/no and multiple choice type questions.

▷ 2   Once you have conducted your questionnaire, enter the information under different field headings – one for each answer. If you have at least five questions (five fields) and ten respondents (ten records) you will be able to use the information to gain part of the NEAB Certificate in IT.

One of the ways to make sure that the data you collect is useful is to present it in a format that makes it more 'user friendly' – like a table, a chart or a graph.

▷▷ 3   Using the graph tool on your chosen software, make as many different types of graph and chart from your information as you can.

▷▷   Which do you think is the most useful and which the least useful? Explain why.

The fourth chart shows how easy it is to present information in a meaningless way. The graph has been produced by a computer but this does not make it right – sometimes computers can produce meaningless rubbish from perfectly good data!

Once a business has analysed its position in the market and conducted market research on its target market, it is ready to decide on a total marketing strategy. This, the 'Four Ps', is discussed in the following four units.

SWOT ANALYSIS

A SWOT analysis is used by firms to analyse where it stands in its own market and can allow it to plan future business strategies. To do this it has to look at both the internal and the external factors that affect its position.

- Internal factors are those over which the firm has some control
- External factors are those over which the firm has no control.

SWOT stands for

internal	**S**trengths and
	Weaknesses and
external	**O**pportunities and
	Threats

Internal strengths and weaknesses

Some information about a business may not be publicly available or published and the firm may not be able to put a measurement on it. Such things as the firm's reputation is extremely important for its success. If a firm, for example, has a good reputation for after sales service and customer care, or is known to deliver on time, or has a staff who are always friendly and helpful, then this will be one of its strengths. These are all things that the company can achieve through training, planning and care. On the other hand, firms can have a very bad reputation and this can do them commercial harm in the market. British Gas, for many years, suffered a bad reputation for after sales service and repairs. They have gone to great lengths to turn this reputation into one of efficiency and concern for

Did you know? Some businesses aim for a particular reputation. Harrods of London has a reputation for quality and high prices while Woolworths has a reputation for low prices. The first Woolworths store was opened by F. W. Woolworth in America in 1879. Everything was priced at 5 or 10 cents (2.5p to 5p) which established its reputation as a no frills store giving value for money.

Researching the market

the gas consumer because of the commercial harm that this bad reputation was doing to them.

In the car market, Rolls-Royce have always been able to rely on their reputation for quality and service, as have Volkswagen for efficiency and reliability. Lada and Skoda, on the other hand, are the butt of many jokes due to their poor reputation. Volkswagen had the task, on taking over the Skoda car company, of burying the Skoda's poor reputation under their own good one. This was rated as a high priority because of its importance.

Firms need to know how well they are doing in terms of efficiency, reliability and customer care. To do this, they have to compare themselves with competitor firms. Is our business better or worse at customer care or after sales service than a rival? Is the rival's reputation better than ours?

If a business can recognise those strengths and weaknesses that it can do something about, then it is in a much stronger position for marketing its product.

Did you know?

Rolls-Royce has said that, should a car ever break down, it would provide a lorry to take the car to be repaired so that no Rolls-Royce was ever seen being towed on the road!

External opportunities

The other half of the SWOT analysis is concerned with the external opportunities and threats to a business. These are things over which the firm has no control. The opportunities could be things like new markets, new manufacturing materials or methods, or new ways of reducing costs in order to reduce price. It may be that a new government rule or law or an EU directive could be to the benefit of the firm. A law stating that the government was going to put extra resources into making

Activity

Read the passage and answer the questions.

This summer saw more people flying abroad for holidays as they spent their building society windfalls. The strong pound also helped to make up the minds of a lot of families. The early season flight delays caused by industrial action were soon forgotten although two tragic air crashes served to make some people think again about flying.

Memories of the fire in the Channel Tunnel and of further emergency stoppages and delays as a false fire alarm was set off reduced the traffic in the tunnel to less than that predicted by its owners. The early part of the summer saw a mini-heatwave while, towards the end of August, rainfall was frequent and widespread. The two main holiday village companies reported that demand was buoyant – their busiest periods, and highest prices, are reserved for school holidays. Center Parcs has a good reputation on its well-established sites. There are excellent facilities and a high rate of return custom (families coming back for more than one holiday). Oasis will be hoping to match this success. A holiday village break is not seen as the main holiday for many visitors and the structure of four day weekend breaks and five day midweek breaks encourages this. Problems can arise, however, as the older villages are modernised as building work and closures of facilities can interfere with holidaymakers' enjoyment.

1. Draw up a 4 column table headed internal – strengths and weaknesses, external – opportunities and threats and put the factors mentioned above into the correct columns.

2. Draw up a market research questionnaire that could be used to help improve the enjoyment of holidaymakers.

3. Suggest why older holiday villages might have more internal strengths and weaknesses than new villages.

4. How would you advise the new villages to build on the strengths and avoid the weaknesses?

sure every school and college had a certain number of computers would be of great benefit to computer sellers.

External threats

External threats to a business are likely to come from three main sources:

- **Government:** new laws or taxation. An EU directive, for example, which said that all cucumbers sold would have to be straight is an advantage for those who already grow straight cucumbers, but a distinct disadvantage to most cucumber growers. Changes in taxation can also have an effect on a firm. High taxes are set on tobacco products, for example, in a deliberate attempt to cut down demand.
- **Competitor firms:** firms competing in the same market may have new ideas or innovations or special advertising or sales campaigns. Merely by undercutting the market price, rival firms will often be able to take an extra share of the market before a business can react. Sometimes innovations can wipe out an existing market. Reel-to-reel tape recorders, for example, were quickly replaced by cassette tape players. When video cassette recorders were first introduced there were two systems, VHS and Betamax. When VHS established itself as the standard, Betamax soon went out of business.
- **Changes in the factors affecting consumer demand:** the most volatile or changeable one of these factors is fashion or taste. If the fashion for this season was thigh length leather boots, then this would be of great benefit to leather manufacturers. However, they would suffer a large drop in business if the fashion then changed to wooden clogs. The BSE scare (mad cow disease) in the UK in recent years meant that the demand for beef fell and cattle farmers suffered.

> **Handy hints**
>
> Remember that while price is within the control of the business, the other factors affecting demand are not. A change in the price of a complement, a substitute or a component will affect demand, as will a change in taste or fashion.

> **Codebreakers**
>
> **SWOT:** An analysis of the internal Strengths and Weaknesses of a firm and of the external Opportunities and Threats.
>
> **Point of sale:** the actual place where a good is sold – in some cases this may not be a shop or store but could be, for example, a catalogue.
>
> **Secondary data:** information that has been previously collected or published.
>
> **Primary data:** information not previously collected or published.
>
> **Qualitative:** quality answers to questions are answers in depth, with a lot of detail. These may be very useful but difficult to analyse or graph.
>
> **Quantitative:** measurable responses that can be easily graphed and analysed.
>
> **Response rates:** the number of people per hundred or thousand asked who actually answer.

SUMMARY

Ten points to remember:

1. Businesses collect market information before marketing a good or service.
2. Businesses have three main sources for this information, SWOT analysis, internal information and market research.
3. A SWOT analysis measures the firm's position in its market.
4. SWOT looks at internal Strengths and Weaknesses and external Opportunities and Threats.
5. Internal information is provided by the business's own systems.
6. Market research is used to identify and question the target market.
7. Published information – secondary data – is collected by desk research.
8. New information – primary data – is collected by various types of questions asked of a target market.
9. Questions need to be carefully constructed and scientifically targeted.
10. The analysis and presentation of answers is crucial to a business's success.

Unit 38
Consumer behaviour

When a firm wants to sell a product or service it must take into account how a **consumer** will make the decision whether or not to buy. There are a number of factors that influence the consumer's decision as to whether they will demand the product. These factors include the price of the good or service, the price of other goods or services, the income of the prospective customer and their tastes.

How would you decide whether to buy the jacket that is shown here? What factors do you think would influence your decision? Firms may have a great deal of market information but the final decision is always down to the consumer. Consumers are faced with a great deal of choice, with many different firms competing for their spending. All consumers (even the extremely rich) have to make a choice as to what they will and what they will not buy.

HOW CONSUMERS BEHAVE

Consumer behaviour is how a consumer makes the decision to buy a good or service, or decides to buy an alternative, or not to buy at all. Some purchases are based on need – without this good you may not survive – such as food, water, protection from the weather. Other purchases are based on want – a desire to have something even though it is not essential.

The basic economic problem and opportunity cost

The basic economic problem is that however much any consumer has to spend, there are always some things they cannot afford. This means that consumers are always

There is only one alternative to spending money, and that is to save it or (unlikely) give it away!

> **Did you know?**
> A psychologist called Abraham Maslow put everybody's wants and needs into certain categories. It is like climbing steps from one level of needs to the next. It is called a 'hierarchy' of needs as consumers will not go further up the steps unless they have fulfilled the needs of the step they are on (see *Unit 14*).
>
> Step 1 is physical needs – food and drink for survival
>
> Step 2 is security – the need to feel safe
>
> Step 3 is social needs – the need for friends and family
>
> Step 4 is status needs – the need to be respected
>
> Step 5 is success needs – the need to achieve ambitions and goals.

having to make choices as to what they will or will not buy. Whenever a consumer makes a choice to buy something, to spend a certain amount of money on it, then that means that there is something else that they can not now afford. In order to buy one thing, the consumer must give up buying an alternative. This is called the opportunity cost of the purchase and is a big factor in making purchasing decisions.

To a firm therefore, consumer behaviour is very important. It is the measure of:

- what goods or services a consumer will buy
- how much of a good or service the consumer will buy
- how often the consumer will buy
- how much the consumer will be willing to pay.

The firm's estimate of these will determine:

- what goods or services they will produce
- what price they will try to sell them at.

Consumer demand

What is a consumer? You are! You have been a consumer since the day you were born – eating, drinking, wearing clothes, using services. Later you played with toys and games, had a cot, a pram, a pushchair, a building set, a bicycle. These things were bought for you by relations or friends so you were not the customer, but you were the consumer. You also had a range of services that were provided for you. Later, when you first had money of your own, you started to make your own purchasing decisions. It is at this point that you became both customer and consumer.

A consumer is anyone who uses goods or services and therefore wants them to be available. Consumer demand

Did you know?

Advertisers often have to put out a 'double' message in their advertising. This is because the advertisement needs to be aimed at both the customer and the consumer. Often, especially where young children are involved, the consumer will be different from the customer. A new toy must be 'safe', 'educational', 'inexpensive' – an appeal to the customer (the parent or relation); it must also be 'exciting', 'colourful', 'attractive' – an appeal to the consumer (the child).

is when this 'want' is backed by the means to make it real. Generally this means that the 'want' is backed by money or other acceptable forms of exchange.

Factors affecting demand

Look at the jacket on the previous page. Did you decide whether or not you would buy it? Did you have enough information on which to base a decision? What sort of questions did you ask? Were they questions like 'Can I afford it? Do I like it? What else is there on offer? Is it good value?'

As a consumer, you answer all these questions before making a purchase, even though you may not necessarily run through them consciously.

Activity

> When you went home last night, or went out at the weekend, what did you buy? What else could you have bought? Make a list of all the possible things that you could have bought with the money that you spent. What opportunity costs were involved? What was the next best alternative?

Price

One of the first considerations for a consumer must be – 'Is it value for money?' Some goods are acceptable in a particular price range. If chocolate bars, for example, were put on sale at £300 each, it is unlikely that many would be sold – they are just not worth it. If, on the other hand, they were priced in an acceptable price range – 15p to 50p – then sales would be normal. Consumers look at the amount of satisfaction or enjoyment they are likely to get out of consuming or using a product. They match that enjoyment with the price, and if they don't think it's worth it, they don't buy. It is unlikely that anyone would get £300 worth of enjoyment out of a chocolate bar! In the case of the jacket shown, a reasonable price might be in the range £25 to £50.

Activity

> 1. Make a list of ten goods that you might buy in the course of a week. Next to each good write the price range that you think would be reasonable for that good.
> 2. Under what circumstances would you expect the good to be near the top of the price range? Near the bottom?
> 3. Did any of your price ranges go down to £0? Why do you think this is the case?

Price of other goods

Consumers then look at the other goods that are on offer. There are two main categories for these.

- **Substitutes:** these are goods or services that might be bought instead. They are in competition with other goods and services. Substitutes for the jacket might be fairly close – a similar jacket by a different manufacturer, a similar jacket but in a different colour – or they might be goods that are not close substitutes – a duffle coat, a donkey jacket or even clothes other than a jacket. The more similar the goods are, the greater will be their influence on the consumer's decision. A jacket the same as the one pictured, priced the same but in black, would have a big effect on how many white jackets were bought. A jacket the same as the one pictured, but £10 cheaper, would be bought in preference to this one.

If the price of substitute goods falls, then more of the substitute is demanded, so less of the original good or service. If the price of a substitute rises, then less of it is demanded, so more of the original good or service.

- **Complements:** these are goods or services that must be bought at the same time. In some cases they are close complements – a car is no good without wheels or

Activity

Use a spreadsheet program to draw and label graphs.

> 1. Collect some information appropriate to this unit such as how the people in your group or class would react to a change in the price of school or college meals.
> 2. Enter different prices in one column.
> 3. Enter the numbers of people who would be willing to buy at each price in a second column.
> 4. Produce and print out a demand graph.

This activity partially fulfills the requirement of the Software Applications Unit of the IT Certificate of Achievement in IT.

Codebreakers

Consumer: someone who uses goods and services.

Demand: the ability to back up a want with (usually) money to make a purchase.

Opportunity cost: the cost of the alternative that has to be given up when a choice is made.

Substitutes: goods and services that are bought instead of each other (fish + pies).

Complements: goods and services that tend to be bought together (fish + chips).

petrol so the price of rubber and of oil will affect the price, and thus the demand, for cars. If, for example, it is essential that this jacket has silk buttons, then the price of silk will affect the price of the jacket. If the price of complementary goods falls, then more of the original good will be demanded. If the price of a complement rises, then less of the original good will be demanded.

Income

Can I afford it? This is not just a question of whether or not the price is right, but whether I have the disposable income to be able to purchase the jacket. Consumers have a range of purchases that they will consider making, because the price is within their income. Outside this range, they will not even consider purchases.

For example, 15 or 16-year olds' range of purchases, on an income that consists of Saturday earnings, paper round, birthday money and whatever they can manage to extort from parents and relations, will include CDs, sports equipment, sweets and chocolate, magazines, make-up, computer games, electronic toys and novelties, entertainment, bus fares and clothes – the jacket illustrated is likely to be at the top end of their range of purchases. There are things more expensive than this that they would not consider purchasing because they are too expensive, even though they would like them, for example a mobile phone, a holiday abroad, a motor bike. There are other things that are too cheap to be considered – for example unbranded trainers sold on a market stall or clothes from a charity shop. As income increases, there are certain types of goods which 'drop out' of the consumers' range (cheap cuts of meat for example) and others that come in (such as eating out in restaurants).

Did you know? The range of expenditure of the super-rich is well outside that of most people. The actress Elizabeth Taylor decided that she would like to go to the Alton Towers theme park for a birthday bash. She hired the entire park for a day!

Taste or fashion

Do I like it? This is obviously a major question for a consumer to ask. The size, style, colour etc. must be right before any purchase is made. It is the main part of an advertiser's job to try to persuade the consumer that products or services are fashionable or tasteful. The images associated with this jacket are of sport, youthfulness and success (*see section on advertising in Unit 41*).

The size and structure of the population will also affect general levels of demand. If a country has a young population – a greater number of people in the 15–25 age bracket – then goods and services will be produced to appeal to this age group. This happened in the 1960s as the 'boom' of babies born just after the war started earning and spending. Britain's population currently has a higher proportion of people in the older age groups so that catering for the demands of 55–65 year olds is important to many firms.

Firms also target products on those sections of the population with money to spend. For example, although much music is targeted at young people, new bands tend to come and go quite quickly. The most important music sector is called 'AOR' – Adult Oriented Rock – which accounts for more than half of the music market. Bands therefore try to get into this sector (Tina Turner, Sting,

Activity

'The beer market in this year was affected by a number of factors. There was a mild winter, there was the football World Cup, there was a dry hot summer. This was followed by a war in the Middle East and snow in February.' *Extract adapted from a brewer's Annual Report.*

1. Explain which of these factors would increase the demand for beer and give reasons for your answer.
2. Draw a graph to illustrate the effect of one of these factors on the demand for beer.
3. Taking all the factors into account, would you expect the market demand for beer to have grown or shrunk?
4. Give reasons for your answer.

Consumer behaviour

U2, Elton John, Meat Loaf, Michael Jackson are all examples) as this guarantees them steady sales over a number of years from the section of population with the most money to spend on music.

Did you know? Bands established over a long period of time build up greater album sales – the real measure of a band's success. The highest number of British sales is still The Beatles' *Sgt. Pepper's Lonely Hearts Club Band* with 4.5 million sold; the highest number of sales for a British band world-wide is the 25 million for Pink Floyd's *Dark Side of the Moon*. The highest selling album of all time is Michael Jackson's *Thriller* which sold 47 million copies.

Demand curve

The combination of all these factors will determine whether the consumer will buy the product or not. It is possible to predict, in general terms, what will happen to demand if any of the factors changes. This means that firms will be constantly checking on changes to the market in which they are selling. Some factors, such as the price of the good, are within their control. Others, like the price of a substitute good, are outside their control.

Handy hints

Drawing graphs in coursework
You can use IT applications to make your graphs colourful and attractive but, be careful! Sometimes graphs are so complicated (in 3-D and many colours) that they are hard to read, and sometimes the computer produces a graph that looks good but is meaningless. You must make sure that graphs are relevant to your coursework and that you explain, in your text, what the graph is meant to show and why it is relevant. A lot of time is wasted in coursework by students producing graphs that might look good but are not related to the text. These do not gain any marks.

The general behaviour of consumers to a change in price can be plotted on a table and then shown on a graph. If the price of a good is high, then consumers are likely to demand less of it; as the price falls they will be willing to buy more.

Price	Bought
High	Less
Low	More

It is possible to put some figures on to this to give a better idea of how demand changes as price changes. For example:

Price (pence)	Quality demanded
100	1
90	2
80	3
70	4
60	5
50	6
40	7
30	8
20	9
10	10

These figures can be transferred to a graph which will look like this:

This means that, in this market, if the price of the product was 100p, only one would be bought, if it were 50p, then 6 would be bought, if it were 10p then 10 would be bought. As the price changes, so does the quantity demanded.

Handy hints

Drawing graphs in examinations
When faced with a graph to draw, make sure that it is both neat and clear. Use a pencil and a ruler. You will gain marks for correct labelling of both axes, correct numbers on both axes and a correct title for the graph as well as for the correct graph. Even if the graph is incorrect you can still usually gain the marks for labelling.

Consumer behaviour

Changes in demand

Changes in the other factors affecting demand will move the demand curve to the left or to the right. If there is an increase in income, for example, then higher priced goods may now come into the range of purchases which the consumer will consider buying. There will be more demand for the good or service at all prices. This is shown like this:

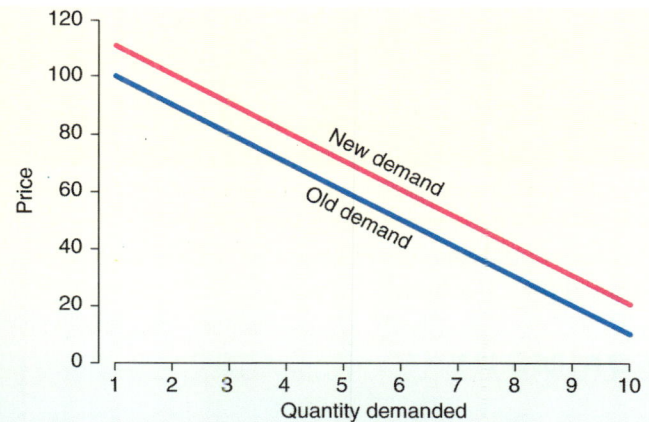

A fall in income will move the line to the left. A good becoming more fashionable, or a change in tastes towards a good or range of goods (healthier foods for example, or the effect of a successful advertising campaign), will move the line to the right. Goods and services which become less fashionable or popular see demand decrease at all prices – a move to the left.

Look at this example to see how demand changes if there is a change in the price of substitutes and complements.

- Fish and chips are complements – they are goods which tend to be bought together
- Fish and pies are substitutes, one tends to be bought instead of the other.

How is the demand for fish affected by an increase in the price of a complementary good (chips), or by an increase in the price of a substitute good (pies)?

Increase in the price of chips = fall in demand for fish

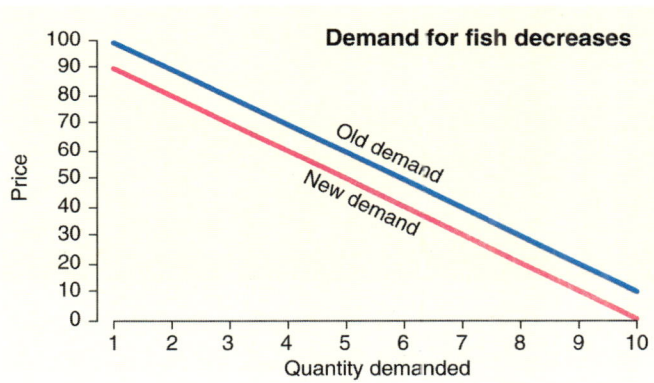

Increase in the price of pies = increase in demand for fish

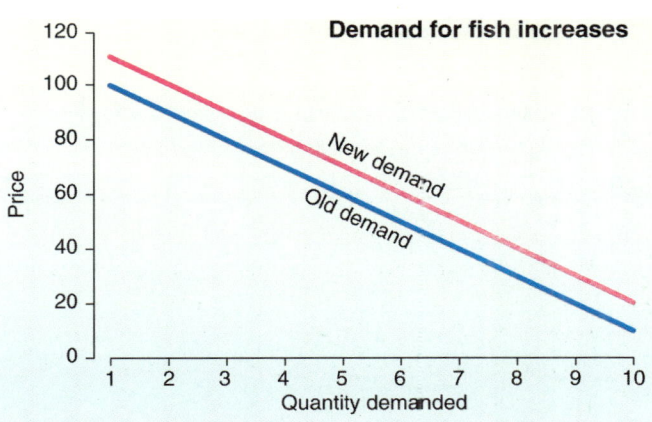

Activity

A coursework title such as 'What are the most important factors influencing the demand for a particular product?' would give a lot of opportunity to study patterns of consumer behaviour. You could choose a product such as, a mobile phone or a current CD and study:

- the differences in demand between the product and its competitors
- what you think causes those differences in demand
- what strategies are used by sellers to try and make the demand as inelastic as possible.

You could

1. Show how consumers are encouraged to buy – for example, impulse buys, repeat purchases, planned purchases.
2. Interview buyers of the good and find out which of the factors that affect demand are most important to them.
3. Explain which factor you think is the most important, and why.
4. Interview sellers of the good and find out which of the factors that affect demand are most important to them.
5. Explain which factor you think is the most important, and why.

Consumer behaviour

Price elasticity of demand

The fewer substitutes there are for a good or service, the less effect any change in price will have on the demand for that good or service. Goods with very few or no substitutes have demand which hardly alters with price changes. Salt is an example of one of these goods with **inelastic demand**. If the price of salt falls to an all time low, people will not rush out to stock up on it; should it rise to an all time high, people will still buy a certain amount. With goods such as this, price is unimportant. Try asking friends and relations how much salt is per kilo – it is unlikely that they will know as they will only buy a certain amount, regardless of its price.

Goods with many substitutes will be very sensitive to price changes. These are goods which have **elastic demand**. If the price of black Adidas jackets, for example, goes up, then people will quickly switch to other colours as they are almost perfect substitutes. Firms try to create a brand image for their product to make it different from other products. This is so that consumers will not see other brands as a suitable substitute *(see brand loyalty – Unit 41)*.

Codebreakers

Inelastic demand: goods and services for which a change in price has little effect on demand.

Elastic demand: goods and services for which a change in price has a great effect on demand.

Handy hints

When you are doing a test or examination, don't just think about what you've learned – think about what you already know from your own experience. If you were trying to think of goods that were inelastic in demand, think about those goods that you don't even know the price of, because changes in prices are unimportant. It is a fair bet that these goods are demand inelastic. Always use your own experience where you can.

The closer the relationship is between one good and another, the greater will be the effect of a change in the price of one good on the demand for another. One brand of petrol is a perfect substitute for another so a change in the price of one brand will have a big effect on the demand for other brands.

SUMMARY

Six points to remember:

1 Consumer behaviour is how the consumer makes a decision whether or not to buy a good or service.

2 This is important to the firm in deciding what to produce and how to price it.

3 All consumer decisions involve a choice between alternatives.

4 The cost of the alternative not bought is called opportunity cost.

5 Consumer demand is affected by four main things:
- The price of the good or service: the higher the price, the less will be demanded
- The price of other goods: substitutes (bought instead of) and complements (bought with)
- The disposable income of the consumer: the higher the income, the higher the demand
- Taste or fashion: more 'fashionable' or 'likeable' products will have increased demand.

6 Price elasticity of demand is the measure of how much the demand for a product reacts to a change in price.

Unit 39
The marketing mix: price

The marketing mix is the term given to the way in which firms have to mix together the elements that go into the successful sale of a product. They are usually known as 'The Four Ps' – Price, Product, Promotion and Place. The four of these are looked at in detail in the following Units. When a firm has a product or service to sell, it must decide at what price it is going to be able to sell it. In theory, this will be the point where what the firm is willing to supply is equal to what the consumer is willing to demand. In fact, there are a large number of other factors that are involved and many different ways in which businesses can decide on what price to charge.

Firms must look at how much the good is costing them to make, how much profit they want to make, and how easily they can persuade consumers to pay the price that they are asking, rather than buying their goods from a competitor shop. They will also see what competitors are charging and what special offers or promotions are being offered.

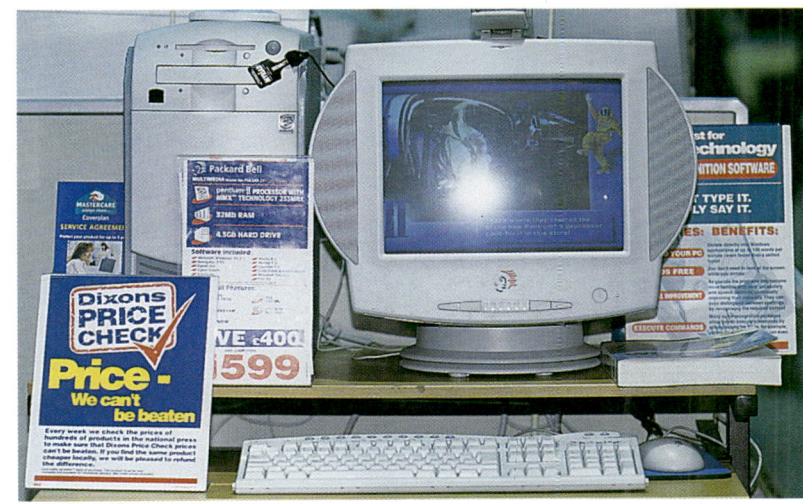

Activity

1. How do you think the prices of the various goods on display here have been arrived at?
2. What factors do you think the business has had to take into account before deciding on a price?

PRICING IN THE MARKET

This is how businesses juggle the various factors in order to set prices so that they reach the targets they have set. This may be a certain number of sales, a certain level of **profit**, a certain proportion of the market share or a price set at a level to prevent their rivals from competing.

> **Did you know?**
> Critical point pricing is when suppliers price goods at just below what is seen as a 'critical point'. £99.99 is only 1p less than £100 but sounds cheaper and can be advertised as 'less than £100'. By knocking off tax, some computer sellers get price down to 'less than £1 000' – usually £999. These are psychological price points; in consumers' minds, goods are cheaper and it is therefore also known as psychological pricing.

This means that, to a firm, setting the right price – pricing – is important because it determines

- how much the firm can sell
- what level of **revenue** they will make
- what sort of profit they will make.

PRICE SETTING IN THEORY

Market theory looks at what should happen for markets to 'clear' – that is, for all the goods that are on sale in a market to be bought. Imagine a market stall selling fresh flowers. At the start of the day the stallholder charges a price that he or she knows will make a healthy profit on the goods. Some of the flowers are sold as some people demand them at this high price. As the day draws on, the stallholder has to drop the price to try to sell the rest of the flowers. Towards the end of the day prices are exceedingly low but the quantity bought, as a result, is high. (*Review Unit 38 on Demand.*) By the time the stallholder packs up, not all the flowers have gone – the market has failed to clear and some flowers must be thrown away. Had the stallholder known the price that would, in theory, clear the market, then he or she could

The marketing mix: price

have supplied exactly the right amount of flowers to satisfy demand and been confident that all would be sold.

> **Handy hints**
> Don't forget how important your correct use of terminology is. There are marks specifically given for this in both examinations and coursework. Remember, for example, that revenue and profit are not the same thing.

Supply

Price	Quantity supplied
High	High
Low	Low

While demand shows the quantity that a consumer wants at each price, **supply** shows the quantity which a supplier is willing to supply. In the same way as demand, supply can be plotted on a table and then on to a graph. In general, the higher the price, the more of a good or service a supplier is willing to supply to the market.

Price	Quantity supplied
1	1
2	2
3	3
4	4
5	5
6	6
7	7
8	8
9	9
10	10

Figures can be added to this to make a table showing what a business is willing to supply at each price. Imagine this is the price for a bunch of flowers. If the price the seller could get was only £1 then they would only be willing to supply one bunch. At £5, they will supply 5 bunches. If people are willing to offer £10, then they are willing to supply 10 bunches.

This can then be transferred on to a graph:

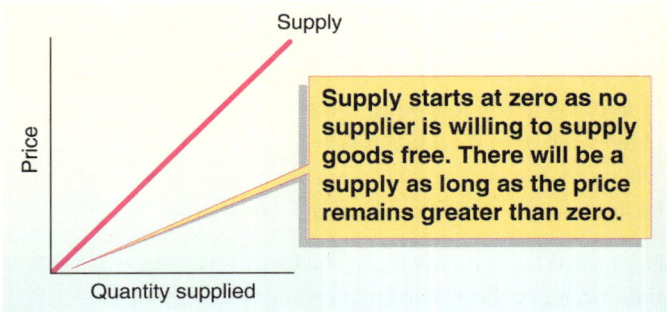

> Supply starts at zero as no supplier is willing to supply goods free. There will be a supply as long as the price remains greater than zero.

This shows that the higher the price of a good, the more the business will be willing to supply. This is called a supply curve.

Demand and supply

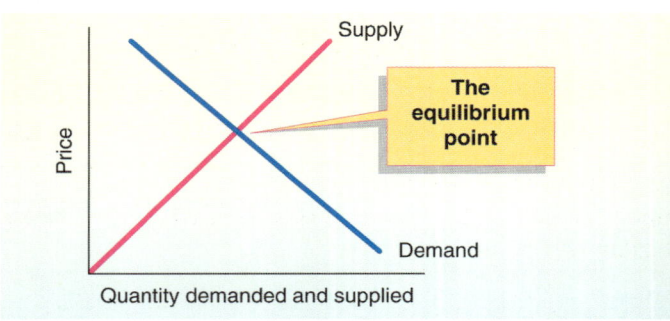

The equilibrium point

If this is plotted on the same set of axes as the demand curve, then we can see that the two lines, supply and demand, cross. It is at the point where the two lines cross that the market is said to be in **equilibrium**. This means that suppliers have agreed to supply to the market, at a particular price, exactly the amount that consumers will demand at that price. Everything will be sold, both supplier and consumer will be satisfied and the market will have cleared.

> **Handy hints**
> Don't mix up equilibrium and equals. The equilibrium point is like the balancing point on a set of scales. It means that there are no forces pushing demand or supply in either direction. The lead in the picture doesn't equal the feathers – but the scales are in equilibrium.

Theory and practice

Why, if everyone is so happy with the outcome, does this not happen in practice? The main reason why this perfect state of affairs does not happen is that the information required to draw either the demand or supply curve accurately is not available. While it is possible to draw such lines in theory, in practice markets consist of many suppliers and many consumers, all buying and selling for different reasons. It would be necessary for all consumers and all suppliers to know exactly what all other consumers and all other suppliers were doing, and for them all to be able to react instantly to any changes in the market, for equilibrium to be reached.

Such perfect markets do almost exist for certain commodities – the price of gold, for example, is set daily by a London committee that collects all the information on that day's supply of gold and on what gold is demanded before announcing the day's price. This is the price for wholesale gold and does not, of course, change the price of jewellery in the shops. It is also worth remembering that many, on both sides – whether consumer or supplier – will benefit from equilibrium not being reached.

Activity

> What other factors do you think need to be taken into account when setting prices? Think about when you would expect to find the price of ice-cream at its highest, or the price of heating fuels?

PRICE SETTING IN PRACTICE
HOW FIRMS SET PRICES

It is likely that the firm will be trying to **maximise** its profits, but there are other things that it may be targeting. It may want to maximise its share of the market, it may want to put a competitor firm out of business, it may want to introduce a new product on to the market or it may want to maximise its sales. These are just some of the possible targets for a firm *(see Unit 9)*. In many cases firms will set prices at the level that will keep them in business, without trying to maximise anything else.

Handy hints

An easy way to remember the correct way to draw demand and supply is that demand is D for Down and sUPply has UP in it – demand is drawn going down from left to right, supply is drawn going up.

Cost-plus pricing

The most common way for firms to decide on a price is through cost-plus pricing. This means that they add up the cost of the raw materials and labour that have gone into the making of a product or the provision of a service in order to determine its cost. They then add on an element for profit, an amount over and above the cost, and often set as a percentage of the cost. This is called the **mark-up**. The diagram below shows a typical simple example.

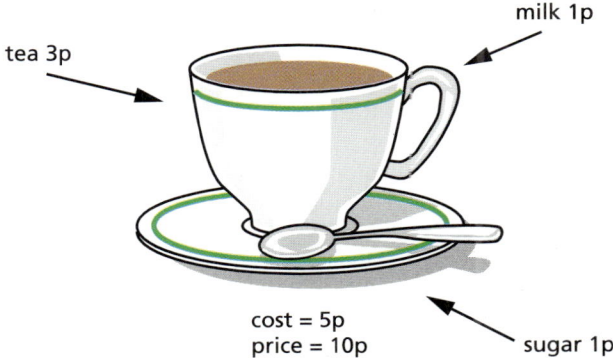

A cup of tea on sale at a school or college event – a parent's evening or a show or concert – or at a church fête or jumble sale might be sold at a price of 10p and make a profit of 5p per cup. This is because, for example, 40 teabags bought at £1.20, give an average cost for each cup of tea of 3p. Similar working out has been done with the sugar and milk. This puts the cost of each cup of tea at 5p. A mark-up of 100% means that 100% of the cost is added. 5p + 5p = 10p.

This is a straightforward example of cost-plus pricing. It is deliberately placed at a college concert or church fête as these are the sort of occasions where such simple pricing takes place. This is because not all costs are taken into account. People are, for example, providing their labour for free, or providing free loan of cups.

Codebreakers

Profit: the difference between costs and revenue if revenue is higher than cost.

Revenue: the amount of money received from a sale.

Equilibrium: the point where there are no forces pushing supply or demand in either direction.

Supply: the amount of a good or service that sellers are willing to supply to a market in a given time period.

Maximise: 'make the most of' – if you maximised your GCSE grades you'd get all 'A's!

Mark-up: the extra added on to cost in order to make a profit.

The marketing mix: price

Look at this more realistic example, where the tea is being made in a commercial organisation:

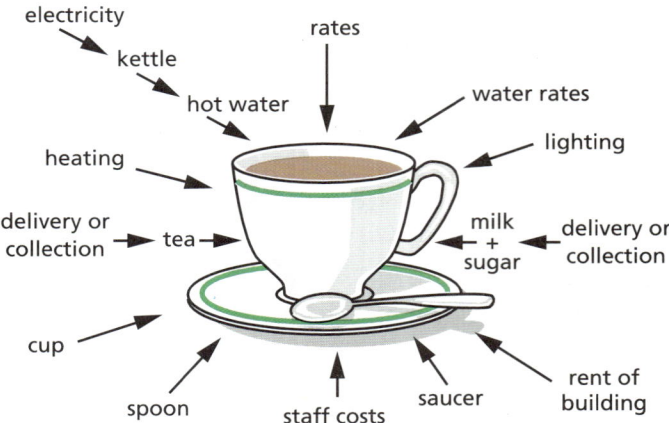

The costs involved fall into two types *(see Unit 23)*. **Fixed costs** are those which do not change as production changes; variable costs are those that do change as production changes. In this case the costs are as follows:

Fixed costs	Variable costs
Kettle	Electricity
Water rates	Tea
Lighting	Milk
Cup + saucer + spoon	Sugar
Rent of building	Staff
Heating	Delivery/collection charges

All these costs have to be averaged out per cup of tea sold. The more cups of tea are sold, the less the average fixed cost per cup will be, while variable cost will remain much the same. As long as a cup of tea is priced at greater than the variable cost then the price is making a contribution towards fixed costs.

In this case if sales were 1 000 cups per year then average fixed cost would be 50p. Variable costs are 10p. The price, with a percentage mark-up of 10% would be:

Average fixed cost 50p + variable cost 10p = 60p

10% (mark-up) of 60p = 6p

60p + 6p = 66p

Any price that covers all costs in this way is called total or full cost pricing.

Any price that covers variable costs and is making a contribution towards fixed costs is called contribution pricing.

The mark-up will differ from one type of good to another. The mark-up in catering, for example, is usually quite high as is that for perfumes and alcohol. The mark-up for retailers on newspapers and tobacco products is very low.

Activity

Jayne White has run a market stall selling flowers for the past few years. She is at the market on Fridays and Saturdays only. Her main costs are her market pitch licence, paid to the local council, the hire of a van for the two days, her wages and the cost of the flowers.

Jayne estimates that her fixed costs for the two days are £200. The cost per bunch of flowers is £1 and she is able to sell 100 bunches a day.

1. Explain which of the costs outlined are fixed and which are variable.
2. What price should she charge if she has a 25% mark up? A 50% mark up?
3. What price would you recommend she actually charged if she had a 50% mark up? Explain your reasoning.

Competitive pricing

178 The marketing mix: price

> **Did you know?**
>
> There's an awful lot of coffee in Brazil! **Price leadership** in a market may mean that the major producer of a good is responsible for setting prices. If Brazil has a good coffee crop then it will set a low world price for coffee. Other producers have no choice but to follow that price, however good or bad their own crop is. Brazil supplies so much of the market that it controls price. Sometimes the major firms in a market will join together and agree to fix prices; this is called a 'cartel'.

How else could a firm decide what it was going to charge for a good or service? Look at these advertisements for computer systems. While they are offering different makes or models of computer and different special offers, they are all asking around the same price – a price that is just under £1 000 before tax. This is an example of companies pricing by looking at what other firms in the market are charging. This is called competitor based pricing. These firms have to compete with each other by using non price competition, because their products are very similar and there is no one firm in the market big enough to be a price leader. Try asking people with a PC what make it is – it is unlikely that they will be able to tell you as it is not the make that is important, but its speed and efficiency.

Promotional pricing

Sale! Special offer! Final reductions! Buy one, get one free! Half price! 25% off! These are all examples of promotional pricing or non price competition (see Unit 41). The idea is to increase sales in the short term, possibly (as with autumn sales for example) in order to clear space for new lines or new stock. It could also possibly be in order to undercut a rival, or to clear stock that is no longer in demand (sales of Easter eggs after Easter or of fireworks after Bonfire Night, for example). The feature of promotional pricing is that prices are, or appear to be, a lot lower than usual.

Some retailers have seized on this and advertise the fact that, on many lines, they cannot provide promotional prices as their prices are already at 'rock bottom'.

Entering new markets

When a firm is trying to gain a foothold in a new market it has a number of possible pricing strategies. It can try to enter the market at a low price in order to gain custom from competitors, or it can try to enter the market at a high price, particularly if it has a new or innovative product. These methods are:

- **Loss leaders:** this is when a firm sells a product at cost price (in other words, with no mark-up at all) or at less than cost price (at a loss), in order to gain a share of the market. Once the company has established a customer base – a section of the market that is buying their product – they will raise the price in order to make a profit. This method is also used by firms who know that the good that they sell will lead to the consumer having to make further, more expensive and profitable, purchases. For example, a satellite television company may well sell dishes cheaply or even give them away, knowing that subscribers will only get the best use out of them by paying for specialist channels such as sport. BSkyB, the major company in the UK, actually gave many satellite dishes away through newspaper promotions in the early days of the company. Now they are introducing pay-per-view events as well as their subscription channels.

> **Did you know?**
>
> The Asda supermarket chain says in its annual report: 'Our commitment is to provide permanently lower prices which means that on a full weekly shop the average family will make significant savings by shopping at Asda. We continually monitor our prices to ensure that they stay low...'

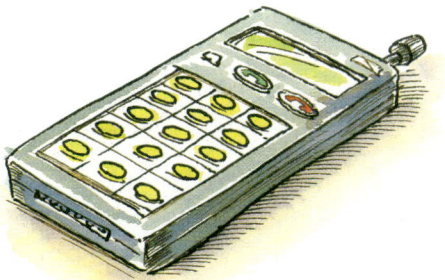

The marketing mix: price 179

A second example is mobile telephones – often the telephone itself is really cheap but the use of it soon recoups the telephone company's losses.

Supermarkets and other large stores also use loss leaders in order to attract customers into a shop. Once the customer has bought their 'strawberries at 50p' in a supermarket or '99p growing bag' in a garden centre, it is likely that they will make further purchases and the profits from these will wipe out the loss on the loss leaders.

> **Did you know?**
> A price war is when competing firms keep undercutting each other to try and gain a larger share of the market. Price wars can be very good for the consumer in the short term, but tend to be bad in the long term. In the short term, prices will be very low, with firms often selling at a loss. In the long term, the weakest firm or firms will be forced out of business. The remaining players in the market can then resume their higher prices (often even higher than before in order to recoup their losses) and the consumer is left with less choice.

- **Penetration pricing:** this is similar to loss leaders in that it is a deliberate attempt to undercut rivals' prices in the market. A penetration price is a price that is lower than competitors are asking. It may not be a price that is making a loss, but it is a price that gives a large enough gap between it and its lowest priced competitors for customers to be attracted to the new entrant to the market. This may have enough of an effect to cause the other suppliers of the market to lower their prices. If this happens then it can spark off a price war as firms try to undercut each other.

If, for example, there was a new entrant to the PC market who could supply similar specifications to those shown but charged £500, there would be two possible outcomes:

– the manufacturer could gain a market share and then raise prices
– other manufacturers could be forced to lower prices as they lost market share.

- **Creaming:** many new technology devices are first introduced to the market at a high price. This has been true, over the years, of televisions, calculators, compact disc players, video cassette recorders, personal stereos, video cameras, mobile phones, computers, modems and many others. The idea is to introduce the item as a luxury good, charging a high price for it so that only the wealthy, or organisations, can afford it. Often companies need the initial top price in order to recoup development costs and to fund further research. Later, price is lowered in order to reach another part of the market. This is called creaming or skimming the market. The diagram shows how this helps to increase the revenue of the company.

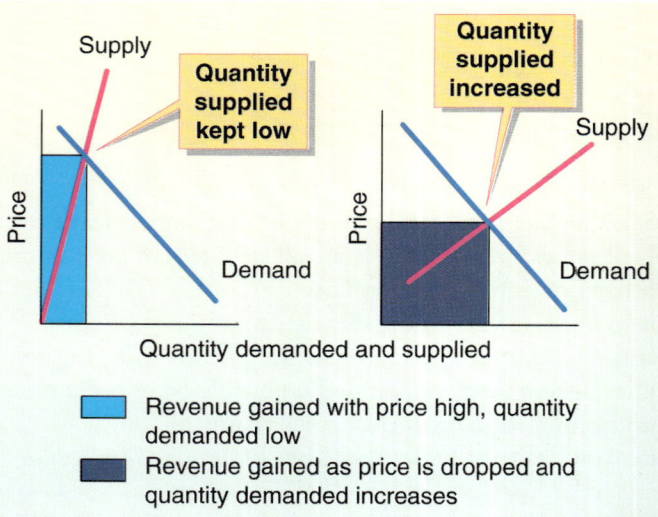

In some cases – calculators for example – the rapid development of the technology meant that the price fell very quickly. In other cases, companies were forced to bring prices down in order to create a mass market. Some of the goods mentioned above are at different stages of this process. Calculators are now so cheap that they are often given away in promotions. Televisions are no longer thought of as luxury items, nor are CD players or videos. Video cameras and mobile phones are becoming increasingly part of the mass market. Computer modems are just beginning to fall in price.

Price discrimination

This is where a firm can gain extra revenue by being able to sell to different people at different prices. This only works if the markets that they are selling to are separated and consumers are not able to buy in one market and sell in another.

There are so many different reasons why people travel – business, holidays, visiting, interviews, shopping etc. – that transport providers are a good example of price discrimination. On a train, for instance, there could be the following people:.

- a businessman who has to attend an 8.30 meeting
- a student visiting his girlfriend
- a lady attending an interview
- a family going for a day out
- a retired couple going on holiday
- a man whose car has just broken down
- a regular traveller, who uses this train daily
- a regular traveller, who uses this train once a month.

It is likely that each of these have paid a different price for their seat, either because they have been able to pre-book

Activity

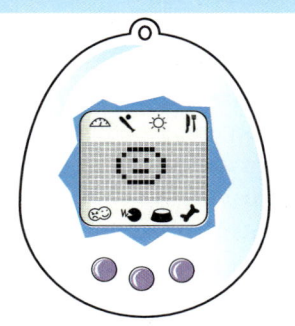

The inventors of 'virtual pets' (miniature computer pets that need to be fed, walked, put to bed, etc. or they die) were able to launch their invention into a market with no competitors.

> **1** What type of price do you think the pets were introduced at?
> **2** What do you think happened to price as competitors copied the idea and entered the market?
>> **3** What would have happened if the inventors had been able to keep the largest slice of the market?
>>> **4** Draw the supply and demand curves that you would expect if the inventors had been able to keep the largest slice of the market. What has happened to price? Explain why this is so.

it, or because they are entitled to a railcard, or because the circumstances of their journey means that they have only just decided to travel. In this case, if they were unable to plan ahead, it is likely that they have paid a higher price.

On an aeroplane flight, the opposite may be true. Look at this example:

- business people who have decided that they must travel on that particular plane
- holidaymakers booking as part of a holiday package
- holidaymakers who booked early
- holidaymakers who booked after discounts were offered
- 'last minute' fliers
- airline staff and their relatives entitled to cheap flights.

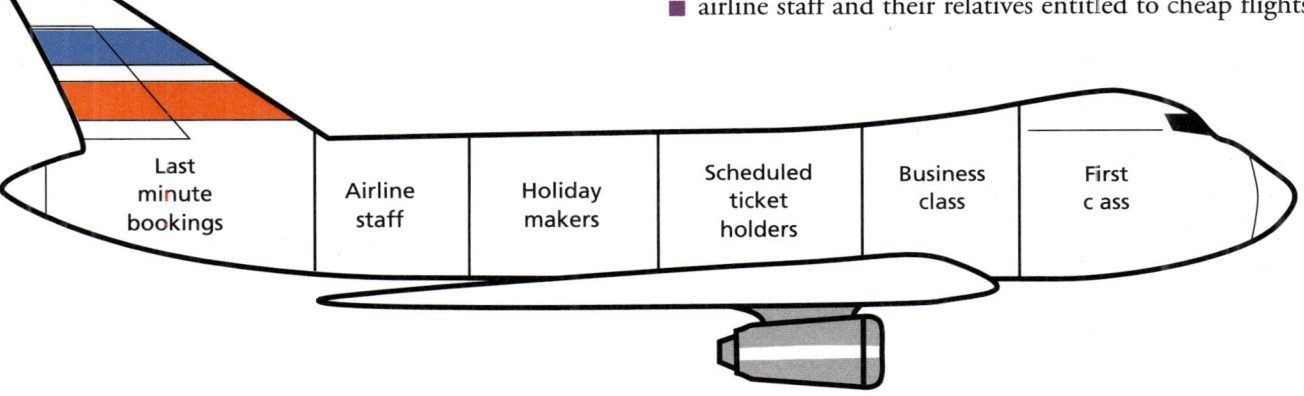

In both cases, different prices are being charged in different markets. The business market is kept separate from the holiday market and so on. If a member of the airline staff could obtain a ticket and sell it on to a businessman, then the discrimination would no longer work. This is why the markets must be kept separate. They can be separated geographically (different prices charged in one part of the country to another), by time (telephone charges are at their highest during business hours, falling at evenings and weekends), or by only making certain concessions available to certain markets (student railcards, family railcards).

Consumer led pricing

In some cases it is the consumer that decides on the price level by having a particular view as to what something ought to cost. A butcher who decided to reduce the price of all his beef to 10p a pound would find few takers for his products. Consumers would be suspicious that there was something wrong with the meat, or something illegal about the transaction. Each product has a **price plateau** – the general price where consumers think it should be. While this may change over the years, it is unlikely to change in a short time period. Thus the butcher may find that either increasing or decreasing his prices for beef has the same effect of lowering demand.

Codebreakers

Fixed cost: costs that don't change with the amount produced (e.g. rent).

Variable cost: costs that do change with the amount produced (e.g. raw material costs).

Non price competition: competing through special offers, promotions, gifts etc.

Price leader: the firm that has enough of a market to be able to set the price.

Cost price: the price that just covers the total cost to produce a good or service.

Price plateau: the 'usual' price range for a good or service.

Activity

Gold prices are set by information being collected from gold suppliers and gold buyers around the world. This used to be done by telephone.

> **1** Write down how you now think that it is done.
>
> **2** State three advantages and three disadvantages of this method of communication.

(Your answer can be word processed.)

This activity partially fulfills the requirements of the Communications section of the NEAB Certificate of Achievement in IT.

SUMMARY

Ten points to remember:

1 Price is just one of the parts of the marketing mix.

2 In theory, prices are set by the interaction of demand and supply.

3 Equilibrium is where demand and supply meet and the market clears.

4 In practice, firms set prices according to the market information they have.

5 Cost-plus pricing means that a mark-up is added to costs to arrive at a price that gives a profit.

6 Competitive pricing is where prices are set by looking at what competitors are charging.

7 Promotional pricing is special price reductions for short periods.

8 Loss leaders and penetration prices are low prices used to take a share of the market.

9 Creaming or skimming is a high price used to take a share of a market.

10 Price discrimination is where different prices are charged to different consumers for the same good or service.

Unit 40

The marketing mix: product and the product life cycle

The product could be said to be the most important part of the marketing mix. Without the product there is no need for price, promotion or packaging and certainly no need for a place to sell from! The product can be either a good or a service; in a service industry, such as banking, the product is the customer's account and the different accounts and schemes on offer. In an industry producing goods, the product is the goods that are for sale.

Usually a firm will not concentrate on a single product, but will produce a range of products. Polo, for example, well known as 'the mint with the hole' and a **market leader**, is produced by Nestlé, whose other products include coffee, condensed milk and breakfast cereal! The Polo story is typical of a product that was going into decline as it became less popular. Polo had been market leader for over 10 years when, in 1992, Trebor Extra Strong Mints became the market leader with 17.4% of the market to Polo's 16.2%. This meant that the product had to be developed if it was going to survive.

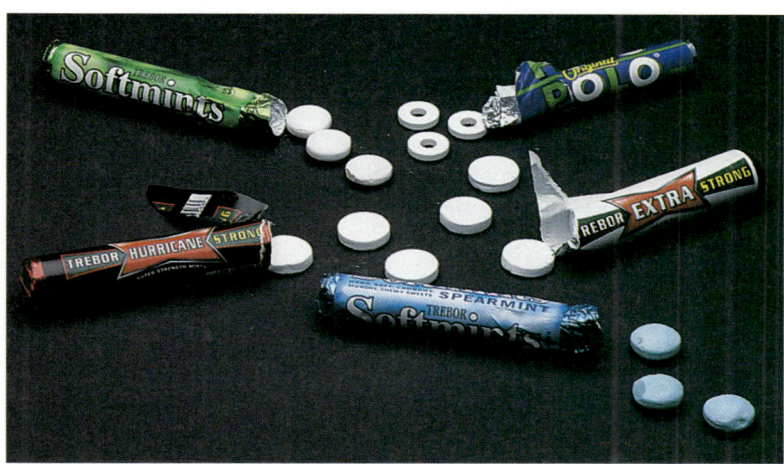

WHAT IS THE PRODUCT?

The product is what the firm is trying to sell. The product life cycle is the natural growth and eventual decline of the product in the market.

This means that, to a firm, the product is:
- the good or service that they are selling
- the reason they are in business.

Product joins price, promotion and place in the marketing mix

The product life cycle is:
- the launch of the product
- the growth of the product
- the eventual decline and often
- the death of the product.

Products and segments

A small firm will target a particular market segment with its product. This segment may be a geographical one (all the people who live within walking distance) or a specific segment because of the goods supplied, such as a health food shop or specialist record store. They may be the only firm which supplies a particular product because the market is a niche market – handmade shoes and customised cars are an example.

A large firm, like Nestlé, will produce a **product range**. This means that if one part of the market goes into decline, they can still rely on other goods. Cigarette manufacturers, in recent years, seeing the decline of tobacco sales, have moved into other markets. This is called **diversification**. Because of the decline in sales of Polo mints, the product had to diversify into different market segments or die.

Did you know? There is a difference between product range and product mix. Product mix can be wide (as with Nestlé, producing many different kinds of product) or deep (as with a bank, who produce many different types of the same thing – financial services).

Activity

1. Look at the confectionery on sale in your local shop or supermarket. Write down as many different brand names as possible.
2. Now see how many different manufacturers' names you can find.
3. What conclusions can you come to?
4. What else do these manufacturers produce apart from confectionery?
5. Explain why you think that this is so.

Handy hints Often your best resource for homework investigations or for coursework will be a local firm – a retailer, newsagent's or confectioner, where it is easy to see what current brands and current trends are.

Product life cycle

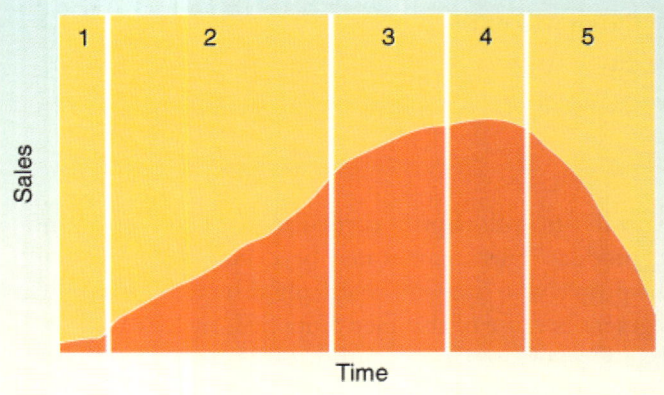

Products have a natural life cycle which starts with when they are first launched on to the market – the introductory or launch stage (1). This is then followed by a period of rapid growth (2) as the product establishes its position in the market. A mature product (3) is one where the product is well established but sales are no longer growing as rapidly. In many cases this is due to other products copying the successful product and coming on to the market at lower prices. These products have not had the research and development costs associated with a new product (see below) and are therefore able to charge a lower price. At stage (4), the market has become saturated – this means that there are now so many different variations of the original product for sale that there is no room at all for sales growth. Finally (5) the product rapidly loses sales and goes into a period of decline, until it reaches the end of the product life cycle.

The cycle is: launch, growth, maturity, saturation, decline.

Activity

Draw up a table like the one below and fill in as many products as you can under each heading. For homework you could try to get someone from the older generation to help you with products that have declined. The examples given may have moved further through the life cycle by now!

Launch	Growth	Maturity	Saturation	Decline
cyberpets	health foods	trainers	personal stereos	record players

Product failure

Some products do not live up to the company's expectations and may suffer an aborted life cycle, being withdrawn from the market at short notice. The Sinclair C5 was a one-person electrical vehicle developed for town travel in the 1980s. The product was not popular as people felt very vulnerable in it due to being near to the ground and production was quickly halted. The life cycle would look something like the following diagram:

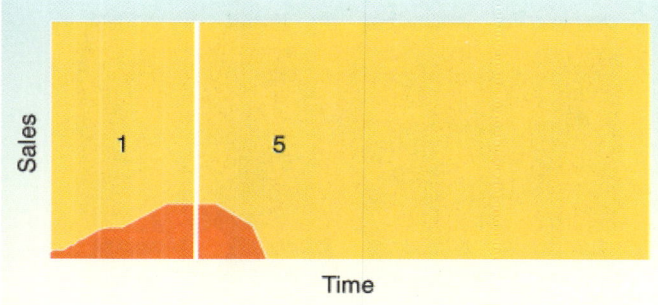

Product development

Product development will take place at two points in the product life cycle. The first point is at the very beginning when the product is being developed. The product will be one of two things:

- **market led:** there is a gap in the market and the product needs to be developed to fill it. An example is telephone banking. Midland Bank spotted that customers did not visit branches but preferred to do their banking transactions over the telephone and therefore produced the product which customers wanted – First Direct, a telephone banking system.

- **product led:** an inventor or developer comes up with a new product that they think the public will buy – the personal stereo is a good example.

Whichever of these it is, it is likely that there will be development costs. Large firms have **research and development** departments which are given over to producing and improving products. These tend to be costly and developers need to charge high prices to start with in order to recover these expenses. Product development may also take place when a product is seen to be in decline. Changes may be made in order to try to give the product a longer life.

Extending the life cycle

This is the way in which a product is changed in order to prevent it declining or dying. As sales of the product fall, researchers will try to identify what features of the product

ACTIVITY

Meredith's are a company whose core product has been the production of record sleeves for long playing records. It has been the market leader in this for over twenty years. Designs are sent to them by cover artists and the company prints them on to card, which is then coated in plastic. The move away from records and towards CDs has badly affected Meredith's trade.

1. How could Meredith's alter its product range in order to recover sales?
2. What other short-term strategies could Meredith's use, apart from altering its product range?
3. What would you recommend as a long-term strategy to ensure that Meredith's stays in business?

are liked, what are disliked and what can be changed. In the case of Polo mints, the competition was spending more on advertising and had introduced a better product range whereas Polo had not changed its image at all. Polo decided to diversify its product so that it would appeal to more market segments. The company launched spearmint Polo to appeal to the younger age group, strong polo to appeal to adults (and to compete directly with Trebor's Extra Strong) and Sugarfree Polo to appeal to the more health conscious market. At the same time it re-launched its **core product** as Original Polo. Advertising and promotion of

Did you know?

A firm can make quite small changes in a product in order to boost its sales. These are called cosmetic changes and may be such things as alterations in colour or packaging. Larger changes could be what are called real changes – alterations in design or performance. Technological changes may alter the product so much that it can no longer be considered to be the same product. In the case of a personal stereo, for instance:

- a cosmetic change could be a new range of colours
- a real change would be the introduction of mega bass
- a technological change could be the introduction of personal CD players.

The marketing mix: product and the product life cycle

each brand was aimed at its own target market segment. The result of this was that within a year of the launch, Polo had regained its position as **market leader** with almost 20% of market share – higher than at any time previously. Polo has since further extended the product range, and therefore the life of the product by selling, as a novelty, Polo holes (the middles from the mints) and soft Polos.

The diagram below shows where a firm has been successful in extending product life.

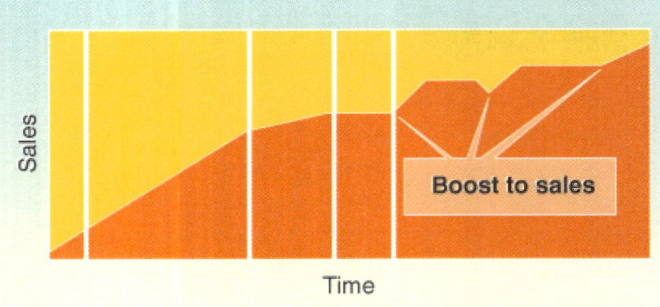

Activity

1. Roller skates were a product with a long and successful sales history but sales were in decline so a replacement product was introduced. This was roller blades. These went through a period of growth and popularity as they were heavily promoted. As sales began to go into decline, they were renamed 'in-line skates' and sales again recovered. Think of three other products that have been changed as they started to decline.

2. Look at the products that you have chosen and at the information in 'Did you know'. Write down in what way the products were changed.

3. If Polo was once again losing market share, how would you suggest it might recover it? Think about new product lines, new market segments and other methods that could be used, other than extending the product range.

Branding

Branding is the way in which products are identified with the firms that make them. Branding is used to give the consumer a feeling of safety and security, a feeling that they are getting the best. A brand may be a distinctive name, a logo, a symbol, a set of colours or a method of writing. Firms protect their brands and **trade marks** by registering them. Copying brands or styles may be illegal. Coca-Cola took Sainsbury's to court for making their Cola look too similar to Coca-Cola. As you can see, from the photograph, the distinctive colours and style of writing were extremely close to the original.

Some brands have become generic names for products in that market. This means that all products in that market have come to be known by the market leader's name. Hoover and Biro are examples, brand names that are used to describe all vacuum cleaners or all ball-point pens. This is not good for brands as they are no longer distinctive; firms will therefore try to prevent this happening or try to make their own brand distinctive again. Sometimes this may mean introducing and establishing a completely new brand name.

Leading brands tend to keep their position at the top of the market, for example, Kodak for cameras, Kellogg's for breakfast cereal, Wrigley's for chewing gum. Their strong **market position** makes it extremely hard for any newcomer to the market to gain sales. Often, the only way to break into a market is through new technology. Dyson, the vacuum cleaner manufacturer, has taken a large share of the market by introducing (and protecting in law) a system that maintains suction levels on its appliances.

Some products are known as generic products. This means products that are difficult to brand because consumers see no difference between one type and another. Fresh fruit and vegetables, for example, would be difficult to brand – although some firms still try!

Activity

1. Look at the goods in your refrigerator, freezer or pantry at home and draw up a three column list. In column one list all the branded goods that you have, in column two, all the unbranded goods, in column three all the generic goods.
2. Which column has the most in it? Why do you think that this is so?
3. Which column has the least in it? Why do you think that this is so?

Packaging

Codebreakers

Market leader: the number one in the market for a particular product measured by its percentage share of the market.

Product range: the different types of product that a firm produces to try and reach different parts of the market.

Diversification: moving into the production of different types or ranges of product other than the core product.

Research and development: trying out new ideas and developing new technology to come up with better products.

Core product: the main product that a firm produces, often the one that it depends on most.

Trade marks: the symbol, name or logo by which a product is recognised. Trade marks are registered and protected in law. TM is used to show where a trade mark is used, (r) for a registered name.

Market position: the place of the product in the market: the market leader is first.

Packaging is often referred to as the 'Fifth P' of the marketing mix – Price, Product, Promotion, Place and Packaging. It is an essential part of the marketing of a product and can be the difference between success and failure. Some colours and styles, for example, do not work. Imagine selling washing powder in a dark brown box. This gives out all the wrong messages. Colours that are used are whites, yellows, greens and blues, all of them in light or bright shades. The packaging gives the product an image and as such it is essential that the right appearance is given.

Mint Munchies and After Eight mints are essentially the same thing, a soft green mint filling inside a dark chocolate case. The packaging of the product is, however, entirely different. After Eights are aimed at the upper end of the market as an after dinner mint; Mint Munchies are a middle range confectionery. The packaging is the difference.

Activity

1. Choose a well-known brand of a product (Smarties, for example, or Heinz beans or Walkers crisps) and redesign the packaging so that the product would appeal to a totally different market.
2. Explain what market you have aimed the product at.
3. What other changes do you think you would have to make in the marketing mix to make this product a success?

SUMMARY

Six points to remember:

1. The product is probably the most important part of the marketing mix.
2. Products are aimed at particular market segments.
3. The product life cycle is the natural growth and decline of a product.
4. Product life cycle can be extended by altering or promoting the product.
5. Branding is how a firm gives a product a distinctive name or image.
6. Packaging is vital in reinforcing that image.

The marketing mix: product and the product life cycle

Unit 41
The marketing mix: promotion

Promotion is the third part of the marketing mix. This is how a firm tells its likely customers what products it has for sale, where they can be bought and why it would be in the interests of the consumer to buy them. This means that promotion includes any way in which a firm tries to sell goods and services to the consumer and ranges from **advertising** through to free gifts and public relations.

A band may be thought of as a particular product that needs to be promoted. In 1996 the band Upside Down released two singles and were heavily promoted in the music press. There was also a promotional television programme showing how boys were auditioned for the band. The promoters had a particular idea of what would make a successful combination. They were compared, at the time, with groups such as The Spice Girls and Boyzone, who went on to chart and international success. In the case of Upside Down, the product did not live up to the promotion and they were not as successful as these other bands.

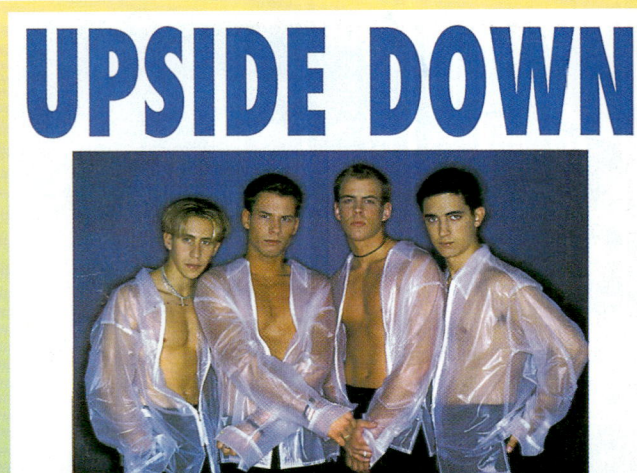

WHAT IS PROMOTION?

Promotion is telling the public about a product and persuading them to buy it.

This means that, to a firm, promotion is how they:
- inform customers about what products or services are available
- inform customers about what benefits the products or services will bring
- persuade customers to buy.

Advertising

Advertising and **public relations** are the way in which the public are first informed about the existence of a product or service. The advertising may be purely informative – a box in a local paper to say that such-and-such a firm is now taking orders for such-and-such a good or it could be a full-blown **advertising campaign**. In either case there is a sender – the advertiser, the message – the advertisement itself, the medium – the channel through which the advertisement is sent and the receiver – you, the consumer. As with all forms of communication there is no way of knowing whether the target audience has been reached. Even if sales of the product do go up, it may not be due to the advertising.

An example of an informative advert . . . or is it trying to persuade?

Handy hints

For a topic like advertising it is easy to collect a lot of information – posters, magazine advertisements, point-of-sale material and so on. In your coursework you must show that you have the skill to be able to select the most useful pieces of information rather than use everything that you have.

Types of advertising

These include:

Classified advertisements – 'small ads' selling goods or services locally

Informative advertisements – announcements giving information

Persuasive advertisements – advertisements designed to influence people

Generic advertising – advertisements produced by a whole industry, for example: 'eat more fish and chips'.

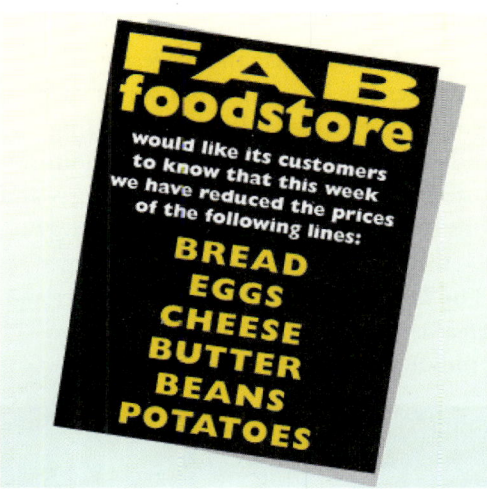

Activity

> Look at the informative advertisement for Fab Foodstore. By changing the lettering and using more adjectives (like smashing, wonderful, special, amazing, astounding, awesome, remarkable, excellent) make it into a persuasive advertisement.
>
> When you bring your advertisement back, you could try to make it even better and brighter by using computer graphics and fancy fonts.

Smashing

looks good in this font for example. It is called 'smashed'.

WINTER SALE NOW ON

could be in this style called 'ice display'.

THE MEDIA

This poster was the image used to promote Upside Down's single 'Never found a love like this before'. The same image was used on magazines, posters, and on the packaging for the record. The medium is the way the message is passed on. **Media** is the plural of medium and refers to all the ways of passing on advertising messages. In many cases the same image will appear on all the media used so that the message is reinforced many times. One of the most effective ways of getting a message across is by word of mouth, so telling your friends is one of the things advertisers will encourage. Other than word of mouth, advertising media are either broadcast or printed.

Broadcast media

- **Television:** expenditure on television advertising has continued to rise and now accounts for almost a third of all expenditure on advertising. TV commercials are generally expensive to make and expensive to show. Even a regional commercial television station (such as Yorkshire TV or Central) will charge more than £1 000 per second at peak periods. The advantage lies in the effectiveness of TV advertising.
  It can be targeted to hit particular market segments and it can reach millions of people.

- **Radio:** more commercial radio stations are broadcasting than ever before as the government has allocated wavebands for them. Radio advertising is a lot cheaper to make and to broadcast and, as most commercial radio stations are already aimed at a particular market segment, it is easy to target advertising. Adverts are much cheaper than television at £10 to £20 per second (usually in 30 second slots).

The marketing mix: promotion

Activity

1. At what time of day would you show advertisements for the following products?
   - a toy for a four-year-old that will also help them learn
   - a personal computer
   - the latest album from a country and western singer
   - the latest album from a boy band
   - a car.
2. Give reasons for the choices you have made.
3. Explain why it is difficult to give a single time slot for a car?

- **Cinema:** cinema advertisements can be longer versions of TV advertisements or may advertise things that are not allowed to be advertised on TV. There are also cinema slots for local businesses, which could be slides projected on to the screens or short videos made semi-professionally.

Did you know? Most newspapers have a low cover price because of the amount of advertising they carry. Some newspapers are delivered free. These free papers are almost all advertising which is how the cost of producing and delivering them is met.

Printed media

- **Newspapers and magazines:** this accounts for well over half of all the expenditure on advertising. Mass circulation dailies are the most expensive – a full page advertisement in *The Mirror*, for example, will cost £27 500 – with local classified advertising being within the reach of everyone's pocket. Magazine advertising has the advantage of being easily targeted (*see Unit 36*).

- **Trade press:** there are specialist magazines and journals for almost all trades and occupations. Some are 'in house' magazines, produced for a particular firm, while some are aimed at particular trades or professions. Many examples of trade press are free, being paid for by the advertisements they carry.

- **Customer magazines:** these are given away to customers using a particular business and generally carry a large percentage of advertising. Asda, for example, produces a regular full colour magazine. *Livewire* is the free magazine for rail travellers on GNER.

- **Posters and billboards:** the biggest billboards are called '64 sheeters' as this is the number of sheets of paper needed to cover them. Poster advertising accounts for about 5% of advertising expenditure. While posters can be striking and interesting – and for some goods like cigarettes are now the only way to advertise – they cannot reach a particular target market. The message must be short and direct and there is great competition to come up with eye-catching pictures and catchy **slogans**.

- **Anywhere there's a flat space:** advertising will appear on the side of buses, in train and bus stations, on envelopes and in postmarks, on racing cars, on team players' shirts, at the side of pitches and anywhere else that there is space for it. One advertiser even offered to pay for an advertisement to be placed on the space shuttle! Much of the sports advertising is sponsorship, explained on page 193.

190   The marketing mix: promotion

Activity

> Some of the most famous slogans may no longer be well known:
>
> *A Mars a day helps you work, rest and play* – Mars Bars
>
> *Just Do It* – Nike
>
> *Just for the taste of it* – Diet Coca-Cola
>
> *A million housewives every day pick up a tin of beans and say 'Beans meanz Heinz'* – Heinz baked beans
>
> *Guinness gives you strength* – Guinness stout
>
> *It takes up to 40 dumb animals to make a fur coat but only one to wear it* – LYNX, fighting the fur trade.
>
> Pick five goods and services that are currently popular with young people and write three advertising slogans for them as follows –
>
> - to give the impression that the good is a luxury good
> - to give the impression that the good is aimed more at females
> - to give the impression that the good is aimed at older people.

Activity

> Direct mail is often personalised. This means that a name and address can be inserted into a standard document to make it seem personal. Find out what this process is called and how to do it on your word processing package and then produce a document like the one below.

Direct mail

Direct mail or 'junk' mail is a way of targeting particular customers. A profile of a customer can be built up from the preferences that they have shown either by filling in questionnaires or guarantee cards or by buying particular goods or services. Information about customer preferences will be stored on a database so that likely customers can be approached. Do you buy dog food? Then you are likely to be interested in other pet products. Are you a member of a book club? Then perhaps you'd like to buy records through the post as well.

The most successful direct mail company is Reader's Digest. Direct mail selling or **direct marketing** cuts out wholesale and retail costs. When DeWitt Wallace first took subscriptions to Reader's Digest in 1921 in America, he also invented direct mail selling. Reader's Digest now has a world-wide readership of over 100 million and is published in 19 languages!

Did you know? The Data Protection Act means that you can have your name removed from anybody's database list so that you can cut down the amount of junk mail that you receive?

THE MESSAGE

The message is reinforced by **brand image**, slogans, logos and the repetition of the advertisement. While one classified advertisement in a local newspaper might be enough to sell on your unwanted bicycle, one showing of a commercial advertisement will never be enough. An advertising campaign will be a combination of advertisements placed in many different media and often repeated.

AGENCIES

Most advertising campaigns are actually put together by specialist advertising agencies. These are companies that bid for the advertising accounts of major advertisers. Gaining a large account (such as Kellogg's, Cadbury's, Procter and Gamble or Pedigree Petfoods) can be the difference between success and failure.

Agencies will produce a campaign – slogan, image and storyboard ideas for example – according to a brief given to them by the advertiser. In a large agency there will be a separate creative department, responsible for ideas and rough outlines, a media buying department, responsible for buying advertising space and air time and a television department, responsible for commissioning and instructing a production company. A successful campaign means repeat business and a successful agency!

BAD ADS

These fall into two categories:

Some advertisements fail to reach their target audience because they are badly made, too repetitive or annoying; such advertisements will lead to a fall in the sales of the product.

Some advertisements either make false claims or are offensive or illegal. 'Whizzbang petrol makes your car go faster' is unlikely to be true; 'Vroom cars – a car for men – no good for women 'cos they can't drive' is likely to cause offence. There are laws and Codes of Practice to prevent such advertisements being used.

> ### Activity
> 1. Is the direct mail document advertising the HOLIDAY OF A LIFETIME legal, decent, honest and truthful?
> 2. In what way would you criticise it?

ADVERTISING STANDARDS AUTHORITY

The Advertising Standards Authority is a group paid for by the advertising industry itself to keep a check that advertisements are 'legal, decent, honest and truthful'. The British Code of Advertising Practice describes what is meant by this. They investigate complaints from members of the public if advertising appears to be:

- illegal – e.g. advertising the sale of fireworks to under 16-year-olds
- indecent – e.g. using nudity in advertisements
- dishonest – e.g. telling lies about products
- untruthful – e.g. making false claims about what a product can do.

PUBLIC RELATIONS

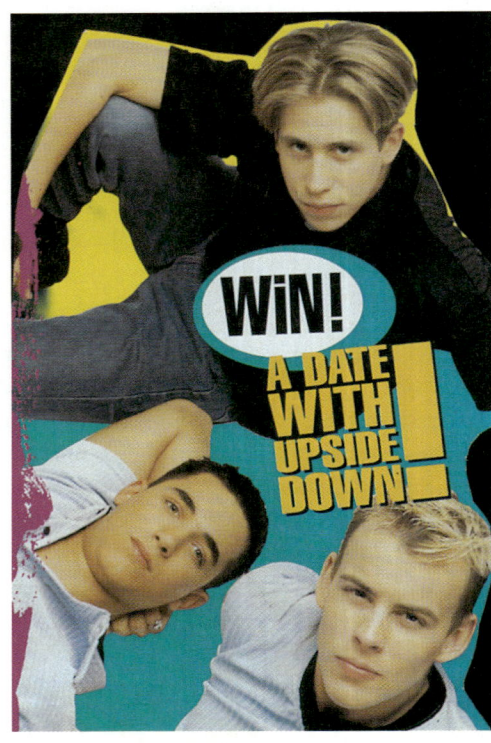

Often known just by its initials as PR, the public relations specialists have the job of making sure that the product has a good image in the eyes of the public. This may be done by one person, the public relations officer (or PRO) or by a PR department. Have a look at the picture showing part of the PR exercise that surrounded the promotion of Upside Down in 1996. PR often involves making news around the product – reports of two members of a band falling out, for example, may be written by the PR department with the intention of creating some media interest. PR will also organise visits, press releases, press conferences and photo opportunities. The main parts of PR are:

- **Customer relations**: making sure that customers are treated with courtesy and politeness, whether face-to-face or on the telephone, gives a good public image. Pledges that 'every telephone call will be answered within two rings' or 'money back if not satisfied – no questions asked' guarantees are now common and help to give companies an image of efficiency and caring. Many firms develop a corporate image, with uniforms, transport, notepaper, and even furniture in the company's colours. The reputation of a company may be more important than its actual production.

- **Endorsements**: getting famous people to say that your product is good is another way of giving a good image with the public. If a famous photographer, for instance, says he always uses XYZ cameras then this will encourage anyone who wants to be a good photographer to buy them.

- **Competitions**: prizes involving the product (as you can see in the picture opposite and below) or items of clothing, jewellery etc. worn by stars, are popular in the music and film world. Other competitions will be designed to increase sales or public awareness of certain aspects of the product.

- **Gifts and samples**: give-aways such as free posters, stickers or calendars are common in magazine publishing. Other firms will give away items with their name or logo on so that people will remember them when they come to use a pen, or a key fob or a mouse mat. Company and product names can be put on to almost anything. Firms may also provide free samples, delivered to homes or available to try in stores.

> **Did you know?**
> There are more subtle ways of keeping a product in the public eye. Product placement is when a company manages to get its product seen in films and on television without actually paying for advertising. It might be that the watches worn by Sean Connery or Sylvester Stallone are all supplied free by a particular company as long as they are seen to be wearing them in public. Car companies often supply cars to film companies for free so that the car's performance and image is seen every time the movie is shown.

- **Awards**: the advertising industry has awards and presentations. These are used by the companies winning them for extra publicity. In some cases, companies will use the awards even if they haven't won them. 'Nominated for ten Oscars' doesn't mean that the film concerned has actually won any, but looks good on publicity.

- **Sponsorship**: the most common sponsorship deals are with sports companies keen to promote their corporate image; football teams wear their sponsor's name on their shirt, grounds and stands are named after sponsors (the Alfred McAlpine Stadium, the Reebok Ground) and, in fields such as motor racing, sponsors' logos cover every inch of the car and the driver. Many sports would not survive without sponsorship so the link between sponsors and sports or competitions (such as the Cornhill Test series, the Nationwide League, the Coca-Cola Cup) is seen as a good one. In America, most television programmes are sponsored and the products

Activity

Emma runs a small business making cakes for special occasions. She has been in business for just over a year and has successfully built up sales of novelty birthday cakes for children. She now believes that the business could be more profitable and is considering three ways to increase sales:

- a small advertising campaign using a leaflet drop to local households and an advertisement in the local paper
- a link with local hotels to provide cakes for conference dinners
- expanding into additional product lines such as greetings cards and flowers.

> 1 Describe the advantages and disadvantages of each of these possible actions.
> 2 Suggest a further alternative idea for Emma.
> 3 Describe which action you think would be best for Emma, giving reasons for your decision.

The marketing mix: promotion

'placed' in the programme. Sponsorship of some television programmes has started in the UK. Even the weather forecast is sponsored! Sponsorship will also happen in other areas, where companies want to give a good public image. The advertisement offering free anti-smoking packs to teenagers was sponsored by the companies listed at the bottom of it.

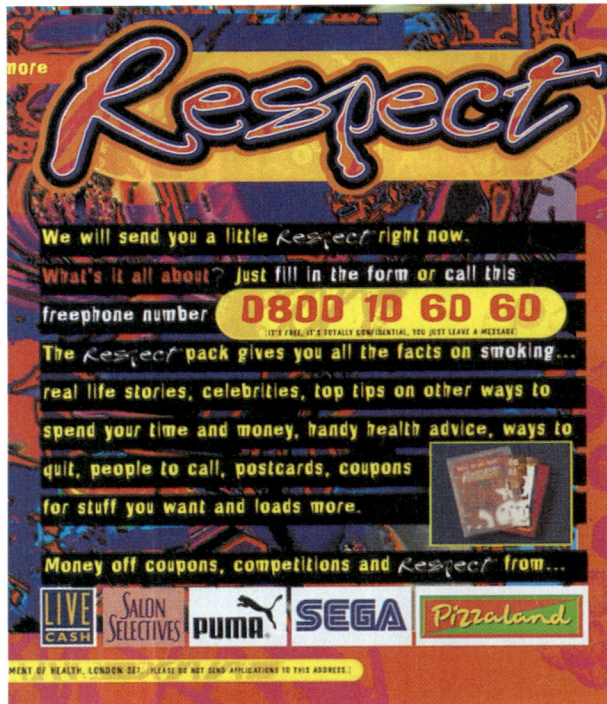

| Activity | hw |

> 1 You have been given the job of advertising the new single from the latest boy band – 'The Ladz'. Write a report to the record company which includes:
> - what media you would use and why
> - what public relations you would suggest (competitions, appearances, photo-opportunities, etc.)
> - what sales promotion techniques you would use.

>> 2 Write a press release for the launch of the band's single 'Luvvin' You', aimed at the teenage music press.

>>> 3 Re-write the press release so it is now aimed at a serious music magazine.

| Activity | hw |

> 1 There is some controversy over allowing companies like tobacco and alcohol manufacturers to sponsor sporting events.

> 2 Name three events or competitions sponsored by tobacco or alcohol companies.

Do you agree that these should be sponsored in this way? Give your reasons.

SALES PROMOTION

Sales promotion is the term applied to the various methods used to persuade the consumer to buy the product. It includes:

- **Special offers:** buy two, get one free; buy now, pay later; 25% extra free.
- **Discounts and price reductions:** 10% off; special low price.
- **Money off coupons:** either published in the press, delivered to homes, provided as part of the packaging of goods or to be sent away for.
- **Savings and discount stamps:** savings stamps are not as popular as they once were. Customers would collect so many stamps for purchases made and stick them in a book. The promoters published a catalogue of gifts which savers could buy using completed stamp books. This has largely been replaced by ...
- **Customer loyalty cards:** customers collect points electronically every time they make a purchase and are rewarded with money off or cash coupons. These cards are meant to ensure that customers will keep returning to the same store. They also enable the store to build up a database of their customers which will help when planning advertising or sales campaigns.
- **Free gifts:** products will sometimes contain such things as small toys, games or other gifts. This is particularly popular in manufacturers of breakfast cereals. Often such inserts are part of a ...
- **Joint promotion:** this is where one firm joins up with another one so that they both benefit from the publicity. Kellogg's might run a competition with Sega games as the prize or Nestlé might offer Disney videos at cut price. The 'Zone Passes' shown here are a joint promotion between a bowling alley and Sega games.

- **Point-of-sale material:** this is the display material used to attract customers to the product in the store. It may include posters and other special displays, such as special areas for the product. Even in small shops, manufacturers will provide special display stands for their product. The packaging itself can be seen as a part of point-of-sale material.

Activity

Handling structured information

1. Design a questionnaire to collect data about consumer preferences in your class – choose a particular range of products, like favourite breakfast cereal, favourite computer game and favourite band.
2. Enter the information into a suitable database.
3. Decide from the information which joint promotion would be most likely to succeed and design a direct mailshot promoting the campaign. Remember that you need to save and print out your work regularly to show how it has developed.

This activity partially fulfils the NEAB Certificate of Achievement in IT.

Codebreakers

Public relations: keeping the image of the product in the public eye in ways other than advertising.

Advertising: bringing a good or service to the attention of likely consumers.

Advertising campaign: the use of different types of advertising, following the same theme, to increase sales and reinforce brand image.

The media: the methods by which advertisements are presented to consumers.

Slogans: catchy 'one-liners' meant to help consumers remember the product.

Direct marketing: selling directly to the consumer, rather than through a sales outlet.

Brand image: the 'picture' which a manufacturer wants people to see when their brand is mentioned e.g. modern, sporty, fashionable.

The British Code of Advertising Practice: the voluntary code that controls British advertising.

Corporate image: the brand image of a firm.

Sales promotion: methods of encouraging consumers to buy.

Handy hints

Remember that not all promotions are necessarily linked to the final consumer. If you remember what you know about the chain of production, you will realise that trade promotions, for wholesalers and retailers, will also be important. These will include discounts, free gifts and sale or return offers.

MERCHANDISING

This used to be the term used for all aspects of selling products to the consumer and included sales promotion, advertising and public relations. It is now more often used to mean the spin-off goods that are sold as the result of a successful product launch. Disney is probably most successful at this, selling mugs, pens, T-shirts, caps, pyjamas, duvet covers, books, tapes, posters, dolls, drinks, lunch boxes and much more linked to their most well-known characters. Often the merchandising from, for instance, a movie, will make more money than the movie itself *(see Unit 11).*

SUMMARY

Seven points to remember:

1. Promotion is how a firm informs customers that products are available and how it persuades the customers to buy.
2. The main part of promotion is advertising.
3. Advertising involves choosing the right media to get the message to the target market.
4. Advertising must be legal, decent, honest and truthful.
5. The Advertising Standards Authority is the industry body that regulates advertising.
6. Public relations is the way in which a firm creates and keeps a good public image.
7. Sales promotion methods are used to persuade consumers to buy.

The marketing mix: promotion

Unit 42
The marketing mix: place – distribution

The final part of the marketing mix is the place where the product is to be sold to the final consumer and, more importantly, how the product is to get to that place. Products travel from the manufacturer through a **chain of distribution** so that products are available in the right place, at the right time and at the right price for the target market.

In the autumn of 1997, the Huddersfield Canal Company received £15 million from the Millennium Commission in order to reopen the Standedge canal tunnel under the Pennines. This was part of a complex Victorian distribution system. At the same time, railway companies were talking about opening up the two rail tunnels that run under the Pennines from Yorkshire to Lancashire, parallel with the M62 motorway. These could again be part of a freight distribution network and relieve some of the pressure on the congested road system. Such schemes are all about getting raw materials to manufacturers and getting the finished goods to a place where the final consumer will buy them.

Standedge Tunnel

PLACE

The place that a product is sold must provide the right setting for the consumer to buy the product and involves a firm in choosing the right channel of distribution.

This means that, to a firm, place is:
- choosing the right channel of distribution
- choosing the right method of distribution
- choosing the right sales outlet.

Supply

Where promotion concentrates on the demand side – trying to influence consumers to buy the product – place concentrates on the supply side. Good distribution means that products arrive at their final destination intact and on time. Different types of transport will be used according to what is being transported. If a product is perishable, or breakable, or urgently needed, then transport can be chosen accordingly – canals, for example, were traditionally used to carry very heavy cargoes like coal, or breakable ones like pottery where speed of delivery was not important.

Did you know? Canals were the major form of long distance transport at one time. They were safe and could transport large quantities of fragile or heavy goods. Their major disadvantage is that they were slow, although they were faster than road. The invention of the steam engine and the growth of railways meant that canals fell into disuse.

Activity

> Which methods of transport would you recommend for the five products below? Briefly explain why in each case.
- a human liver for transplant surgery from Glasgow to London
- bananas from Africa to England
- frozen fish fingers from Liverpool to Manchester
- cigarettes from America to England
- coal from Germany to London.

CHAIN OF DISTRIBUTION

This is the means by which products reach sales outlets. The most common chain is

This is sometimes altered to cut out either or both of the wholesaler and retailer. They may be replaced with agents, or either producers or wholesalers may deal directly with the public. For example, the producer of fitted furniture made to a customer's specifications, will deal directly with the customer or a wholesaler might also act as a retailer (carpet warehouses, for instance).

Producer

The producer or manufacturer makes products in large amounts and will usually sell them on to a firm that will buy them in large amounts. In some cases, part of production is sold directly to the consumer – as in the case of farm shops, for example, or garden centres who both grow and sell their own stock.

Wholesaler

The **wholesaler** buys from producers and manufacturers in bulk, and usually provides both transport and a storage site. Wholesalers often face paying the bulk of distribution charges as they transport goods to warehouses. It is likely to be wholesalers who would be interested in a cheaper and quicker way of crossing the Pennines than road transport. Because they are buying in large amounts, they are able to buy at relatively low prices. When they sell the goods on, they will have to recoup their transport and storage costs as well as the cost of their services.

Cash and carry

One of the more recent developments has been **cash and carry** stores. These are where a wholesaler displays goods in a warehouse sized shop for **retailers** to come and buy what they need. Retailers are still buying in bulk and receiving their discount but, instead of ordering from a wholesaler and having to wait for delivery, they can collect exactly the goods that they want. The wholesaler has cut down on delivery costs and can also use the fact that the warehouse is designed like a shop to encourage retailers to buy using special offers, point-of-sale material and other promotions *(see Unit 41)*.

> **Handy hints**
>
> Think of the stores along your local high street. How many of them would you expect to see in the high street of a neighbouring town? These are all likely to be chain stores – stores which have different branches in different towns. You need to know that some of the stores are franchises (like McDonald's or The Body Shop) and remember the names as it is almost impossible to tell them apart from chain stores.

Retailer

A **retail outlet** is anywhere where the consumer can purchase the good. Most retailing takes place through shops of various kinds. These range from giant superstores to independent small corner shops. They include:

- Department stores: for example Harrods in London, where the shop is divided up into different departments.
- Multiple stores: for example Marks and Spencer and Boots, where the company has many different branches of the store.

> **Activity**
>
> One of the coursework titles asks 'How does a small retailer survive despite competition from larger retailers?'
>
> Look at the reasons given in this unit and apply them to a retailer that you are familiar with locally.
>
> 1 Which do you think are the most important reasons for them?
> 2 What threats do you think are being posed by the larger competition?
> 3 Do you think that this retailer will continue to survive?
> 4 What evidence can you collect to support your views?
> 5 How will you use the evidence in forming your views?

The marketing mix: place – distribution

These can be further subdivided into:

- Variety chain stores: selling a range of different goods – Woolworths, for example.
- Specialist chain stores: concentrating on a core range of goods – Dixons for cameras and electrical goods for instance.
- Franchise chains: Mcdonald's hamburger bars and Body Shop are examples of chains owned by franchisees *(see Unit 4)*.

Not all retail outlets have to involve shops; vending machines, mail order catalogues and direct mail selling are common. Being able to buy goods by telephone or television ordering or via the Internet are methods that are becoming much more common.

Survival of the small retailer

Why does the small retailer continue to survive despite the competition from much bigger retail outlets? There are a number of reasons, many of them based on the **non price competition** that small shops can make.

- **Personal service:** one of the attractions of many small retailers is that they have personal knowledge of the customer and, rather than self-service, will personally serve the customer. This can be a very important social contact for people who live alone, especially the old.
- **Convenience:** the location of small **retail outlets** is generally a great deal more convenient than large stores. Large stores are designed for people with their own transport. They are also designed for large purchases, so everyday goods such as bread and milk are deliberately placed as far away from the door as possible which means that customers must pass all the other goods before getting to where they want. Checkouts are impersonal and often have long queues.
- **Providing community service:** the small local retailer will often provide such things as a board for local 'for sale and wanted' advertisement cards, savings clubs and a space for posters advertising local events.
- **Opening hours:** local shops often have longer and more convenient opening hours than large stores (although some supermarkets are trying to counter this with 24 hour opening).
- **Informal credit:** local shops may allow people to take goods and pay for them another day. In many cases, this informal credit (sometimes called 'on tick' or 'on the slate') helps families to budget.
- **Delivery services:** local retailers may pack orders up for customers and may also deliver them.
- **Specialist goods or services:** some local retailers offer specialist goods which people prefer to buy from a specialist rather than mass produced versions. This could include butchers, bakers and greengrocers. Many local shops are based around a particular local service, such as newspaper delivery, confectionery or a post office. Many also provide other services such as video rental or lottery ticket sales.

Activity

> Using a CAD or drawing package, design a supermarket layout that will encourage people to buy as much as possible. Note where particular goods will be and how your layout is designed to cut down on theft.

198 The marketing mix: place – distribution

> **Handy hints**
>
> Bulk is not a word that is often used these days, except in business! It means a 'large amount'. The bulk of a weight lifter is muscles, for example. Materials bought 'in bulk' are those bought in large amounts. It is the use of words like this that can gain you extra marks in both examinations and coursework.

Breaking bulk

Both retailers and wholesalers **break bulk**. This means that they buy in large quantities and provide the service of selling in smaller amounts. A wholesaler buys by the container or lorry load from the manufacturer and provides storage space in warehouses. This means the manufacturers or producers do not have to store their own goods. The retailer will buy by the case or box from the wholesaler and the consumer then buys single items from the retailer. The retailer and the wholesaler both benefit from lower unit prices because they are buying in bulk.

Direct sales

Not all products are sold to the final consumer through a shop, store or by mail or machine. Some are sold directly on a door-to-door basis, with a salesperson calling with samples, for example, Avon cosmetics. Others may be sold by agents who will receive a commission, such as Tupperware (through Tupperware parties). Door-to-door sales are less common than they used to be but have been largely replaced with telephone sales, where a salesperson rings up and tries to sell goods via the telephone; this is particularly popular amongst manufacturers and fitters of double glazing and kitchens.

Many sales to retailers or wholesalers are made by sales representatives, who will be able to offer discounts and special deals and are probably paid on commission according to the amount of sales that they make. **Network marketing** is the use of salespeople's networks of friends, neighbours or work colleagues to provide likely consumers.

Shopping malls

In the United States of America, these have been common for a long time. They are huge areas where a large number of shops are all together under one roof, linked by pedestrian areas. Inside are major national chains and also smaller retailers providing food, or 'market stall' type goods. There are large areas available for display and large car parking areas. You will now find such centres in all of Britain's major towns. A further development has been the out-of-town shopping centre. These are even larger sites with extensive parking facilities and other special transport arrangements – some with their own bus services and even their own train stations! They house many shops under the same roof. The first of these in the UK was the Metro Centre in Newcastle but this has since been overtaken by such massive developments as the giant Meadowhall Centre, on the M1 motorway just outside Sheffield.

The Meadowhall Centre

> **Activity**
>
> ▷ What do you think are the advantages of such shopping centres:
> - to shoppers
> - to the shops themselves.
>
> Can you think of any disadvantages?

The marketing mix: place – distribution

DISTRIBUTION CHANNELS

To get from manufacturer to consumer involves different channels of distribution. The channel will depend on both the type of product and the type of customer. The traditional channel of distribution is as outlined in the producer to consumer chain we saw earlier. For some products and for some customers this is not appropriate. Buying fresh produce from a farm shop, for example, is a much shorter distribution channel, with the farmer acting as producer, wholesaler and retailer and the consumer paying a lower price. Direct mail from a producer is also likely to keep prices down. Many major companies will have their own channels of distribution – Asda, for example, has its own warehouses and fleet of delivery vehicles. The longer the channel of distribution, the more people have been involved and the more expensive the final product will be.

IT and distribution

Computerised distribution and stock control systems are making it much easier for manufacturers, wholesalers and retailers to ensure that the chain of distribution is efficient. A supermarket system will not only tell the supermarket management when to order stock, it will probably order it automatically itself. Bar coding allows IT systems to know how much is sold, how much is stored on the premises, what is available in the warehouse and when to have goods delivered. This means that large stores can keep a constant flow of goods to their shelves and should never run short of stock. IT systems are also used in distribution centres to work out the best and most efficient routes for distribution.

International networks

Many distribution networks are not just national, but international. International distribution involves customs and excise, shipping laws and regulations and a lot of forward planning. Bananas, for example, are picked in their green state, are too heavy to be flown in and are therefore shipped to arrive just as they are beginning to ripen. Flowers, on the other hand, will be flown in as they are reasonably lightweight. Manufacturers have to choose between speed, security and expense when deciding which international methods of transport to use.

Activity

Volume through our food distribution network has been growing at the rate of 12% per annum for the last three years. Last year we increased grocery capacity by building a new warehouse.

We have also reconfigured the remaining network to provide 30% more space for fresh and frozen storage. Further efficiencies will be obtained as we focus on reducing supplier direct deliveries, and introducing stockless distribution techniques.

– Asda Group Annual Report

The passage is taken from the Annual Report of the Asda supermarket chain.

1. Explain why you think that Asda has built a new warehouse.
2. Explain what is meant by the phrase 'reconfigured the remaining network to provide 30% more space . . .'
3. Explain why you think that Asda is trying to increase the volume of goods through its food distribution network.
4. Explain what is meant by 'supplier direct deliveries' and 'stockless distribution'. Why does Asda wish to encourage these?

Did you know? Some international distribution networks are so large that you will find the end of them in some unlikely places. The Europort for goods arriving across the channel is at Wakefield, several hundred miles to the north. This is because the network of motorways here makes it easier to distribute goods around the country.

Activity

Think of a product that you have bought recently. It might be an item of clothing, or a magazine, or an ice cream, or a drink, or a game …

▸ **1** Explain, in detail, how the marketing mix has been used to persuade you to buy this product. Don't forget to mention all four parts of the marketing mix (and anything else that you think might have affected your decision to buy).

▸▸ **2** Explain how you would improve the marketing mix for the product you have written about. Which parts would you concentrate more on, and why?

▸▸▸ **3** How would you be able to afford to change the marketing mix?

▸ **1** Interview a member of your family about a major purchase they have made in the last year or so. Ask them what influenced their decision to buy.

Looking at their answers, explain what you think is the most important part of the marketing mix and why.

Codebreakers

Chain of distribution: the way in which goods get from the manufacturer or producer to the consumer.

Wholesaler: a link in the chain, buys from the producer, sells to the retailer.

Cash and carry: a wholesale warehouse set up as a retail outlet for certain customers.

Retailer: a link in the chain, buys from the wholesaler, sells to the consumer.

Non price competition: competing on service, or selection or other things when price competition (selling at lower prices than competitors) is not possible.

Retail outlet: anywhere where a consumer can purchase a good.

Breaking bulk: selling in small amounts goods bought in large amounts.

Network marketing: using friends and families as your target market then asking them to introduce their friends and families to you, thus creating a network.

MARKETING MIX

The four elements are Price, Product, Promotion and Place. They are known as the 'Four Ps'. It is the mixture of these that is important when marketing a good or service.

Finding the right **price** to appeal to your target market

Developing a **product** for which there will be demand

Using **promotion** in order to persuade people to buy the product *and*

Making sure that it is available by being distributed to a convenient **place**.

If the producer can get the mix of these right, then their product will be a success.

SUMMARY

Seven points to remember:

1 Place is the final part of the marketing mix.
2 Place actually refers to the distribution of a product.
3 Distribution is getting the product to the consumer at the right time and price.
4 The traditional chain of distribution is producer to wholesaler to retailer to consumer.
5 More modern distribution systems may cut out some of these stages.
6 Wholesalers and retailers buy in bulk and break bulk.
7 IT helps to make distribution more efficient.

The marketing mix: place – distribution

Unit 43

The marketing mix: protecting the consumer

There are certain practices in marketing that are not allowed as they are unfair, illegal or morally wrong. Some of these practices are forbidden by UK law, some by European Union law and some (as with the Advertising Standards Authority – Unit 41) are controlled by voluntary bodies. Both legal and **voluntary codes** are designed to make sure that the consumer is treated decently, fairly and honestly.

A firm will try to meet high standards of both product and service. Many of these standards are enforced by the law. The page shown here is taken from the catalogue of Lowe Alpine, a mountain equipment and clothing supplier. The clothing which they retail must conform to the highest standards of safety and comfort. It is tested both in the laboratory and also 'in the field' on mountains and at extremes of temperature and weather. The claims that they make for their clothing must be true, and the descriptions of its performance must be accurate as it is often just the standard or performance of clothing that means the difference between life and death. For Lowe Alpine, it is essential that protecting the consumer is uppermost in their minds when planning advertising, sales brochures or catalogues.

PROTECTING THE CONSUMER

Protecting the consumer is making sure that the customer is getting goods and services that do what they are supposed to do as described, are fit for use and are not dangerous. The consumer should not be put at a disadvantage by sales techniques or misleading information.

This means that, to a firm, protecting the consumer means:
- telling the truth about goods and services
- not attempting to deceive the consumer
- complying with the law relating to what they sell
- complying with any voluntary codes relating to what they sell.

PROTECTING YOURSELF

Caveat emptor are the Latin words that are often used when talking about protecting the consumer. The two words mean 'let the buyer beware' and are used to show that the best people to judge consumer fairness are often the buyers themselves. If they 'beware', in other words, if they are careful about what they buy, then many consumer problems will not arise. You can help yourself as a consumer by making sure that you:
- read instructions and follow them
- read ingredients
- read the small print.

Likely to be true?

202 The marketing mix: protecting the consumer

Take note of the claims made for the product, either in the way it is described or in the way in which it is advertised and ask yourself:

- does it do what you want it to do?
- do the claims sound genuine?
- is there any after-sales service?
- are there any guarantees?

Make sure that, as a consumer, you know your rights. How would you complain if goods you bought were faulty or dangerous? Who would you complain to?

> ### Activity
>
> Look at the picture of mountain clothing on the previous page.
> 1. Write down three reasons why it is important for the company to describe their goods accurately.
> 2. Write down three reasons why it is important for the consumer that products are described accurately.

What should you do?

If you buy a good that is faulty, or doesn't work, or doesn't do what it is claimed to do, then you have the right to have it replaced or receive your money back. In the case of a service that is not carried out properly, or as described, or in a reasonable time, then you have the right to withhold payment until it is done properly or to have another firm complete the work to your satisfaction and at the expense of the first firm.

With goods, the first thing to do is to take the item back to the retailer. As the people who sold it to you, it is the retailer who is responsible to you. It is not the manufacturer who should meet your claim. It is up to the retailer to claim their money back from the manufacturer.

If you find that the retailer is not willing to give you your money back, you can contact a trade association or organisation if they belong to one. Most trade associations will handle complaints about their members, especially if a member is not upholding the law or is not behaving according to the association's rules or code of practice.

As a last resort, if you cannot gain satisfaction elsewhere, you can take the retailer to court. As long as the sum

involved is less than £1 000 then you would go to the small claims court. This is made extremely easy and inexpensive so that people do not have to instruct lawyers or pay out large amounts of money. A magistrate makes the decision as to who is in the wrong and often makes the loser pay the winner's expenses as well.

WHAT IS THERE TO HELP THE CONSUMER?

Voluntary codes of practice

In many cases it is voluntary codes of practice, set up by the industry itself, that lay down what is or is not acceptable. The Advertising Standards Authority (ASA), for example, has stopped advertisers from using 'hidden' persuaders or from exploiting racial issues in adverts. The newspaper publishing industry has recently laid down a code of practice regarding the privacy of famous people. There are associations like the Association of British Travel Agents (ABTA) or the National House Building Council (NHBC) and it is well worth checking that the firm you buy goods or services from has membership, as they can provide many safeguards. There are also professional associations that govern behaviour and what is acceptable in certain professions, for example the General Medical Council (GMC), who can have doctors prevented from practising medicine if they are careless, dishonest or incompetent.

> ### Activity
> - Visit your local small claims court and find out what steps you would have to take to make a claim. How long would you expect it to be before a case was heard? What forms would you need to fill in? Collect an example.

> **Did you know?** There used to be a type of advertising called 'subliminal' advertising. This flashed the name of the product up on to a movie screen while the film was showing for such a short space of time that the eye did not see it. The brain, however, remembered the product name subconsciously and the consumer was therefore hypnotised into buying the product. This is now illegal.

The marketing mix: protecting the consumer

Local authority help

The Local Authority helps to maintain standards by employing Trading Standards Officers. These will check on weights and measures and investigate any traders who have been the subject of a number of complaints. Sometimes they will expose bad practice to the public so that the trader loses business. Sometimes, if the trader has broken a law, they will take them to court. Environmental Health Officers check for food hygiene and investigate other risks to health including things like pollution and illegal waste disposal. Public Health Inspectors enforce the provisions of the Food and Drugs Act (see page 205).

> **Did you know?**
> One of the biggest pollution offenders is noise pollution. If noise near airports, factories or night clubs for example – rises above a certain level, then action can be taken to ensure that it is kept down.

Independent help

There are many independent organisations set up to help the consumer by ensuring that standards are kept. Perhaps the most important is the BSI.

- The **British Standards Institute** (BSI) tests products to make sure that they are safe, reliable and of good quality. The British Standards 'Kitemark' ▽ shows that a product has been tested and meets certain standards. BSI also check quality systems in firms and work closely with ISO – the International Standards Organisation.

- The British Electro-Technical Approvals Board (BEAB) check and approve electrical items for safety and reliability.

Activity

Martin Ashcroft is a student at the college. He is a good climber and is interested in all kinds of outdoor pursuits. He usually only buys his gear from one or two reputable shops, where he is quite well known. Six weeks ago, he went to a canoeing event where a firm he had not previously heard of was selling gear from a van. He bought a jacket at a reduced, sale price of £35 which he would have expected to pay £70 for at a shop. He paid for it in cash and was happy to buy it as it carried a well-known brand name.

When he got it home, he discovered that the side seams had not been sewn properly and that the jacket was therefore useless. He has left it in the boot of his car until today, when he came across the same van at an event. The retailer has refused to change the garment or refund any money as Martin:

- does not have his receipt
- should have brought the jacket back straight away.

Also, he claims:

- it's the manufacturer's fault
- as it was in a sale, Martin has no right to a refund.

> 1 For each of the four statements above explain whether it is true or not, giving reasons for your answer.
> 2 Advise Martin of his legal rights in this situation.
> 3 Explain who you could report the trader to and what action they would be able to take.

- Citizens' Advice Bureaux provide free help and advice in all sorts of matters including consumer rights and will assist in making complaints, getting replacements, or taking traders to the small claims court. The address of your nearest one will be in the telephone directory.

- **The Consumers' Association** is an independent body and publisher of *Which?* magazine. In this magazine, products are consumer tested and reported on and the best buys are pointed out. The magazine also exposes bad or unfair practices and helps to prevent dishonest or underhanded dealing from happening.

- There are also television consumer programmes which expose bad practice, dishonest trading and faulty or dangerous goods.
- The Office of Fair Trading was set up in 1973 to provide information and advice to consumers. Much of this is in the form of leaflets, which may be obtained free from Citizens' Advice Bureaux or Local Authorities. The Director General of Fair Trading has the job of constantly examining consumer problems, consumer law and consumer credit.
- OFTEL, OFGAS, OFWAT are examples of consumer protection organisations, set up to make sure that when certain industries were privatised they did not exploit their monopoly position by charging prices that were too high. OFTEL is the office for telecommunications, OFGAS for the gas suppliers and OFWAT for the water supply industry.

EUROPEAN UNION

The European Union now sets many standards in food, safety, health and hygiene. Often these cause argument and debate, for example the EU does not want British sausages to be called sausages but 'cereal and meat filled tubes' as they do not meet the standards of other European sausages. The EU is also against things like doorstep deliveries of milk, for health reasons.

THE MAJOR ACTS

The government lays down the law in many areas of consumer protection covering health, safety, criminal acts and general fairness. Listed here are the major Acts of Parliament relating to consumers. The years given are the dates when the Act was first passed and dates on which it has been amended.

Handy hints

You don't have to learn every part of every Act by heart! It would be useful, however, to put together a list of the major consumer rights that you have and match them against the appropriate Acts.

- **Food and Drugs Act, 1955/1984.** The main part of this Act is that it is illegal to sell goods which are 'unfit for human consumption'. It also covers the way in which goods should be described, so that misleading descriptions are not given. For example whether orange juice is orange juice, or orange squash or orange flavoured depends on the amount of pure orange juice

Activity

Magnus Taylor is in the sixth form. Last weekend he was asked to join his friends at the local swimming pool to try out the new slides and wave machines. He decided that he needed some new swim shorts so bought some that looked fashionable. Imagine his embarrassment when he got into the water and found that the shorts turned completely see through. He rushed to the changing rooms to get changed and, as he took the shorts off, they came apart in his hands, the material disintegrating until only the waistband remained. The following day he took them back to the shop.

The shopkeeper told him that he couldn't have his money back because he didn't have a receipt and, anyway, these were fashion shorts which were not meant to be used in the water and were not resistant to chlorine. He pointed to a notice by the till that read 'swim shorts sold in this shop are not resistant to chlorine'.

1. What should Magnus do now? Write down the steps that you would take if you were in this situation.
2. What rights does Magnus have in this situation?
3. What rights has the shopkeeper got in this situation?
4. Write down which laws you think would apply in this situation and explain why.

Magnus decides to pursue a claim for compensation.

5. Write him a letter from the Citizens' Advice Bureau explaining what steps he needs to take.
6. Explain, giving reasons, what chance Magnus has of gaining compensation.
7. Outline whether his experiences at the swimming baths would have any bearing on the case, and why.

The marketing mix: protecting the consumer

> **Did you know?**
>
> The power of a reputation is so great that, at one time, China named one of its steel producing centres 'Sheffield' so that it could call its steel 'Sheffield steel'!

used. A meat and potato pie with more potato than meat in it must be labelled as a potato and meat pie; the largest ingredient must always come first so that the consumer has a better idea of what they are buying.

- **Weights and Measures Act, 1963/1985.** This gives inspectors the power to check scales and weights and says that all weights (plus the price per weight – £ per kilo for instance) should be stated on pre-packed goods.

- **Resale Prices Act, 1964.** Suppliers can only suggest the lowest price at which their goods should be sold (MRP – Manufacturers' Recommended Price) but retailers are allowed to sell at less if they wish. Suppliers may not refuse to supply goods to someone selling at the lower price.

- **Trades Descriptions Act, 1963/1968/1972.** States that accurate descriptions of goods must be given, whether in advertisements, as verbal descriptions or at the point of sale. Real champagne must be just that, Sheffield steel must be steel made in Sheffield. The Act laid down what information had to be provided on labelling such as 80% wool, 20% nylon, colourfast and the country of origin for foreign goods.

- **Unsolicited Goods and Services, 1971.** If goods that you have not ordered are delivered to your home you are entitled to keep them for free if they have not been collected in six months. This period reduces to thirty days if you tell the firm to collect them.

- **Fair Trading Act, 1973.** This set up the Office of Fair Trading (see page 205).

- **Consumer Credit Act, 1974.** This refers to goods which are bought on credit. Full information of what the cash price is, what the annual percentage rate of interest (APR) is and what the total credit price is must be given to the consumer. If buying goods from home, they are allowed a 15-day cooling-off period in which they can decide not to go ahead with the purchase. This is to stop people being pressured by salespeople into buying things they do not want.

- **Consumer Protection Act, 1978/1987 / Consumer Safety Act, 1978.** There must be clear displays of price, to include things such as VAT. With sale prices, goods must have been on sale at the higher (pre-sale) price for a period of 28 days. This is to stop traders from just making it look as if prices have been reduced. There are also certain goods such as night-dresses, electrical goods, paints, toys, cots, etc. that must be safe or must carry appropriate warnings. Consumers can claim damages if faulty goods, or goods on which there was insufficient warning, cause harm. Poisonous and dangerous goods (poisons, solvents, medicines, irritants) must be clearly marked as hazardous and first aid advice given on the packaging.

- **Sale of Goods Act, 1979/1994 / Supply of Goods and Services Act, 1982.** Goods sold from a business must be fit for the purpose for which they are sold, must match the description given to them and

> **Activity**
>
> ▷ Look at the questions involving Martin Ashcroft and Magnus Taylor. Choose one of these situations and, using a word processing package, write a letter outlining the situation to a television consumer programme. If you save and print the letter and then change it by:
>
> - deleting some words, sentences and paragraphs to edit it
> - adding at least one paragraph
> - moving at least one paragraph
> - using underlining, emboldening and italics
> - altering the margins
> - altering the justification to left, right and centred
>
> – then you will have fulfilled the requirements of the Word Processing Unit of the NEAB Certificate of Achievement in IT.
>
> **1** As an extension exercise for homework, exchange the letters written with someone else in your group and write them a reply from the television programme explaining what you intend to do.

> **Handy hints**
>
> One of the commonest ways to test you on your knowledge of consumer law is to ask, in an examination paper, what you would do in a certain situation. Shut your eyes and put yourself in that situation. Who would you complain to? What organisations could help you? What backing would you get from the law?

must be of 'merchantable quality' – in other words, fit to be sold. Consumers who buy goods do not have a contract with the seller if any of these conditions are broken and are entitled to their money back or to replacement goods. These rights cannot be taken away by a retailer putting up signs such as 'no returns'. This law also states that it is the retailer's responsibility to put the situation right. The 1982 Act extended these rights to services as well as goods – consumers should expect reasonable standards from tradespeople. The 1994 Act changed the old word 'merchantable' to 'satisfactory' and strengthened consumers' rights so that they are entitled to their money back and do not have to accept a replacement or a credit note.

- **Unfair Contract Terms 1980.** Contracts between consumers and traders must be reasonable, and unreasonable disclaimers do not count. An example of an unreasonable disclaimer would be if a plumber said that his work was not guaranteed against leaks. For example, if a trader offered to fit a new kitchen in a two-week period and the customer accepted this but the fitter then took several months, the reasonable contract would be upheld – even if the contract said 'this work may not be completed on time'. This would be seen as unreasonable.

MORAL CONSIDERATIONS

There is a moral argument against the sale of certain products and there are laws in place to protect people. Tobacco products now carry a large government health warning, telling of the risks of cancer, heart disease and smoking whilst pregnant. Fireworks may only be sold to people over sixteen years old. Certain glue-based products are restricted as is alcohol and the advertising of alcoholic drinks.

Green issues

There are other issues that affect marketing. Environmental issues have become much better known in recent years so that manufacturers now find it helpful to claim that they are being 'green'. Recycled packaging is used, or ozone friendly aerosols, or bleach free washing powders or statements that 'no animal testing is involved in production' or that 'trees for paper are taken from managed sources' are made. This has come about as consumers have become more environmentally aware so that highlighting such things will increase consumer demand for the products involved.

SUMMARY

Five points to remember:

1. Most firms strive to meet high standards of product and service.
2. Customers who are dissatisfied can get help to gain satisfaction.
3. The retailer is responsible for the sale, therefore responsible to the consumer.
4. Voluntary organisations exist to help the consumer.
5. The law, at local, national and international level, exists to help the consumer.

> **Codebreakers**
>
> **Voluntary codes:** agreements between members of a particular industry to police themselves, rather than have laws passed to control them.
>
> **Caveat emptor:** the Latin words that are used in consumer law. They mean 'buyer beware' and are used to show that the consumer must always be careful.
>
> **British Standards Institute:** a non-governmental body which, nevertheless, receives government funding to carry out testing and certification.
>
> **The Consumers' Association:** an independent body which carries out testing and reports its findings in its magazine *Which?*.
>
> **Office of Fair Trading:** a government organisation set up to uphold fair trading laws.
>
> **Privatised:** companies that have been taken from government control and sold into the private sector.
>
> **Monopoly:** a single company which has enough control in a market to be able to set prices at its own level.

Unit 44

The external costs and benefits of business activity

When a firm produces goods or provides services it creates many costs and benefits. While many of these costs and benefits directly affect the firm and appear in the profit and loss account, some of them may be felt by the wider community and environment outside the firm. When this happens they are known as external costs and benefits, sometimes shortened to the single word **externalities**. In many cases it is very difficult to put a money value on these externalities. While **external benefits** add to the welfare of the community outside the firm, external costs cause many problems especially in finding ways to prevent, control or stop them.

Most communities have examples of developments which have created **external costs** and benefits and which have led to heated debates. In Northumberland, Wansbeck District Council together with the County Council have planned a road that will arguably be an important link between Ashington's new Business Park and the A1 trunk road about seven miles away. Part of the link road will create a generally welcomed bypass for the village of Pegswood but the planned route will cut through some of the village's existing recreation land. There are also coal reserves lying under the route on the southern edge of the village. This coal must be extracted by opencasting before the road can be built. Nearer the A1 itself, an ancient woodland will have to be cut down, at least one farm will be cut in half and a smallholding made uneconomic. The debate has been fiercely fought in the council chambers and in the local newspapers with an action group formed to try and stop the road. An enquiry has been started into the need for opencasting with the final decision on the road likely to be made by the Department of the Environment.

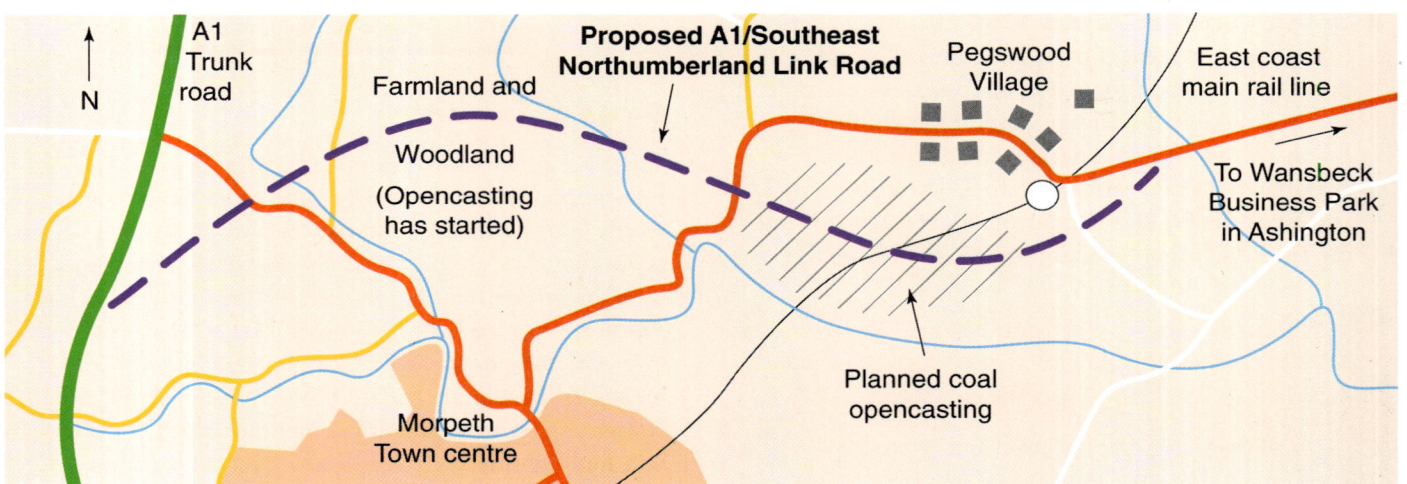

Activity

1. Try to identify all the groups of people and organisations that might be affected by the building of this link road.
2. For each group or organisation, identify any costs and benefits they might receive.
3. Put yourself in the role of an inspector from the Department of the Environment. What sort of information would you need to decide whether the road, and therefore the opencasting, should go ahead?

EXTERNAL COSTS

The exact nature of external costs depends on the development that takes place and where it takes place. The list below gives the full range of possible external costs but most developments will create only some of the costs.

Pollution:
- noise from factories and traffic
- smell from factories and traffic
- waste in the forms of smoke, gases, solids and liquids
- the unsightliness of buildings and developments
- safety hazards from factories and traffic.

Business closure:
- lost employment in that business
- lost incomes for those made unemployed
- lost expenditure on goods and services by the firm and its workers.

Other:
- lost amenities if a business closes or buildings are knocked down
- a loss of our heritage if new developments are built on historical sites
- overcrowding and overstretching of resources if too much development takes place in one area
- lost peacefulness of a rural area.

You might be able to increase this list of possible costs by thinking about developments in your area. When you look at this list, try to decide which ones could have a money value easily calculated and which would prove very difficult to do this.

EXTERNAL BENEFITS

As with external costs, the exact nature of the benefits depends on the type of development and where it takes place. Placing a money value on these benefits is probably more difficult than for external costs. Typical external benefits include:

- The creation of jobs and incomes from a new business.
- If jobs and incomes are being improved, the standard of living for these families should be improving.
- Extra spending from these families will create income and possibly jobs for other groups of people.
- Some developments will improve transport, communications and facilities within an area which may benefit the whole area.
- More businesses being created may help to regenerate a run-down area and give the people more confidence for the future.
- Some benefits are quite accidental, such as the good fishing in areas of the sea where power stations cool their generators.
- Some benefits are quite imaginative, such as using the heat created from waste burners to run central heating for nearby housing estates or social facilities (see diagram on page 210).

Think of developments in your own local areas to see if you can extend this list.

What can be done about external costs?

There is no magic formula to apply to developments that create external costs. In some cases, it is very difficult to measure the cost to the community or environment, and in some cases it is difficult to prove what has caused it. Possible methods include:

- Pressure groups or local action groups might cause so much bad publicity that an organisation decides to do something about the external cost being generated.
- Laws might be passed that create rules preventing or limiting external costs. If the rules are broken the organisation might be taken to court and fined if the case is proven.
- Government policies might be introduced that change the way we think about issues. For example, there seems to be a change in policy that will make it more difficult to build out-of-town shopping centres; and there may yet be new policies to encourage public transport and discourage car users.
- The government can use taxes to 'punish' polluters. For example, taxes on petrol have been increased to try and reduce the use of cars and therefore help the environment.

The external costs and benefits of business activity

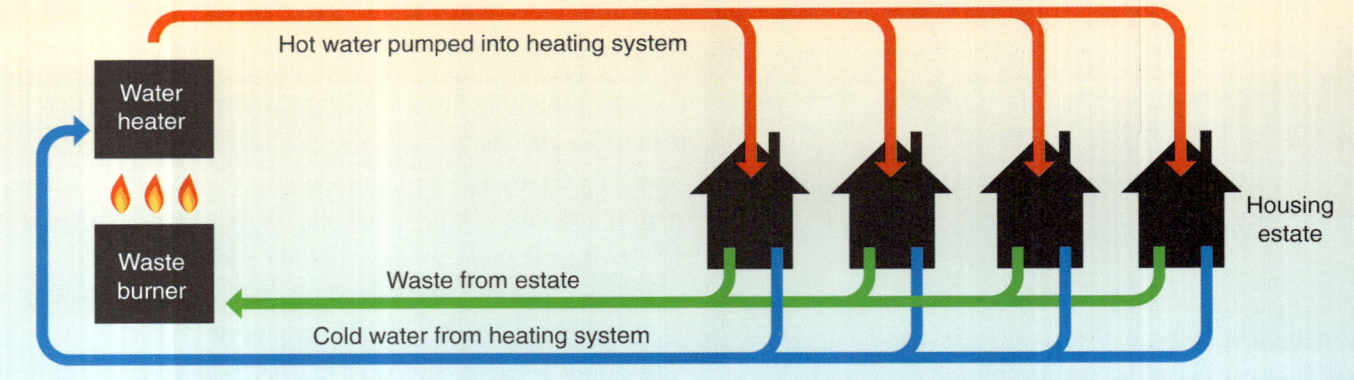

A closed system for effective use of resources and waste

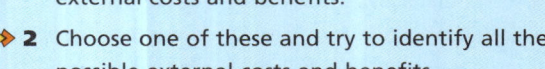

Activity

1. As a class, make a list of existing and proposed projects or developments in your local area which might be generating external costs and benefits.
2. Choose one of these and try to identify all the possible external costs and benefits.
3. Produce a grid on a poster to show which groups or organisations are being affected by which costs/benefits.

Codebreakers

Externalities: something that results from a production activity or development that is felt by the community or environment outside the producer. They may be a cost or a benefit to the community.

External costs: these are costs felt and paid for in some way by the community or environment and not by the producer of the costs.

External benefits: the community or environment gains when some sort of productive activity or development takes place. The producer of the benefit does not directly benefit from this.

- It is possible to introduce a complete ban to stop some developments. Some buildings, for example, are listed as historically important and cannot be changed. Some waste incinerators have been identified as too dangerous and planning permission has not been granted.

Handy hints

In an examination paper, a question might ask you to describe the possible external costs and benefits from a particular development. A slightly more difficult question might ask you to weigh up the costs and benefits. If this is the case, try to show which benefits might balance out which costs and decide if the costs are likely to be greater than the benefits overall. For a coursework assignment, you may find many new business developments being proposed which you could investigate. New shopping centres, pedestrianised areas, the introduction of parking charges or even the closure of a major local employer could all be investigated using external costs and benefits.

SUMMARY

Four points to remember:

1. When a production activity or some other development takes place, it may generate an externality that is felt by the outside community and environment.
2. These externalities may be costs to the community or may benefit the community.
3. It may be quite difficult to calculate the money value of these costs and benefits.
4. Pressure groups, laws, taxes and changes in government policies may all be used to limit the effects of external costs.

Unit 45

Business and changes in economic policies

When a firm is operating, it may find its operations are unexpectedly affected by changes in government policies. This unit concentrates on changes in the government's spending and taxation policies, and changes in interest rates which are triggered by the Bank of England. Both of these sets of changes will have direct and indirect effects on business activity.

Since the election of the Labour government on 1 May 1997 there have been a series of small increases in interest rates. The higher interest rates were attempting to reduce consumer spending in the economy. Bank of England figures showed that in the second quarter of 1997, consumer spending had risen by 1.5% while spending on durables was up 6.8%. Some of this extra demand was caused by the proceeds of building society share sales. Total consumer spending remained strong right up to October. By November 1997 interest rates were 1.25% higher than in May and the impact was just beginning to be felt. In November, high street stores began to report that sales figures were down on those in the same period in 1996. Many companies believed that the higher interest rates had slowed consumer spending in the run up to Christmas and were not confident of another record in Christmas sales figures for the year.

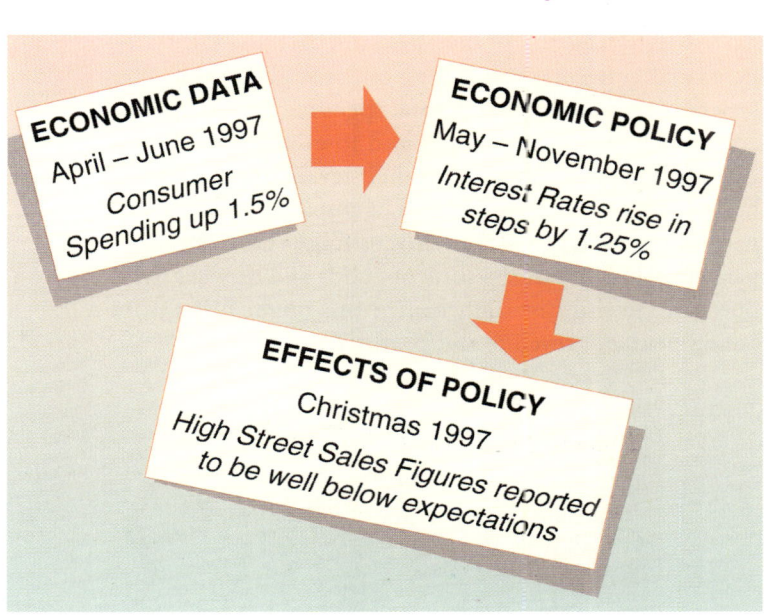

FISCAL POLICY

The budget secrets on the way to the Commons

Fiscal policy is the name given to the government's policies on its spending and taxation activities. Normally, once a year, the Chancellor of the Exchequer will announce the government's spending and revenue plans in the House of Commons. Once this **Budget** speech has been debated and agreed, the policies will begin to affect both consumers and businesses.

Changes in government spending

There are three broad categories of government spending. They are **transfer payments**, current goods and services and capital spending:

- **Transfer payments:** spending on benefits and help for the sick, old, disabled, unemployed and young.
- **Current goods and services:** spending on goods and services, and wages for workers in education, the Health Service, defence and law and order.

- **Capital spending:** the building of new roads, hospitals and schools.

Very roughly, 75% of this expenditure is carried out by central government and 25% by local government. Changes in the three categories of spending can have quite different effects on business activity and it is not always easy to predict the extent of the effects.

A cut in benefits to some groups of people, such as a reduction in unemployment benefit, would have an almost immediate effect on the unemployed's ability to spend. They would have to cut out spending on unnecessary items and concentrate spending on basic goods and services. This might reduce total spending in the whole economy which in turn could lead to even more unemployment if firms found their revenue and profits both falling. On the other hand, a cutback on the rate of pensions paid to our senior citizens might have only a particular impact on the sorts of goods and services they purchase. In this case, only some firms might suffer from falling demand, revenue and profits.

If the government decided to increase spending on the Health Service by raising wages for those employed in the Health Service and by increasing the number of doctors and nurses employed, the impact on businesses might not be immediately obvious. In time, some of the extra income received by Health Service workers will generate extra spending on a variety of goods and services. This extra spending will create income for businesses and they may decide to increase production and take on more workers, but such decisions depend on many factors. These include:

- How much extra spending has been created?
- Will there be a permanent increase in spending?
- Are other groups of workers benefiting from higher wages?
- Will some of the wage increase be saved?

Increases in capital spending on roads and buildings often take a long time to affect business. It will obviously help to guarantee jobs in firms that undertake such work, but whether more jobs are created depends on these firms' order books. It takes several years to plan and build many of these projects, so any increase in such spending may be spread over a long time and may not have a large effect on employees spending in the shops.

Changes in government taxation

Businesses are probably most affected by three broad types of taxes. These are:

- **Taxes on income:** the two main taxes on income are income tax and employees' national insurance contributions both of which affect workers' **take-home pay**.
- **Taxes on expenditure:** Value added tax (VAT) which is placed on most goods, except food and children's clothing, at 17.5%, and excise duties on alcohol, tobacco products and fuel for vehicles are the two main forms of taxation on consumers' expenditure.
- **Taxes directly placed on business:** profits are subject to corporation tax, while businesses also have to pay rates on their premises to local councils, and national insurance contributions for each employee.

Any changes in these taxes will have quite a range of effects on a business. A change in income tax will affect workers' take-home pay. This in turn will affect their ability and willingness to spend money, which will therefore affect sales, revenue and profits for business in general. In this case, any business is indirectly affected because it depends on how workers react to the tax change.

A change in expenditure taxes will directly affect a business in the first place. Changes in the rate of VAT, for example, will affect the price that the firm has to charge. Any change in price may then have an impact on consumers and the quantity they are prepared to buy. In this case, the change in tax also has an indirect effect on business activity.

Changes in corporation tax, business rates and employers' national insurance contributions will all have direct effects on businesses. Changes in the last two will affect a firm's costs and therefore probably its prices. Changes in corporation tax will affect the amount of profit after tax and therefore a firm's willingness and ability to invest, especially if the firm prefers to use retained profit as a source of finance.

Activity

> 1 Try to find out some of the existing rates of tax for the main taxes such as income tax, national insurance, VAT, corporation tax and the duties on beer and tobacco.

> 2 Try to find out the main items of both central and local government expenditure.

> 3 If you find out enough information about government taxes and expenditure, try to draw charts and graphs to show some of this information. Use IT programs to help produce colourful displays.

> 4 Try to find out how some of these taxes work and report back to your class.

Monetary policy

A range of policies that try to control the amount and cost of money in the economy are called a government's **monetary policy**. There are some complex policies that try to control the ability and willingness of banks and financial institutions to lend money. Other policies are used to influence interest rates which should be thought of as the cost of borrowing money. For GCSE Business Studies we can limit ourselves to the effects of interest rate changes on business activity. Changes in interest rates are triggered by an independent committee of the Bank of England setting a central rate each month. Any changes in this central rate will eventually influence all other rates in the financial markets.

Changes in interest rates will have both direct and indirect effects on business activity. Many of the effects cannot be predicted with great certainty because people and business may react in quite different ways. To explain the possible effects, we will look at a rise in interest rates.

The indirect effects of interest rates on business will be felt through the reactions of consumers to higher rates. Consumers buying goods and services on credit will find that the full price of these, including the cost of interest payments, will be higher. It may be that consumers do not feel particularly affected by this or they may decide to spread the payments across a longer period of time. If the increase in interest rates is high enough, however, it is likely that consumers will eventually reduce their spending. Additionally, consumer spending will probably be reduced because the higher interest rates will push up mortgage rates on people's homes so reducing spending power. Generally, higher interest rates slow down spending thus reducing revenue and profits, and possibly leading to lower employment.

Interest rates are a cost of production to most firms. A rise in interest rates will therefore raise costs which may lead to higher prices. This shows us another way in which a firm is indirectly affected by higher interest rates, this time through higher prices when inputs are purchased, as well as directly through the higher interest rates it pays on its own borrowing.

Higher interest on a firm's borrowing may be analysed in two ways. Overdrafts are likely to be immediately more expensive thus raising costs and squeezing profit margins. Existing loans may be unaffected if they have been agreed at a fixed rate, but any new loans will be arranged at higher rates and therefore may make the investment less profitable. If the firm also believes that demand for goods and services is falling because of higher interest rates in the economy, it may view investment projects as being more risky and it may halt the investment.

A fall in interest rates will more or less work in the opposite way to the process described above. Consumers' spending will probably rise and therefore so will firms' revenue and profits. At the same time, production costs will fall a little as will the cost of financing new investment by borrowing. Falls in interest rates should improve the confidence of both consumers and producers.

Handy hints

For the examination, you do not need to know in any detail how individual taxes work. Nor do you need to know the rates of tax, the amounts the government spends on different services, and nor do you need to know the actual rate of interest. What you *do* need to try and understand is how firms might be affected by changes in taxation, government spending and interest rates. This includes both direct effects and indirect effects such as the way consumers react to these changes. Try to think through changes in both directions; for example, an increase in VAT and a decrease.

Business and changes in economic policies

Codebreakers

Consumer durables: these are products bought by consumers to last a long time, so examples will include fridges, televisions, washing machines and furniture.

Fiscal policy: the use of government spending and taxation to control the state of the economy.

The Budget: an annual announcement by the Chancellor of the Exchequer in the House of Commons explaining the government's plans for taxation and government spending in the next 12 months.

Transfer payments: money paid in goods, services or benefits to those in need, such as people who are unemployed, sick or retired. Money is transferred to them from the taxpayers.

Monetary policy: this attempts to control the amount of money available in the economy and the cost of borrowing money which is more usually known as the rate of interest.

Take-home pay: this is the money left to a worker after deductions for tax and pensions have been made from gross pay and before any money is actually spent.

Activity

» Try to explain how each of the firms described below might be affected by the following changes:
- a decrease in the rate of income tax
- an increase in VAT from 17.5% to 19%
- more government spending on school textbooks
- a fall in interest rates by 1% over six months
- a rise in excise duty on cigarettes by 25p per pack of 20.

Firm A: a large electrical retailer
Firm B: a large supermarket chain
Firm C: a medium sized housebuilding company
Firm D: a book publisher
Firm E: a tobacco manufacturer.

SUMMARY

Four points to remember:

1. The government has a range of economic policies that it can use to control the economy, but two of the most important are fiscal and monetary policies.
2. These policies will change taxes, government spending and interest rates.
3. Changes in any of these three items will have both direct and indirect effects on firms.
4. Some of the effects are difficult to predict because people and firms often react in quite different ways.

Business and changes in economic policies

Unit 46

Business and the state of the economy

When a firm is operating it will be affected by the state of the country's economy, as well as having some influence on the economy itself. Most economies throughout the world go through a business cycle, moving from **boom** to **recession** and back to a boom. During this cycle, firms will be both benefiting and suffering from changes in unemployment rates, inflation rates and growth rates.

It is quite useful in this unit to look at some of the changes in the UK economy in the last few years. Output of all goods and services grew at 2.3% in 1993 and 4.5% in 1994. It remained quite steady at 2.8% in 1995 and 2.5% in 1996. The forecast for 1997 was an annual growth rate of about 3%. This **growth** in 1997 was particularly noticed in the service sector, with business services such as computing doing best of all. **Inflation** figures are more usefully looked at monthly. Headline inflation, which includes all items, stayed around 2.2% between May and September 1996. A sharp rise to 2.7% in October 1996 then led to some fluctuation in the rate with a low of 2.4% reached in April 1997. Since then, there have been small increases each month which led to the interest rate increases described in Unit 45. Unemployment rates can be shown monthly but are more easily described annually. From a peak of 10.5% at the start of 1993 they have decreased very steadily to around 5.7% in the middle of 1997. Not only has the rate of unemployment fallen but the number of job vacancies has increased, suggesting that firms are keen to recruit. In some areas there are quite noticeable skill shortages.

THE BUSINESS CYCLE

The typical business cycle for the UK is shown on the right. The usual amount of time from peak to peak is four or five years, although there have been occasions when it has been nearer seven or eight years. Throughout this cycle the economy will be growing at different rates. The continuous straight line labelled as the average growth rate shows the average rate achieved over the period.

If the UK achieved an average of 3% growth in its national output each year for 24 years, the country would benefit from a doubling of its living standards. Businesses would benefit from this because they would be supplying the goods and services to meet the rising demand, thus revenue and profits would both increase. The problem for business is, however, that the overall, upward rise in demand and output is not smooth. As the economy moves through the business cycle, growth speeds up and then slows, matched by changes in unemployment rates and inflation rates. These fluctuations affect firms in many ways, causing them to change their plans and policies.

The UK business cycle

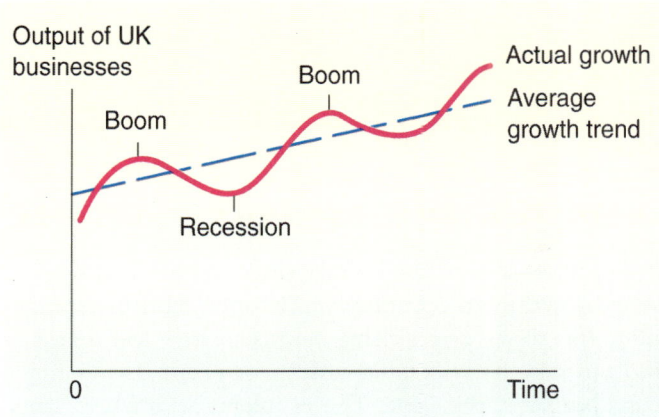

Unemployment and business activity

As the economy moves out of a recession, unemployment will begin to fall. Demand for goods and services will be rising giving firms some confidence to start increasing output. This might require more workers, so that average incomes will begin to rise. More income means more spending power so demand for all goods and services is likely to continue to rise.

Activity

1. Keep a record in the classroom of the rates of unemployment, inflation, growth and any other changes you read or hear about.
2. Decide what other data could be collected and decide how to record the data.

Handy hints

Try to think of the effects of changes in unemployment in small, logical steps. One way to show this is in a flow diagram. As the economy moves out of a boom and towards a recession, increasing unemployment might have the following effects:

Rising unemployment → Falling incomes → Falling demand for all goods and services → Fewer goods/services sold → Falling revenue and profits → Falling demand for labour → Lower investment → More unemployment → Fewer services as shops close / Higher social security payments/benefits / Lower government tax revenues

Inflation and business activity

Inflation is a rise in the average prices of goods and services within an economy. Sometimes, a business might quite like to see prices rising because it may feel that it too can raise its prices and earn more profit if sales and costs both stay the same. The problems arise when firms find that their costs are rising because of inflation and they are losing their competitiveness on price. Some of the effects of inflation on business can be shown in a series of logical chains.

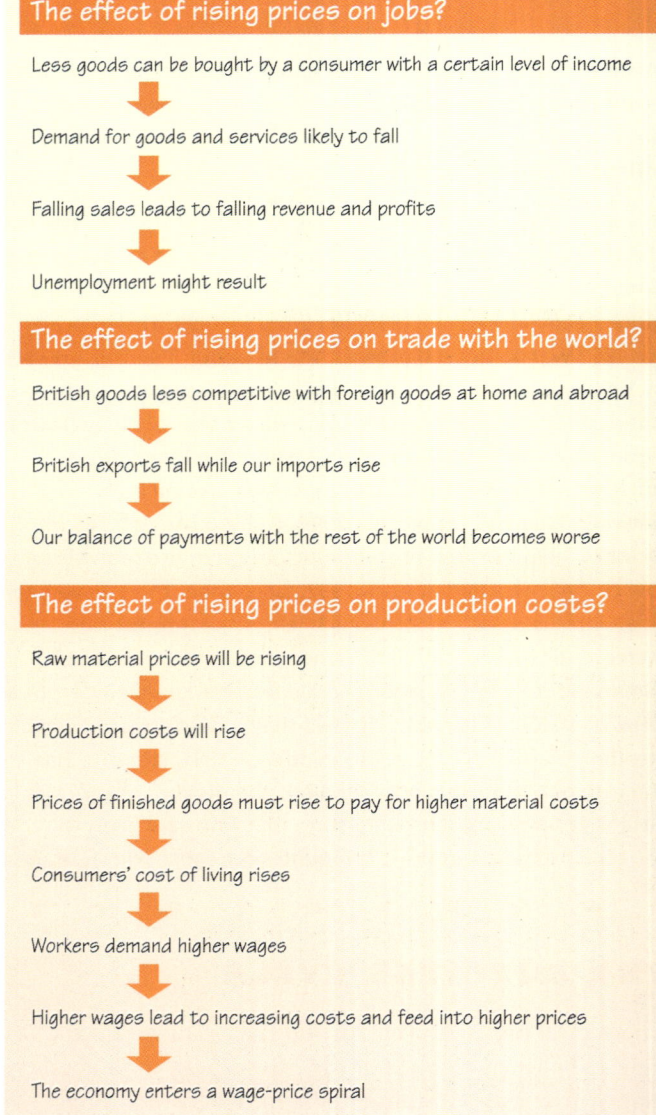

The effect of rising prices on jobs?
- Less goods can be bought by a consumer with a certain level of income
- Demand for goods and services likely to fall
- Falling sales leads to falling revenue and profits
- Unemployment might result

The effect of rising prices on trade with the world?
- British goods less competitive with foreign goods at home and abroad
- British exports fall while our imports rise
- Our balance of payments with the rest of the world becomes worse

The effect of rising prices on production costs?
- Raw material prices will be rising
- Production costs will rise
- Prices of finished goods must rise to pay for higher material costs
- Consumers' cost of living rises
- Workers demand higher wages
- Higher wages lead to increasing costs and feed into higher prices
- The economy enters a wage-price spiral

This last chain of reasoning shows the major fear with inflation. Price increases may create conditions in the economy that lead to ever higher inflation, with the country becoming less and less competitive with foreign companies. These fears have helped persuade governments in the last 20 years to make the control of inflation their number one target. Some of the policies used to control inflation are explained in Unit 45.

216 Business and the state of the economy

Activity

>> In Unit 45, the final activity looked at the effects of economic policies on five imaginary companies. Those companies were:

- A a large electrical retailer
- B a large supermarket chain
- C a medium sized housebuilding company
- D a book publisher
- E a tobacco manufacturer.

For each company, try to think through and explain the possible effects on the company of the following separate changes to the UK economy:

1 A rise in unemployment from 5.7% to 8%.
2 An increase in growth from 3% to 3.3%.
3 A rise in the rate of inflation from 3% to 5%.

Codebreakers

Boom: this occurs when demand for, and the output of, goods and services in an economy are high. Employment and levels of income are likely to be high and price increases might be accelerating.

Recession: a lack of demand for all goods and services means that output levels are low, leading to rising unemployment although price increases are likely to be slowing down.

Growth: this is the economic growth of an economy measured by the increase in total output of all goods and services over the period of a year.

Inflation: is the rise in average price levels of goods and services measured by the retail price index.

Wage-price spiral: wage increases will eventually start to put up production costs and therefore push up prices. Higher prices will lead to workers demanding higher wages which may then start to push up prices even further. There is a spiralling relationship between wages and prices.

SUMMARY

Four points to remember:

1 The UK economy, like all others in the world, goes through a cycle as demand and supply rise and fall.

2 As the economy moves through this cycle it moves from boom to recession and back to boom.

3 Throughout this cycle, growth rates, unemployment rates and inflation rates will change.

4 Changes in these rates will affect all firms and their activities, although the decisions the firms make will also affect the actual levels of growth, unemployment and inflation.

Unit 47
Business and Europe

When a firm is operating in the UK it needs to remember that it is also operating in the European Union (EU). There are now 15 countries that are full members of the EU with at least six more applying to join. This has created a single market of over 370 million people for firms to sell in, while many regulations, policies and directives exist both to help and to control business activity.

The creation of the European Single Market has increased competition in UK domestic markets while it has created new opportunities in European markets. All companies, whether they export or not, have had to review their marketing strategies in particular. Companies like Reckitt & Colman, who manufacture well-known brand names like Harpic, Haze, Steradent and Dettol, have reorganised their company's approaches to competition in Europe. New management structures, a European Supply Organisation, 12 National Business Units to target sales and marketing at the needs of local customers, and concentration on key products have all been introduced. This is backed up by extra research and development into new products. The potential rewards are very high for companies like Reckitt & Colman but the risks are even greater if companies do not plan for this huge market.

WHY HAVE A EUROPEAN UNION?

Countries that join the EU are committing themselves to a policy of unification. Gradually, some of the powers of the individual countries have been transferred to the EU's policy makers. The goals of the EU include:

- protecting the rights of each country and its citizens
- creating an economic and monetary union including a single currency
- helping achieve social and economic progress
- common citizenship shown by the common passports for all the countries
- co-operation in justice.

WHAT DOES THE EUROPEAN UNION DO?

The EU is a very large and complex organisation which both directly and indirectly affects our lives and the actions of business organisations. Some of the main functions and how they affect the UK are outlined below.

- Since the Single European Market was established on 1 January 1993, companies, goods and people can travel between the member countries without being stopped at the borders. There are no barriers to trade such as tariffs or quotas, nor the more hidden differences in safety or environmental standards, between the member countries. This should make it easier for British firms to trade in the EU although the difficulties of language, transport costs and consumers' tastes may still create some problems. Of course, the single market makes it easier for EU firms to trade in the UK, so we might find an increase in imported goods and services.
- The EU works together to create jobs and to improve training. It is now quite easy to work in another EU country.
- If you visit another EU country and fall ill you can get medical help as if you were in your own country.
- The EU is setting increasingly higher standards on environmental matters. Standards are now fixed for water purity, seawater and beach cleanliness, noise levels, and the use of chemicals by industry and farmers. This has affected some UK industries. For example, the water companies have had to invest many millions of pounds into sewage treatment plants to meet minimum standards on bathing water.
- Consumer laws have been made in addition to those in the UK which extend the rights of and protection for consumers, especially on food and toys.
- The Common Agricultural Policy (CAP) helps farmers by making sure they get enough money for growing crops and providing other farm produce; but the EU is now trying to find ways to reduce the famous

'mountains' and 'lakes' of stored foodstuff. For some UK farmers this has meant cutting back on milk production or setting fields aside, leading to some economic hardship for the farming community in some areas.

- The Social Charter sets out basic principles for workers' rights and regulations in the workplace. Gradually, these principles are being put into practice although not every country has fully adopted all the ideas. The UK has not yet signed up fully to The Social Charter. The final goal is to set minimum standards in such things as health and safety matters, hours of work, benefit rules, pension rights, working conditions, redundancy arrangements, equal opportunities and perhaps minimum wages. For UK firms, the introduction of some of these requirements might increase costs although in some cases British workers have rights above the intended minimum already.

- A major help to some regions of the EU, including parts of the UK, has been its regional policy. In regions such as Northern Ireland, which have been lagging behind economically, there is an emphasis on providing financial help to modernise transport and communication links, to improve energy and water supplies and to help small business development. Regions such as North East England or parts of the Midlands and South Wales, are seen as declining industrial areas. Here the priority is to provide finance to support existing UK help through creating jobs, improving the environment and encouraging research and development. In rural areas such as North West Scotland, Mid-Wales and parts of South West England the focus is on encouraging new jobs outside farming both in small businesses and in tourism. Transport improvements are also targeted.

- With the creation of a single currency, the Euro, economic and monetary union is perhaps receiving most headline treatment in the media. It is planned that most EU countries will join this union and adopt the Euro but to do so, each country must have its economy under strict control. The UK is working towards this but the government has said that it will allow the people to vote saying whether they want to replace the pound with the Euro. A single currency will mean that travellers and firms will no longer have to exchange pounds for other currencies in the EU. There will be no fluctuation in the exchange rate between member countries so there will be less uncertainty for business. The Euro will have the combined strength of all member countries so it should be able to withstand the fiercest international monetary shocks. Most exporters want to see the UK adopt the Euro. The concerns mainly rest with the idea that we are giving away the country's rights to make many of its own economic decisions.

Activity

> Try to find out more about the EU and how it affects you, your local community, and the businesses in your area. One of the best places to start is your public library. Most now have access to detailed information about the EU and this is available in many different forms. You could also contact your local Member of the European Parliament (MEP) by looking in the telephone directory.

Handy hints

You might be able to do a coursework assignment linked to the EU but you will need to discuss this with your teacher as it is not linked into one of the agreed titles in the syllabus. For the examination papers, you need to be able to understand how the EU might affect business organisations. This will include the effects of the single market, the possible effects of policies controlling business activities, of how help for consumers or workers, for example, might affect firms, and of the help for UK businesses such as EU regional policy. As we move towards a single currency, listen to the debate and try to understand some of the points for and against its introduction: in particular, try to decide how firms might be affected.

SUMMARY

Two points to remember:

1 All UK firms now operate in a single market of over 370 million people.

2 These firms are increasingly controlled and affected by policies made by the EU as the organisation slowly moves towards greater unification.

Business and Europe

Unit 48
Business within the international environment

When a firm exports any of its goods it is competing within world-wide markets. The sale of goods and services abroad enables the UK to pay for the goods and services we do not produce or cannot produce as well as other countries. Trading means exchanging British and foreign currencies, so any changes in the value of the pound will affect British firms. British firms will also be affected by unexpected international events. Sometimes countries may try to slow down or stop the inflow of goods to protect their own domestic industries.

An increasing number of firms now operate within global markets. This involves markets that are even larger than those of the Euorpean Union described in Unit 47. As people travel ever greater distances for their holidays, they find company and brand names littering every location as if they were back at home. McDonald's restaurants are now very popular in the old communist bloc countries while Coca-Cola appears to be drunk in every country of the world. Kellogg's cereals, Ford cars, Kodak films are just three other names that you will see all round the world. This has come about partly because of improved communications and partly through the decline of **barriers to trade**

Activity

> 1 As a class, try to add to the global products and companies listed above.
>
> 2 Sometimes a firm may decide to adopt a single name to help a product sell in global markets. For example, 'Opal Fruits' was changed in 1997 to 'Starburst'. What advantages and disadvantages would this create for the parent company Mars Confectionery?

IMPORTS AND EXPORTS AND THE BALANCE OF PAYMENTS

Imports are goods and services that are brought into the UK with payment flowing out to the foreign producers who supplied them. When UK producers sell goods and services abroad they are called **exports**, with the money earned coming back into the UK. These flows of money are recorded on the country's **balance of payments** with the sale of actual goods described as **visibles** and the sale of services called **invisibles**.

In 1996, the UK imported £12 228 million of goods more than we exported. Our invisible earnings were much higher than our invisible payments so that overall the current balance was only a £14 million deficit. This was a good year for the UK especially compared to 1989 when our balance was a massive £22 398 million deficit.

THE EXCHANGE RATE

Each country in the world has its own currency. This means that firms trading in international markets will have to exchange one currency for another at some point in the trade deal, just as holiday-makers do when they travel abroad for holidays. The value of the UK pound against other currencies is called its exchange rate. The value of the pound may be calculated against all other currencies, but we usually compare its value to major currencies like the US dollar and the Japanese yen. Exchange rates will vary each day and they will affect a firm's ability to trade competitively.

If the pound is valued highly or its value is rising, our exports become more expensive while our imports become relatively cheaper. This may result in falling demand for British goods both at home and abroad. A low value for the pound, or a falling value, will make British goods cheaper at both home and abroad. In this case, British firms might expect to sell more goods and services. This can be shown by a simple example using some fictional figures:

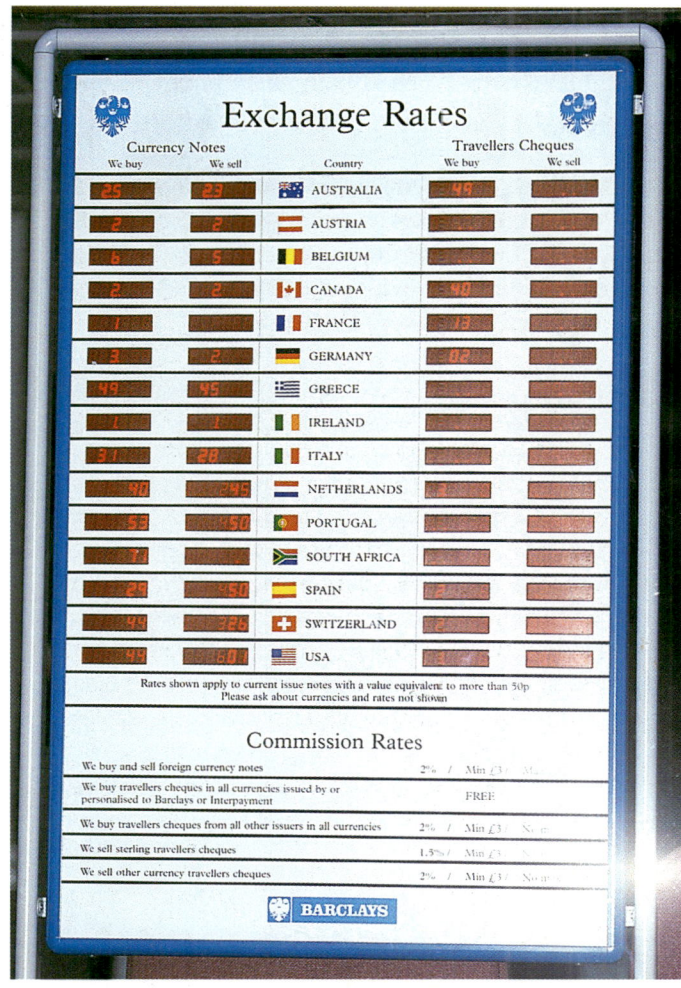

Original exchange rate £1 = $4

A UK good priced at £100 would sell at $400 in the USA while an American good priced at $200 would sell in the UK for £50.

Exchange rate falls to £1 = $2

The £100 UK export would now sell in the USA for $200 while the import from the USA would now sell in the UK for £100.

As a result, sales of UK goods both here and in the USA should rise if consumers are at all sensitive to price. These figures are quite deliberately unrealistic but they show you the effects of changing exchange rates on business activity.

SHOULD WE EVER PROTECT BRITISH FIRMS FROM FOREIGN COMPETITION?

In the past, when British firms have struggled to compete with foreign firms at home and abroad, there have been calls for special help to be given. Tariffs, which are a tax on imports, could be put on imports so raising their price and making them less attractive to the British public. Quotas, which are a restriction on the amount or total value of imports, could be placed on particular goods to help out specific UK industries. Subsidies on our exports,

Did you know? Most of the calls for protection for a country's industry are the result of major shocks. Towards the end of 1997, South Korea found itself under economic pressure for a number of reasons. One reaction in that country was by a group of women who called upon South Koreans to stop buying goods from other countries. Similarly, late in November 1997 a Japanese stock-broking firm collapsed, creating a great deal of concern about the stability of many other Japanese companies. Western countries waited nervously to see whether some of those Japanese companies would solve their cash problems by selling their investments in Western companies. Some economists warned of a possible major world-wide depression as a result. By the time you read this you may know the full extent of the problems resulting from the collapse of Yamaichi Securities.

Business within the international environment

by giving grants to exporting firms, will reduce their costs and therefore help them lower prices. Some countries use more subtle controls such as high safety or environmental standards on imports to make it difficult for any foreign firm to sell there. The UK is very limited in what it can do to help its firms. As members of the European Union and as signatories to the General Agreement on Tariffs and Trade (GATT) we are committed to reducing restrictions on trade; and much of British industry prefers the benefits of free trade with the rest of the world.

Codebreakers

Barriers to trade: these are ways used to discourage or stop the import of goods. They include tariffs which are a tax on imports, quotas which are a limit on the amount of imports and the use of safety and environmental standards to make it difficult to sell goods.

UK imports: the purchase of foreign produced goods by UK consumers and businesses with the money paid for them flowing out of the UK.

UK exports: the sale of UK produced goods in foreign markets with the money earned flowing back to the UK.

Balance of payments: a record of our trade with the rest of the world that also includes all transactions and movements of money.

Visibles: this is the trade in actual, physical goods.

Invisibles: these are earnings and payments from trade in services such as banking, travel and tourism and shipping.

Exchange rates: this is the value of the UK pound in terms of foreign currencies such as the dollar.

Activity

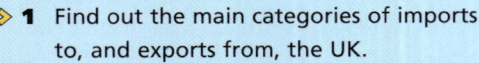

1. Find out the main categories of imports to, and exports from, the UK.
2. Find out who are the main countries we trade with.
3. Display this information in pie charts.
4. Try to find out which local businesses import and export goods.
5. Find out what sort of help is available for firms wanting to export goods.
6. Record the changes in the exchange rate of the pound against four other currencies over a month and chart the changes.

SUMMARY

Four points to remember:

1. An increasing number of firms are now operating in world-wide or global markets.
2. Changes in the exchange rate of the pound affect the ability of UK firms to compete on price with foreign goods at home and abroad.
3. Some countries may use trade barriers to help their domestic firms and industries to compete against imports.
4. Sometimes shocks such as wars or international disasters can cause many problems for countries and their trade.

Unit 49

The examination papers

Most examination papers are set in a real-world or realistic context. This means that a case study is created that allows questions to be asked that need candidates to apply their business knowledge and understanding. Each examination board will have its own style of papers and questions but they all have to cover the same assessment objectives. This tends to limit the range of questions that are asked on any particular topic; so while this unit will be making specific reference to the NEAB's GCSE Business Studies examination papers, the general advice and guidance may be used to help you prepare for any examination board papers.

SOME DO'S AND DON'TS

➡ **Do** try to write clearly. Several candidates each year limit their potential marks because it is impossible to read some of their answers.

➡ **Do not** use a pencil, red or green pen to write your answers. Most examiners actually prefer black ink to be used, although blue ink is acceptable.

➡ **Do** read the question carefully and make sure you answer the question that is being asked – and not the one you would like to be asked. This is particularly important when the question appears to be similar to one that has been asked in the past.

➡ **Do not** write in the margins and do not try to squash your answers in when you run out of lines. Use the extra blank pages at the back of the exam paper or ask for additional sheets from the exam invigilators. If you do use additional sheets, make sure you number each response correctly.

➡ **Do** read the data carefully as there may be clues to help your response, or the question may require you to select specific information from the data.

➡ **Do** use the number of marks per question to guide you on the length of response needed and keep an eye on the time. If you do not answer all the questions you will automatically reduce your potential mark.

➡ **Do** read the instructions on the front cover. They include important reminders before you start to put pen to paper.

➡ **Do** answer using sentences and paragraphs – unless the question specifically asks you to give a list.

➡ **Do not** use general words and phrases, but always try to use business terms. For example, 'money' is often used by candidates when 'revenue', 'costs' or 'profit' would have been the correct specific term. Try not to mix up terms such as 'borrow' and 'lend', 'price' and 'cost' or 'revenue' and 'profit'.

➡ **Do** look out for the 'command' word in each question. It will be telling you how to frame your answer. This is particularly important for questions using 'explain', 'why' or 'describe'. Answers to these questions mean you have to make some points but then you need to develop or expand them. This does not simply mean that you rewrite the data provided. You have to say something extra about the point without getting repetitive. Using examples is one way to help you explain or develop an answer.

➡ **Do not** rewrite the question but try to find a quick way to introduce and start your specific answer. Some candidates take three or four lines of writing before they actually start to answer the question. Remember – most introductions will not help you to score marks.

➡ **Finally, do** remember that all examination papers in Business Studies will have 5% of the marks allocated for spelling, punctuation and grammar (SPG). While this means you must try to improve your English before your GCSEs, keep concentrating on SPG as you write in the exam room. It is very easy to let your standards slip as you rush to show your understanding of the subject.

THE NEAB GCSE PAPERS

Choosing the right Paper for you

Candidates doing the full course will take Papers one and two, and may take Paper three as an alternative to submitting a coursework assignment. Those candidates taking Business Studies as a combined subject with, for example, IT or D&T will take Paper one and may also substitute Paper three for the coursework assignment. Papers one and two are tiered, meaning that candidates must be entered either for the Foundation Tier or for the Higher Tier. The possible grades for the Foundation Tier are C – G while for the Higher Tier they are A* – D.

This means that grades C and D overlap; but most importantly, if you do not quite reach a grade D on the Higher Tier you will be ungraded, while on the Foundation Tier the highest grade possible is a C. You must discuss which tier to enter with your teacher. Our advice is, that if you are predicted as a sound grade C then the Higher Tier is the most appropriate. Candidates predicted to be on the C/D borderline are probably best advised to enter the Foundation Tier. There are no tiers for Paper three or for the coursework assignment.

Use of case studies

All three papers use real-world or realistic case studies in which to set the questions. In Paper one there is a continuous case study which is common to both tiers. Paper two may have two or three different case studies, but they are again common to both tiers.

Paper three will be a single case study that asks candidates to solve a business problem or situation in a very similar way to the demands of coursework. For example, in 1996 candidates were asked to advise a burger chain which site out of a possible choice of three was the best location for a new fast food restaurant; while in 1997 candidates had to advise a kitchen manufacturer and installer on how to improve labour turnover problems. This paper will assess your abilities to select and use data, to interpret that data and apply your business understanding, and to evaluate the evidence so that you make reasoned judgements and draw appropriate conclusions. In other words, it tests exactly the same things as the coursework assignment does. The paper lasts for an hour but you would be expected to spend 15 minutes of this reading and thinking about the data and 45 minutes responding to the three or four-part task.

Question styles

The first question in both Papers one and two is often referred to as the 'friendly opener'. It is designed to help settle candidates down by giving them a reasonably easy question that they can respond to positively. Look at the extract below which shows part of Data A from the 1995 paper.

Colin Thain is a fully trained furniture maker. He worked for 10 years for a large furniture manufacturer. In 1992, he decided to make greater use of his skills and opened his own business. He believed there was a gap in the local market for a shop selling good quality, handmade, pine kitchen furniture.

Colin prepared a detailed business plan. He estimated that he needed £25 000 to start up as a sole trader. He had £10 000 savings and he arranged a bank loan of £15 000.

Colin rented a building just off the main high street. The front shop area was used to display and sell the kitchen furniture. He used the larger, rear area to make and store the furniture.

The first question asked, 'Why might someone like Colin decide to start his own business?' with up to (8) marks available. Clearly the data suggest some of the reasons such as 'he was trained' and 'he wanted to make greater use of his skills'. These could be developed as could the idea about a 'gap in the local market'. Other points not in the data could also gain marks like 'he wanted to be his own boss' or 'perhaps he thought he could make a higher income from his own business'.

Calculation questions are normally asked in both papers. It is important that you use a calculator so that your answer is exact, but you must always set out your workings to show the process in arriving at the answer. If you make a silly mistake you may still gain part of the marks for showing some knowledge even if you got the final answer wrong. Calculation questions are an important part of any Business Studies paper because they test key parts of the syllabus, and by carrying out these calculations and using their results you are acting like real-world business people.

In the 1995 paper, Data C set out the following figures for Colin Thain's business:

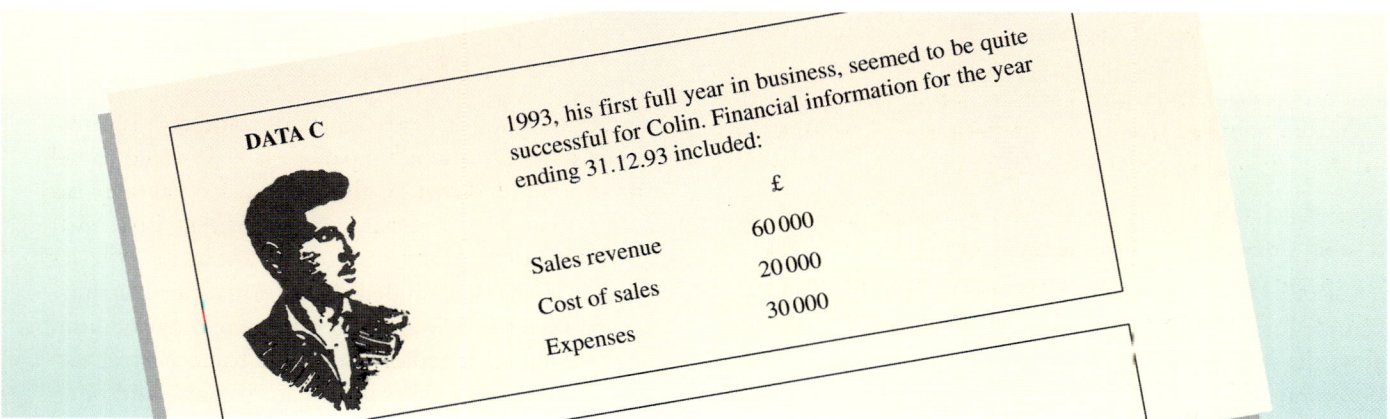

DATA C

1993, his first full year in business, seemed to be quite successful for Colin. Financial information for the year ending 31.12.93 included:

	£
Sales revenue	60 000
Cost of sales	20 000
Expenses	30 000

The questions based on this data were:

10 Showing your workings, calculate Colin's:

(a) gross profit for 1993 .... (4)

(b) net profit for 1993 .... (4)

11 Showing your workings, calculate Colin's:

(a) gross profit to sales revenue ratio .... (5)

(b) net profit to sales revenue ratio .... (5)

The examination papers 225

These questions were therefore assessing knowledge of the formulas and the ability to select data and to apply knowledge using the data. A total of (18) marks could be achieved for four correct answers but remember, by showing your workings you could have still gained marks even though you might have made small mistakes.

Some questions are just assessing your ability to recall key knowledge. For example, Question 9 on that 1995 paper asked:

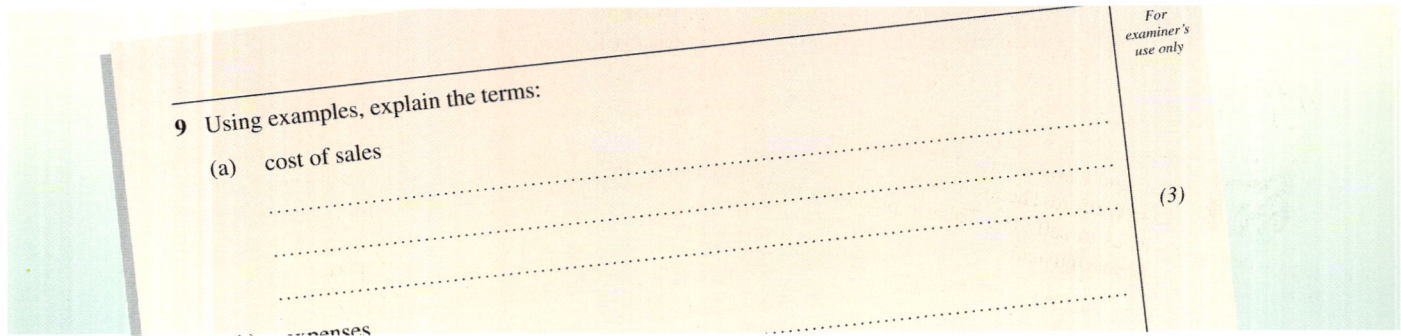

In both cases, a definition was needed with at least one example for the maximum marks to be achieved. This shows the importance of learning key terms together with appropriate examples.

To test a candidate's ability to evaluate and draw conclusions, at least one question per paper is set that requires some advice to be given. Such a question will not normally be asked until you have already answered several other questions that help you to get a feel for the firms involved in the case study. For example, Paper one in 1996 was based on the case study of a bakery called Big Buns. Question 8 was written:

The data available included the information that the planned investment was to go into increasing the number of bakers' shops, together with a full balance sheet to allow candidates to select information that could be applied to the question. To answer the question successfully, the advantages and disadvantages of each method had to be given together with some weighing up of their suitability for Big Buns and the planned investment. This question required a lot of thought and a lengthy answer with (12) marks allocated.

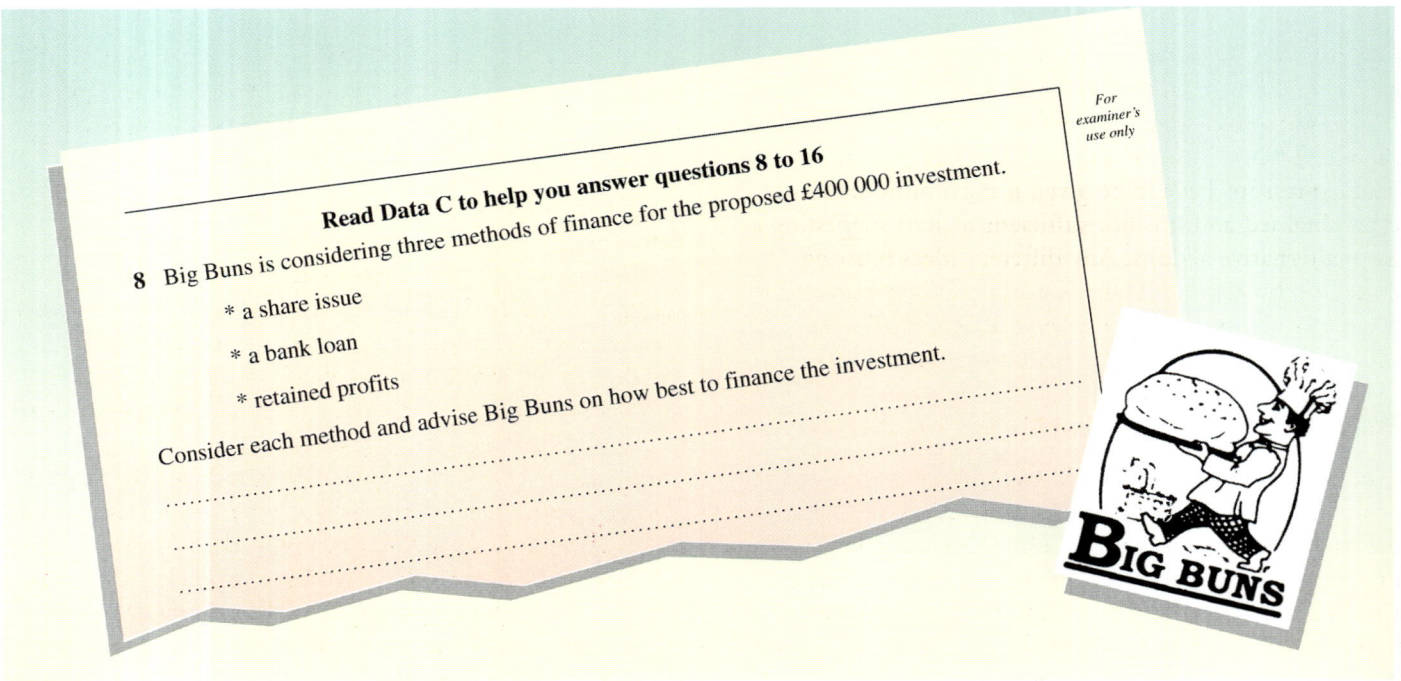

A similar style of question that is often asked will look like the following one set in Paper 2 in 1996. The case study looked at Carol Garner who had bought Welford Theatre, having previously owned the wine bar located in the theatre.

This question is asking candidates to explain how each option might help increase revenue whilst also asking how costs might be affected. By considering this, a candidate can advise Carol how she can best improve profits. Detailed reasons have to be given if maximum marks are to be obtained and it is not sufficient to start suggesting a list of alternative actions. Any different ideas must be backed up by reasons. There is no correct option for Carol to take; rather, the examiners want to test candidates' abilities to use knowledge, to reason and draw conclusions.

Revision and exam practice

Candidates often ask 'What should we revise?' The answer is quite simply everything that is included on the syllabus! It is impossible to assess the whole syllabus content in any one year's exam papers but something from each section will normally be included. In one year there may be more emphasis on one or two sections because of the case study that the questions are set on. It is impossible for you to try and question spot but you can be sure that the papers will include questions that ask you to recall key knowledge, to select data, to apply your business understanding and to evaluate business problems and situations.

Make key notes of all your work so that you have definitions, examples, formulas for business calculations, and lists of basic features, advantages and disadvantages across the whole syllabus. Your teachers will give you exam practice and this is important so that you build up your speed of thought and writing. Reading out your written answers so that people can listen to the points and the way you have constructed your answer is one useful way of preparing for the exam. This is particularly helpful if your teachers explain how an answer is marked. By learning what the examiner is looking for and how marks are awarded you will learn how to answer the question to achieve the most marks. Examples of exam papers and marked candidates' answers are included in the teacher's pack to go with this textbook. Ask your teacher to see these examples.

Unit 50

Coursework

Coursework accounts for 25% or a quarter of the marks available at GCSE so, if you choose to do coursework, you must make sure that you do it well. The NEAB provides an alternative for coursework which is designed for those students who decide that they do not wish to take it, but would rather do another examination. This is discussed in Unit 49. For those who decide to do coursework, this is a guide to help you obtain the highest possible marks.

GETTING THE BEST OUT OF YOUR COURSEWORK

What can I do?

Titles are published by the examination board. Your teacher will be able to give you a copy of the current ones from the syllabus. From time to time some titles change in order to keep up with changing trends in business. Some titles are always appropriate so will always remain on the syllabus. The titles for those taking the examination in the year 2000 are as follows:

a) ● Is there scope for a new business in the local area?

b) ● How can a business proposal for a new business be planned and presented?

c) ● How can the success of a business be measured?

d) Assess the effect of a business development of your choice on the local community.

e) ● What strategies could be used to help a small business survive in spite of competition?

f) Compare and evaluate the effectiveness of recruitment, selection and training of personnel in two businesses.

g) Compare and evaluate the success of the marketing strategies of two firms in the same market.

h) ● Compare and evaluate the objectives of two different businesses.

i) ● Is Firm X better at motivating workers than Firm Y?

j) ● How effective is Firm X's quality control?

k) Will the social benefits of a business development outweigh the social costs?

l) How have external factors affected Firm X?

m) ● What are the most important factors that affect demand for a product or service? Suggest how a local business could influence demand.

n) Why and how could Firm X expand?

o) ● Assess the effectiveness of *either* recruitment *or* marketing *or* production methods at a Work Experience placement. What advice would you give your employer on how to make improvements?

p) ● Evaluate the possible ways to market a new product.

The titles marked with a ● are those that can be used for the GCSE Combined subject syllabuses. This is a Business Studies element that can be added to a short course in Languages, Geography, Design and Technology and Information Technology to make a full GCSE. The element requires a shorter piece of coursework. If you find that you have a really interesting piece of work that you would like to do, then your teacher can present a title other than the ones shown here for approval by the board. It will receive approval as long as it allows you to gain marks in the way outlined on page 230.

How do I get started?

This is often the most difficult part of coursework, but here are some ideas to help you get started:

- Look at the titles that are available and get your teacher to explain any that you don't understand.

- Think what resources you have –

    Have you been or are you going on a work experience placement?

    Do you have a part-time job or a Saturday job at a business?

    Where do your parents or elder brothers and sisters, uncles and aunts, work?

    Can you use any of these businesses as a starting point for your investigation?

- Do you have a local newspaper? –

    Can you get archive material from it?

    Can you get photographs from it?

- Do you have a local council? –

    What information can they provide you with?

- Do you have a local library?

    Does it have CD-ROM?

    What facilities does your school library have?

- What local business developments are there? –

    new supermarkets or shopping centres?

    new sports or leisure facilities?

- Any other resources or sources of information? –
  If you are actually working for a business, or know someone who is, then that first contact is so much easier to make.

How much do I have to do?

For the NEAB full course you need to do approximately 3 000 words. For the element this is reduced to 2 000 words. For other GCSEs you will need to refer to the appropriate syllabus. You may think that this sounds like a lot, but it is really not all that much when you think that it is worth a quarter of the marks. To give you some idea, this unit is just over 2 500 words long.

Some detailed examples

1 Is there scope for a new business in the local area?

Purpose of assignment

State what you are looking for to help you make your decision. Are you seeking a gap in the market or to expand an existing market? What sort of evidence would make you conclude that there is, or isn't room for a new business? What evidence will be, in your opinion, the most useful to you? What evidence do you intend to collect and how do you intend to collect it?

Research and collection of data

Define what is meant by the 'local area'. Draw up a list, or show on a map, what businesses already exist. Collect evidence by questionnaire, survey, observation and interview from current businesses, residents and prospective customers. What other data could you collect, for example on the costs of setting up, on licensing or other regulations, on location, on sources of finance?

Sorting and analysis of data

Can you identify a gap in the market? Is there enough consumer interest for you to consider a new business? What evidence do you have to help you make your decisions? Would you be able to find a suitable site, comply with regulations, or raise the finance?

Presentation

Present your data and evidence clearly and attractively. Use different forms of presentation, graphs, charts, photographs, maps etc. Your presentation must include appropriate business terms and methods and an evaluation of the data you have collected – which is most useful, which least useful?

Judgements and conclusions

Is there scope for a new business? Assess the evidence that you have collected and come to a conclusion. Explain your reasoning and the judgements you have made. What were the strengths/weaknesses of your research? What advice or recommendations would you make to anyone wishing to open a new business?

2 Assess the effect of a business development of your choice on the local community.

Purpose of assignment

State what you are looking for to help you assess the effect. You should be looking for both the positive effects and the negative ones, for short-term effects and long-term ones. What different groups of people, different businesses have been affected? What evidence will be, in your opinion, the most useful to you? What evidence do you intend to collect and how do you intend to collect it?

Research and collection of data

Decide which groups of people might have been affected. What evidence have you based this on? Use observation, surveys and interviews to collect evidence. Other statistical information might also be useful. Have traffic flows been affected? Can you get the information from your local council? Can you get accident statistics from them? Can you get pictures or stories from newspaper archives that give you a picture of what it was like before the development? Ask residents – do they remember?

Sorting and analysis of data

Assess the data you have collected. Which is most useful to you, and why? Collate the opinions you have collected in order to give an overall impression of general opinion. Are there opposing views about the benefits or otherwise of the development? Why do you think that this is? Were some of the benefits only short term – employment during construction for instance? Will some be longer term, like accident reductions? Will some of the effects get worse as time goes on?

Presentation

Present your data and evidence clearly and attractively. Use different forms of presentation – you might like to tape or videotape interviews. This can be presented as evidence as long as you provide a brief written summary as well. Your presentation must include appropriate business terms and methods and an evaluation of the data you have collected – which is most useful, which least useful? Can you balance personal opinion against statistical evidence? Which carries most weight, and why?

Judgements and conclusions

Assess the evidence you have collected and come to a conclusion. Explain your reasoning and the judgements you have made. What were the strengths/weaknesses of your research? Is there any crucial evidence which you feel you should have but were not able to obtain? Has the effect been a good one – if so, for whom. Has it been a bad one, if so, for whom?

3 Compare and evaluate the objectives of two different businesses.

Purpose of assignment

Choose two different firms. It is often best to choose those firms with which you already have some sort of contact as outlined above. A work experience placement or somewhere where you work part-time is an ideal starting point. State what you mean by objectives and which groups of people connected with the firm are likely to have different objectives or aims. Say how you intend to compare the objectives – which are different, which are the same, and why? State how you intend to evaluate the objectives – which are realistic targets? Which are positive aims?

Research and collection of data

Interview the various different groups – owners, managers, customers, suppliers and so on at the two firms. Find out what their objectives are and why. Do any of the objectives clash? Collect any published material that the businesses have on which their aims are stated. Do they have particular policies in operation, or a mission statement? Are targets long-term or short-term? General or specific?

Sorting and analysis of data

What aims or objectives would you expect the firms to have? Use this textbook to help you in this. What aims and objectives do they actually have? Assess the data you have collected. Which is most useful to you and why? Collate the opinions that you have collected – do different groups have different objectives or the same ones? Why do you think this is? Can you categorise the objectives using business terminology?

Presentation

Present your data and evidence clearly and attractively. Use different forms of presentation – you might like to tape or videotape interviews. This can be presented as evidence as long as you provide a brief written summary as well. Your presentation must include appropriate business terms and methods and an evaluation of the data you have collected – which is most useful, which least useful? Is there other information you would have liked to collect but were not able to?

Judgements and conclusions

Come to a conclusion regarding the objectives you have found out. How sensible or attainable do you think the targets are? What other targets would you recommend? Which business objectives did you expect to find? Which *did* you find? Why do you think they are the same, or why are they different? Always use the evidence you have collected to back up your reasoning.

What do I get marks for?

Your work is marked under five headings.

1 How well can you design and carry out practical research? How well have you planned your work? How much useful evidence have you been able to collect?

This is 14 % of the marks.

2 How well were you able to select information, organise information and use information? How many different sources did you go to for your information? Were you able to use different methods of presentation and keep the presentation appropriate to the information?

This is 27% of the marks.

3 How well were you able to use the specialist language that is used in business? Did you use the proper terms, the proper theories and the proper methods for doing tasks? Did you use all the terms and methods that were appropriate to the assignment?

This is 27% of the marks.

4 How well were you able to draw conclusions? Were you able to say which, of the evidence you collected, was the most useful and why? Were you able to show that you had made judgements and come to decisions based on the evidence that you had? Were your conclusions all linked to the evidence you had collected?

This is 27% of the marks.

5 Can you spell, punctuate and use the rules of grammar properly?

This is 5% of the marks.

Some do's and don'ts

Many candidates make the same mistakes each year. Many also do excellent pieces of coursework which are extremely professionally produced. There are always candidates who score maximum marks on coursework, meaning that they already have a quarter of the available marks before they even sit down to an examination paper.

➡ **Do** start your coursework early in order to be able to collect as much information as possible. If you are writing to companies, for example, it can sometimes be four or five weeks before a reply is received.

➡ **Don't** start too early, or you will not have enough knowledge or expertise from your course. Early in the second year of the course is probably the best time to start.

➡ **Do** plan your work properly. Do an outline of what you intend to do and a timescale for when you intend to do it.

➡ **Don't** leave everything to the last minute!

➡ **Do** collect as much information as possible. You need to be able to show that you have the skill to be able to select from the information you have collected.

➡ **Don't** use everything you've collected, otherwise there has been no selection. Say why you have chosen to leave certain information out.

➡ **Do** some primary research: use questionnaires, surveys, interviews and observation.

➡ **Don't** include everything you have done. A couple of questionnaires and the analysed results is all the evidence that is needed, not the hundred questionnaires actually filled in.

➡ **Do** some secondary research from books, articles, company reports, leaflets and other publications.

➡ **Don't** include company reports, leaflets and so on when presenting your work.

➡ **Do** reference your material. Extracts from CD-ROMs, textbooks and encyclopaedias need to be acknowledged. A bibliography should be provided.

➡ **Don't** overdo the presentation. Often there are too many pie charts, graphs, bar charts and so on, all produced on computers, few of which have any relevance.

➡ **Do** present work clearly and accurately, using IT where appropriate. Work does not have to be word processed, but it does have to be readable.

What will get me top marks?

The best candidates:

- Use several methods of practical research that are well designed, properly carried out and appropriate to the task. Traffic counts for statistical information and interviews where in-depth answers are required are good examples.

- Select and use information from a variety of sources, organise it well and present it in a professional manner.

- Use terms and concepts associated with Business Studies in a professional manner and are able to apply and interpret those terms in relation to the research work they have done.

- Evaluate evidence throughout their work and come to reasoned conclusions based on the evidence they have collected. They are aware if their evidence is imperfect and can comment on how this affects the accuracy of their conclusions.

Index

Codebreaker definitions for each Unit appear in the index in bold type.

Absenteeism 72
Acid test ratio 128
Actual cash flow 116
Advertising 157, 188-195
Advertising campaign 195
AGM 12
Appropriation 120
Appropriation account 121
Arbitration 94
Articles of Association 12
Assets 122-124
Assets, current, fixed, net current 123
Assisted areas 152
Authority 53
Average costs 111

Balance of payments 222
Balance sheets 122-124
Barriers to trade 222
Batch production 140
Board of directors 11, 12
Bonuses 90
Boom 217
Borrowed funds 99
Brand image 195
Break even analysis 112-114
Break even point 114
Breaking bulk 201
British Code of Advertising Practice, The 195
British Standards Institute 207
Budget, The 214
Building society conversions 24
Bureaucracy 35
Business objectives 41-49
Business rates 27

Capital 122-124
Capital employed 123
Cash and carry 201
Cash deficit 116
Cash flow 115-117
Cash flow forecast 116
Cash inflow 116
Cash outflow 116
Cash surplus 116
Caveat emptor 207
Chain of distribution 201
Changing work practices 144
Co-operatives 21-24
Collective bargaining 94
Commission 72
Complements 170
Conciliation 94
Conglomerate 39

Consultation exercise 60
Consumer 170
Consumer co-operative 21, 23
Consumer demand 168-174
Consumer durable 156, 214
Consumer/retail co-operative 24
Consumers' Association, The 207
Contract 85, 89-91
Contract of employment 91
Contribution 114
Controlling interest 12
Core product 187
Corporation 27
Cost of sales 119
Cost price 182
Costs 107-111, 208-210 (and Benefits)
Costs, external, internal 66
Costs, fixed, variable, average, total 111
Council tax 27
Creaming 180
Credit rating 35
Creditors 123
Current assets 123
Current liabilities 123
Current ratio 128
Customer protection 202-207

Data, primary, secondary 167
Debentures 100
Debtors 123
Decision making 63-66
Deed 9
Deed of Partnership 5
Delayering 53
Delegation 6, 9, 52, 53
Demand 170 (elastic, inelastic) **174**
Demerger 39
Demotivate 72
Depreciation 120
Deregulation 28, 30
Direct marketing 195
Disciplinary matters 94
Diseconomies of scale 34, 137
Dismissal 75
Disposable income 156
Distribution 196-201
Diversification 38, 39, 187
Dividend 24, 121
Dividends 121
Division of labour 5
Divorce of ownership 12
Downsizing 60

Economies of scale 33-35, 136-137
Elastic demand 174
Endorsements 193
Enterprise Zone 152
Entrepreneur 1, 5, 134

Equal opportunities 95-97
Equal opportunities policy 94
Equilibrium 177
Equity capital 44
European Union 218
Exchange Rate 219, **222**
Expenses 121
Exports, UK **222**
External benefits 210
External costs 66, 210
Externalities 210

Factoring 12, 100
Finance, short, medium and long-term 101
Financial sources 98-103
Fiscal policy 211, 214
Fixed assets 123
Fixed costs 111, 182
Flow/mass production 140
Franchise 20
Franchisee 17-20
Franchiser 20
Franchises 17-20
Fringe benefits 90, 91
Funds 98-99

Grants 27, **99**
Grievance matters 94
Gross profit 119
Gross profit to sales revenue ratio 128
Growth 36-40, **217**

Head-hunting 81
Health and Safety 95-96, (**Policy**) **97**
Herzburg's Theory 70
Hire purchase 100
Human resources 68, 72
Hypothesis 66

Imports, UK 222
Incentives 71-72
Induction training 88
Industrial relations 92-94
Inelastic demand 174
Inflation 49, 215-217
Infrastructure 152
Integration 37-38, 39
Internal costs 66
Invisibles 222

Job production 140
Just-in-time (JIT) 140

Labour 73-76
Labour turnover 76
Lack of continuity 9
Laissez-faire 59
Leasing 20, 100

232 Index

Limited companies 10-16
Limited liability 10, 12
Line manager 85
Liquid assets 128
Liquidation 14, 16
Liquidity measures 128
Loans 100
Local government 27
Location 148-152
Long list 85
Long-term finance 101

Majority shareholder 11, 12
Management buy-out 60
Managers, Management 47, 55-60, 145-147
Manufacturing methods 138-140
Mark-up 177
Market leader 187
Market position 187
Market pricing 175-182
Market research 159-167
Market segments 156
Maslow's Theory 69
Maximisation 44
Maximise 177
Maximising 49
McGregor's Theory 70
Media, the 195
Mediation 94
Medium 66
Medium-term finance 101
Memorandum of Association 12
Merchandising 195
Metropolitan council 27
Minimum wage 76
Monetary policy 214
Monopolies 34
Monopoly 30, 207
Motivation 68-72

National insurance contributions 26, 27
Nationalisation 28, 30
Natural wastage 76
Nepotism 80
Net assets employed 123
Net profit 121
Net profit to sales revenue ratio 128
Network marketing 201
Networking 66
Non price competition 182, 201

Off the job training 88
Office of Fair Trading 207
Official Receiver 14, 16
On the job training 88
Operational decision making 66
Opportunity cost 170
Organisational structure 53
Owners 47
Owners' funds 99

Partnerships 6-9
Pay 71, 90-91
Payment by results 91

Perfect monopoly 35
Performance linked payments 60
Performance related pay 76
Perks 71
Point of sale 167
Portfolio 12
Premiums 24
Price leader 182
Price maker 44
Price plateau 182
Price taker 44
Primary data 167
Primary production 134
Privatisation 28-30
Privatised 207
Producer co-operative 24
Product range 187
Product, Production and Productivity 56, 60, 73, 76, 132-144, 183-187
Production resources 134
Production, job, batch, flow/mass, project, just-in-time 140
Production, primary, secondary, tertiary 134
Productivity 60, 76
Productivity deals 144
Profit 110, 111, 118-121 (and loss), 125-131 (and profitability), 177
Profit after tax 121
Profitability measures 128
Project production 140
Promotion 194-195
Public relations 195
Public sector 25-30

Qualitative 167
Quality assurance 147
Quality control 147
QUANGOs 25, 30
Quantitative 167

Ratios 125-128
Receiver 66
Recession 217
Recruitment 78-85
Redundancy 24, 75
Research and development 187
Resources 132-134
Response rates 167
Retail co-operative see Consumer Co-operative
Retail outlet 201
Retailer 197-198, 201
Retained profits 121,123
Retirement 75
Return on capital employed (ROCE) 128
Revenue 35, 110, 111, 177
Royalty 20

Salary 60, 90, 91
Sales promotion 195
Satisficing 43, 44, 49
Secondary data 167
Secondary production 134
Secret ballot 94

Sender 66
Separate legal identity 10, 12
Share capital 123
Share of the market 36, 39
Short list 85
Short-term finance 101
Single status workforce 72
Situational interviewing 85
Sleeping partner 9
Slogans 195
Socio-economic group 156
Sole proprietor 1, 5
Sole trader 1-5, 61
Span of control 52, 53
Specialisation 5
Sponsorship 193-194
Stock Exchange 16
Stock turnover 144
Stockholders 46, 49
Stocks 119
Strategic decision making 66
Strikes 92-93
Subsidies 30
Subsidies 30, 44
Substitutes 170
Summary dismissal 76
Suppliers 48
Supply 177
SWOT analysis 165-167

Tactical decision making 66
Take-home pay 91, 214
Target market 153-158
Taxation 211-214
Teamworking/cell production 144
Tertiary production 134
Time rates 91
Total costs 111
Total quality management 147
Trade credit 100
Trade marks 187
Trade unions 92-93
Trading account 119
Training 86-88
Training and Enterprise Councils (TES) 2
Transfer payments 214
Transferable skills 76
Transmitter 66

Unit costs 39
Unlimited liability 5

Value added 134
Value Added Tax (VAT) 5
Variable costs 111, 182
VAT threshold 5
Visibles 222
Vocational qualifications 85
Voluntary codes 202, 207

Wage-price spiral 217
Wholesaler 197, 201
Work study methods 144
Worker co-operative 24
Working practices 94

Acknowledgements

The authors and publisher are grateful to the following for permission to reproduce illustrative material:

Abbey National page 24; ACAS page 93; Air Mauritius page 188; Alfred McAlpine Stadium page 47; Alliance and Leicester page 24; ASDA page 200; Birds Eye Wall's page 138; Blue Circle page 73; Body Shop pages 14, 17; Britannia page 24; British Alcan page 148; BSM page 17; Burger King page 17; CBI page 92; CWS page 23; Café Direct page 22; Cambridge Collection (Libraries) page 209; Canadian Muffin page 17; Christian Aid page vi; Coca-Cola page 41; Colorific Photo Library page 211; Companies House page 12; Domino Pizza page 17; *The East Anglian* page 156; First Direct page 41; Ford page 34; GNER (*Livewire*) page 190; *The Guardian* (Don McPhee) page 196; Her Majesty's Stationery Office (on behalf of Parliament) page 26; Halifax page 24; Hanson page 115; Holiday Inn page 17; ICI page 125; Investors In People page 88; KFC page 17; *Live and Kicking* Magazine pages 188, 189, 192, 193; Lowe Alpine page 202; Marks and Spencer (Andrew Molyneux) pages 41, 68; McDonalds page 17; Meadowhall Centre pages 29, 199; Nation All Coverage page 190; Nationwide page 24; News Corporation Ltd pages 31, 32; News International Associated Services Ltd page 57; North News page 92; PA News pages 139, 184; Philips page 141; Oasis Lakeland Forest Village, Cumbria page 159; Remploy pages 86, 95; Safeway page 138; Sainsbury's page 122; Sega page 194; *Shoot* page 156; Somerfield page 10; Sony pages 34, 39; Swinton page 17; Snappy Snaps page 17; *Telegraph* Colour Library pages 25, 87, 90, 135, 139, 141, 143, 146, 148, 166, 177, 184, 209; Tesco page 122; Tetley's page 130; The Co-operative Union page 21; *The Independent* page vi; *The Fellrunner* page 154; *The Voice* page 155; *The People's Friend* page 154; Virgin pages 4, 37; Walkers Crisps page 138; Wimpy page 17; *Woman* page 155; Woolwich page 24; Woolworths page 4; WYPTA/Metro page 44; Zuken-Redac page 78.

Thanks are also due to the following illustrators:

Sheila Betts (colour diagrams) pages: v, 2, 3, 5, 7, 11, 13, 14, 15, 16, 26, 27, 29, 32, 37, 38, 40, 42, 50, 51, 52, 53, 57, 58, 60, 63, 65, 66, 70, 71, 76, 79, 80, 81, 82, 84, 86, 89, 93, 101, 104, 105, 108, 109, 113, 115, 116, 118, 119, 120, 126, 127, 130, 132, 133, 134, 139, 140, 144, 149, 150, 157, 160, 162, 164, 165, 172, 173, 176, 178, 180, 184, 186, 191, 197, 200, 203, 204, 208, 210, 211, 212, 215, 216, 224, 225, 226, 227; Charlie Gray (photographs) pages: 8, 36, 46, 50, 55, 61, 62, 65, 81, 90, 98, 99, 108, 116, 118, 124, 129, 130, 135, 137, 138, 143, 145, 149, 153, 154, 160, 163, 168, 172, 175, 181, 183, 185, 186, 187, 198, 205, 207, 209, 218, 220, 221; Tim Oliver (cartoons and drawings) pages: 1, 2, 4, 6, 19, 21, 26, 33, 43, 47, 48, 51, 55, 56, 58, 59, 61, 62, 63, 64, 66, 71, 72, 74, 79, 80, 83, 84, 85, 87, 89, 101, 102, 103, 106, 107, 112, 113, 117, 121, 122, 131, 133, 136, 142, 145, 146, 147, 151, 153, 158, 161, 163, 164, 168, 169, 170, 171, 173, 174, 176, 177, 178, 179, 181, 183, 192, 197, 198, 199, 201, 202, 204, 205, 206, 210, 212, 219.

Every effort has been made to trace copyright holders but this has not been possible in all cases; any omissions brought to our attention will be corrected in future printings.

Special thanks are also due to Ros Horton, Liz Knox and Sue Nicholas for their help in producing this book.